ITALY IN THE AGE OF DANTE AND PETRARCH
1216–1380

A LONGMAN HISTORY OF ITALY
Volume Two

Italy in the Age of
Dante and Petrarch
1216–1380

JOHN LARNER

LONGMAN
London and New York

Longman Group Limited London

*Associated companies, branches and representatives
throughout the world*

*Published in the United States of America
by Longman Inc., New York*

© John Larner 1980

First published 1980

British Library Cataloguing in Publication Data

Larner, John
Italy in the age of Dante and Petrarch,
1216–1380. – (Longman history of Italy; vol.2).
1. Italy – History – 13th century
2. Italy – History – 1268–1492
I. Title
945'.04   DG531   79–41509
ISBN 0–582–48366–2

Set in 11/12pt V-I-P Garamond No. 3
Printed and bound in Great Britain by
William Clowes (Beccles) Limited
Beccles and London

First issued in paperback 1983
ISBN 0 582 49149 5

For Margaret McHaffie

Ahi quanto a dir qual era è cosa dura
esta selva selvaggia e aspra e forte
che nel pensier rinova la paura!
Tant' è amara che poco è più morte;
ma per trattar del ben ch'i'vi trovai,
dirò de l'altre cose ch'i' v'ho scorte.

Dante, *Inferno*, i, 4–9.

Abbreviations

Contents

List of Maps, Tables and Plates

(The plates appear between pages 150 and 151.)

Acknowledgements

The author would like to thank the Carnegie Trust for the Universities of Scotland and Glasgow University for generous grants to study in Italy. He owes a large debt to the staff of Glasgow University Library and in particular to Isabel Neilson who read the manuscript of this work and suggested many improvements in it. Finally he gratefully acknowledges the valuable criticism given by Denys Hay, the general editor of the series.

Map 1   Italy *c.* 1300

CHAPTER ONE

The idea of Italy and the sources of Italian history

I

The majority of Italians who lived in the thirteenth and fourteenth centuries never heard the word 'Italy'. It was a country in which only the literate lived. Consciousness of its meaning arose from three sources: the classics, xenophobia, and exile. The study of classical literature gave the idea of the old Roman province, praises of *Italia* from the Latin poets, and a belief that the peninsula formed a territory with natural boundaries:

> 'the fair land
> That the Apennines divide and the sea and Alps surround.'[1]

These learned insights could blend easily with a hatred of non-Italians, of peoples whose language could not be understood and whose soldiers devastated native fields and towns in some claim to lordship over them. It is the emotion expressed in his song against the followers of the emperor by Peire de la Caravana:

> Granoglas resembla
> En dir 'broder guaz?'
> Lairan, quant s'assembla
> Cum cans enrabiaz.
> No voillaz ia venga!
> De vos los loignaz!
>   Lombart, be.us gardaz
>   Que ia non siaz
>   Peier qe compraz
>   Si ferm non estaz[2]

> 'Frogs they resemble
> With their *'Bruder, ach so?'*
> Barking they assemble,
> Like mad dogs they go.
> Fight and dissemble!
> Far off with this foe!

1

> Lombards stand with me
> For you will be
> Worse than unfree
> If you fail our company.'

Sentiments like this were played upon in the hope of forming political loyalties. From the time of Gregory VII the Papacy had appealed to 'all Italians' against the pretensions of the German emperors, and some communes had answered with a call for 'Italian liberty' in their resistance to a foreign lord. The Lombard communes came together, they claimed, 'for the honour and freedom of Italy and for the preservation of the dignity of the Roman Church'. In the later thirteenth century the cry of 'Italy' was to be raised again by the Hohenstaufen Manfred against French popes and princes.

It was from outside Italy that the word found the strongest response, among merchants and exiles. In an alien world and without the protection of their cities' laws, Florentines, Venetians, and Milanese were likely to draw together and to find in one another men whose minds and habits were less strange, men with whom it was sometimes necessary to form working alliances and with whom, perhaps, the pleasures of nostalgia could be shared. Brunetto Latini, forced in 1260 to take refuge from the Ghibelline rulers of Florence, had gone to France and there had written of French as being the most delightful of all languages. Yet on his return to his native city he expressed his new consciousness of nationality in the lapidary judgment: 'Italy is a better country than France'. In his chronicle, Giovanni Villani, who had spent six years as an agent of the Peruzzi bank at Bruges, found it normal to write of a city faction-leader as being a man of the greatest renown, not in Florence or Tuscany or Christianity, but *in Italia*.[3] Above all, it was from the circle of Italians resident at Avignon that Petrarch drew his intense consciousness of Italy and hatred of foreigners.

The exile from his native town who stayed in Italy might, like Dante in his search for the elusive 'panther' of a common literary language, find there some unity: 'very simple standards of manners, dress, and speech by which our actions as *Latini* are weighed and measured'.[4] The close interdependence of town and countryside in the peninsula, the frequency with which nobles engaged in trade, the high level of urban literacy and education, all contrasted strongly with anything found north of the Alps. Elements of cohesion could be seen too in the common legal culture, even, it has been suggested, in the provincial alliances of city factions, and, certainly, in the interchange of officials, such as *podestà*, among different communes. A man like Uguccione della Faggiuola (d. 1319), who came from the remote Apennines of southern Romagna and during his life served as *podestà* of Arezzo and of Vicenza, as Imperial-Vicar at Genoa, and as Lord of Pisa, could, perhaps, be presented as 'an Italian'.

These are not negligible factors. Yet neither Dante nor Uguccione knew personally the South or many other parts of Italy. Looking at the peninsula as a whole the conclusion is inescapable that it was elements of disunity which predominated. Geographically the area is divided by sharp contrasts in land-formation and climate. Lines drawn between Spezia and Rimini along the crest of the Apennines or from the Tuscan Maremma to the Abruzzi would serve for as good 'natural frontiers' as the Alps. It was a land with no linguistic unity. (One Barnabò of Reggio (d. 1285), a chronicler tells us, was an accomplished linguist, speaking French, Tuscan, and Lombard fluently.[5]) Until Dante there was no common vernacular literary language (and even then no common language in prose but only in verse). To move from one town to another less than 30 miles away called generally for sharp revisions of attitudes and knowledge. Weights, measures, currencies, could all be different. So varied, for instance, were the towns' calculations on when the year began that a traveller, leaving Lucca on the 20 March 1300 and taking a day for his journey, would arrive at Florence on 21 March 1299. From there, after a leisurely week's trip, he would enter Pisa on the 28 March 1301. If he then took ship to Naples he would have had to discover on what day Easter fell before knowing in which century he would arrive.

Finally Italy was politically divided. If men could hate non-Italians they could hate Italians of the neighbouring and of their own city as fiercely and could without compunction call upon non-Italians against them. In these circumstances, even for the literate, national feeling was a tender growth. Just how frail is illustrated by the verse of Peire de la Caravana which has been cited. It is written not in Italian but in Provençal; it is addressed not to 'Italians' but to Lombards; and its primary purpose was to appeal to those Lombards who were in alliance with the Germans. Even the memory of Rome hindered in many respects the growth of national feeling, for it carried with it a reverence for the Medieval Empire which, it was believed, was a direct heir of the Roman Empire. As the example of Dante shows, a passionate reading of the *Aeneid* could lead Italians to see men with names like Rudolf, Albrecht, and Heinrich as their natural leaders in succession to Augustus. In the last analysis not even Petrarch or Cola di Rienzo succeeded in rising above a conception of Italy as a province, albeit the leading province, in a restored empire. In the thirteenth century, some Italians, it is true, had already begun to break with the tradition which identified the Roman and Holy Roman Empires. The Florentines, seeking perhaps to justify their 'imperialism' in Tuscany, declared that it was Florence itself which was 'the new Rome'. Yet this formulation, while destructive of the imperial myth, replaced it by a symbol of communal, not national, loyalty.

The truth is 'Italy' was nothing more than a sentiment or – it is what must justify the title of the present volume – a literary idea. The reality was not unity, but a mass of divided cities, lordships, and towns, dominated by particularist sentiments and local interests.

Since Italy hardly existed, it is understandable that it has proved difficult to write its history in this period. In particular while writers on the fortunes of France, England, or Scotland in these years can form their accounts – however distorting the process may be – around the role of central government, the Italian historian is denied that possibility. First to attempt the task was Flavio Biondo in his *Historiarum ab inclinatione Romanorum imperii Decades,* a work begun about 1440. Biondo had started to write the *Decades* with the intention of telling the story of all the nations which had succeeded the Roman Empire, but by the time he reached the thirteenth and fourteenth centuries his vision had largely narrowed to Italy. In his narrative can be seen the apparently insuperable difficulties which the subject presents. Without any central theme to articulate the material, the reader meets only a riot of discrete facts and a work whose sole form is that dictated by annalistic progression. No better was the *Enneades sive Rhapsodia historiarum*, published in 1498, by the Venetian humanist Marcantonio Sabellico, an attempt to emulate the *Decades* by expounding a world history as seen from the standpoint of Venice. The humanists produced no satisfactory, unified portrayal of the Italian Middle Ages. What they did do with some success was to combine in one volume histories of the individual regions and towns. Here again Biondo set the pattern with his *Italia Illustrata,* first published in 1453, where, moving from region to region, he describes in turn their geography, history, famous men, and monuments. This was the model for Leandro Alberti's *Descrittione di tutta Italia* (Bologna, 1550), and for the first *History of Italy* in English, written by the Welshman, William Thomas, and published in 1549. Of the form of these works the subtitle of the last volume tells all: 'A Book Exceedingly Profitable to Be Read Because It Entreateth of the State of Many and Divers Commonwealths How they Have Been and Now Be Governed'. Already, that is to say, it seemed to have been tacitly agreed that Italy could be considered only by dividing its story into a series of individual histories of its 'many and divers commonwealths'.

One man at least refused to join this consensus, the Modenese scholar, Carlo Sigonio (1523–84). In the introduction to his *Historiarum de regno Italiae Libri XX* he complains that France and Germany had their national histories (and, of course, by then he could have added Poland, Hungary, Spain, and England) but that none, 'kindled by love of his native soil or the sweetness of domestic praise', had bestowed one upon Italy. Biondo da Forlì, he claimed, in writing a universal history, had diffused concentration upon what should have been his central theme, and Sabellico had been even less satisfactory both in research (*diligentia*) and style (*elegantia*). He therefore proposed to write a history 'from the coming of the Lombards and the first Italian kingdom up to those times in which the Italian cities freely waged great wars and initiated most powerful revolts against it, until the various princes of the kingdom attained by commendatory grants of the Kings that state which they now hold'. This plan betrays the essential formal weakness of the work. The history of Italy, at least from the tenth century, is seen as a branch of imperial history, and consequently the story ends in 1286 where Sigonio conceives of the Emperor Rudolf as making a conscious decision 'to yield Italy its entire freedom'.[6] Whatever his original intention – which one suspects was rather different – Sigonio had been forced, as were so many others after him, to construct his narratives of the thirteenth century upon the fortunes of the German Empire, and to conclude that in the fourteenth century there was no national history but only the history of 'the various provinces'.

For two centuries there was no significant attempt to follow or surpass Sigonio, until, that is, the coming of another Modenese, the great Ludovico Antonio Muratori. Muratori offered two models of how the work might proceed. The first is found in the *Annali d'Italia*, published from 1738 to 1749, which took the story from the birth of Christ to his own day. These volumes followed the tradition of Biondo's *Decades*, though with very much greater learning than Biondo, and consisted of a compilation, year by year, of the political events which had taken place in the peninsula. It has been assumed that this was planned merely as a work of reference. Yet given the view of history stated in the introduction, which was still in part that of the classical world and of Biondo: *cioé di lodare il merito, di biasmare il demerito altrui*, to assign, that is, praise or blame, one can see that this is not necessarily so, and that the annalistic form could very well serve Muratori's ends. Indeed the final moral to be drawn was perhaps even enhanced by the overall impression of formless chaos. For, apart from a sigh of relief that one lived not in the past but in the age of the enlightened despots, this moral was not patriotic and political (and so not classical) but rather religious. Here, Muratori declares, where wars had become the everyday food of Italians and one saw the insane and violent factions of Guelfs and Ghibellines, one came to an understanding of the sole reality, namely that God, in creating this world, had mingled there more weeping than laughter in order that men should be stirred to seek that other world of which Holy Faith gave hope.

None the less, what he offered was not a true history of Italy as a unit but a '*storia universale d'Italia*', as if one were to write of 'a universal history of the world', a conglomerate, a bringing together of the vicissitudes of opposed political centres. Yet immediately before writing the *Annali* Muratori had produced one of the most remarkable books in the history of historical scholarship, a work which stands alone in the age and until recently almost alone in Italian historiography, and one which finally succeeded in treating Italian life in the past as a unity. This was the *Antiquitates Italicae Medii Aevi* (Milan, 1738–42).

Here, by largely eschewing political narrative, and by considering rather topics – mints and exchequers, usury, hospitals, trade, mercenaries, law, ranks, institutions, literature, education – by writing essays in what was in effect social history, Muratori was, for the first time, able to present a unified vision of medieval Italy.

The pioneering solution of the *Antiquitates* was not followed up. With the nineteenth century came nationalism and liberalism, and historians turned to the search for a national history conceived in political terms. Curiously, at first sight, this history was sought not in the Roman but in the medieval past. Whereas histories of England normally begin with the Roman occupation of Britain – even though its later effects were so slight and even though the English race had not then come into existence – Italian history, as exemplified in the series of which this present volume forms a part, is always taken to start with the fall of the empire. Perhaps the explanation lies in a reluctance to see as specifically Italian a political order which came to embrace the whole of Europe, and whose rulers, and intellectuals too, were sometimes Spaniards and Africans and other non-Italians. Possibly it lies merely in academic convenience, in the belief that both the Roman and later Italian worlds are all too much to encapsulate in one survey, however extended. But more probably what is seen here is the inheritance of the idea of absolute dichotomy drawn by the humanists between the Roman world and 'the Age of Darkness' which was deemed to succeed it, a dichotomy which dictated the form of Biondo's and Sigonio's works, and established a tradition with which later writers were unwilling to break.

It was a tradition particularly appropriate for Italian historians in the dawn of the *Risorgimento*. Here they could find – and particularly in the story of the twelfth and thirteenth centuries, which was interpreted as the struggle of native Italians against foreigners – a stimulus and guide much more relevant to the needs of the day than a story of imperial triumphs. What all sought was 'a poem', an epic which would excite emulation. The newly rediscovered work of Vico (1668–1744) too, with his belief in the Middle Ages as 'the youth of the new Europe', blended with the romanticism of Chateaubriand to direct attention to these centuries. To the Catholic Liberals or 'neo-Guelfs' of the age this was a particularly happy development, since it harmonised well with their own hopes for the future political development of their country. What these men sought was not unity but an Italy free from foreign domination, a federation of states under the presidency of the pope. As an exemplar of the federal ideal worked out in historical terms they already had before them the *Histoire des républiques italiennes du moyen âge*, published between 1807 and 1818 by Jean Charles Léonard de Sismondi. Sismondi was a citizen of Geneva and a Protestant republican who had suffered imprisonment in early life at the hands of both the French Revolutionaries and the Austrians. Understandably his history judged societies by the liberty they permitted. By this standard the Italian communes, with their autonomous power to create law (a power which was vital, for it was laws rather than race which created character) and with their resistance to central domination, came close to being ideal communities. But an Italian national state, Sismondi believed, would have been disastrous because it would have suppressed local legislative freedom.

This synthesis was taken up by the neo-Guelfs and refurbished with a Catholic interpretation. The story of the twelfth to fourteenth centuries, as told by Cesare Balbo (*Storia d'Italia*, 1836) and Cesare Cantù (*Storia degli Italiani*, 1849–50), was one of how the communes under the guidance of the Church had resisted the emperors from beyond the Alps. Inspired by this vision, Luigi Tosti, Abbot of Montecassino, in his *Storia di Bonifazio VIII e dei suoi tempi* (Montecassino, 1846), was even able to portray that pope in the remarkable guise of an Italian patriot seeking the independence of the city-republics. For the men of this school the political history of Italy was still the sum of its parts. Yet none the less they held that there existed a particular unity in the culture and society of the peninsula which flourished only when free from outside control. Accordingly, in what could be seen as a development of the tradition of Muratori's *Antiquitates*, they also wrote, and more successfully, works which concentrated on general aspects of Italian life in the Middle Ages transcending regional differences: works such as those by Balbo on Dante, by Ricotti on the Italian military spirit, and by Cibrario on Italian commerce.

Against the neo-Guelfs, the neo-Ghibellines, who were anti-clerical, and hoped for a united Italian state, had much less success in their treatment of this period, partly because the thirteenth and fourteenth centuries were so obviously much more difficult to see in terms of their own contemporary hopes, and partly because they lacked the genuine scholarly concern of the Catholic party. The one exception – though it is not, perhaps, really accurate to see him as a member of the school – was the brilliant Michele Amari, who in *La guerra del Vespro siciliano* (Palermo, 1842) portrayed the revolt against Charles of Anjou as not merely a Sicilian but as a national uprising. This revolution – against foreigners who were in league with popes – was, he asserted, not merely an incident but represented a great tradition, an eternal characteristic, of the Italian people. The part was made a symbol of the whole.

With Pio Nono's abandonment of the Revolution of 1848, the neo-Guelfs relapsed into a despairing silence and of the neo-Ghibellines too, as if incapable of survival without the presence of their enemies, no more was heard. During the 1850s a significant element in the mood of the age was reflected in the thesis of Giuseppe Ferrari's *Histoire des révolutions d'Italie, ou Guelfs et Ghibellines* (Paris, 1858). His vision of Italian history was one which it must have been very easy for anyone who had read works in the tradition of Biondo's *Decades* and Muratori's *Annali* to draw. Between the years 1100 and 1530, Ferrari counted 7,200 revolutions and 700 massacres in the peninsula. Herein, he believed, lay the key to the understanding of the essential Italy. If English history were made meaningful and given form by the story of its parliament or the history of France by its monarchy, what characterised Italian history was precisely its lack of any coherence, was precisely the eternal struggle of Guelfs and Ghibellines, by whatever name they passed under, which took place within its boundaries. Nor was this necessarily to be deplored, for might it not be that out of the very violence of the ages had been born the great manifestations of the Italian genius? Without revolution and massacre, exile and political turbulence, where is the *Divine Comedy*, etc.?

Finally national unity was achieved. At the same time profound changes were coming too in the world of historical study. In these years Italy and the whole of Western Europe were subject to a new invasion and once again the invaders were those of old, the Germans. This time, however, they marched not with buckler and spear but with powerful magnifying lenses; they deflowered not maidens but archives; they lusted after not blood but precise, verifiable facts; they acclaimed as their Gods not Wodin and Thor but Niebuhr and Ranke. The arrival of the philological-positivist school brought great benefits, notably in the scientific publication of sources and in archive study. Less happily it led to new general histories of Italy based upon the new methods. For Ranke, after all, the totality of universal history was very much bound up with the identification of individual races in political unity, and such a belief was seconded by the teaching of middle-class nationalists under the leadership of Pasquale Villari, who proclaimed the patriotic duty of 'creating Italians' by creating an Italian history. Hence the *Storia d'Italia scritta da una società d'amici* and the *Storia politica d'Italia scritta da una società di professori*, learned and scientific works which yet failed to find a centre around which to unfold and suffered as a result from a certain notable aridity.

With the 1890s new bands broke in upon the Italian world from the North and new names were inscribed upon the banners of the intellectuals. The doctrines of

Marx and Engels were elaborated by their Italian apostle, Antonio Labriola, founder of the *scuola economica giuridica*. Members of this school combined historical studies on Marxist or vulgar-Marxist lines with a particular interest in institutions derived from Savigny. Labriola lectured on the thirteenth century but rejected the possibility of writing about 'articifial entities' such as Italy. Against the Marxists came the Hegelians and the followers of Crocean idealism. But Croce too followed his one-time mentor, Labriola, in dismissing as springing from 'sentimental' and 'poetic' origins any hope of arriving at 'the hoary Utopia of a general history of Italy'.

In the twentieth century historians who have attempted to defy these judgments have seemed only to vindicate their essential justice. However great their ingenuity or learning they found themselves in the sights of a double-barrelled rifle of unfailing accuracy. If like Salvatorelli (*L'Italia communale*, 1940) they narrated a mass of events from all regions they were shot from the barrel marked 'unity'. (Like Sigonio and the neo-Guelfs Salvatorelli saw the thirteenth century as the age of 'the war for Italian liberty'; faced with the fourteenth century he could do no more than comment that 'the moral unity' of Italy was lost.) If like Valeri (*L'Italia nell' età dei principati*, 1949) they isolated and selected what they considered to be significant regional incidents as representative, they fell to the barrel marked 'diversity'. If like Simeoni (*Le signorie*, 1950) they thought to meet the problem by dividing up their work into alternating sections, some concerned with unifying features, some with regional, they were accused of writing two books and enjoyed the distinction of being blasted twice over.

Can then the history of Italy in these centuries be written? If Biondo and Sigonio and Sismondi, and two score others, have failed; if Labriola and Croce have condemned the enterprise, it seems unlikely. Moreover, today, the very attempt to evoke a specifically Italian (or British, French, or German) history must seem as reminiscent of the nineteenth century as the plumes in the dress hat of a carabiniere under the glass dome of the *Galleria*. Yet thinking again of the success of Muratori's *Antiquitates* one hesitates before abandoning hope. The basic failure of the tradition of Biondo's *Decades* springs from the attempt to see significance in groups of men as being primarily Italians. The success of the *Antiquitates* lay in its willingness to consider simply the actions of men, of men, that is, who happened to be Italians. In that way the *Antiquitates* was the first example of a search for a truly human history. It is in that spirit too that in the past decade a brilliant group of Gramscians, other Marxists, and liberals *di pura sangue* have combined to produce the *Storia d'Italia* issued by the Einaudi publishing house.

In a tighter chronological framework than was available to those authors this present work will consider within a loosely defined region (an Italy which may or may not include Trieste, Nice, Corsica, etc.) and arbitrary period of time (*c*. 1216–*c*. 1380) how some five or six generations of men and women contrived to live. Two introductory chapters will narrate the failure of Frederick II to create a united Italy and the subsequent disintegration of all wider political unity. A third will review the family and the fortunes of women and children. From there three chapters will examine the nobility, their attempts to monopolise political control against the *popolo,* and the emergence of both *signorie* (that is, governments controlled by single families) and new, more highly developed communes. One will turn then to the rural life of the *contado* (that area in the countryside subject to the town) and to that economic and social development of the towns which can be seen as the key motor of change in this period. Then, after describing the effects of agrarian and commercial growth on the relations between subjects and government, there follow chapters on the Church and, finally, on 'the crisis' of Italian society in the uneasy last forty years of the period.

II

By comparison with most other areas, Italy has preserved an unusually large body of written source materials from this period. Her history has dictated that these should not be concentrated in any one principal centre, such as the Public Records Office in England, but rather in over twenty *Archivi di Stato* whose geographical distribution today reflects broadly the pattern of governments as they existed during the later medieval period. Among the *Archivi di Stato* one may pick out for the bulk of their collections: Venice, Genoa, Mantua, Milan, Pisa, Florence, Bologna, Siena, Perugia, and Rome. The general pattern here is to find documents in large numbers from the 1250s and in often unmanageable quantity after the 1340s. Side by side with the *Archivi di Stato* are over 800 communal archives, administered by the local town councils, which frequently contain relevant records. As examples, thirty-five of the 285 communal archives in Tuscany and sixty-eight out of 246 in the Marche hold at least some manuscripts for this period.[7] Often they are few in number and slight in importance, but sometimes – and this is particularly true of the Marche – they make up considerable collections.

In addition there are the Vatican Archives with a wealth of sources referring to the Papal State and papal–Italian relations, while the 260 dioceses of the country each have an episcopal and chapter archive. Finally there are private libraries and archives. So in Florence, for example, there is the *Archivio di Stato*, archives of the Archbishop, of the Chapter, of the cathedral works, and of four charitable foundations. Then there are fourteen among numerous family archives still in private hands which hold material for this period. Again, the Biblioteca Nazionale di Firenze (incorporating the archives of suppressed monasteries,and the Magliabecchiana and Palatine libraries), the Biblioteca Laurenziana (incorporating, among other collections, the Ashburnham Library), and the Biblioteca Riccardiana (incorporating the Moreniana library), all contain a large variety of important sources.

There have been great losses over the centuries. The last war saw many, notably in September 1943, when a group of soldiers, seeking to relieve the tedium of military life, destroyed by fire the Angevin Archive of Naples. More recently the flooding of the Arno in November 1966 wrought havoc among certain sections of the *Archivio di Stato* at Florence. None the less, by the standards of contemporary

Europe, medieval Italy was an immensely literate, legalistic, and bureaucratic society in which a great deal was written and from which much survives. Among the survivals governmental documents predominate: town statutes, conciliar deliberations, decrees of administrative boards, court and fiscal records, and material concerning diplomatic relations. From commercial life there are account books, merchants' *ricordanze* or diaries (though these only in Tuscany), handbooks on trade (*Pratiche di mercatura*), and some letters, though these all appear in great numbers only at the end of our period. Particularly interesting are the contracts found in the notarial archives, through whose formulaic language one discovers a wealth of detail on sales, loans, wills, apprenticeships, marriage settlements, commissions for works of art, land transfers, labour agreements, and every aspect of social life.

Turning to literary sources, the writing of chronicles, which normally have a range of interest limited to their author's own region, was unevenly distributed. The towns of Umbria, Latium, Rome, and the Campagna produced few men to catalogue their fortunes. (It is a curious fact that more is to be learnt about thirteenth-century Rome from Matthew Paris, resident at St. Albans in England, than from any native chronicler.) Yet these areas are exceptional, and over 150 chronicles written in this period and dealing with its events are in print. They vary greatly in length, merit, and manner. There is the chivalric rhetoric of Martin da Canale's *Estoires de Venise* and the lively anecdotal narrative of the Franciscan friar, Salimbene de Adam. There were those who committed their work to verse, like the Milanese theologian, Stefanardo da Vicomercato, or the historian of Aquila, Boezio di Rainaldo. Some, like Ferreto Ferreti, looked for the spectacular; others, like Jacopo da Voragine, for examples of sanctity. Yet more and more in this period chronicles come to be written by men of the administrative class at the centre of affairs. One thinks of Riccardo da San Germano and Niccolò da Jamsilla, imperial notaries of the Hohenstaufen court; of the Sicilian lawyer and ambassador, Bartolomeo da Neocastro; of the Venetian Chancellor, Raffaino de' Caresini; of the authors of the *Annali Genovesi* whose work was commissioned by their commune; of the notaries of the Trevisan March in the thirteenth century, above all Rolandino of Padua and Albertino Mussato. Almost everywhere chronicle writing was increasingly taken over by laymen reared in the culture which was diffused by the Bolognesi schools of law and rhetoric.

In Florence a slightly different tradition appeared. Here in the thirteenth century historical writing had a rather weak growth. Two Florentine works in the past have been much praised for their colour and detail in describing events around 1300, but of these the *Cronaca* of Riccardo Malispini has, after a century of academic debate, been finally exposed as a forgery, while that of Dino Compagni, though still generally accepted as authentic, may well be a late fifteenth-century refashioning of earlier material.[8] It is only with the combined world history and chronicle of Giovanni Villani, given final form in the 1330s and 1340s, that Florentine historiography attained any distinction. What in some ways marks off this work from the notarial chronicles of the Bolognese school is the fact that its author was both a member of the Florentine oligarchy and a merchant and company director, and had a merchant's interest in such things as statistics of population, revenue, expenditure, and food supply. Two other rather similar Florentine chroniclers can also be singled out: Giovanni's brother, Matteo Villani and Marchionne Stefani.

Other surviving literary sources are numerous. From the ecclesiastical world there are lives and letters of saints, sermons, studies of liturgy, and a variety of pietistic and mystical writings. Canon and civil lawyers poured out treatises in great profusion. Then there are encyclopaedias, descriptions of cities, accounts of travels, mathematical textbooks, handbooks on agriculture, on cookery, on keeping fit, on treatment of disease. Just as in this age are found the first true portrait-representations in art, so now appeared the first biographies of men who were neither saints nor rulers. Finally there are works of prose and poetry, conceived as literature – this is the age of Dante, Petrarch, and Boccaccio – works which often throw the strongest light upon the feelings and thought world of the day.

III

More source materials survive than a hundred scholars could adequately master. From the fifteenth to the eighteenth centuries only a few among those who have drawn upon them have remained in the memory of general European scholarship. Of these the humanists of the fifteenth century, men like Bruni in his Florentine, and Sabellico in his Venetian history, whatever their attractions in their own time, have today little to say to us about our period. In the sixteenth century Machiavelli's *Storia fiorentina* stands by itself for the penetration of its insights (the speech ascribed to Michele di Lando in 1378 is the first and most powerful evocation of the voice of the revolutionary proletariat) but was constructed with an almost total indifference to factual accuracy. In the *Lives of the Painters*, another remarkable book, of which the first edition appeared in 1550, Vasari extended the boundaries of history, and adumbrated a plan for the interpretation of art in our period destined to have a long future.

In the seventeenth and eighteenth centuries the leading names of European historical scholarship in the Italian field were generally celebrated for learning and compilation rather than for the uses to which they put their materials. Rainaldo (1595–1671) continued the *Annales* of Baronius from 1198 in a work still useful to the historians of the Papal State. The Florentine Cistercian Ferdinando Ughelli (1595–1670) documented the history of the Italian bishoprics in his *Italia Sacra*, and the Irish Franciscan Luke Wadding (1588–1657) collected considerable Italian materials in his history of the Franciscan order. With 'the age of erudition' Dom Marténe and Dom Durand from the school of Saint Germain published documents relating to the history of the Papacy in Italy; the Dutch philologist, Johann George Graeve, issued his collection of chronicles, the *Thesaurus Antiquitatum et Historiarum Italiae* (Leyden, 1704–25); and Muratori edited the *Rerum Italicarum Scriptores ab anno aerae christianae 500 ad 1500* (Milan, 1723–51).

Yet to mention these men is by no means to encompass the totality of historical work done during the period. For Muratori did not stand alone. He was not at the beginning but rather in the middle of a tradition, and it is this tradition, it should be added, which helps to explain the extraordinary success of his *Antiquitates*. What gave Muratori sustenance was a long line of local scholars, abbés and gentleman *rentiers* with antiquarian tastes, who passed their long afternoons in the leisurely investigation of muniment rooms and the chronicling of the history of their towns.

Anyone who has worked in Italian medieval history knows the ubiquity and the immense value of these studies. At Ravenna, to cite the example of one town, the historian finds a tradition of local history which runs from the medieval chroniclers up to the present day. In the fifteenth century there was the humanist antiquarianism of Desiderio Spreti's *De amplitudine, eversione, et restauratione urbis Ravennae* (Ravenna, 1498); and in the sixteenth the elegant Latin of Girolamo Rossi's *Italicarum et Ravennatum Historiarum Libri XI* (Venice, 1572, reprinted there 1586, 1589, 1603); Tomaso Tomasi's *Istoria di Ravenna* (Pesaro, 1574; Ravenna, 1580); and the unpublished *Storia di Romagna fino al 1522* of Vincenzo Carrari (1540–1620). The seventeenth century saw Giorolamo Fabri's *Effemeride sagra et istorica di Ravenna antica* (Venice, 1664; Ravenna, 1675), his *Ravenna ricercata* (Bologna, 1678), and Serafino Pasolini's *Lustri Ravennati* (Bologna, 6 vols., 1678). In the following century came Antonio Zirardini with his *Degli antichi edifizi profani di Ravenna* (Ravenna, 1762) and his manuscript *De antiquis scavis Ravenne aedificiis* (published only in 1908–9). Pier Paolo Ginanni, Abbot of San Vitale and correspondent of Muratori, left his *Memorie storico-critiche de' scrittori ravennati* (Faenza, 1769) in print, and in manuscript six huge volumes cataloguing the Archiepiscopal Archive. From the same archive Giuseppe Amadesi wrote his history of the archbishops, the *In Antistitum Ravennatum Chronotaxim* (Faenza, 1793). Then in the era of that Jacobinism which he so detested, Count Marco Fantuzzi produced the magnificent six volumes of the *Monumenti ravennati de' secoli di mezzo* (Venice, 1802–4).

One could continue to document the tradition up to the twentieth century. Let us end with Camillo Spreti, who, in addition to producing his *Memorie intorno i dominii e governi della città di Ravenna* (Faenza, 1822), also translated into Italian the history which his ancestor had written in the fifteenth century. Part of these men's importance lies in their preservation of knowledge: their transcriptions of documents now lost, their descriptions of buildings now destroyed; their pointers to materials still in the archives. But there is something more than this too. What moved them was something which Sismondi and the neo-Guelfs were correct in sensing to be, if anything can be said to be so, characteristically Italian, that is intense local pride. From this it came that these men, possessors of a flowing classical Latin style, did not disdain the Latin of 'obscure' ages. Long before Walter Scott or Chateaubriand they could love their town and chronicle its vicissitudes even in the Middle Ages, even in the thirteenth and fourteenth centuries. And, again, their passion forbade them to limit themselves to great issues, to questions of war and peace, or to those genealogical studies which might flatter their friends. For them apparent trivialities too were important: the passing of sumptuary laws, the appointment of schoolmasters, the operation of pawn banks. In that way long before anyone had heard of social history they documented it. It was a tradition carried into the age of the *Risorgimento* by the foundation of over thirty local historical societies with their own periodicals and publication of sources. And still in the twentieth century a citizen army has survived among the forces of what might be called Italian and barbarian mercenaries, the national historical institutes, the German students of the empire, the French investigators of the Papacy.

Among professional historians of Italy in recent years there have been two significant developments. The first – though it is in a tradition or traditions which go back to the *scuola economica giuridica* – has been the development of socio-economic studies which either give a primacy to the character of society over politics or seek to place political developments within their social setting. The second – obviously connected with the first, yet more original – is what might be called 'the return to the land'. Some twenty years ago very little attention was given to the countryside. The Italian academic was essentially a man of the town and unlikely to be impressed by stories of R. H. Tawney's 'stout pair of boots' (the first requirement, he believed, for the student of history). Since then, even as Italian peasants have flocked to the cities, scholars have moved to the fields. Here a principal influence has been the publication of Philip Jones' first systematic synthesis in the second edition of volume 1 of the *Cambridge Economic History*. Work has begun too upon the type of evidence used by historians of the French and English economies: landscape, field systems, deserted villages, topography, place-names, rural housing, and the weather. As a result there is a movement away from an earlier emphasis upon the 'bourgeois' and 'capitalist' elements in the Italian communes, which are now being considered more in terms of their 'feudal' and agrarian elements.

In the fields of cultural and artistic history the traditions of Tiraboschi, Burckhardt, and Venturi are still strong. There has been much study, at least in their aesthetic aspects, of the towns, buildings, paintings, sculptures, and minor arts of the period. (Though more mundane survivals – one thinks of old factories, such as the fulling mill at Remole on the left bank of the Arno – have too often been neglected.) Of early Humanism a great deal is known. Yet here too there are important gaps in knowledge. Though art and literature are the subject of intense research, what so often underpins their understanding, namely knowledge of the religious society and sentiments of the time, has been passed by. Ecclesiastical historians, always keen to censure those clerics in the past who deserted their flocks to seek emolument and office in the *curia*, have themselves tended to concentrate on the central machine of the Vatican as a world power rather than on the local diocese. Yet here again the foundation of the *Rivista di storia della chiesa in Italia* in 1947 and the establishment of the *Centro di studii sulla spiritualità medioevale* at Todi in 1957 augur new developments.

It is all too easy to complain of researches not undertaken and of areas neglected. Yet the thought of the richness of the material which is available for study, combined with what are often great problems in its interpretation, will still any voice of discontent. Coming to attempt a consideration of human experience in Italy in these centuries one is struck constantly by the immensity of study devoted to the subject, a volume of work in face of which all must feel diffident. Every introduction to a book written upon the period must end, as I too end, with two notes: the first of respect and gratitude to all those scholars upon whose labour it is based; the second of apprehension for trespassing in fields of which others know so much more than the author.

NOTES

On **national consciousness** W. Goetz, 'Das Werden des italienischen Nationalgefühls', *Sitzungsberichte der bayerischen Akademie der Wissenschaften: Philosophisch-historische Abteilung*, 1939, pt. 7, gives a good introduction. For the problem of an **Italian national history** see D. Hay, *The Italian Renaissance in its Historical Background*, 2nd edn, Cambridge, 1977, ch. iii; B. Croce, *Storia della storiografia italiana nel secolo decimonono*, Bari, 1921; and E. Sestan, 'Per la storia di un idea storiografica: l'idea di una unità della storia italiana', *RSI*, lxii, 1950, pp. 180–98.

Among **recent histories of Italy** are Volume 1, 'Il medioevo', of the *Storia d'Italia*, ed. N. Valeri, 2nd edn, Turin, 1959; and the Einaudi *Storia d'Italia*, 6 vols. in 12, Turin, 1972–6. In English there are B. Pullan, *A History of Early Renaissance Italy from the mid-thirteenth to mid-fifteenth century*, London, 1973; D. Waley, *The Italian City–Republics*, 2nd edn, London, 1978; and J.K. Hyde, *Society and Politics in Medieval Italy: The evolution of the Civil Life, 1000–1350*, London, 1973.

On **chronicles** the only extended overall survey is that of U. Balzani, *Le cronache italiane nel medio evo*, 3rd edn, Milan, 1909; but see the article of O. Capitani, 'Motivi e momenti di storiografia medioevale italiana' in *Nuove questioni di storia medioevale*, Milan, 1964, especially pp. 770–92. Important local studies are G. Arnaldi, *Studi sui cronisti della Marca Trevigiana nell' età di Ezzelino da Romano*, Rome, 1963; G. Fasoli, *Cronache medievali di Sicilia*, Catania, 1950; *La storiografia veneziana fino al secolo XVI. Aspetti e problemi*, ed. A. Pertusi, Florence, 1970; B. Capasso, *Le fonti della storia delle provincie napolitane dal 568 al 1500*, Naples, 1902.

Among recent **bibliographical surveys** are Hyde, *Society and Politics, cit.*, pp. 200–16; E. Dupré Theseider, 'Literaturbericht über italienische Geschichte des Mittelalters: Veröffentlichungen 1945 bis 1958', *Historische Zeitschrift*, 1962, Sonderheft I; and N. Rubinstein, 'Studies on the Political History of the Age of Dante', *Atti del congresso internazionale di studi danteschi, Relazioni* i, Florence, 1965; and G. Martini, 'Basso medioevo' in *La storiografia italiana negli ultimi venti anni*, Milan, 1970. The annual *Bibliografica storica nazionale*, Rome, 1942–9, Bari, 1950 ff., records only works published in Italy, and should be supplemented by the bibliographical volumes of the *Revue d'histoire écclesiastique* (1900 ff., not confined to ecclesiastical history).

For an introduction to **archaeology** in the period, see T. Mannoni, 'Medieval Archaeology in Italy: A survey in *Papers in Italian Archaeology I: The Lancaster Seminar*, Part ii, ed. H. McK. Blake, T.W. Potter, D.B. Whitehouse in *British Archaeological Reports. Supplementary Series*, 41, 1978.

1. Petrarch, *Canzoniere*, cxlvi.
2. G. Bertoni, *I Trovatori d'Italia*, Modena, 1915, p. 207.

3. Goetz, 'Das Werden', *cit.*, p. 24; G. Villani, *Cronica*, ed. G. Dragomanni, 1844–5, VIII, p. 96.

4. *De vulgari eloquentia*, i, xvi, ed. A. Marigo, Florence, 1957, p. 138.

5. Salimbene de Adam, *Cronica*, ed. G. Scalia, Bari, 1966, p. 864.

6. Carlo Sigonio, *Historiarum de regno Italiae Libri XX*, Frankfurt, 1591, *Praefatio* and pp. 122–3. The edition of Bologna, 1580, is composed of fifteen books and continues only to 1200. The edition in volume ii of the *Opera Omnia*, Milan, 1732, shows other variations which perhaps indicate a change of plan in the course of the writing of the work.

7. I base these figures on a rough count in *Gli archivi storici dei comuni delle Marche* (Quaderni della Rassegna degli Archivi di Stato, 6), ed. E. Lodolini, Rome, 1960; and *Gli archivi storici dei comuni della Toscana*, (Quaderni, *cit.*, 22), ed. G. Prunai, Rome, 1963.

8. Despite the defence of L. Minervini 'Un problema ancora aperto: La cronaca malispina', *ASI*, 1971, pp. 143–80, the arguments of C. Davis, 'The Malispini question', *Studi medievali*, X[3], 1969, pp. 215–54 are decisive. My reserves before Compagni spring only in part from the type of arguments forwarded by P. Scheffer-Boichorst, 'Die Chronik des Dino Compagni, eine Fälschung' in his *Florentiner Studien*, Leipzig, 1874, pp. 45–218 (answered by I. del Lungo, *Dino Compagni e la sua cronica*, Florence, 1879, I, 2, 1043 ff.) but more from the discussion of its syntactical forms in G. Folena, 'Filologia testuale e storia linguistica' in *Studi e problemi di critica testuale*, Bologna, 1961, pp. 29–31.

CHAPTER TWO

Frederick II

I

As knowledge of Arabic learning spread within the West it was more and more coming to be believed that the lives of men on earth could be, if not ruled, at least interpreted through magic. Those sages who claimed skill in the art never wholly succeeded in dispelling all doubts that they might be, as individuals, either heretics or charlatans, but very few of their contemporaries would have asserted that they were pursuing a discipline which was entirely false or unlawful. The magician indeed, in his attempts to comprehend, dominate, or reduce to a formula the whole fabric of experience, in his search to give unity to all the myriad, seemingly unrelated, aspects of existence, was one of the most characteristic figures of the age, comparable in this with the civil lawyer and the scholastic theologian.

Pre-eminent among those who exercised the craft in Italy was Michael the Scot, servant of popes and of the Emperor Frederick II. Fat-bellied, thin-shanked; a typical Scotsman of the *diaspora*; one imagines him in Messina dreaming of the low light on Ettrick Water or back at Balwearie wistfully reminiscing of days in Toledo and sun-drenched Palermo. He portrays himself in the character of one born under Mercury:

He is serious and a great reader, notes important questions, and wants to know all the answers. He is interested in miniatures, painting, sculpture, school-teaching, and wants to be able to instruct scholars or disciples in white magic, to engage in business, and to perform tricks and subtleties which give pleasure to others.

He is anxious to save his soul and, as he grows older, is very conscientious. Sometimes he may sin like others, but he is extremely anxious to live morally.

He delights particularly in astronomy, natural science, law and divinity, and in adulterine arts such as interpretation of dreams, auguries, and lots.[1]

Although Michael's knowledge of and versions from Arabic scientific treatises were very largely dependent upon Jewish translators his studies in the new learning were comprehensive. They embraced cosmology, psychology, physiognomy, together with alchemy and all branches of magic: nigromancy, aeromancy, hydromancy, and the twenty-four other variants of the art which he

16

distinguishes. At Frederick's request he prepared two works on astrology: a *Liber Introductorius* written in a spirit of indefatigable pedagogy 'for all men of gross intelligence' and then a *Liber Particularis* addressed to those – among whom he gives a prominent place to the emperor himself – learned in the art.

He was to have a host of distinguished followers. There was Arnaldo da Villanova, who gave Boniface VIII the ring enclosing a spirit that had once been owned by Manfred. There was Cecco d'Ascoli – a martyr for his science, but the only one of the age – who overstepped into forbidden boundaries with his claim that Christ himself had been the victim of stars of ill omen. There was Pietro Buono of Ferrara whose *Pretiosa Margarita Novella*, a voluminous study of alchemy, almost endears through its final admission of failure to discover the secret it sought. There was Dionigi di Borgo San Sepolcro, early humanist and astrologer to King Robert the Wise, and the 'mathematician' (a word often used synonymously with 'astrologer'), Paolo Dagomiri, whose reading of the heavens was thought to have brought victory to the Florentines in the battle of Cascina. There was Tomasso da Pizzano (the father of that brilliant lady, Christine de Pisan), professor of Astrology in the University of Bologna, who was called as astrological adviser to Charles V of France. And there were scores of other remarkable men.

This is not to say that the occult arts were the exclusive preserve of the learned, for merchants' handbooks had their sections of astrological information, with advice on when to buy corn and engage in trade.[2] Nor does it imply that they did not have their own hierarchy of respectability. Least reputable was ritual magic: the imprisonment of demons in rings, mirrors, and phials. It was a practice condemned by John XXII, a French pope, who thought that many Italians (among them Matteo Visconti and Dante Alighieri) were, by these means, plotting against his interests. (Similarly, Clement VI was to complain that Cola di Rienzo communed with a demon called Fiorone whom he had trapped within a steel mirror.) By contrast, astrology enjoyed the esteem of all. Ristoro d'Arezzo's *Della composizione del mondo* (written in 1282) spoke for many of his contemporaries: 'We know how to design and work gold and silver and we know how to design and apply colours; these arts we know and understand and they delight us much, almost more than any others, saving only the science of the stars which is above all'.[3] Even those like the Augustinian friar, Agostino Trionfo, author of the *Contra divinatores et somniatores*, who launched general attacks upon the study of magic, normally accepted the search for meaning in the stars as valid, and like him asserted indeed that it would be sinful for a doctor to treat a patient without reference to the phases of the moon or for an astrologer to allow sailors to set out from port in the face of a storm which their art had presaged. There could be, of course, false astrologers, but as Pietro of Abano pointed out in his *Conciliator*, it would be absurd to judge the whole of a science from its unworthy practitioners. Hence, by the end of the thirteenth century every court boasted its resident astrologer; by the end of the fourteenth, theologians competed in proclaiming the nobility of the art and its full compatability with true religion.

The principal difficulty which appeared to face the astrologer was, as Abano explains, the precision which his craft demanded. Human error was always liable to upset the most careful attempts at calculation. The notary and historian, Rolandino of Padua, tells of how Master Theodore, imperial astrologer in succession to Michael the Scot, was led to choose the wrong hour for the departure of Frederick's army in its march upon Castelfranco:

He stood with his astrolabe on the tower of the commune, waiting, so it was said, for the ascent of the first phase or horoscope of Leo, believing Jupiter to be within it. But since, through overhanging clouds, he could not examine it with the astrolabe, he was deceived in his election. For Jupiter was not in Leo nor was Leo in the ascendant but Virgo and since Scorpio was then in the third house of its progress neither the army nor emperor were permitted to create offence. It was almost as if the tail of Scorpio, known to be untrustworthy and poisonous, had this effect.

Again, he tells of how Frederick in 1247 founded the siege-town of Vittoria against the city of Parma:

And because he knew that great men of old looked at the ascendant when they wished to found cities . . . he began under the ascending sign of Aries, both because it is the sign of Mars, known as the God of War, and because it was in opposition to the declining Libra which is the symbol of Venus, said to be the planet of Parma and its fortune. In this perhaps he thought, as it were, that the fortune of the men of Parma, in opposition to it, should decline. For among astrologers and those who follow astrological subtlety, the first house is given to the operative, the seventh to the oppositive. I think, however, he must have failed to note that Cancer was fourth from the ascendant. For the fourth designates buildings, houses, and towns, and a town begun under such an ascendant, had to be cankered.[4]

The answers of the astrologer, it had to be faced, were notoriously liable to error; as liable, we might say, as those of a computer. Then again, as with a computer, the answers were always dependent upon the questions set, the information fed in. Any hopes, that is, of a scientific, supra-mundane answer to the problems of the world always finally resolved themselves into the recognition that life was still ruled by the play of contingency, the irrational movements of the heart, the quirks of individual human beings, notably, at the beginning of the thirteenth century, by the mind and heart of the emperor.

II

His father had died when Frederick was three years old; his mother a year later. As heir to the Sicilian throne he had passed his childhood as a captive pawn of those German, Norman, and papal factions contesting the domination of the kingdom. In early 1212 he was seventeen years old, already a father, politically still largely helpless. In that year, representatives of the German princes came to Palermo to offer him the election to the imperial Crown. The Sicilian magnates sought to dissuade him; the success of any attempt to dispossess the reigning Otto IV was by no means certain; and if victorious in Germany, the Papacy would expect him to renounce the Sicilian throne in favour of his son. On the other hand

18

to be emperor was the greatest of secular honours. Control of Germany, to put the matter at its lowest, would prevent any renewed invasion of Sicily by an imperial claimant. More than this, Frederick was after all a Hohenstaufen and the tradition of his house dictated acceptance. He accepted.

Within a few years of his arrival in Germany it became obvious however that Hohenstaufen traditions, here at least, were to be abandoned. Calculating, perhaps, that by now any genuine re-establishment or royal authority north of the Alps was impossible Frederick triumphed simply through a massive series of concessions. Prêmyd Ottokar I was granted a golden bull which virtually freed Bohemia from any feudal relation to the empire; the claims of Waldemar II of Denmark to lands north of the Elde and Elbe were recognised and sanctioned; almost all imperial rights in respect of the ecclesiastical princes were abandoned. In the years 1212–20 Frederick set aside any plans he might originally have had to act as an effective ruler in Germany and offered the German princes vast alienations of his lands and regalian rights. In return he sought two things. The first was the imperial title which would give him *de jure* authority over the communes of northern Italy. The second was a claim upon German gratitude when he moved to make that authority a reality. Towards the Papacy, however, he adopted a stronger line. He informed Pope Honorius III that, though he would keep his promise never to bind Sicily in formal union with the empire, he did intend to continue to hold both, himself, in his own person. Whatever doubts or fears this announcement raised in the *curia* it was, perforce, accepted, above all in the hope that Frederick would lead, as he repeatedly promised to do, a new crusade. In November 1220, he returned to Italy and was crowned emperor at Rome.

In the event the crusade was long delayed. In the years 1220–5 Frederick devoted himself, instead, to the establishment of order in the Sicilian kingdom. It was a remarkably successful operation. Lay and ecclesiastical feudatories who had seized royal rights during the king's minority and absence were stripped of their usurpations. Castles built since 1189 were destroyed. All charters issued in the royal name since 1189 were subject to enquiry and abrogation. Defiant nobles on the mainland, notably among them, Tommaso, count of Molise and Celano, were crushed and exiled. The extravagant commercial privileges of the Genoese were abolished. For four years a war was fought against Muslims who had established, virtually, a brigand state around Girgenti in the centre of the island. With their surrender they were transported to the mainland and settled at Lucera in the Capitanata. This new colony, now in great dependence upon the emperor, was turned into a centre for the raising of Saracen troops for his service. Over the Church, in defiance of his promises to the popes, Frederick exercised that autocratic control customary among his Norman predecessors. He intervened in episcopal elections, seized the revenues of vacant sees, and maintained them vacant in order to continue drawing their revenues. He taxed the clergy and brought them to justice in the royal courts. At the same time royal government expanded. In 1224, Frederick founded a University at Naples and staffed it with teachers from Bologna, 'mother of the laws', in order to train the bureaucrats necessary for his administration.

Encouraged by these successes Frederick then moved to bring imperial control to northern Italy which hitherto he had neglected. A diet was summoned at Cremona for Easter 1226 whose purpose, it was announced, was 'to restore imperial rights'. A generation had passed since anyone had sought such a programme, and the answer of almost all the communes was a flat defiance. On the 6 March the Lombard League which had resisted the empire in the twelfth century was re-formed. On Frederick's arrival at Ravenna in April he learnt that the Brenner had been closed to the troops which he had ordered to his aid from Germany. His sole allies were Cremona, Parma, Reggio, Modena. Thwarted, he climbed down and made an humiliating peace which seemed to acknowledge imperial impotence. Worse was to follow. In March 1227 Honorius was succeeded as pope by Gregory IX, a forceful personality and aggressive politician. From the outset of his pontificate, Gregory abandoned that policy of appeasement or Christian passivity pursued by his predecessor and determined to unleash war. He was well able to calculate the dangers which the Papacy would face were there some imperial triumph in Lombardy which would render the whole of Italy subject to Frederick. He feared in particular for the intergrity of the Papal State, so recently formed by Innocent III. The *curia* had received with particular apprehension the emperor's suggestion of March 1222 that Spoleto and the Marche should be returned to the empire. It observed with indignation that in March 1226, on his way north to Ravenna, he had actually called the nobility of these regions to his banner as his vassals. Quite apart from these things Gregory also sought the restoration of 'ecclesiastical liberties' in Sicily, the end of those abuses or, as the Crown would have put it, 'ancient customs', which the young Frederick had indeed sworn to forgo.

Politically there was sufficient motive for war. The pretext for its declaration was found in Frederick's failure to fulfil the crusading vow which he had taken in 1215. In the summer of 1227 the emperor's crusading fleet was in fact gathered in the harbours of Apulia, ready to set forth. But it was a year of famine, and famine-diseases attacked the assembled army. Frederick, who claimed to have, indeed may have, himself fallen ill, thereupon postponed his own departure until May of the following year. Gregory at once seized the opportunity to excommunicate him. Frederick replied by setting out for the East in June 1228, and was thereupon re-excommunicated for having sought to go on crusade while in a state of excommunication. Gregory followed up this stroke by taking the remarkable step of declaring his own crusade against Frederick: 'that a mighty persecutor of the Church may be driven from his kingdom'. The 'crusading tenth' was raised from the clergy of Europe to finance it; and, though somewhat ineffectively, a papal army began to wage war within the kingdom.

While this, the, as it were, official crusade proceeded with little success, varying fortunes attended what must be thought of as the unofficial expedition. Frederick's rather clumsy assertion of imperial suzerainty over the barons of Cyprus between July and September 1228 ensured that he should receive no unanimous welcome among their factious and legalistic cousins who held fiefs in the Holy Land.[5] In these circumstances and in the tradition of most of the native Frankish politicians of the Holy Land, Frederick sought his ends by negotiation rather than force. As Richard Coeur de Lion had parleyed with Saladin, so Frederick held a series of conferences with Saladin's nephew, the Sultan Malik al-Kamil. These discussions finally achieved a ten-year truce and the cession by the Muslims of Jerusalem, Bethlehem, Nazareth, and two corridors linking these places with the coast. It might at first sight have seemed a satisfactory solution. Yet for Frederick the episode was an error. From the point of view of a monarch the purpose of a crusade was not simply to regain the Holy Places for Christendom, it was, much more, to appear in an heroic light, to have one's Christian virtues praised by every troubadour in Europe, to return to one's country and one's clergy in the image of an ideal knight. Such a knight the Papacy would have found much more difficult to oppose, excommunicate, or depose from imperial power. If there had been, as with King Richard, a battle before the negotiations began, Frederick would for the rest of his life have been in a much stronger position vis-à-vis the spiritual power.

He returned to Sicily in June 1229. He drove the papal army from the kingdom, but in the following year came to peace with the pope by promising the surrender — the very considerable surrender — of royal control over the Sicilian Church. A chapter was closed in the history of the reign. Frederick, now thirty-five years old, stood at a cross-roads, in which the broad possibilities of any future policies — intervention in Germany, in northern Italy, in the Papal State, in the East — had all been tested. He could examine these possibilities again — though none seemed particularly promising — or he could simply concentrate the rest of his life in Sicily, bringing there that order, perhaps even some measure of prosperity, which had marked the reorganisation of 1220–5. All depended upon his personal decision and character.

That character has exercised and continues to exercise a perennial fascination. For Matthew Paris he was: *'Principum mundi maximus Frethericus stupor quoque mundi et immutator mirabilis'*, words which perhaps mean: 'Greatest of the princes of the world, Frederick who bewildered the world and brought extraordinary change'. It was not a judgment intended as praise, though later generations have taken it as such. Frederick had strong intellectual interests, rare enough in rulers, and hence has made an instinctive appeal to scholars. He fought against the Papacy, which has widened his attraction considerably. He lost, which allows the luxury of reflections on 'if only' themes. In the event, when considering his career, historians have tended both to exaggerate his (in fact very considerable) abilities and to recreate the man in the image of their own age. In the eighteenth century, he was cast as an enlightened despot; in the twentieth as a romantic, blond, Teutonic nationalist. With this there goes the urge to proclaim his modernity (as in Burckhardt's 'the first man of a modern type who sat upon a throne') and hence, given that he lived in the thirteenth century, his astounding originality, a contention expressed in that often-repeated and most unhistorical of all phrases: 'he was born before his time'.

To seek the reality of the man, the evidence of the thirteenth century requires careful sifting. Frederick was a Mediterranean ruler, brought up in a world conquered from the Muslims, where Muslim traditions were still strong. Like other such rulers, like those 'baptised sultans', the Norman kings before him, he had some working knowledge of Arabic, and he maintained a court of oriental splendour and exoticism. We hear of a menagerie; Saracen girls who danced upon moving balls, singing and beating cymbals; blacks playing upon silver trumpets; queens secluded in the atmosphere of a harem: all 'the astonishing novelties' which Richard of Cornwall reported from his visit to Palermo. To the Northern world he was inevitably an exotic, and as such he attracted exotic gossip, the gossip of Matthew Paris and Salimbene, sometimes perhaps true, sometimes certainly false. Again, according to who was paying them, troubadours and Minnesingers poured out a wealth of conflicting evidence on his virtues and vices, which has muddied the waters still further. He was moreover for the best years of his life the object of a sustained propaganda vilification by the Papacy, which, though often received with a certain critical scepticism by contemporaries, was, by its volume and persistence, influential in forming opinion of the day. More than this, it has often profoundly influenced modern biographers who have frequently praised Frederick precisely for those things which the Church slanderously or tendentiously attributed to him.

Against these attacks Frederick relied upon the eulogies and propaganda of his rhetoricians but ignored the chronicle. Though some pro-imperial city histories are extant their principal theme is never the deeds and mind of the emperor but rather the fortunes of the local imperial party. The one chronicle by a supporter, that of Mainardo of Imola, which apparently took the emperor as central to the narrative, has not survived. While not exaggerating the importance of chronicle evidence, the historian, if only from fellow feeling, would have felt much more at home in Frederick's world had he appointed Matthew Paris to be his historiographer rather than Michael the Scot to be his astrologer. Certainly, in considering the emperor's character, there is much less evidence upon the thought behind his everyday political actions than upon his cultural and intellectual interests.

On these latter, much is known. In the world of the visual arts, it is difficult, taking into account the length of his reign, to see Frederick as an important figure, despite large claims made by his admirers. Not all that much has survived from the milieu of his court; one thinks of the miniatures in the Vatican codex of the *De arte venandi*, perhaps the engraving of the gold *augustales*. In architecture numerous hunting lodges were built for him, and several castles in a uniform, rather featureless, style. Two works only stand out. The first, Castel del Monte, set amidst the bleak landscape of the Basilicata, has exquisitely proportioned octagonal walls and a curious blend or clash of classical and later elements, a linking of pediment and Corinthian pillars, Lombard lions, and Gothic bosses and windows. The second is the triumphal portal at Capua, now wholly destroyed, which appears to have had strong classical elements in its composition. It is indeed likely that there was some link between the work undertaken at Capua and that of certain sculptors of the second half of the thirteenth century in Tuscany. Yet the inference that Frederick's court was in any major way responsible for those changes in Italian art brought about during our period seems to be based on very little evidence.[6] The coming of the new styles of the thirteenth and fourteenth centuries was largely bound up with developments in civic and ecclesiastical feeling with which Frederick had no sympathy. The final word, perhaps, should rest with Tommaso da Gaeta, who complained that the poor were being oppressed for the construction of castles and that 'it would have better become your majesty, for the sake of Him who suffered poverty for mankind, to have offered the first fruits of your building in some work pleasing to God'.[7]

As a patron of literature, Frederick's rôle is much more impressive. Like all politicians of the time he gave money to troubadours. It was the equivalent in that age of buying a newspaper, and does not necessarily imply any interest in Provençal or German lyric poetry. The Latin *littérateur*, Henri d'Avranches, and various Greek poets from the Terra d'Otranto wrote panegyrics upon his virtues. No doubt he rewarded these authors; whether he burdened himself with reading them is unknown. What is much more significant is his interest in Italian poetry. Some at least of the early Italian verses ascribed to the emperor – in themselves rather flat exercises – seem indeed to have been written by him. Certainly, it was at his court, and presumably with, as Dante believed, his encouragement that Italian speech was first systematically developed in literary forms.

Everything, however, suggests that Frederick's particular bent of mind was one which took pleasure, above all, in the new learning of the natural sciences, studies in which his grandfather, King Roger, had shown an early interest. Although Palermo could never be thought of as a major centre – comparable with Toledo – for the transmission of Greco-Arabic learning to Europe, Frederick's court played some part in the movement. He was the patron of translations from the Arabic and of original works on hygiene, biology, and magic written by Michael the Scot and Theodore of Antioch. Lionardo of Pisa's treatise on mathematics and Giordano Ruffo's study of the diseases of the horse were dedicated to him. Moreover he was himself responsible for a remarkable ornithological work: the *De arte venandi cum avibus*. Those who have asserted that this is 'a work of modern science' are, predictably, in error, for although (the basis of their claim) Frederick does assert the right to correct Aristotle when inaccurate (and who did not?), he sees the anatomy of the bird in an Aristotelian, *a priori*, teleological, functional manner. Yet, this said, what remains is a very remarkable book indeed, 'the best book on birds ever written',[8] composed after formidable research and inspired by powerful intellectual curiosity. It is unfortunate that we do not know how much of it – something no doubt, but, one suspects, by no means all – derives from the treatises of his Arab falconer, Moamyn, which Theodore of Antioch translated for the emperor.

With this too went some interest in philosophy, a series of curious questions addressed to the Arab world on such matters as the number of categories and the eternity of matter, and then again, correspondence with the learned commentator on Maimonides, Moses ben Solomon of Salerno. The new learning, of course, derived principally from Arab sources and Frederick's interest in it, though by no means unique to himself or his court, gave the Papacy an easy pretext to accuse him of adherence to Islamic belief. This claim was accompanied – illogically enough, as Matthew Paris pointed out – by suggestions that he was a complete sceptic, that he held Moses, Christ, and Mohammed to be three impostors. Any certain resolution of Frederick's real religious sentiments is impossible. Certainly the character of his patronage to the arts was extremely secular: churches did not benefit. Again when he was in the East Ibn-al-Jawzi remarked that: 'one saw from the way he spoke that he was a materialist who made a simple game of Christianity'. It is a comment perhaps of a man who is interpreting Frederick's anti-clericalism as anti-Christianity or who is insensitive to the irony with which the emperor might speak to Muslims of his own faith as being that of 'the polytheists'. Against it one sets the Frederick, who, admittedly as a young man, impetuously and very unwisely took the cross, who, member of a Cistercian prayer community, loaded the order with gifts, and who promoted devotion to his relative, St. Elizabeth of Hungary. The position of Holy Roman Emperor was so closely bound up with Christianity that it must have been difficult for the emperor, psychologically, to have been doubtful of its doctrines. Perhaps he professed a Hohenstaufen piety, one which eschewing enthusiasm and making few demands, gave its possessor the conviction that his life was justified and sanctified from outside. What certainly accompanied this was a fierce public intolerance before 'heresy' and an insistence that any deviation from the Catholic faith 'in the least way' should be punished by the fire.

In all, Frederick's personal intellectual and cultural interests and attitudes suggest a most brilliant and wide-ranging mind but one which it would be truer to think of rather as *avant garde*, as very sharply attuned to current developments, than as in itself strikingly original or unorthodox. The same judgment might be given upon the use he made in the public field of the two most important, native-Italian or, more precisely, Bolognesi branches of study of the age. The first of these was the type of rhetoric evolved by the *dictatores* of the school of Boncompagno. At Capua this was developed in the works of Taddeo da Suessa, Riccardo of Traetto, Andrea da Cicala, and, above all, in – if one may parody his own style – the amphigonic discourses of the protreptical protonotary and logothete logorrheic, Pietro della Vigna, those resonant compositions designed to suggest to an awed world the magniloquent voice of a Roman emperor. The second was the study of law in the spirit of the great renaissance of Roman jurisprudence initiated in the eleventh century. That he employed men skilled in these two fields showed awareness of the contemporary intellectual climate but no particular originality for both his grandfather, Barbarossa, and the Papacy had done the same. None the less, here was an intellectual in politics, and one has only to think of his contemporary sovereigns to grasp the measure of how cultivated he was and how cultivated the world from which he came.

Intellectual cultivation, it is a truism, is, however, no guarantee of ability in the coarser world of political calculation. Here Frederick had to formulate plans both as Roman Emperor and as king of Sicily. As emperor he inherited a structure of grandiose early-medieval theoretical formulations which asserted the sacred, religious, divinely-ordained character of his rule, and his right and duty to exercise secular lordship over all men. In this rôle his panegyrists told him that he was Lord of the four Elements, the Deity of the Sun, and one destined to bring back the Age of Gold. Niccolò of Bari spoke of him as born of the House of David, elected to be Aaron the Priest. He was Judas, son of Jacob, prefiguring Christ, to whom applied the prophecy of Jacob (*Genesis*, 49:10), interpreted thus: 'None shall take away the sceptre from the hand of the Lord Frederick, nor the staff of leadership from his loins, that is to say the Empire from his line, until Christ shall be sent in Judgement. That is to say, until the end of the world shall this family rule . . .'. In the letters of his rhetoricians (though in those addressed to other kings the words are muted) there feature large assertions of universal predominance. 'Albeit', he writes to the Romans in December 1243, 'not everywhere corporeally present, our reins extend to the furthest ends of the earth . . . Rome shall be subject to us, to us whom the land serves, the seas favour, and for whom, at our nod, all desires are fulfilled'.[9]

Whether this rhetoric or propaganda was too traditional and conservative or too much at variance with observed facts to be effective in the world of the thirteenth century; whether, alternatively, the hints of contemporary Joachite millenarianism which have been discerned within it made it either potent or too *outré* to be potent, it is not easy to say. It was an age of extravagantly formulated claims. There was no pope, hastening to exile as the result of the importunities of the Roman mob or an insurrection of Viterban street-boys, who could not find time to pause in flight and declare himself to be Lord of the World. But Frederick himself, it can hardly be doubted, had not lost all grip upon reality, did not, that is, pay much attention to the flatteries of legal or mystical formulation. He probably conceived himself, as his grandfather had done, as being in some way the heir of Caesar and Augustus – hence the 'Roman' rhetoric, the minting of the would-be classical *augustales*, perhaps the classical influences in the Capuan gate – but he had, one can be sure, no ambition to recreate their empire, of which indeed, like his contemporaries, he can have had very little knowledge or understanding. The most he hoped for, as some distant goal, might have been to enjoy the rôle of final arbiter in Christendom, similar to, perhaps even stronger than, that which had been exercised by Innocent III. It was this which (if he really took any notice of the rhetoric of his *dictatores* or clerks) he might have thought of as 'the restoration of the ancient glory of Rome'. But his policy in Germany, with its continued concessions to the princes, its virtual abdication of royal power, particularly in the years 1213–20 and 1231, show that, however much his official letters might suggest it, he had no interest in the direct domination of the whole world, even more, one might say, that he had learnt the lessons which in this had been dealt out to his grandfather, the first Frederick, and his father, Henry VI. For Frederick the Roman Imperial title meant nothing more than the right to rule in northern Italy, some prestige, and some claims to independence of the pope in areas of temporal dominion.

In addition to his father's inheritance, and before he was emperor, he was king of Sicily: heir to his Norman mother and the Norman feudal monarchy. By the end of the twelfth century, southern Italy, which, notably at Messina, Gaeta, Bari, and Salerno had once enjoyed a certain flowering of commercial activity, had begun to sink into that economic lassitude which still characterises it today. Even as the towns of the north of Italy were rising to become the dominant elements in European commerce the hand of a centralising fiscalism had throttled the enterprise which was bringing prosperity to Tuscany, Liguria, Lombardy, and Venice. At Frederick's accession the wealth of the kingdom was found only in land: on the mainland in the wheat-fields of Apulia; on the island in the corn regions around Agrigento, Licata, Sciacca, and Castrogiovanni or the vine-covered hills near Messina. Trade, which by now amounted to little more than the export of corn, had fallen into the hands of the Pisans and Genoese. There were few skilled craftsmen; the silk industry of Palermo had withered away; textile manufacture satisfied only some small local demand and was faced, even here, with the competition of superior north-Italian products; the working of cotton was giving way to the simple sale of the raw material.

In these circumstances, without imagining any solution to 'the problem of the South' the historian of today, with all the advantages of hindsight, might see the best strategy for a ruler who sought the prosperity of his people as one which encouraged native trade, gave glory and profit to merchants, which sought the growth of private industry and private banking, which promoted vast individual wealth and, inevitably if unwillingly, the vast social change which went with it. The aim of the king would be to make of Messina a Venice, of Palermo a Barcelona, draining off part of the trade which was to flow into those ports. It would be, that is, the sort of policy which Jaume I and Pere II were pursuing in Aragon. In Aragon the monarchy, in alliance with the merchants of Catalonia and Valencia, was seeking new markets in Italy, new access to the ports of the East, and the creation of a native capitalism from whose benefits foreigners were to be excluded. It was the policy followed – largely because they had no superior effective *de facto* ruler – by the great Italian cities of the north in the thirteenth century.

Yet Frederick was too much a Norman king, too much an Hohenstaufen emperor, to follow such a course. In his Italian kingdom such developments might indeed have brought prosperity to his subjects but they would have implied no particular benefits and many certain disadvantages to the ruler. For although the Normans had crushed possibilities of economic growth in the South, they had (indeed the two things were intimately connected) exploited to the full its fiscal possibilities. Immense sums – towards the 1270s they were to be in the region of 200,000 *oncie* (say 1,000,000 gold florins) annually – flowed to the Crown which had therefore no real imperative to increase the taxable wealth of its subjects. This was the truer in that any promotion of the economy could have sprung only from such measures as the abolition of the *casaticum* (the obligation to store exports in royal warehouses), reduction of taxes upon merchants, very pronounced preferential tax discrimination in favour of native against north-Italian entrepreneurs, and the abandonment of royal monopolies in dyeing, iron, steel, pitch, and hemp. Yet all these would have bitten sharply into royal revenues. Moreover, what effect the growth of powerful commercial towns in Sicily would have had upon royal power was amply demonstrated by the political difficulties which had already attended Frederick in his attempt to impose his imperial power upon the North.

Understandably if any such course of action were ever considered it was wholly rejected. Instead Frederick devoted himself in Sicily to expanding and sharpening the traditional Norman policy. Early in his reign he cut down the privileges of over-powerful foreign merchants. The Genoese, who in the early 1190s had been enfeoffed with the whole city of Syracuse and with 250 knights' fees in the Val di Noto, were dispossessed. But no corresponding benefits were given to native traders. At no point did Frederick seek commercial privileges for the men of his kingdom in Germany, Venice, North Africa, or the Levant. Instead, the burdens upon their commerce were increased; the growth of any private mercantile shipping was inhibited by the construction of a privileged royal navy which took part in trade; royal monopolies were extended. At the same time the administrative controls upon the collection of revenues by the Masters of the *Dohane de secretis*, the *quaestores*, the collectors of excise, were made more efficient. Any surplus wealth in the already wretchedly poor kingdom came to be soaked up in the *subventio generalis*, a property tax, originally levied only in times of crisis but from 1235 transformed into an oppressive annual levy.

In return the monarchy gave an increasing measure of efficiency in the adminstration of justice and an answer to that problem of public order which as in the whole of Italy or Europe of the day was, at least from the point of view of the governing classes, the central issue of contemporary politics. Like his grandfather, Roger II, or like Henry II in twelfth-century England, Frederick saw the key to monarchical power as the establishment of a centralised legal authority. This, it was hoped, would break down the anarchy implicit in local traditions of obtaining justice by self-help and provide an alternative and superior justice both to that of feudal courts and to the private search for vengeance. In the imposition of royal justice the Great Court, composed of the higher officials of the realm, sat under the Master Justiciar in criminal and under the Master Chamberlain in civil cases. At the same time the Master Justiciar presided over the regional justiciars of the eleven provinces into which the kingdom was divided. These men, chosen, by preference, from the lower nobility of the royal demesne, and working with a staff of notaries, castellans, and sergeants from the castles where they held sway, were responsible for all criminal cases. Civil cases were made the responsibility of chamberlains and bailiffs subject to the Master Chamberlains of the Great Court. All judges, notaries, even advocates, were appointed by the Crown.

The thought behind these arrangements was spelt out in the *Constitutiones Augustales*, issued at Melfi, after Frederick's return from Palestine, in 1231. This collection of decrees (known sometimes as the 'Constitutions of Melfi' or, from the nineteenth century, as the *Liber Augustalis*) reveals more clearly than any other source the presuppositions of Frederick and his advisers and the aims and purpose of his government. Its heavy 'Capuan' style, so much in contrast to the style of the contemporary statutes of the north-Italian towns, and the powerful influences which the Bolognese revival of law has exercised on that style (its insistence upon how the *Quirites* have conferred *jus et imperium* upon the *princeps Romanus* by the *lex regia*, etc.) have perhaps led later historians to overemphasise its originality. There was, in truth, nothing particularly new in this age in governments, whether papal or secular, claiming a legislative right. Over seventy years before the four doctors of Bologna had greeted Frederick I as *lex animata*, as 'the personifier of law'. Nor was there anything new in legal codes drawing upon the traditions of Roman law. What was new was the precision and explicitness, the comprehensiveness and coherence with which the claims of the monarch were set forth. The principal interest of the work, that is, does not lie so much in what might be new within it as in what it reveals of the mind of the ruler of Sicily.

The basic content of the *Constitutiones* is procedural law. The principal aim of government is to secure *pax* (public order) by the *cultus justitiae* (the establishment of effective legal processes). With minor reservations (for the use of the ordeal and trial by battle were restricted though not abolished), the continued existence of the various legal codes and local customs, whether Frankish, Langobard, Romano-Byzantine, under which men lived in the kingdom, was fully accepted. But over these was extended a system of royal courts and judicial procedure which would make these various codes effective and would guarantee a large measure of that *pax* which the king saw himself as destined to provide. This programme, accompanied by the direct prohibition of private war and restrictions upon the bearing of arms, sought to make of the king: 'the father and the son, the lord and the servant of justice; father and lord in dispensing justice and in maintaining what has been dispensed'.

Anyone aware of the breakdown of public order within the communes of northern Italy or who remembered the anarchy of the interregnum in Sicily could realise the benefits offered by the royal ideal of 'the cult of justice'. For the monarch too it increased revenue and gave justification for those high-sounding phrases which set forth his absolute power. Yet reading the *Constitutiones* it is clear that the purpose of this absolutism was not in any way revolutionary but rather designed to preserve an existing predominance of feudal custom. *Pax* was to be secured by internal immobility, by the preservation of the kingdom from those changes and tensions which were tearing northern and central Italy apart. The independent commune is seen as a principal enemy; it is the source of heresy and the breeder of usury (i.e. any capitalist activity). Towns must, therefore, be exclusively under the control of officials appointed by the Great Court. Any official, '*podestà*, rector, or consul elected by the men of a town' shall suffer death; the town where such an election has been made shall be given over to 'perpetual desolation', and 'all men of the same town shall be held as serfs in perpetuity'.[10] Against the danger to the existing order posed by the towns the monarchy looked to traditional allies, first to the Sicilian Church (if possible, under royal control) whose jurisdictions (except in case of treason) were confirmed and to whom the payment of tithes was strictly enjoined; and second, and above all, to the nobility.

In the *Constitutiones* the traditional privileges of the nobility, which in northern Italy were already under attack from the *popolo*, were emphatically confirmed. 'In order that the accustomed honour of each and every noble of our kingdom should be wholly preserved', the trial of 'counts, barons, and other knightly men' was reserved to their peers. The oaths of fealty by vassals to their lords were strengthened. Their right to exact aids from vassals was confirmed and extended, and the seigneurial right to disseise vassals reaffirmed. Other sections of the *Constitutiones* look to the interests of the nobility in the grant of fiefs in dower, wardship, and treatment of fugitive serfs. In some cases higher penalties attach to offences against nobles by non-nobles; and the credence given to testimony in courts is graded according to the rank of him who gives it. The caste character of Frederick's mind appears, perhaps, nowhere more clearly than in the reissue of his grandfather's decree which asserted that none should be a knight unless born into a family of knights. This is then, in part, emended: those who have become knights since the edict of king Roger may continue to hold the rank 'as long as they live in a knightly manner', and, then again, men may become knights by royal licence. Yet, he continues, none may be a judge or notary, who is of low rank, or a serf, or illegitimate. In addition, 'anyone indifferent to shame, who seeks to dishonour knighthood, the foundation of any dignity he has' may be stripped of his status. Striking a fellow knight, habitual gaming, or haunting taverns, could lead to deprivation of the rank.[11]

However original the clothing of Roman-law allusions, the *Constitutiones* in their nakedness were immensely conservative. Any north-Italian lawyer who was involved in politics and who read the collection would perhaps fasten his attention first upon those passages in which the absolutism of the emperor was exalted, such flights as:

When the imperial clemency turns the eyes of his forethought to the paths of justice and exalts the throne of his government by arming the imperial majesty with the defence of law, he relieves both the burdens and oppressions of his subjects, who only after God breathe through the mildness of their generous prince.[12]

Alternatively he might brood on those sections where it was declared 'sacrilege' to question the emperor's decisions. Such words certainly carried with them the message that any extension of imperial power to Lombardy would spell death to the consultative regimes of the communes. For many, already, this thought may have held no terrors. The rule of a generous prince may well have been seen as preferable to that anarchy provoked by a communal oligarchy. Although the rhetoric which was to surround such a ruler was fawning, the price to pay for the restoration of social harmony within the towns might have been deemed slight. What for many readers would have made the reaffirmation of imperial power in Italy supremely undesirable was not so much the possibility of absolutism as the presuppositions which would inform that absolutism. It could be argued – probably wrongly – that the rigid feudal ideal of the *Constitutiones* was a suitable solution for the problems of the kingdom. But that the man whose mind was expressed in them should seek to rule the world of the north-Italian cities with their complex mercantile interests, where merchants were not subordinate to the feudal classes but fused with them, where economic interests often openly directed the course of politics, augured ill. Such a mind might have operated very well in England or France but it was unlikely to establish by agreement *pax* in northern Italy. Two different societies and ways of life here faced each other: the one, authoritative, romantic, employing all the learning of the present to preserve the venerable practices of the past; the other individualistic, violent, often squalid, creating the world of the future.

Yet what the *Constitutiones* made abundantly clear was that Frederick, now in 1231, was planning once again to assert his rule in the North. Within them all idea of separating the empire and the kingdom of Sicily, of distinguishing between emperor and king, had been put aside. These constitutions, ostensibly for the kingdom of Sicily, are issued by the most sacred Roman Emperor, whose Caesarian and Augustan splendour is constantly referred to, and their formulation is justified by the Roman people's grant of absolute power to their prince in the *lex regia*. What is made obvious is that these decrees were not simply drawn up for Sicily, but were designed, as well, for the imperial possessions of the North, when they came into Frederick's power.

It would be easy, with hindsight, to dismiss Frederick's attempt to dominate the North, to create – though the word is never mentioned – an Italy, as irresponsible, as doomed to failure. Would it not have been better to have made Sicily the scene of his life, to have lived on its vast revenues, dividing his time between the cares of administration, his hunting lodges, the poetry of his courtiers, and conversation with his astrologers? At least the peninsula would have been spared yet more war. It was not what troubadours expected of kings and emperors, for whom war and diplomacy were seen as a sport or a game of chess; but it was what, at least in the past, the Papacy had hoped of him; and, after all, there were pious kings. It was not, however, within the character and ideals of this Hohenstaufen whose ancestors had been so powerful. In law, after all, the North was his. If his grandfather had failed to defeat the Lombard Communes, he had not lost all power there; if his father's influence had been swept away at his untimely death, could it not yet be reconstructed? The precedent of 1226 looked unpromising; the enmity of the Papacy was now more uncompromising; yet did not that enmity make the union of North and South Italy now more imperative? And would not war divert his own Sicilian feudality from thoughts of resistance to their king? In history there were many precedents for poor, backward societies with disciplined military strength becoming masters of rich, fat lands, whose peoples were divided among themselves. Looking north, Frederick could see a world of virulent anarchy, town against town, faction against faction within towns, a world looking – surely? – for a saviour. What he did not see, for he was an alien to it, was the immense vitality of that violent world, the strength and resilience of those warrior merchants of the north who would seek to retain this wealth with all the courage with which they had gained it.

III

In the event some four to five years were to pass before Frederick was to meet with any success in Lombardy. His immediate attempts to make something of the empire were abortive. He summoned a diet of the towns at Ravenna for November 1231 at which none of the Lombard League appeared. In the negotiations which followed Pope Gregory imposed on the two parties that same form of indecisive peace negotiated by Honorius III in 1226. Meanwhile, to secure the continuing support of the German princes, Frederick made yet more concessions to them. In the *Constitutio in favorem principum* of May 1231, comfirmed and promulgated by the emperor in the following year, the privileges of the German towns were abrogated in the interests of the nobility and the princes were virtually accorded a *de facto* independence of the empire within their own territories. It was an important landmark in that process by which Germany became simply a confederation of princes, 'the lights', as Frederick curiously called them, and protectors of the empire. When, three years later, his son, Henry, aghast at this destruction of royal power, resisted and revolted, Frederick raced to Germany and crushed the rebellion with the aid of the grateful princes. Like Abraham, the emperor showed no hesitation in preparing his first-born for sacrifice in obedience to the requirements of that which he most loved; Henry was stripped of his kingship and condemned to a perpetual imprisonment from which he would only be released by suicide.

Shortly the father was to receive his reward. Confident now of German support, at the Diet of Mainz in November 1235, he declared what he affected to believe was 'not war but an execution of justice' against the Lombard League. Those who 'preferred the luxury of a certain imprecise freedom to stable peace and who placed that above equity and justice' were to be taught a lesson; 'the shoots of hateful freedom' were 'to be trampled underfoot'.[13] The opening of the war brought great successes. The estrangement of Ezzelino III da Romano, ruler of Verona, from the Lombard League had given the emperor a new ally and a new foothold at the outlet of the Brenner. In May 1236 he sent to the aid of his Italian friend a force of 500 German knights and 100 crossbowmen under Gebhard von Arnstein. With this decisive new weight in the party struggles of the Veneto, Ezzelino was able, rapidly, to conquer Vicenza, Padua, and Treviso. As imperial forces moved south from Augsburg, the communes of Mantua and Ferrara hastened to side with the emperor. With troops from these towns, with contingents from his older allies (Parma, Cremona, Reggio, Modena), and with a force of Saracen mounted archers from Lucera, he inflicted a massive defeat upon the Lombards in the battle of Cortenuova (22 November 1237). It seemed a decisive blow. The six towns remaining in the League (Milan, Alessandria, Brescia, Piacenza, Bologna, Faenza) offered to yield on terms. In Tuscany both Pisa and Florence submitted. Meanwhile the emperor sent his illegitimate son, Enzo, to espouse the queen of Sardinia and to seize the island.

It was the highest point in Frederick's fortunes, but amidst the hubristic rhetoric of his triumphant proclamations any real advantages he might have gained were thrown away. Frederick refused a negotiated peace with the Lombard League and insisted instead upon an unconditional surrender which its members found impossible to concede. How fragile his position was in fact was shortly to be demonstrated. This ruler of the earth at whose nod all desires were fulfilled deemed himself insufficiently powerful to strike at the heart of his enemies' power at Milan and chose instead the prospect of securing an easier victory at Brescia. From July 1238 the attack was set in motion. The siege towers rolled forward with prisoners bound to their sides in an attempt to dissuade the defenders from using ballistas against them. War was total. Yet as winter came on it was obvious that there would be no success. In October the imperial army withdrew. It was an ominous portent. Meanwhile, in secret contact with the League and in alliance with Genoa and Venice, the pope waited, judging the moment to intervene. On

20 March 1239 Gregory launched his excommunication of the emperor. The Papacy and the Hohenstaufen had entered on that twenty-nine-year war which was to bring disaster upon Frederick and all his descendants.

That war could be considered under three aspects. First it could be looked at from the point of view of the local factions of the communes. Already in each town of northern Italy there existed two parties struggling for supremacy, who, in the course of the papal-imperial struggle, came to call themselves 'the party of the Church' (later 'Guelfs') and 'the party of the Empire' (later 'Ghibellines'). It would perhaps be unjust to dismiss these terms as wholly meaningless, to see in them nothing but a specious cloak for personal and immediate interests. For some men the words may have had real significance. The spiritual authority of the Church could easily promote political loyalty. Even though it can rarely have implied for laymen those theocratic ideals elaborated with progressively greater emphasis by successive thirteenth-century popes, adherence to 'the Church' party could carry with it a belief that papal authority was a force for the suppression of heresy, for a just settlement of ecclesiastical 'rights', for the propagation of true religion in the world. The popes, at least, had enough propagandists in the clerical order, whether theologians or popular preachers, who could place such beliefs in persuasive terms before laymen. So too did the imperialists have their loyalty, a belief, older than that of the papalists, in the need for some final secular tribunal, presided over by one who, like the pope, was marked out by Heaven for its purpose, and who was in a broad sense a descendant and continuator of the rule of Caesar and Charlemagne, one who, within the secular world, should be free from any divisive ecclesiastical control. If such an allegiance might savour, or at least by its enemies be said to savour, of a certain hostility or disrespect to the spiritual powers, it drew, in compensation, glamour from its link with the emperor himself, head of the blood-nobility of Europe, a man in his person much more compelling to a world living by aristocratic ideals of honour than a pope who might at best be a mere scion of Campagna nobility, at worst the offspring of a shoemaker. Yet having said that it must be admitted that in the ultimate analysis it was private interest, sometimes no more than scores to be paid off in tribal blood feuds, which determined the leanings of the mass of the 'political nation' of the communes. A man like the Lord Ezzelino, as contemporaries were the first to point out, was not struggling for the glories of the empire; he was fighting for himself. The first necessity of pope and emperor alike was to make an appeal to the interests of the local warring parties.

At this level, the second aspect of the war, the direct confrontation of pope and emperor, the Papacy had a clear advantage. For whereas the emperor was claiming allegiance and rule over the communes, the popes, outside the Papal State, were asking for nothing more than alliance and friendship. Moreover, one has the sense that papal diplomacy was much more attuned to local issues than that of the emperor. The families of papal legates, of the popes themselves, were frequently powerful in the towns, and were able to exercise a greater influence than Frederick's councillors. Looking at the names of those who subscribe imperial documents one meets the curials, those men who produced the rhetoric, Piero della Vigna and suchlike; then members of the royal family; finally great nobles of 'Palatine' houses, linked through many generations to the interests of the emperors. They are not men who were representative of the most powerful forces in the thirteenth-century world nor were they well-chosen for the all-important task of winning the local loyalties of the towns. Enzo, king of Sardinia, Frederick's Legate General of all Italy, was chivalrous, an imperial bastard, and one who in his own person enjoyed great prestige. Yet that prestige counted for less than the influence of the Fieschi family and those allied to it in Parma, Reggio, and Genoa, men who, whatever their former loyalties, decided for the party of the Church when Sinibaldo Fieschi became Pope Innocent IV. Again, Innocent, a Genoese noble, could understand, even perhaps sympathise with, the world of the north-Italian communes. Frederick, promulgator of the *Constitutiones Augustales*, had much greater difficulties in coming to terms with it.

The third aspect of the war was the propaganda conflict. On the papal side it took the form of accusations of heresy and immorality, finally the identification of Frederick as the Antichrist: attacks made to isolate the emperor diplomatically, to attract, if possible, the intervention of other monarchs against him, and to justify and sweeten that taxation of the clergy of Europe which the prosecution of the war made necessary. Frederick II's counterblows here were, at least in the early stages of the contest, more effective. In urging his innocence, in portraying himself as one for obscure motives ruthlessly persecuted by a malevolent pope (whose person is carefully distinguished from his office), he could make an appeal both to the clergy of Europe, weary of papal exactions, and, too, to other European monarchs who might have cause to fear a Papacy which could excommunicate and depose them. When, however, from the mid-1240s, he began to espouse the cause of apostolic poverty and to suggest a willingness to strip the Church of its wealth in the interests of a purer Christianity, the radical tone of his pronouncements, though ultimately to bring great harm upon the Church, alienated general support. Indicative here is the attitude of the English monk, Matthew Paris, whose early enthusiasm for the emperor as protector of poor clergy rapidly gave way to indignation against him as a despoiler of the rich.

In the event it was not in Europe at large but in Italy that the conflict was to be settled. Frederick had his successes, notably during 1240–1. In these years he seized the Marche, the Duchy of Spoleto, and threatening Rome itself, most of the Patrimony. Further north he pushed into Romagna to gain Ravenna and Faenza. In May 1241 the Pisans defeated Genoa at the naval battle of Montecristo, seized numerous cardinals who had been travelling under Genoese protection, and handed them over to the emperor. By retaining them in custody Frederick was able to prevent the assembly of a General Council called by Gregory. It was, perhaps, through the indignation it gave rise to, only a Pyrrhic victory. Yet all the imperial triumphs had a curiously hollow character. Such areas as transferred their loyalty to Frederick could be preserved in loyalty only by granting them virtual autonomy. Adherents could be gained only by bribes; their allegiance could be preserved only by bribes. It was conquest by concession. Men like Ezzelino remained his followers only so long as they were allowed a free hand. There were very few in the north who felt a greater instinctive loyalty to Frederick than to their own local interests, and – here was his principal weakness – there was no general principle of advantage which he could offer the adherents of his cause. He was left with the argument of force. Though its siege-tactics were weak, his army could, it is true, generally, though by no means always, compel allegiance. But the army could not be everywhere; and in the communes he was faced with a Hydra whose heads it was impossible to lop off at one stroke.

From the death of Gregory IX in August 1241 one has the impression that Frederick was a man longing for peace. Fra Salimbene tells a story which, if not true, seems well invented, in which Frederick's daughter, the countess of Caserta, asks him why he continues to attack the Lombards: 'when you already have everything in your kingdom in which human beings can take delight'. Frederick is made to answer that she is right, but that: 'I'm so far in, I can't get out without loss of face; at least I hope to get some vengeance upon my enemies'. When in June 1243, Sinibaldo de' Fieschi came to the papal throne as Innocent IV, Frederick's hopes of an end to the struggle rose high. But he had misjudged his man. Innocent, cardinal and vice-chancellor of the Church since 1227, was the candidate of those in the *curia* who sought not reconciliation but only the complete destruction of the enemy. For this he was an ideal choice, a man of presence, a brilliant financial organiser, above all, an iron-willed politician. Abandoning Italy, he established the Papacy at Lyons and there convened the Council which (27 July 1245) solemnly deposed Frederick from the imperial office.

The struggle continued. But the imperial rhetoric ('we who as an anvil have so far patiently and loyally submitted, now will take up the office of the hammer') came to ring ever more hollowly. At Frederick's court plots multiplied. There was 'the plot of the Great Functionaries' involving men like the Vicar of the March of Ancona, the former Vicar of Tuscany, and the Captain General of Sicily, in March 1246. There was the extraordinary treason – if treason indeed it were and not some delusion born in the mind of a ruler past his tether – of Pietro della Vigna in February 1249. The emperor's immediate strategy becomes more difficult to discern. Was he in April 1247 planning to march on Lyons in order to purge himself of guilt before the pope or to seize his enemy as a prisoner? The defection of Parma from the imperial cause (June 1247) and the diversion of the imperial army to that city, forbade in fact the pursual of either course. The end was dismal: the defeat of Frederick's army by the men of Parma (18 February 1248); the consequent defection of the towns of Romagna and the Marche; and then, in 1249, the capture of King Enzo. Death, in December 1250, must have come to the emperor as a relief. He had still, it is true, adherents: the counts of Savoy and, in Eastern Lombardy, the Lords da Romano and Pelavicini; but of loyal subjects, at least in northern and central Italy, there seemed to be none.

For the Hohenstaufen and their supporters, as for Germany and Italy, the reign of Frederick II brought great suffering. For the emperor's own family it meant the suicide of an estranged eldest son, the life-long imprisonment of his dearest child, and misery for all his descendants. For Germany it implied civil war and the irrevocable collapse, under imperial auspices, of imperial power. For the kingdom of Sicily it brought yet further impoverishment as year after year money extorted from a wretched countryside was poured into fruitless wars. For north and central Italy it brought the intensification of already brutal faction conflicts and a fearful devastation by rival armies:

At that time there was total war which lasted many years. Men did not plough or sow or reap or tend the vine or harvest the grape or live in villages. This was particularly so in Parma and Reggio and Modena and Cremona. Men worked near the town with a guard of troops detailed to their posts according to the town-gates. Armed soldiers stood on watch the whole day while the peasants laboured in the fields. This was necessary because of the bandits and thieves and robbers who had so much multiplied. They captured and imprisoned men for their ransoms and drove off their cattle to eat or sell. Those who did not give ransoms were hung up by their feet or hands, their teeth were drawn, and frogs or toads were stuck into their mouths to make them ransom themselves more quickly: something more bitter and frightful to them than any death. They were crueller than demons. At that time a man would see another going on the road as willingly as he might see a devil. For he always suspected that the other wanted to capture and imprison him, to make him *the ransom of a rich man's life* (Proverbs, xiii). And the land was reduced to a desert for there was no peasant on it and none passing through. For in the days of Frederick, particularly from when he was deposed from the empire and Parma rebelled from him and raised insurrection, *the paths rested: and they that went by them walked in the by-ways* (Judges, v).

And evils were multiplied in the earth; and birds and wild beasts such as pheasant and partridge and quail, hares and robucks, stags, buffalo, wild boar, and marauding wolves over-multiplied acutely. For they could not find in the hamlets what was their usual prey – lambs and sheep – since the hamlets had been completely burnt down. And so wolves gathered in great packs around the moats of towns, howling for their raging hunger. They entered the towns by night and attacked the men who were sleeping under the porticoes or in carts and women too and children. Sometimes they dug through the sides of houses and stifled children in their cradles.

None could believe, unless they had seen it, as I saw, the vile things which in that time were done, in their own ways, by men and animals.[14]

Such were the fruits of imperial lust for power; such were the wondrous changes brought by the *immutator mirabilis*.

What, as a whole, the reign of Frederick had demonstrated, though perhaps the demonstration was unnecessary, was that imperial loyalty was of too weak a growth in Italy to allow any real union of the peninsula behind an emperor. At the same time it had shown that the southern kingdom was already too remote from the towns of the north to allow the effective domination of the whole land by a king of Sicily. It had revealed that in any real sense the history of Italy no longer existed, that it had been dissolved into the history of its constituent parts. The growth of Italian economic and commercial life had been preserved, for a time at least, from that centralising, governmental fiscalism which had destroyed it in the South. Had men not resisted Caesar, Dante complains in the sixteenth canto of the *Paradiso*, the Florentine who trades and trucks would have been sent back to Simifonte where his grandfather was a beggar, the Conti would still own Montemurlo, the Cerchi would still be in Acone, the Buondelmonti, perhaps, in Val di Greve. It is a just observation: without the defiance against Frederick the old order would have survived. through that defiance, for good or ill, the vitality, enterprise, individuality, and cultural development of towns unique in the world were allowed to go forward and were preserved from the autocratic dominance of a feudal court. There was, moreover, to be no one capital draining off and moulding to its own image all that was powerful in Italian life; instead Italy was to be the land of an essential political disunity: the world of Venice, Genoa, Florence, Milan, Naples, Rome, and a hundred other cities.

NOTES

On **astrology** see L. Thorndike, *Michael the Scot*, London, 1965; *idem, A History of Magic and Experimental Science*, vols. ii and iii, London, 1923–4; and E. Garin, *Lo zodiaco della vita: La polemica sull' astrologia dal trecento al cinquencento*, Bari, 1976.

For recent discussion of **Frederick II** see *Stupor Mundi: Zur Geschichte Friedrichs von Hohenstaufen*, ed. G. Wolf, Darmstadt, 1966; *Probleme um Friedrich II.*, ed. J. Fleckstein, Sigmaringen, 1974; and D. Abulafia, 'Kantorowicz and Frederick II', *History*, 1977. All still take as their starting-point the work of E. Kantorowicz, *Kaiser Friedrich der Zweite*, Berlin, 1927–1931 (abridged translation into English *Frederick the Second*, London, 1931). Basically derivative, in sentiment at least, from this study is T.C. Van der Cleve, *The Emperor Frederick II of Hohenstaufen*, Oxford, 1972. G. Pepe, *Lo stato ghibellino di Federico II*, 2nd edn, Bari, 1951, serves as some corrective. But the best account is still that given in E. Jordan, *L'Allemagne et l'Italie aux XIIe et XIIIe siècles*, Paris, 1939.

Much of the original source material is to be found in J.L.A. Huillard-Bréholles, *Historia Diplomatica Friderici Secundi*, Paris, 1852–61. There is no complete critical edition of the *Constitutiones Augustales*. The most satisfactory is *Die Konstitutionen Friedrichs II. von Hohenstaufen für sein Konigreich Sizilien*, edited and translated into German by H. Conrad, Thea v. der Lieck-Buyken, and W. Wagner, Cologne, 1973. J.M. Powell, *The Liber Augustalis*, New York, 1971, gives an English translation from the edition of Huillard-Bréholles. Both works have valuable introductions. A useful guide to the literature on the theme is H. Dilcher, 'Die sizilische Gesetzgebung Friedrichs II. eine Synthese von Traditionen und Erneuerung' in *Probleme um Friedrich II., cit.* The same author's *Die sizilische Gesetzgebung Kaiser Friedrichs II.*, Cologne, 1975, discusses its sources and analogues.

On the culture of the court, see particularly: C.A. Willemsen, *Kaiser Friedrich II. Triumphator zu Capua*, Weisbaden, 1953; B. Panvini, *La scuola poetica siciliana (Biblioteca dell'Archivium Romanicum*, ser. 1, 43), Florence, 1955, pp. 139 ff.; C.H. Haskins, 'Latin Literature under Frederick II', ch. v. of his *Studies in Medieval Culture*, New York, 1929, and *idem, Studies in the History of Mediaeval Science*, 2nd edn, Cambridge, Mass., 1927, chs. xii–xiv.

Amidst a wealth of monographic literature on the Emperor particularly useful are J.L.A. Huillard-Bréholles, *Vie et Correspondance de Pierre de la Vigne*, Paris, 1865; F. Graefe, *Die Publizistik in der letzen Epoche Kaiser Friedrichs II.*, Heidelberg, 1909; J.M. Powell, 'Medieval Monarchy and Trade: The Economic Policy of Frederick II in the Kingdom of Sicily', *Studi medievali*, s.3, iii. 1962; A. Nitschke, 'Friedrich II. Ein Ritter des Hohen Mittelalters', *Historische Zeitschrift*, 194, 1962; and the articles in *Atti del Convegno internazionale di studi federiciani*, Palermo, 1952. With F. Gabriele's assessment of 'Federico II e la cultura musulmana', *RSI*, 1952, compare N. Daniel, *The Arabs and Medieval Europe*, London, 1975, ch. vi.

1. Thorndike, *Michael the Scot, cit.*, p. 14.
2. R.S. Lopez, 'Stars and Spices: The earliest Italian Manual of Commercial Practice', *Explorations in Economic History*, vii, 1969–70, pp. 40–1.
3. Milan, 1864, p. vi.
4. Rolandino da Padova, *Cronica in factis et circa facta Marchie Trivixane*, ed. A. Bonardi, *RIS*, viii, i, pp. 66, 84.
5. See Philippe de Navarre [sic], *Les gestes des Chiprois*, ed. G. Raynaud, Geneva, 1887 and, in English translation, edited by J.L. La Monte, *The Wars of Frederick II against the Ibelins in Syria and Cyprus by Philip de Novare*, New York, 1936. Cf. too J. Riley-Smith, *The Feudal Nobility and the Kingdom of Jerusalem 1174-1277*, London, 1973, pp. 159 ff.
6. See E.M. Angiola, 'Nicola Pisano, Federigo Visconti, and the Classic Style in Pisa', *The Art Bulletin*, 1977, esp. pp. 21 ff.
7. C.A. Willemsen and D. Ollenthal, *Apulia: Imperial Splendour in Southern Italy*, transl. D. Woodward, London, 1959, p. 36.
8. This is the judgment of my friend, the late M.F.M. Meiklejohn, formerly Stevenson Professor of Italian in the University of Glasgow, and a very considerable ornithologist, in a typescript translation and commentary upon Book I of the *De Arte* from his hand. In defect of the critical edition promised by Professor Ströhl of Zurich, one depends upon *De arte venandi cum avibus*, ed. C.A. Willemsen, Leipzig, 1942. The English version of this book, *The Art of Falconry*, undertaken by C.A. Wood and F. Marjorie Fyfe, Stanford, California, 1943, suffers from an inadequate knowledge of birds.
9. H.M. Schaller, 'Die Kaiseridee Friedrichs II.' in *Probleme um Friedrich II.*, *cit.*, pp. 118–19; Huillard-Bréholles, *Historia Diplomatica, cit.*, vi, i, pp. 145–6.
10. *Die Konstitutionen, cit.*, I, 50.
11. *Ibid.*, I, 47; III, 18, 59–60, 43.
12. *Ibid.*, I, 73.
13. Huillard-Bréholles, *Historia Diplomatica, cit.*, iv, i, p. 873.
14. Salimbene de Adam, *Cronica*, ed. G. Scalia, Bari, 1966, i, pp. 274–5.

CHAPTER THREE

Popes, emperors, and communes, 1250–1380

If the reign of Frederick II represents the final blow to any attempt to create a united Italy before the nineteenth century, the 130 years which follow his death present a picture of ever-increasing disunity and disintegration of the larger political units. The southern kingdom is divided, and its separate parts fall to a wretched anarchy. The Papacy, unable to secure a firm hold in a turbulent countryside, is driven from the peninsula and takes refuge in Avignon. Despite the immense expenditure of blood and money which are poured out to achieve its control, the Papal State, the supposed guarantor of papal independence from secular control, throws off its master's rule. The Guelf alliance, dominated by the pope and seen by its members as a means of bringing peace to the peninsula, disintegrates. Emperors, when they intervene in Italy, appear as ghosts feared at first through their re-evocation of the past, yet soon mocked with the swift realisation of their impotent insubstantiality.

The larger the institution in this period, the more extensive its claims, the more historic its past, the more hallowed its traditions, the less successful it is: in particular if the criterion of its success be taken to mean its contribution to human happiness. The word 'Italy' is heard more and more but the men whose lips pronounce it are rootless intellectuals, dreaming rarely of the future, more often seeking an escape from the chaos of the present into the imagined greatness of a Roman past. What survives, what flourishes, what has growth, are small units, pragmatic policies, the rhetoric of the possible rather than the ideal. These, the fields, the farms, the business houses, the *popolo*, the commune, the *signoria*, we must examine later. For the moment, if only to provide a thread of chronological continuity along which their development can be traced, it is to the larger political institutions that we shall look: to the decline of the old great powers up to that point when new younger forces are coming to achieve their own maturity.

I

Eighteen years were to pass after the emperor's death before the Hohenstaufen were wholly eliminated from the southern kingdom. On his return to Italy

Innocent IV gave the impression of a man utterly weary of that political activity in which he had so long excelled. In northern Italy he withdrew from the support of factions in the cities, and allowed the Lombard League to wither away. He confined his activities here to the strengthening of certain families which, generally allied to him by blood or marriage, might serve as centres of support, should future circumstances make papal involvement absolutely imperative. In the Papal State he eschewed action, leaving the towns in anarchy. From 1252 the Romans, with Brancaleone degli Andalò as their senator, launched fierce attacks upon those of the nobility who supported papal authority, and marched out to seize land from or extend their dominion over the neighbouring communes. In Umbria and the Marche, war and party struggles continued. For ten years the empire had allowed the towns a virtual autonomy which they were not now willing, lightly, to abandon. Nor did Innocent, apparently, possess either the will or the power to constrain them to obedience.

Innocent's successor was Rinaldo Conti, a nephew of Gregory IX, who adopted the title of Alexander IV (1254–61). Devoted to the Franciscans, he wrote verses in honour of St. Clare, was obese, good-humoured, relaxed, averse to political decisions. He found it easy to follow the policies of Innocent's later years. Between 1250 and 1261 the Papacy was provoked to action and engagement in North Italian affairs on only one occasion. This was in 'the crusade' directed against Ezzelino da Romano and Uberto Pelavicini, an enterprise whose outcome seemed to justify all too strongly the wisdom of passivity. These two men had grown in power as lieutenants or allies of the Emperor Frederick and both claimed to rule their territories in the name of the emperor. In 1254 Uberto Pelavicini, still flaunting the title of 'Vicar General of the Holy Empire in Lombardy', held Cremona, Piacenza, Pavia, and Vercelli, an impressive lordship dominating the waters of the middle Po and the meeting of the via Emilia and the Padua–Turin road. At the same time Ezzelino ruled Verona, Vicenza, and Padua. In persuading Innocent to declare a 'crusade' against them, the local leaders of 'the party of the Church' pointed to Ezzelino's notorious cruelties, the attacks of both men upon ecclesiastical liberties, and the suspicion that they were guilty of heresy. Pelavicini was certainly an anti-cleric. He had refused to receive the inquisition, had exiled the bishops of Cremona and Piacenza, and was the protector of Count Egidio da Cortenuova, a notorious supporter of Catharist heretics. Ezzelino's father had in his day been accused of heresy, and so his son could plausibly be tarred with the same brush. He had behind him too a long career of violence against clergy and churches.

With Innocent's death, the organisation of the venture devolved upon Alexander. Volunteers flocked in; Venice, fearful of Ezzelino as a neighbour, gave its assistance. During the next three years the crusaders had some success, gaining Padua, Pavia, and Piacenza. By January 1259, however, Pelavicini had secured the alliance of Manfred, ruler of Sicily, who sent 200 German mercenaries in his aid. Together with Ezzelino, he seized Brescia and defeated and captured the papal legate at the battle of Gambaro d'Oglio.

At this point there occurred an amazing reversal of alliances. Finding that Ezzelino had successfully edged him out of control of Brescia, Pelavicini in solemn treaty transferred his loyalties. The new papal legate stood impotently by while the crusaders welcomed to their ranks one of the two excommunicate heretics against whom they had been crusading. Three months later, in September, Ezzelino was killed in battle, and his power collapsed. The victors of the crusade – now revealed to be, what for the lay nobility it had always been, namely a struggle for their own territorial interests – attempted with varying success to secure the spoils. Most successful among them was Pelavicini himself, who between 1259 and 1261 built up a much stronger lordship than he had previously held. Meanwhile, at the end of 1259, Alexander, having learnt an expensive lesson in the character of Italian party conflict, had written to his legate advising him that all further action would be in vain and ordering him to withdraw in peace to the papal court.

In the South, Sicily remained in the hands of 'the race of vipers'. Frederick's son, Conrad IV, who had made his way from Germany to claim his inheritance there, had died in May 1254. His heir, Conradin, was at the time only two years old, and still in the North. During the next four years, amidst confused events, attempts by the popes to gain the kingdom by negotiation, a disastrous invasion by a papal army, revolts, and treasons, Manfred, Frederick's illegitimate son, gradually built up his power. By August 1258 he was strong enough to set aside Conradin's rights and, amidst the mosaic splendours raised by his ancestors in the cathedral of Palermo, to have himself crowned as king of Sicily.

Manfred was in many ways as remarkable as his father and, like him, attracted a legendary aura. 'His dead father lived in him', wrote Jamsilla, 'He was Manfred, the *manus Frederici*, the hand of Frederick, heir and universal successor to the graces and virtues of his father'. He had the same passion for the chase and the same interest in the new sciences, those interests to which, together with his courtesy, Jamal-ad-din paid eloquent tribute in an account of his embassy to the Sicilian court. He too was a poet and patron of poets, one whom Dante was to place by the side of his father as founder of the Sicilian school. He had other gifts which contemporaries had not particularly stressed in his father. Friend and enemy alike commented on his physical grace: 'blond and handsome and of noble mien he was'. Adam de la Halle, Charles of Anjou's own minstrel, sang of him in nostalgic praise:

> Biaus chevaliers et preus et sages fu Manfrois,
> De toutes bonnes tèches entèchiés et courtois . . .[1]

They are lines which cannot be translated outside the rhetoric of chivalry (see pp. 95–9). 'With all good qualities well qualified', it was his reputation for *courtoisie*, above all, which laid its spell upon contemporaries and successors. Faced by it, Guelf propaganda against 'the monstrous son of a monstrous father' – whether the frontal attack by Dante's master, Brunetto Latin, that he had murdered his father, half-brother, and two nephews, whether, more personal, that he was weak, vainglorious, and preferred threatening to fighting – could avail nothing. Even among his enemies his legend carried over into the fourteenth century as one who was a genial, poetic, libertine. So the Guelf Giovanni Villani saw him as a musician and singer, surrounded by minstrels, entertainers, and fair concubines ('for he was lustful more so than his father'), as generous and courtly and with a great manner, as much loved, an Epicurean all his life, caring nothing for God or the saints but only for the delights of the body.

Though it was not an emotion which he could feel himself, he bore the fortunate nimbus of those destined, effortlessly, to attract intense loyalty. He had some concern too for the improvement of the kingdom. To replace Siponto in its malarial marshes, he built Manfredonia, described in the fourteenth century as: 'today the best port between Venice and Brindisi'. More, he was a diplomat of great skill, with a hard sense of political reality. If he eventually failed, it was perhaps because his main opponents were less interested in realities.

In the face of Manfred's power, Innocent and Alexander could, as many in Europe, as many in the *curia* wished, have come to an arrangement with him to hold the kingdom as a papal fief. Their reluctance to accept this course sprang perhaps not so much from an instinctive rejection of one whose father had been the Antichrist, as from, first, a suspicion that a Hohenstaufen could never accept that his ancestors had alienated central Italy to the Papal State; and, then again, from a well-merited distrust of Manfred himself. Yet they seemed to have no means to rid themselves of him. Having abandoned north-Italian politics, they had no allies within the peninsula to call to their aid. In this situation Innocent had begun to look around Europe for a champion willing and able to snatch the kingdom for himself in the name of the Church. Richard of Cornwall, brother of Henry III of England, was approached and declined the honour ('As well ask me to unhook the moon from the sky!'). The offer was passed on to Charles of Anjou, brother of Louis IX of France, who, as count of Provence from 1245, had already entered the politics of neighbouring Piedmont and had obtained there remarkable successes. At this stage, he was tempted, but unable to pursue matters. Innocent returned to England again, this time urging the crown upon Henry III's second son, Edmund. Henry, to be condemned by Dante as *il re de la semplice vita*, accepted the bait. Yet to little avail. Any dreams of powerful armies marching down the peninsula to place the banner of St. George upon Palermo were dispelled with the English baronial insurrection of April 1258, a revolt largely generated by the fiscal consequences of the Sicilian offer.

In these circumstances Alexander was helpless. Meanwhile Manfred's power grew as, throughout the peninsula, he built up a body of allies and clients to put pressure upon the Papacy. He despatched money or troops to Guglielmo Boccanegra at Genoa and to Uberto Pelavicini at Piacenza. In October 1258 Neapolitan officers began to occupy the March of Ancona in the Papal State. But his greatest success was to be in Tuscany. Here Manfred had at first hoped to gain the alliance of Guelf Florence whose rulers had been excommunicated in September 1258 for the summary execution of a delinquent cleric. But the Guelfs were cool; perhaps the memory of their hostility to his father was still too much alive. As a second-best he received the offers of the Sienese Ghibellines. In May 1259 he accepted the lordship of their city and sent Giordano d'Anglona, count of San Severino, with a considerable force of mercenaries, as his vicar in Tuscany. It was an alliance from which the Tuscan Ghibellines were to gain a remarkable predominance. On 4 September 1260 the Sienese and Florentine armies met in battle at Montaperti, and the Guelfs were decisively defeated. The Florentine Ghibellines re-entered their city; Sangimignano, Pistoia, and Volterra opened their gates to the triumphant party. Within the province Lucca alone stood with the Guelfs. Everywhere in the peninsula men turned to the insignia of the black eagle on the silver shield. In Piedmont Manfred began to draw the marqueses of Monferrato and Busca into his orbit. Within Europe as a whole his prestige rose to new heights when in July 1260 his daughter, Constanza, was betrothed to Pere, heir to the Aragonese throne, an imposing international recognition of his power and status. At Rome itself, he was one of the two Senators appointed in the disputed election of 1261.

Unlike his father, Manfred sought in Italy not subjects but allies, and as a result by 1261 he was more powerful than his father had ever been. Yet his victories were, in a curious way, counter-productive. In order to persuade the Papacy to recognise his kingship in Sicily, he had to intervene in the North. Yet the more he was successful in encircling the Papacy, the less were the popes willing to grant him peace. It was in these circumstances that Urban IV (1261–4) ascended the papal throne. Alexander had been an Italian, a noble, and was, it was said, 'unwilling to build Sion in blood'. Urban was a Frenchman, with no experience of Italian politics, of uncertain origins, perhaps a cobbler's son, who though now in his seventies suffered from a compulsive restlessness. ('Even when I sleep', he writes to his sister, 'the silence of the night brings no peace to my troubled heart.') He had been patriarch of Jerusalem and his mind was conditioned to seeing politics in terms of crusade: a world of blacks and whites and the *gesta Dei per Francos*. He brooked no discussion of his plans; he took no counsel; he resolved to build Sion in blood. Everywhere in Italy he allied with those factions calling themselves 'Guelf' or 'of the party of the Church' against the supporters of Manfred. Once again (it was perhaps easier for a Frenchman than for his two Italian predecessors to come to such a decision) the Church was to descend into the arena of Italian politics. It was, perhaps, unavoidable but it had unfortunate consequences for the Papacy's spiritual rôle and it intensified the impulse to see resistance to the political aims of the *curia* as heresy. It was Urban who gave their rule to the *Cavalieri Gaudenti*, the lay-order designed to bring an end to faction strife in the towns, but it was he who aligned the Church with a faction.

All the diplomatic and spiritual resources of the Papacy were brought to the task. Early in 1262 Urban ordered all Christians to renege on their debts to Sienese banking houses that supported Manfred. In July 1263 he commanded the seizure of all goods of Florentine Ghibelline merchants throughout Europe. He allied with the Pisans against the Genoese, with the Visconti against the della Torre family in Milan, and with the Este against their enemies in Emilia. Above all he began negotiations to secure a new candidate for the Sicilian throne. These achieved their end in June 1263, when Charles of Anjou accepted the papal call. The terms were severe. In return for the investiture of the kingdom as a papal fief, Charles promised an annual census of 5,000 *oncie* of gold (over seventeen times as much as that claimed from Frederick II); the cession of Benevento; absolute 'ecclesiastical liberty'; and service of 300 knights for three months each year within the Papal State.

Urban died in October 1264. It was still not certain that his policies would be carried forward. Manfred still bore all before him. In August Lucca had fallen to the Ghibellines in Tuscany, and the Papal State was in confusion. Many still sought reconciliation. In 1261 Michael Paleologus, the schismatic Greek emperor, had recovered Constantinople from its Latin rulers. Both the titular Latin emperor, Baldwin II, and his Venetian allies looked for an alliance with Manfred to continue the struggle. If Filippo da Fontana, archbishop of Ravenna, had, as he believed he was going to, attained the papal throne, their pleas would probably have prevailed. Yet here Urban's posthumous influence triumphed. In his brief pontificate he had created fourteen cardinals, of whom six were French, and three counsellors of the French king. In the new election their weight told. In February 1265, Clement IV, a former servant of Louis IX, emerged as the new pope. The plans of Urban were to be followed through.

A principal difficulty was the financing of Charles's expedition. Here Clement's untiring energy was of immense value. 'Seek a loan', he writes to his legate in France, 'Seek a loan. Seek it from the king, from his brother, from prelates, from monks, from bourgeois, from usurers, from everybody, even if you've already had ten refusals.' By a mixture of threats and promises the bankers of Rome, Florence, Siena, Lucca, Arezzo, and Perugia were persuaded to produce mighty sums (500,000 florins from Tuscany, 125,000 florins from Rome) for the expedition. Meanwhile, in May 1265, Charles proceeded by sea to Rome with a small force, and was elected Senator. Since Genoa was hostile, however, the main body of his army was forced to march through the peninsula. It did not set out until the second half of November and reached Rome only at the end of December. In the interval – it seems in retrospect a fatal error – the Sicilians forbore to strike at the enemy. In January the newly united army marched south. On the 26 February King Manfred entrusted the fortunes of his house to battle with the invaders at Benevento. His army was cut to pieces and he himself killed.

Charles of Anjou, his French and Provençal followers, were now the masters of the kingdom. Their triumph was sealed two years later, when the young Conradin, the last legitimate heir of the Hohenstaufen, invaded from Germany, was defeated at Tagliacozzo, captured, and executed (August–October 1268).

II

The final destruction of the Hohenstaufen and the triumph of Charles of Anjou were to have momentous long-term consequences. Until 1435 scions of the Angevin dynasty were to rule from Naples; in 1494 the Angevin claim upon the throne was to initiate that cycle of international war which established the political form of the peninsula in the early-modern period. Nearer the event it established 'the Guelf League', a tradition of alliances which was, if only broadly and with intermissions, to last until the 1330s. Though its members surrounded the idea of 'Guelfism' with a wealth of rhetoric they had little in common ideologically. What sustained the league was the simple recognition of a need for

43

collective security. Its centre was the Papacy, and its alliance with the Angevin royal houses of France and Naples. With them stood their commercial allies in Tuscany, above all Florence. In return for their financial assistance in its conquest these virtually took over the trade of the southern kingdom and at the same time came to exercise a powerful influence in the money-markets of France. Against the Guelfs, the Ghibellines seemed, with the decay of the empire, much less powerful, though with the passage of time their true strength was to be strikingly demonstrated.

The last effect of the Angevin conquest, perhaps the most important, was to weaken the stability of the southern kingdom. In the event the strains imposed by the coming of a new ruling class were so great as to break its unity, to separate it into two new political units, whose mutual hostility was to bring yet more misery to their luckless inhabitants.

If any usurper could have prevented such an outcome it was Charles of Anjou. His very allies, it is true, found him unlovable. Clement IV wrote of him, with memorable irritation, as 'gracious neither to his own nor to other people, being neither visible, audible, affable, nor amiable'. His admirer, Tommaso di Pavia, describes him as silent, serious, never laughing 'even as a child', indifferent to hunting or dress or the pleasures of the table. He was not uncultured. He wrote poems as a young man, and in later life patronised the translation of medical works from the Arabic. Yet his culture was found rather in the reading of 'le roumans de Godefroy de Bouillon' than in the exciting areas investigated by the Hohenstaufen. With his long nose and olive skin he was physically unattractive and in temperament he was extremely cold. This all said, it should be added that he possessed a certain sense of justice and honour, utterly alien to his Hohenstaufen predecessors, and that in political energy and ability, he was their superior. His overriding passion was of course power; but who, without this, would ever in the first place have accepted the conquest of the kingdom?

For the moment he prospered. Once established on the throne he began to build up his strength in northern Italy. The alliances forged there as a means of resistance to the expected attack of Conradin were continued after Conradin's defeat. In Lombardy he united the various Guelf factions and sought, though unsuccessfully, to secure lordship over them. To Tuscany he sent troops and officials, and by 1270 had assumed the lordship of most of its towns. At Rome he held the senatorship from 1268 to 1278, while in the Papal State his officials came frequently to be appointed as rectors.

In the southern kingdom too Charles established his control. All lands granted after the year 1245 were confiscated to the Crown and redistributed among some 700 of the king's French or Provençal followers. French became the language of government, and most of the highest offices were given to Frenchmen. Fiscal posts were given to Italians, who as it seems, at least in the island, administered them with customary corruption. Despite much written on the subject it would be difficult to say whether on the mainland or island the administration as a whole was more or less oppressive with the coming of Charles, than it had ever been. In most matters he followed the paths laid out by the Hohenstaufen. Support was given to government and alien (particularly Tuscan) commerce at the expense of native entrepreneurs, and financially the screws were once more turned upon native wealth by the reimposition of Frederick II's *subventio generalis*. This taxation was made necessary by Charles's decision – in the event shown to be wildly over-ambitious – to follow out the anti-Byzantine policies of his Norman predecessors. No sooner had he conquered Naples than he unveiled his plan – which was justified on the pretext of ending the Greek Schism – to bring down the Emperor Michael Paleologus and to conquer the Eastern Empire. By the spring of 1282 this project was coming to fruition; his fleet lay at anchor in Messina, preparing to set sail upon a new and yet more splendid adventure. It was at this moment that disaster struck.

In Aragon, King Pere II had not forgotten the claims of his wife, Constance, the daughter of Manfred, upon the Sicilian throne. To his court had flocked those Sicilians dispossessed in favour of French adventurers: men like the landowner Ruggiero Loria, officials such as Riccardo Filangieri, Enrico da Isernia, and Manfred's former chancellor, Giovanni di Procida. King Pere's own emissaries were active both among the Ghibellines of northern Italy and among secret supporters in the island. In May 1281 he was in clandestine contact with at least seventeen of the Sicilian baronage. It was a period when under royal tutelage the growth of the port of Barcelona was making Aragon into a great sea-power and he could rely upon the support of her merchants in any attempt to extend Catalan hegemony to southern Italy. In March 1282, as Charles made final preparations to move East, Pere had assembled a large fleet and had sailed on a crusade against Tunisia. At the same time he was poised to turn to Italy and was calculating whether the departure of Charles upon the Byzantine venture might offer him a chance to invade and seize what he considered to be his wife's inheritance.

As it happened he was overtaken by events. On the Easter Monday of 1282 the approaches of a French soldier to a young Sicilian woman in Palermo provoked his murder by her husband. While the bells called to Vespers, the killing set in motion a chain wave of massacres of the French in the city, which spread rapidly to other centres in the island: to Corleone, Trapani, Caltanisetta and then, on 28 April, to Messina itself. These atrocities – primarily considered perhaps as a protest against a century's misgovernment from the mainland – can have had no direct connection with Pere's plans. Indeed they hindered them for they forestalled Charles's departure. The Sicilian leaders who emerged from the collapse of French government on the island declared not for the Aragonese monarch but for the establishment of communes under papal suzerainty. Only when their stand was repudiated and condemned by Pope Martin IV did they turn to Pere. In August the men of Palermo and Messina called him to the throne of the kingdom. On 4 September he was crowned at Palermo. Charles was forced to evacuate the island, though Pere, after an initial success, was unable to conquer the mainland. It was the beginning of the great 'War of the Vespers' which was destined to last, amid a series of temporary truces and false hopes of peace, for ninety years.

III

Charles of Anjou died in 1285. His successors, Charles II (1285–1309) and Robert I (1309–43), carried on the struggle to regain the whole kingdom. In the island Jaume of Aragon succeeded to his father, Pere, in 1285 and eventually yielded to the pressure of the Angevins and the Papacy. He renounced his Sicilian rights and, as some compensation, was to receive later, by papal grant, the kingdoms of Sardinia and Corsica. But the nobility of Sicily contested his surrender. Jaume's brother was crowned in his place as Federico III (1295–1337), and under his leadership resistance continued.

The Ninety Years War was as disastrous for the South of Italy as the Hundred Years War was for France. It fixed the region in that helpless poverty to which the Normans had first decisively pushed it. In Naples the constant demands of war, particularly during the reign of Robert I, who made five attempts to conquer the island kingdom (1314, 1316, 1325–8, 1335, 1339–42), ensured the maintenance and extension of the burdensome fiscalism of the Norman-Hohenstaufen kings. The kings, it is true, made sporadic attempts to enhance the economy of their realm. In 1308 Charles II even tried to establish the order of the Umiliati, who had played a considerable part in the development of cloth manufacture in Milan and Florence, in his capital at Naples, and drew up plans for the import of English, French, and Tunisian wool. Yet the state monopolies, the royal warehouses, and the devitalising taxation continued and destroyed all possibility of native capitalist growth. External trade came yet more firmly into the hands of Tuscans. Great wealth still flowed to the Crown. The *subventio generalis*, raised each year, almost always produced about 44,000 *oncie*; on the occasion of feudal 'aids' (marriage of a member of the royal family, etc.) this sum could be doubled. Perhaps another 80–90,000 *oncie* came from normal feudal revenues, monopolies, taxes upon trade, and the profits of royal estates. During the fourteenth century a normal year would probably bring the king something in the order of 700,000 florins: that is to say only some 30 per cent less than the Hohenstaufen had raised from the mainland and island together. But this wealth, exacted from the sole productive elements in the kingdom, above all the wretched and impoverished peasantry, was employed to no productive ends. First charge upon it was the payment to the Papacy of the feudal census. Here Robert, being an honourable man, successfully strained every nerve to repay all arrears. What was left was squandered on the attempted reconquest of Sicily; and, again, largely at papal bidding, on an elaborate foreign policy in the north of Italy which by no stretch of the imagination could be thought of as benefiting the inhabitants of the kingdom.

At the same time the War of the Vespers brought a new measure of feudal disorder. There is, perhaps, some danger of exaggeration here. Had historians ever been able to read the Hohenstaufen registers as they were able to read those of the Angevin kings (though since 1943 these too exist no longer) they might have tended to emphasise less the contrast between the character of royal–baronial relations under the two lines and to have been less surprised at the extent of administrative corruption and rural disorder under the Angevins. It is significant, for instance, that many of the concessions granted to the mainland nobility by Charles I after the Vespers in 1283–5 (such as, for instance, the right to give fiefs in dowry, the right to judgment by peers) were merely restatements of rights guaranteed to them in Frederick II's *Constitutiones*. This said, however, it is clear that in the fourteenth century feudal power still grew considerably vis-à-vis the monarchy.

In this period, four main classes of noble can be distinguished. The nobility of the towns: of Naples, Salerno, Sulmona, L'Aquila, Bari, and Trani, who, though in a more overtly privileged way, resembled the town nobility of the North, and who, despite the faction conflicts between them, again characteristic of the North, offered little challenge to monarchical authority. More threatening were those families, notably the princes of Taranto and Durazzo, who, allied to the Crown by blood, sought from it displays of family affection in the form of grants of *apanage* lands and access to power. Third, were a few truly powerful houses: the Estendart, the Bourson, the counts of San Severino, of Aquino, and of Celano, who, closely linked to the court, were dependent upon what they could cajole from the royal bounty for the extension of their broad *latifundia*.

These men threatened the integrity of the monarchy which, when in difficulties, was inevitably tempted to win their allegiance by bribes. The fourth class of nobles presented, more than this, a threat to public order. There were the holders of the 3,455 fiefs (of which only twenty-two were ecclesiastical), remote from the principal towns. The new families of the Conquest lived under French, the older under Langobard, law. Among them was a very widespread class of poor nobles, holding properties from one-eighteenth to one-hundredth *pro indiviso*. [On this tenure, see below, pp. 60–1.] The combination of poverty and nobility, particularly in so poor a world as the Regno, led inevitably to an extremely violent climate, in which 'magnates and brigands' and family vendetta flourished. In November 1340 King Robert, in what one presumes must have been desperation before such conflicts, hit upon the expedient of persuading Benedict XII to write a letter, then to be read in their churches by all bishops and archbishops of the kingdom, wherein 'by apostolic authority' his holiness declared 'shattered, broken, and wholly annulled all leagues and conspiracies of one man against another made between counts and barons, knights, nobles and other persons of the said kingdom'. What effect such words had may be judged by a solemn royal proclamation in the following June announcing that royal functionaries, justiciars or other officers, who abused their office 'especially in waging war with armed men' or in giving aid to those who did so, would be removed from their positions, and that barons, counts, and knights 'who made war within the kingdom' would be deprived of their fiefs. Whether as a result anyone lost office or fief is unknown.[2]

Similar evidence of anarchy abounds. None the less one would hesitate before refusing the title of 'good government' to King Robert's rule. For good government in this context cannot mean, as it might in other places and times, the establishment of order, but rather the determination never to be wholly overwhelmed by the mass of disorder, violence, and injustice, the stubborn willingness always to fight back. Although the terms in which his flatterers spoke of Robert 'the Wise' (Petrarch's 'who in Italy, nay who in Europe, is more illustrious than, Robert?', etc.) evoke instinctive distrust, yet we cannot, like his ex-chancellor, Pope John XXII, dismiss him simply as 'a miserable poltroon'. He does indeed in his domestic life present a figure of a certain humorous pathos. His queen was of such piety that the pope was impelled to write to her, urging that she should not, in her pleasure in the divine spouse, forget the rights and needs of her earthly husband. When in his frustration he turned to other loves, the same pope wrote in schoolmasterly protest. Robert's attempts to engage in the intellectual life of the age, all those lifeless tracts and sermons delivered to the applause of his courtiers, provoke too some derision, that feeling expressed by Dante in dismissing him as '*il re da sermone*', 'the preachifying king'. His inner piety caused him, perhaps, to fall too much under the influence of the Church in his public policy. Yet in his basic good-will, his striving after justice as he conceived it, he seems to be one among that rather small number of rulers in the thirteenth and fourteenth centuries to whom it is possible to give any admiration.

With the accession of his grand-daughter, Giovanna I (1343–82), such authority as Robert had maintained withered away. She came to the throne, aged only sixteen years, under the 'Castilian' law of succession, and the line of the prince of Taranto who would have succeeded under Salic law was resentful. Her husband, Andrew of Hungary, was a year younger than she and somewhat simple. The queen, prey to the factions of the court seeking power, may, as rumour loudly asserted, have taken lovers from among their leaders. However this may be, in September 1345, in circumstances which are obscure, Andrew was murdered. The consequences were serious. His elder brother, King Lewis of Hungary, asserting the collective guilt of the Neapolitan court and the necessity of revenge, invaded the kingdom in the hope of securing it for himself. The country was plunged into civil war (1347–52). There followed a competitive race to encroach upon royal rights, and a massive breakdown of order as the mercenary companies of Conrad of Wolfort, Conrad of Landau, and Fra Moriale ravaged throughout. Amidst the fluctuations of war Giovanna survived; between 1352 and 1365, under the supervision of the Grand Seneschal, the Florentine Niccolò Acciaiuoli, some measure of recovery came about. Between 1354 and 1356 it seemed indeed that Sicily might fall to Naples, and that the old kingdom might be reconstituted. But with the end of Giovanna's reign civil disorder and rebellion broke out again, as the nobility once more rose to challenge royal authority.

To the South, meanwhile, the Sicilian kingdom 'of Trinacria', in rebellion against the Papacy, its feudal overlord, was not, as in obedient Naples, forced to disgorge immense sums into the coffers of Avignon. Yet the revolution of the Vespers brought no amelioration of the island's economic circumstances. Commerce remained in the hands of aliens, even if now Catalans rather than Tuscans predominated. Here too the war with Naples, which had been heralded by the formal recognition by King Pere that he was 'crowned by the will of the Sicilians' (as expressed by a feudal parliament), brought, ultimately, even greater power to the Sicilian feudality than that enjoyed by their neighbours to the North. At the beginning of the thirteenth century the island had been only weakly feudalised. Vast tracts of royal demesne had intersected baronial properties and had made more difficult any noble plans of revolt. But the needs of war, the need to purchase, by lavish concessions, the loyalty of their feudality, forced the kings to a continual policy of appeasement which ultimately impoverished the Crown. Under Federico III the rôle of the monarchy still survived. He still played some sort of part in the politics of the Levant, and, indeed, tried to employ the famous mercenary 'Catalan Company' to conquer Byzantium. With his successors all monarchical strength dissolved.

In the 1340s, there were three major Sicilian noble families. Of these the Ventimiglia who were temporarily in exile as the result of an unsuccessful blood feud with the Chiaramonte, and had allied themselves with the Angevins. The two other houses, those of Chiaramonte and Passaneto – whose heads the chronicler, Michele da Piazza, calls 'semi-kings' – were still ostensibly loyal. Below them were some sixty-seven clans of modest prosperity, and another 144 who could be described as poor. Their moment of power had now arrived. On the death of Pietro II, 'the Idiot', in 1342, the Crown devolved upon his five-year-old son, Ludovico. At once armed struggles broke out on the question of who should fill the office of regent. The newly-arrived nobility of Catalan descent, the Alagona, Caleranado, Moncada, and Peralta, espoused the claims of the dead king's brother, Giovanni; while the older native 'Latins' asserted the rights of the dead king's widow. As the result of unsatisfactory successions the conflicts continued. Ludovico died in 1355 to be followed by his thirteen-year-old brother Federico IV. At his death in 1377 the kingdom passed to his daughter, Maria.

Against this background, local justiciarships fell into the hands of powerful barons; appeal to the *magna curia* against judgments in seigneurial courts fell into desuetude. The king allowed the alienation of fiefs, allowed the claim of the *Parliamento* of the barons that taxation might be levied only with its consent, and accepted its refusal of taxation. Public office such as the ranks of 'Great Admiral' and 'Grand Chamberlain' became hereditary within noble families. Demesne cities were classified as 'Captaincies of War' and placed under the nobility to form part of their lordship; what remained of the royal demesne was subject to progressive illegal occupation. The royal monopoly of corn-export fell into noble hands. Public order broke down. The nobility, united in formal treaties of alliance for *vendette*, usurped ecclesiastical properties, took over the patronage of churches and abbeys, and by maintenance drew the lower orders into their struggles. 'Oh magnates and followers of the king, then', intones Piazza, 'I direct my words to you and ask: "Why should you have a king if the barons acquire the whole kingdom and its jurisdiction?".' In these circumstances, however, he prudently avoids explicit condemnation of individuals and limits his reproaches to the class in general: 'I could say more about these peers, but I keep silence, because it is healthier to confess ignorance of the secret matters of peers and magnates than to assume a perhaps dangerous courage.'[3] In these words he wrote the epitaph of that great kingdom inherited by Frederick II in 1197, a kingdom which, despite its clear weaknesses, had still possessed at that time immense potentialities for fruitful growth.

IV

The empire had collapsed; the southern kingdom limped to disaster. The Papacy and the Papal State were also to suffer harsh blows.

Between 1268 and 1295, there were no less than nine elections to the papal throne. This succession of short pontificates weakened the Church's authority, particularly in relation to its allies in the Guelf League. Charles I's extension of Angevin power in northern Italy had been in technical violation of his agreement with the Papacy in 1263, and Angevin influence was sometimes brought to bear, and, as in the election of Martin IV in 1281, brought to bear effectively in determining who the popes should be. It was natural, in these circumstances, for fears to arise that the *curia* might be faced with something like the dangers posed by the departed Hohenstaufen. For the time being the popes counted upon Charles's personal obligations and undoubted loyalty to the Holy See, and, though with less enthusiasm among those born in Italy than in France, worked together with him. At the same time as some counterweight to his power, they ended the *interregnum* of the empire, accepted Rudolf of Habsburg as King of the Romans, and, in 1278, secured from him the formal cession of Ferrara, Bologna, and the towns of Romagna, to the Papal State. With the coming of the Sicilian Vespers they threw themselves, perhaps over-enthusiastically, into the struggle to restore the island to the Angevins and resisted any plan of settlement which implied renunciation of Angevin rule.

Papal–Angevin co-operation reached its climax in the brief pontificate of Celestine V (July–December 1294). He came to the throne after a two and a quarter year vacancy; the cardinals seem to have made his election in almost a moment of despair at finding an adequate and agreed candidate. He had nothing in common with the other curial administrators of the thirteenth century; he was simply a semi-literate hermit with a reputation for sanctity. He was also a Neapolitan, and soon proved to be almost wholly under the influence of Charles II, for whom he created seven French and two Neapolitan cardinals. In this situation the Roman members of the *curia,* fearing a total subservience of the Church to the Angevins, aghast, as he himself was, at his administrative incompetence, persuaded him to resign. In his place was elected Benedetto Caetani, from a noble family of the Campagna, who took the title of Boniface VIII (1294–1303).

No greater contrast to his successor could be imagined. Now entering his sixties, Boniface was a skilful canon lawyer and experienced administrator with a taste for jewels, rich clothes, and finely-worked statues of himself. A mocking sense of humour, rare among popes ('Could be, could be not', he replied to one who was expatiating on the joys of Heaven awaiting him), a taste for miming the physical disabilities of his cardinals, in all a certain theatricality, weakened the respect in which his *curia* held him. With these traits went a memorable brutality of speech ('Your argument's fatuous, as fatuous as it can be fatuously put, or as a professor can fatuously put it') which mirrored a certain brutality of mind, and which was not, perhaps, the mark of an essentially strong character. Particularly towards the end of his career one gains at times the impression that he adhered to the ideological rhetoric of canon-law theories not so much because he believed in them but because those such as Matteo da Acquasparta who were close to him had persuaded him that he ought to believe in them. With his reign the authority of the Papacy received a harsh setback.

Initially Boniface determined to maintain the Guelf Alliance. The Church continued to support Charles II's attacks upon Sicily. To this end indeed the Pope passed over 750,000 florins to his ally. The Church was to remain in harmony with the royal house of France. Yet at the same time, to balance these powers, and to prevent an Angevin dominance of the *curia*, Boniface planned, first, to restore the power of the Papal State, second, to impose his own party, that of the Black Guelfs, in control of Florence, and third, to build up the power of his family around Rome. None of these was a task likely to be achieved without considerable difficulty. The Papal State, founded by Innocent III and lately augmented by the concessions of Rudolf of Habsburg, had, it was true, a splendid bureaucratic and judicial framework and an impressive financial machine. In these circumstances, it was all the more distressing that so few of its communes obeyed its authority or paid its taxes. At the same time, in Florence, it was the White Guelfs who held power. To meet these and his other problems Boniface turned, in 1301, to Charles de Valois, brother of King Phillip IV of France. Charles was called into Italy with the titles of 'Pacifier' of Tuscany and 'Vicar' of the Papal State. His success was limited. In Florence he did, indeed, secure papal ends. Entering the city in the company of the Black Guelfs in November 1301, his army stood by while the Whites were massacred or exiled and the papal faction came to power. Then, however, he marched south and retreated with some ignominy from an ineffective invasion of Sicily. The Papal State remained unpacified.

Boniface's attempts to build up the power of his family were attended by greater success. The Caetani were from the minor nobility, and to turn them into a great magnate family required a certain ruthlessness. It required both a great deal of money – some half to three-quarters of a million florins gleaned from the pious over Europe were spent in purchases – and a great deal of intimidation and sharp practice. (So, for example, Boniface's great nephew, Roffredo Caetani, was married to Margherita, heiress of the Aldobrandeschi properties of southern Tuscany, divorced when it appeared that she and they would be difficult to control, and then re-married to Giovanna d'Aquila; heiress of Fondi and Traetto.) Inevitably, too, it required a certain indifference to the sensibilities of older houses. Among these the Colonna, who had two cardinals within the *curia*, were particularly incensed at the pope's purchase of land which they themselves sought from the Annibaldi family. At the beginning of May 1297 their resentment boiled over and Stefano Colonna seized the baggage train bearing the monies destined for conclusion of the Annibaldi sale. Boniface replied by ordering that the Colonna castles of Palestrina, Zagarolo, and Colonna should be handed over to him. The cardinals of the family thereupon fled, declared his election invalid, and appealed for the convocation of a General Council to depose him. Boniface retorted by preaching a crusade against the family, with all the privileges of a crusade against the infidel. It was a bizarre procedure (though little more, after all, than declaring a crusade against Saracens), but one which did indeed succeed in crushing his local enemies.

Success here, however, was to be revealed as supremely delusive. From the end of 1301 Boniface rashly embarked upon his struggle with the French king over 'ecclesiastical liberties'. The vast expense of Boniface's policies in Italy made it perhaps necessary that the papal right to tax the clergy of Europe be maintained. Moreover it could have been argued that the French clergy, who had yielded 173,000 florins, and the English, who had given 450,000 florins, must, to remain good milch cows, be protected from the taxation of their kings. Yet it was precisely the heavy clinking of coins into papal coffers during the past century which, above all else, had come to drown the voice of papal authority. Philip IV knew that he could meet this challenge to his Crown with a confidence Frederick II could never have had. Brushing aside any reverence which might once have attached itself to the papal person, he despatched his minister, Guillaume Nogaret, to Italy in March 1303 with orders to seize Boniface. By September Nogaret had assembled at Ferrentino a small army, perhaps some 300 knights and 1,000 foot, from among those hostile to the pope. On the 7th they marched on Anagni, entered its walls, and took the pope into custody. The attackers, it is true, had not reckoned with the gratitude of the citizens of Anagni to the patron who had brought so much wealth to their village. Two days later they rose up and secured his release. Yet the spirits of the old man had been crushed; and he died in Rome in the following month. In his person the Papacy had suffered a profound humiliation; with his death the *curia* seemed to be impotent before the secular world.

What the last act in the drama of Boniface VIII's pontificate had made clear was the extreme fragility of the papal temporal power. The Papal State, founded by Innocent III as a guarantee, a buttress, and defence of the independence of the popes' spiritual authority, had dragged the Church much more deeply into the political arena than ever before, and yet was now shown to be ineffective as a power base. If some thirteen-hundred bandits could seize the papal monarch in the heart of his dominions, what purpose did these dominions fulfil? Clement V, elected in 1305, read, at least part of, the message of Anagni. With or without the Papal State, the popes were immensely vulnerable in Italy; the peninsula was too inhospitable for their government. Two years later he formally transferred the *curia* to Avignon. Here the Papacy was, in fact, to enjoy for the following seventy years that independence which it sought. None the less the ancient tradition of the Church made it unthinkable that this should be a permanent solution to its problems. Ultimately the pope had to return to the city of the martyrdom of St. Peter, to the city of which he was bishop. Hence, the story of the Papacy in the fourteenth century was very largely dominated by the attempts of the popes to re-establish, or, rather, to establish for the first time, an effective control of the Papal State which would allow them to return from what almost all men of the Church, even those most closely linked to France, considered as 'exile'. Tyrants who had seized power within 'the patrimony of the crucified one' must be dispossessed, communes seeking autonomy must be crushed or conciliated; barons must be brought to obedience; peace and order must be established, that the pope might, once again, reside in the Lateran. These needs dominated a large part of the external politics of the peninsula powers in the fourteenth century.

First to attempt this fulfilment was Clement V himself, who with more ingenuity than realism seized upon the ambitions of Henry of Luxembourg, recently elected to the imperial throne, as instrumental to his purpose. Of insignificant wealth and family, Henry hoped to establish the prestige and authority of his house in Germany by coronation in Rome and by the revival of some imperial claims south of the Alps. In approving his projected expedition, Clement required in return the establishment of peace in the peninsula, not by warlike means but through the reconciliation of rival factions. In the event such plans proved a chimera. Henry reached Milan in December 1310; began, in the spirit of an honest broker, his attempts to bring together Guelfs and Ghibellines; and swiftly discovered the impossibility of his task. Any attempt at the harmonisation of different political interests, any restoration of Guelfs to Ghibelline towns or vice versa, implied an overturning of the *status quo*, and would be resisted. In particular, Florence saw any reassertion of imperial power as wholly unacceptable. King Robert of Naples, who had at first accepted the ideals of pope and emperor, was compelled eventually to intervene on behalf of his north-Italian Guelf allies. At the same time Henry was driven inexorably towards becoming the leader of the Ghibellines and was forced into alliance with Federico III of Sicily. At this Clement swung back firmly to his traditional allies of the Guelf League and repudiated the imperial adventure. The great dream was over. Henry's death from disease at Buonconvento in August 1313 while marching on Florence with his army was for Dante, and for all his fellow exiles, a tragedy; for all in power a simple full-stop to a long chapter of idle fantasies.

The papal struggle was taken up, with more directness, by John XXII (1316–34), who adopted a policy of out-and-out war against all enemies of the Guelf Alliance. The Ghibellines – Pisa and Lucca in Tuscany, the Visconti and della Scala powers in Lombardy and the Veneto, the house of Savoy in Piedmont, Federico III in Sicily and all dissidents within the Papal State – were to be struck with spiritual weapons, branded as heretics, and crushed by force. By virtue of the disputed imperial election of 1314, John claimed for himself the right to order the affairs of Lombardy, and planned to make of that region a papal fief which was to be given to France. King Robert, whom he despised but saw as a necessary tool, was, in pursuance of this end, made lord of Genoa (1315) and imperial vicar of Italy (1317). The pope's principal agent, however, was his legate in Italy (1319–34), Cardinal Bertrand du Poujet. For fifteen years Poujet concentrated his efforts within the Papal State. Immense sums – over 3,000,000 gold florins, some two-thirds of the income of the pontificate – were dispensed by the pope for the feeing of men-at-arms who would assert the authority of the Holy See. All in vain. The hostile intervention (1327–30) of an imperial claimant, Lewis of Bavaria, complicated the papal strategy. Above all Poujet's alliance with the son of the Emperor Henry VII, King John of Bohemia, a prince who in the years 1330–3 built up a vast but insubstantial domain extending from Mantua to Lucca, alienated the Papacy's oldest allies. In the Treaty of Ferrara of September 1332 Florence, in a momentous reversal of policy, broke with the pope and adhered to the party of the Lombard Ghibellines against King John. The old

Guelf League, first forged back in the 1260s had begun, finally, to break up. Poujet, abandoned by his allies, defeated in battle at Ferrara (April 1333), was ultimately forced to acknowledge the failure of his long legation. After all these years the Papal State remained unmastered.

John XXII was succeeded by two popes, who were either unwilling (Benedict XII) or unable through financial necessity (Clement VI) to resume the struggle. The task was taken up again by Innocent VI, who appointed as reconqueror of the Papal State the former chancellor of Castille, Cardinal Gil Albornoz. The years 1353–63 in which Albornoz exercised his legations in Italy have been portrayed by some historians in heroic terms and he himself has been hailed as 'the second founder of the Papal State'. This is to magnify the significance of his achievements. After ten years' fierce war, the spending of an immense treasure, the shedding of much blood, Albornoz had, it is true, imposed some order. But it was at the expense of considerable concessions. Many of the tyrants who had usurped power within the papal domains remained; men like the Malatesti in Rimini and the towns of the Marche, the Polenta in Ravenna, the Montefeltro in Urbino. In return for acknowledgement of papal lordship, the promise to pay an annual *census*, and to perform military service, their power was strengthened by their recognition as papal 'vicars'. Moreover, Albornoz's triumph was transient. When, in 1375, Florence declared war upon the Papacy, communes and tyrants alike, at the republic's instigation, threw off their allegiance. Three years later the Church and the Papal State were to be thrown into still greater confusion with the outbreak of the Great Schism.

V

While the southern kingdoms and the Papal State struggled simply to survive, the powers which prospered were the lordships and communes of central and northern Italy. In later chapters we must consider their development under the pressure of the movement of the *popolo* and the growth in their functions and authority as they developed into the *signorie* or into the new-style republics of the fourteenth century. For the moment it is sufficient to point out that this very growth served to emphasise the disunity of the peninsula. The end of the Guelf Alliance is normally dated to the collapse of the Florentine banking houses which had been linked with the Angevins and the Papacy in the 1340s. From then on all possibility of seeing the political history of Italy as a meaningful entity disappears. All that can be discerned are the separate policies and conflicts of the individual governments, each struggling for local supremacy or survival.

Within the generation before the 1380s it would be possible to distinguish five major themes in inter-state relations. The first two were the attempt of Albornoz and his successors to reconstitute the papal State and the disintegration of monarchical power in the southern kingdoms. The third was the bitter struggles between Venice and Genoa for mastery in the Mediterranean. The fourth was the Florentine policy of expansion which led to war against Pisa (1362–4) and, in alliance with the Visconti, against the Papacy ('The War of the Eight Saints', 1375–8). Fifth was the consolidation and extension of the rule of the Visconti. By 1354 the brothers Bernabò (1354–85) and Galeazzo II Visconti (1354–76) held Milan and, for a time, Genoa in common. To the east, Barnabò held the towns of Bergamo, Brescia, Crema, Cremona, and Piacenza. To the west Galeazzo held Como, Novara, Vercelli, Asti, Alba, Alessandria, Tortona, and Bobbio. As their power pushed ominously south, they waged war against the Papacy (1362–4; 1367–9), against a Florentine–papal alliance (1369–70), and then, in alliance with the Florentines, against the Papacy again (1375–8). The growth of their wealth and influence was reflected in the marriages of their children. In 1360 Giangaleazzo, son of Galeazzo, married Isabelle de Valois, daughter of King John of France. In 1365, Bernabò's daughter, Valencia, married Pierre de Lusignan, King of Cyprus. Three years later, Galeazzo's daughter, Violante, married Lionel, duke of Clarence, third son of Edward III of England. If their enemies were to sneer at these splendid *coups* as the triumphs of upstarts, the Visconti could draw consolation from the thought that they had advanced their house to the position of a European power.

Amidst all these changes 'Italy' had disappeared. Perhaps it was for this reason that in no period previously had 'Italy' been so much talked of. These were the years of Petrarch's appeal to the princes of 'Italia mia', the years when Florence could declare war upon the (French-dominated) Church under the slogan: 'Expel the abomination from Italy'. Italy has become a topos in rhetoric. Such rhetoric merged easily with the rhetoric of 'Rome', yet the city itself could now boast only a past glory. Men quoted the prophecy of St. Benedict: 'Rome will not be destroyed by the nations, but, shaken by weather, lightning, hurricanes, and earthquakes, will moulder to decay'.[4] Within the Aurelian walls, grass and wild-flowers spread over the pavements, baths, and triumphal ways. It was a city of meadows in which cattle grazed, vineyards, orchards, interspersed by broken temples, bridges, and colonnades. From the ruins rose up the towers of the Roman nobility: the Orsini at Sant' Angelo and in the remains of the Theatre of Pompey; the Savelli on the Aventine, the Colonna at the Mausoleum of Augustus; the Frangipani on the Coelian and Palatine; the Annibaldi at the Colosseum. Deserted by the Roman court, a class of artisans and innkeepers, deprived of the business which had come to them from curials, litigants, and pilgrims, languished. Such was the scene against which Cola di Rienzo was to play out his brief drama.

Born on the left bank of the Tiber, son of an innkeeper and a washerwoman, endowed with a limitless faculty for fantasy and self-delusion, Cola acquired sufficient education to become a notary, read the standard classical texts of his day with a consuming passion, studied the inscriptions on the monuments about him, and with no less zeal investigated the sacred relics of the city. In November 1342 he was sent on an embassy, composed of the three orders of the city, to offer the dignity of 'Senator' to the new pope, Clement VI, and to urge him to return to Rome. When, in the following January, severe disturbances broke out against the established government he went again to Avignon as sole representative of the people to set before the *curia* their cause: to complain of the harsh domination of a factious nobility and the economic decline of a city from which the Papacy was absent. Here his oratory impressed both Clement and Petrarch ('I felt as if I had heard from the temple the voice not of a man but of a God'). At the same time, writing to his fellow citizens under the titles of 'Roman consul' and 'Legate of widows and orphans', he seized the opportunity to impress them too with his influence and eloquence. The pope sent him back to Rome with the office of 'notary to the municipal chamber', where, at once, he became the focus of anti-noble feeling.

On the Whitsunday of May 1347, after the hearing of some thirty masses 'of the Holy Spirit' (with whom he claimed direct communication), he struck. With the assistance of some hundred mercenaries, he deposed the ruling senators, and persuaded a parliament called on the Capitol to appoint himself, together with the papal legate in Italy, Robert de Déaulx, as joint rectors, in effect *signori*, of the city. Before the week was out a second parliament bestowed upon him the title of Tribune, and he had adopted the style of 'Nicolai, the severe and clement, the Tribune of Freedom, Peace, and Justice, and Liberator of the Holy Roman Republic'. Faced with this coup the baronage temporarily yielded to events. Cola turned to a reorganisation of city government designed to secure the end of faction, and began to extend the power of Rome over the Campagna.

More ambitious designs followed. On 7 June he despatched letters to all the Italian powers, the *universa sacra Italia*, urging them to come to a fraternal parliament in which would be discussed 'the security and peace of the whole Roman province'. Even Cola can, perhaps, have hardly expected a full response, and it is more likely that he sought a wider audience for his verbal skills than that he was, as some have thought, planning an Italian confederation. In fact (it was a testimony to his rhetoric but also to the confused state of the peninsula at the time, the turmoil in which the powers were willing to seek any allies) the representatives of twenty-five Guelf communes appeared. In their presence, within the baptistery of the Lateran, Cola was knighted and assumed the title of 'Radiant knight of the Holy Spirit, Nicolai severe and clement, Liberator of the City, Zealot of Italy, Lover of the World, and August Tribune'. That accomplished, amidst a week's banqueting and festivities, he proclaimed the jurisdiction of the Romans over the whole world and generously conferred freedom upon all Italian cities, to whose members he extended the rights of Roman citizenship. He solemnly forbad, *'pro quiete totius Italiae'*, any foreign power from entering the peninsula, forbad the use of the names 'Guelf' and 'Ghibelline', and summoned the rival emperors to submit to his jurisdiction upon their claims.

The high comedy of these pretensions could not long continue. It was, as Villani remarked, 'fantastic stuff which won't last long'. Pope Clement was swift to turn against his erstwhile protégé, and amidst the general indifference of a people satiated by novelty, the legate Bertrand, in alliance with the nobility, drove Cola in mid-December from the city. ('At least,' wrote Petrarch, shocked at the pusillanimity of his hero, 'he could have died gloriously in the Capitol he had freed.')

Exile brought Cola to prison in the Prague of the Emperor Charles IV who was then planning a descent upon the peninsula. Here he pursued his dreams, forecast the coming reign of the Holy Spirit, and prophesied the union of Italy not now under his own auspices but those of his captor. He was transferred to the papal dungeons at Avignon, and then released through the calculation of Albornoz, who saw in him a potential pawn for the reassertion of papal power in the patrimony. Returning to Rome, in 1354, he was appointed Senator. Yet by this time he was in poor health. With a paunch 'like a satrap of Asia' and a new fondness for the bottle ('In prison, they dried me up'), his grasp on events was soon overtaken. In a little over two months he was faced by a popular revolt which brought him to the scaffold. What he left was a legend for later historians: that he had shown the Roman people the *Lex Regia* which gave them the authority to appoint the ruler of the world, that he had planned a united Italy under the leadership of Rome, that he was the prophet of the *Risorgimento*. The reality is otherwise. The man who, perhaps, believed himself to be the illegitimate son of the Emperor Henry VII, who claimed inspiration in dreams from the theocratic 'holy' Boniface VIII, who hailed Clement VI as the 'angelic angel' of Joachimite prophecy, who came close to seeing Charles IV as 'an Emperor of the Last Days', was firmly rooted in the traditions of the past and saw both Italy and Rome in those terms.

The future of Italy lay not with men such as this, but with the nobility of its communes, the workers upon its land, and the merchants of its cities. Save in so far as they might be affected personally by taxation or the devastation of war the interests of most Italians were utterly remote from these or the other concerns of the great. They saw themselves, primarily, not as Romans or Italians or citizens, but as children or parents, and the centre of their lives was not any political unit but rather the family.

NOTES

Among the more important **regional and communal political histories** which treat of this period are on the **Papal State**: D. Waley, *The Papal State in the Thirteenth Century*, London, 1961; P. Partner, *The Lands of St. Peter*, London, 1972; *Storia della Emilia Romagna*, ed. A. Berselli, Imola, 1975; A. Vasina, *I Romagnoli fra autonomie cittadine e accentramento papale nell' età di Dante*, Florence, 1965; E. Duprè-Theseider, *Roma dal comune di popolo alla signoria pontificia (1252–1377)*, Bologna, 1952; F. Gregorovius, *History of the City of Rome in the Middle Ages*, trans. A. Hamilton, London, 1894–1902 (first German edition, 1859–72), vols. v and vi; P. Colliva, *Il Cardinale Albornoz, Lo Stato della Chiesa, Le 'Constitutiones Aegidianae' (1353–57)*, Bologna, 1977.

On the **southern kingdoms** see S. Runciman, *The Sicilian Vespers: A History of the Mediterranean World in the Late Thirteenth Century*, London, 1958, on which should be consulted the review of Helene Wieruszowski in *Speculum*, xxxiv, 1959, pp. 323–6, which, together with other important, relevant articles, is republished in her *Politics and Culture in Medieval Spain and Italy*, Rome, 1971. See too, O. Cartellieri, *Peter von Aragon und die sizilianische Vesper*, Heidelberg, 1904, and C. N. Hillgarth, *The Problem of a Catalan Mediterranean Empire 1229–1327* (English Historical Review, Supplement 8),

London, 1975. Thought-provoking are B. Croce, *Storia del Regno di Napoli*, 3rd edn, Bari, 1953 (in English translation, 1970) and G. Calasso, 'Considerazioni intorno alla storia del Mezzogiorno d'Italia' in his *Mezzogiorno medievale e moderno*, Turin, 1965. For later developments, there are: E. Léonard, *Les Angevins de Naples*, Paris, 1954; R. Caggese, *Roberto d'Angiò e i suoi tempi*, Florence, 1921–30; E. Léonard, *Histoire de Jeanne I*, Paris and Monaco, 1932–7; V. d'Alessandro, *Politica e società nella Sicilia aragonese*, Palermo, 1963; A. de Stefano, *Federico III d'Aragona, re di Sicilia*, Palermo, 1937; R. Moschati, 'Ricerche e documenti sulla feudalità napoletana nel periodo angiono', *Archivo storico per le province napoletane*, 59, 1934; S. Tramontana, *Michele di Piazza e il potere baroniale in Sicilia*, Messina, 1963; D. Mack Smith, *A History of Sicily: Medieval Sicily 800–1713*, London, 1968.

For other areas there are R. Davidsohn, *Geschichte von Florenz*, Berlin, 1896–1922 (Italian translation, Florence, 1956–68), vols. ii and iii; *Storia di Milano* of the Fondazione Treccani degli Alfieri, vols. iv and v, Milan, 1955; *Storia di Brescia* also of the Fondazione Treccani degli Alfieri, Brescia, 1963 ff; *Mantova: la storia*, ed. G. Coniglio, Mantua, 1958; V. Vitale, *Breviario della storia di Genova: Lineamenti storici ed orientamenti bibliografici*, Genoa, 1955; T. O. De Negri, *Storia di Genova*, Milan, 1968; and F. C. Lane, *Venice, a Maritime Republic*, Baltimore, 1974.

On particular incidents and personalities see E. Jordan, *Les Origines de la domination angevine en Italie*, Paris, 1909; P. Durrieu, *Les archives angevines de Naples. Etudes sur les registres du roi Charles 1er*, Paris, 1886–7; M. Fuiano, *Carlo I d'Angiò in Italia: Studi e ricerche*, Naples, 1974; L. Gatto, *Il pontificato di Gregorio X*, Rome, 1959; T. S. R. Boase, *Boniface VIII*, London, 1933; W. M. Bowsky, *Henry VII in Italy*, Lincoln, Nebraska, 1960; F. Filippini, *Il Cardinale Egidio Albornoz*, Bologna, 1933; and K. Burdach and P. Piur, *Briefwechsel des Cola di Rienzo*, Berlin, 1912 (in *Vom Mittelalter zur Reformation*, pt. ii, 1–5, 1912–29).

1. Niccolò da Jamsilla, *Cronaca* in O. del Re, *Cronisti e scrittori sincroni napoletani*, vol. ii, *Suevi*, Naples, 1868, p. 118; Dante, *Purgatorio*, iii, 107; *De vulgari eloquentia*, 1, xii; Giovanni Villani, *Cronica*, vi, p. 46; Adam de la Halle, 'Roi de Sezile' in *Oeuvres complètes*, ed. E. de Coussemaker, Paris, 1872, p. 291.
2. Caggese, *Roberto d'Angiò, cit.*, ii, p. 359.
3. Michele da Piazza, *Historia Sicula* [1337–1361] in R. Gregorio *Bibliotheca scriptorum qui res in Sicilia gestas retulere*, Palermo, 1791–2, ii, p. 54; i, p. 773.
4. Gregorovius, *History of the City of Rome, cit.*, v, pt. ii, pp. 679–80.

CHAPTER FOUR

The family

I

As men passed through their life they might distinguish its stages in various ways.[1] In harmony with the early Fathers they might divide it into six periods corresponding to the six days of creation and the six ages of mankind. It was in this way that Benedetto Antelami sculpted the theme in the west portal of the Baptistery of Parma at the beginning of the thirteenth century. Following a sermon of St. Augustine, he portrayed life here within the context of the parable of the workers in the vineyard. In six scenes the Master sends out the husbandmen at the respective hours of the day. At the first hour of the morning he speaks to a child called *infancia*. There follows Boyhood at tierce, Adolescence at sext, Youth at nones, and then, at the eleventh hour, Manhood and Old Age, a weary labourer resting upon his mattock. Others, like Dante in his discussion of the virtues which nobility encourages throughout life, might think of four periods. There was *adolescenzia* or growth (to 25), time of obedience, shame, sweetness, beauty and agility of body; *gioventute* (25–45), time of temperateness, strength, love, courtesy, and loyalty; *senettute* (45–70), time of prudence, justice, liberality, affability; and *senio* (over 70), time of religious feeling and gratitude for the past.

Doctors, like Pietro d'Abano in his *Conciliator*, would be less specific. Abano gives the principal ages of life in the medical tradition of Galen and Avicenna: growth (1–16); youth (16–30), beauty (30–40); diminution (40–60); old age (60+), and then recapitulates to subdivide 'growth' into 'infancy' (to 1 year); the 'planting of the teeth' (1–7); the 'concussive age' (when the body is struck by humid humours, 7 to 11 or 12); and 'puberty' (11 or 12 to 16). He concludes, however, that on the whole, because complexions differ in individuals, one could not tie the Ages to any particular number of years. A lawyer had to be less flexible. The Bolognese jurist, Rolandino Passagieri (d. 1300), offered the following scheme:

1. Birth–7   (males and females)   = infants
2. 7–9½   (males)   = those close   minors
   7–10½   (females)   to infancy   (below

59

3.	$9\frac{1}{2}$–14	(males)	= those close	legal
	$10\frac{1}{2}$–12	(females)	to puberty	age)
4.	14–25	(males)	= adolescents	
	12–25	(females)		
5.	25–70	(males and females)		majors
6.	70+			(of legal age)

Outside the literary or learned formulations the pattern of men's life was dictated in the thirteenth — and still more, perhaps, in the later fourteenth — century by the realities of very high mortality rates. Of those born only a minority reached *legitima aetas*, age of full legal responsibility. Males of the upper classes who reached the age of twenty-five could count upon very rapid promotion in politics or business. From the age of forty-five when the risk of death again rose sharply, most survivors of any talent could hope for the highest offices. No particular reverence was paid to age as such — indeed a frequent theme of poetry was the contrast between careless youth and crabbed, preoccupied old age — yet survival, unaccompanied by senility, did bring power, and the government of Venice, for instance, where the office of Senator was reserved for the over-forties, has been well described as 'a gerontocracy'. For men of the lower orders, too, ageing had compensations; at seventy they entered by common consent the years of 'decrepitude' and in many communes would be exempted by a formal legal deed from the burdens of citizenship and enrolled among those who enjoyed 'in all things the privilege of the septuagenarian'.[2]

To whatever age they lived men and women found their principal support in the household. Its size and composition would vary with the varying chances of birth and death. A nuclear or simple household, consisting of husband, wife, and their children, might easily expand. Sons frequently resided with their father until his death. Sometimes one or more of the sons might marry, bring wives to live with them, and have children, to form a three-generation, multiple-family household. When the parents died, the household might turn into a *frérêche* or *fraterna*, with two or more brothers living with their wives in the same house. Or again, were one of these brothers to die, his sons with their families might continue to reside with their uncle or uncles (the 'avuncular' household). Then, as the building grew over-crowded or other accommodation became available, the families might decide to separate and form new nuclear households. There was here no 'progressive nuclearisation' of 'patriarchal families' but rather unending cycles of internal household development.

The normal practice of inheritance might seem, at first sight, to have favoured a prevalence of 'extended' households. In Italy rights of primogeniture were rarely acknowledged. Estates, rights, and titles normally passed to sons *pro indiviso* or *in solidum*, that is to say as a single, undivided entity to be held jointly by all the heirs and exploited in common between them. Were one of the sons to die, his children too would often enter into the inheritance of their grandfather's property. For most classes, however, joint possession of and co-residence in large households were not seen as ideal. Before the house filled up with children and quarrels broke out over the administration of the common properties — quarrels

60

all the more likely in that coheirs could sometimes sell their rights in the inheritance to outsiders – it was natural and frequent for the possessors to come together and arrange a simple division of the properties hitherto held *in solidum*. As a result from the beginning to the end of our period the overwhelming proportion of houses was owned by the heads of simple rather than multiple households.

Such simple households might be extended at the margins with a coresident widowed father, or, more often – since men generally married women much younger than themselves – widowed mother. Or again, for the same reason, a fairly large proportion of women might be sole householders. But most men and women who were married lived for most of their lives in a conjugal family unit, consisting of husband and wife, and their children. The pre-eminence of this simple family over any wider family group was mirrored in both surnames and wills. Outside the upper classes of the commune most men and unmarried women used only their father's name as surname; they called themselves Giovanni di [of] Pietro, Maria di Pietro, etc. In their wills, if one may judge from impressions rather than any systematic survey, they left goods to, or asked that prayers be said for, their spouse, sons, unmarried daughters, brothers, or parents. Save when these were lacking, more distant relatives were rarely mentioned.

To this broad generalisation, there are two exceptions. In certain areas of the countryside, particularly where the structure of land-holding dictated the need for the working of the soil by a labour force of large units, the *frérêche* (joint household of brothers) and the multiple-family household (two or more conjugal units) were more frequent. Here land was frequently leased to 'many brothers and/or blood relatives (*consanguinei*) and/or partners (*participes*) from one patrimony who seek the investiture', and in such cases the sharing of 'one bread, one wine, one hearth' and the gathering 'at the same table' were common.[3] Again, families from the upper classes of the commune divided inheritance less frequently and were more likely to live in large household groups.

From the household, whether large or small, the wider family extended. All Italians who had reached the level of the upper-citizen class were probably comparatively closely inter-related. The Franciscan chronicler Salimbene de Adam, for instance, whose blood sprang from no great social eminence, was, through his sister's marriages (though he makes nothing of this), linked to the powerful Emilian lines of the da Gente, Rossi, Lupi, San Vitale, Enzola, and Cornazzano, and through them to the marquesses d'Este and that scion of the counts of Lavagna, Innocent IV. One could continue from there to trace his affinity throughout the whole peninsula. Widely extended interbreeding among the élite class was reinforced by several circumstances. Though comparatively strong social mobility brought reinforcements to it from below, its numbers were still small in relation to the total population and the 'isolate' or 'pool' from which its members could find mates was further reduced through the adoption of celibacy by those who followed an ecclesiastical career. It was diminished again by the decrees of the Church against marriage within 'the prohibited degrees of kindred'. Up to 1215 these prohibitions had extended to a remarkable seventh degree in canon law. From then on they were restricted to a fourth degree: that is seven degrees in civil law, or up to third cousins. Yet this relaxation was accompanied by the extension of physical to 'spiritual' affinity: that is by the prohibition of marriage when one of the parties had been sponsored at baptism by someone related to him or her within the prohibited degrees.

Theologians and canon lawyers had justified these inhibitions by the argument that through their operation greater areas of society would be united in family love. In fact the upper-class was already very closely intertwined, and in the event, family love could be shared out only between a rather limited section of the population. For most men, no doubt, the function performed by all but the nearest relatives was less than that fulfilled by those in the often no less important relationship of 'neighbours'. In fact neighbours and family were often closely connected. In towns kinsmen of the middle class sought to live in households adjacent to each other or, at least, in the same quarter. To what extent they then acted in common and sought a functional unity beyond that varied from class to class. The wider family, it is clear, loomed very large among those of the nobility or patricians who sought power within the communes. For these men it was an element in social life vital for security and for participation in politics. So too the lineage was of importance for prominent merchants (among whom many were nobles) in their struggle to dominate the commercial and financial world. As with the Alberti del Guidice in Florence or the sixteen households belonging to the Salimbene of Siena the family could turn itself into a banking firm, or, as in the coastal cities, into a company of merchant-adventurers overseas.

Symbolic of the search of such men for family unity was the rise among them of the shared patrilineal family surname. From as early as the eleventh century some noble families had adopted a surname; in the thirteenth the practice became quite common. Sometimes the name of the individual was joined to the family name by the preposition 'da' (Giovanni da Porto), sometimes by the use of the Latin genitive singular (Giovanni Martini, Dante Alighieri), sometimes by the use of the family name in apposition (Brunetto Latino = Brunetto, son of Buonaccorso Latino). In modern Italy these three forms have been seen as characteristic of the south, the centre, and Liguria and the western-Po valley respectively.[4] In our period the usages were still in flux, as too, for new families, was the use of surnames themselves. New men would change their family names at will. For more established families, however, they were becoming virtually unalterable, to be changed only under great political pressure (see below, p. 123), a feature of their members' personality.

Sharing the same cognomen and coats of arms, these men struggled to preserve the wider family. Though it was generally difficult to do so beyond the third generation, they sought as far as possible, sometimes through entails and pacts of *de non aliendo extra familiam*, to preserve joint households and the community of all of or parts of their property. When households divided, they would group themselves as neighbours around a street, piazza, family tower or loggia. (Powerful Florentine families were often described as 'those with a tower and a loggia'.) So in Genoa the piazza of S. Matteo was completely surrounded by the houses of the Doria family; in Florence and Lucca the piazza di Peruzzi and the via de' Guinigi take their names from the respective families who dominated the areas. They would establish, like the Bardi, Pazzi, and Rucellai, in Florence, their own private chapels, and exercise joint rights of patronage over churches they owned in common. In Genoa, again, family houses are found grouped around their own jointly-owned shops, warehouses, and baths.

Or again, households of one lineage residing in the countryside would hold a palace together within the city. So, at Reggio Emilia in 1272, twenty-four male descendants of Manfredo da Sesso and his three brothers, organised in ten smaller family groups (five *frérêches*, two avuncular, and three simple households) are found holding *pro indiviso* a palace called 'The Trebbio [or meeting place] of the da Sesso'. Normally resident at separate villages in the *contado*, at Cavriago, S. Maria del Piano, Novillaria, 'outside Borgo S. Croce' and at the ancestral homeland of Sesso itself, the individual households, at family festivals or moments of crisis, would come together at the Trebbio. Here at the centre of the city, only two doors from the Palazzo Comunale, they would assert, through their numbers in unity, their influence upon the politics of the commune.[5]

In Emilia and Lombardy, at least, still larger groupings are found, which can properly be described as 'clans' (various lineages linked by the reality or assumption of common descent). Characteristic of these are 'those from Canossa' said to have found a common ancestor in one Azzo, living at the time of Otto I, 'the sons of Manfredo', and 'those from Fontana', who, Giovanni de' Mussi explains in his chronicle, 'are in great number and so have diversified their cognomen', being known then as the Arcelli, Malvicini, Zagni, etc.[6] How far any effective unity subsisted within these clans is, however, uncertain. In most communes agnate lineage looms much larger, though, as we shall see in the following chapter, lineages with no close relationship by blood sometimes came together to form artificial clans with a shared surname.

It should be added that though upper-class families sought lineage-unity, it was a condition very difficult to maintain. Inheritance *pro indiviso*, it has been seen, could provide an opportunity for maintaining the cohesion of the family, but it could also have the reverse effect, particularly if several generations passed without some simple division of the properties held jointly. The common administration of properties whose co-proprietors might hold 1/72 or 42/860 parts of a property, the administration of some unit, for instance, like the marquisate of Ceva in Piedmont, which was in 963/4 parts and where more than sixty household-heads held the title of marquess of Ceva, presented particular difficulties, both in initiating policies for the property's development and in the equitable division of profits which came from it. Herein lay fertile grounds for suspicion and dispute. And the ultimate simple division of such unitary properties could also give rise to profound discontent. Hence rivalries within families were frequent, and caused deep political splits and much blood-letting between kinsmen. In Florence, Giovanni Villani describes the families who composed the 'White' party in 1300, and then, with very little exaggeration, remarked that their 'Black' opponents consisted of 'part of all the houses' he had named among the Whites.[7]

Many families, none the less, succeeded in holding together. What the wider lineage could mean for its members can be deduced from the *ricordanze* or family memorials of the Florentine, Donato di Lamberto di Filippo di Bonaccurso di Piero di Berto de' Velluti.[8] They were written between 1367 and 1370. From a prosperous family of merchants who traded in wool in France and England, and who had many times filled the highest functions in the commune, Donato, himself a judge, had held many public posts, had been on various embassies to Italian powers, and had died in office as Gonfaloniere di Giustizia. In his *ricordanze* he notes a family tradition that the Velluti had originated from Semifonte in the Val d'Elsa, but says he does not know when they came to Florence. He knows (though only through a document) the names of his great-grandfather's father and that man's (twelfth-century) grandfather. He names and relates to each other sixty-five third cousins (descendants of his great-grandfather's two brothers) and of many of these he is well-informed, partly through documents, but partly, too, through personal knowledge. He also knows a great deal about the families into which they married. For example, he names and relates eight of the family into which his great-grandfather's eldest brother had married, names and relates twelve of the Antinori family into which one of his third cousins, twice removed, had married; and, more than this, gives the names and families of four other men into which women of the Antinori family had married.

One could multiply examples of Donato's knowledge of his family along these lines at some length. No doubt much of the information does have a 'genealogical' character; it is compiled for the sake of disinterested curiosity or comprehensiveness. (And perhaps, too, third cousins loom so large because he had only two second cousins and four first cousins.) None the less, his interest was also 'functional', based upon the fact that these relationships were of importance. Both aspects are referred to in his apologia for the writing of the work: 'because men want to know of their breeding and its past times, and how their relatives have been, and the goods acquired, and often through this they avoid much damage and flee many errors.'

In his account of his family, for instance, cousins, particularly first and second cousins, are consistently found working together. They lived together in houses grouped around the via Maggio; they are partners together in commercial ventures, and they give aid to each other in law and politics. And, here, third cousinship is still important. Donato tells his readers, for instance, that as Gonfaloniere he has seen to it that a third cousin, twice removed, has not suffered, as he seemed to be about to, from his investments in the state debt. He speaks of the great affection shown to him as a boy by Diana, his third cousin, once removed; he tells of how he was given his name from a second cousin, once removed, of his father; and he deplores the fact that a third cousin should have married into a family 'which has no status'.

Finally the family made vendetta together. Such vendettas could be pursued over a long period of time. The murder of Donato's great-grandfather's brother by one of the Manelli family in 1267 was avenged only when his father, together with his second cousins, once removed, together with others, 'joined to us by love, lineage, and neighbourhood', murdered another member of the Manelli family in June 1295. The long time allowed for the exaction of vendetta, it should be added, promoted family unity over long periods, for faced, always, with the possibility of reprisals, families that slayed together had every reason to stay together.

Turning to lower levels of society, the importance of the wider family lessens. Salimbene de Adam, of thirteenth-century Parma, who gives an account of his family in the course of his chronicle, came from *nouveau riche* stock who showed little interest or participation in politics. He names and relates only sixty-four cognates – something which most urban Scots today could better – and among them none more remote than a second cousin. Even with these he shows real interest only in those who had gone into religion, or those whom he had known in his childhood and early youth. We learn of the families his sisters married into, which were in fact quite distinguished, only through chance references. It could be that as a Franciscan he cultivated indifference to the wider family. Yet the instability of the family name – among his agnates it appears as 'Grenoni', 'Olivieri', 'de Adam', and 'Adde' – suggests that this attitude was characteristic of the family as a whole, that without strong political ambitions or mercantile concerns the wider alliances to be exploited within it were not seen as having any great significance. Among the working class, as Dr. Hughes's researches into Genoa suggest, it seems likely that the meaning and importance of the family diminished still further. In this city artisans, many of whom lived in accommodation rented at short lease, did not settle in houses near to relatives. At death they often willed their property to their wives, even when they had children, and sometimes left their estate outside the family. In Florence again the extreme rootlessness of the poor was likely to have worked against any lineage cohesion.

Whether men looked to the wider family or not the household, on which the communes placed responsibility for taxation and military service, remained the basic unit of society. Within it the eldest male was an absolute ruler, his total power guaranteed by the sentiments of religion and the decisions of jurists. His right to administer corporal punishment to any of its members was acknowledged in law, and he could call upon the commune to imprison recalcitrant sons. Irrespective of the age of the son ('even if he be sixty years old', wrote Accursius) the *filius familias* was bound by the authority of the *patria potestas* for as long as the father lived. In some communal statutes, indeed, it was decreed that both son and father were in the *potestas* of the grandfather as long as he lived. Hence father and son were in a sense one. That being so, jurists discussed at length whether when a property or wealth qualification attached to an office in the commune a *filius familias* could count his father's wealth towards qualifying for it; whether the goods of a father could be seized for the debt of a son; whether a son could be held responsible in law for a crime that his father had ordered him to commit. Or again, whether a father could be held responsible for the crime of a son which he had not authorised; whether, if a son were condemned to lose all his goods for a crime that judgment touched simply his *peculia* (that wealth which he himself had earned), or, in addition, that part of his father's wealth that he might expect to inherit from him.[9]

For men subject to the *paterfamilias* marriage was not a matter for individual choice but a contract entered into on the initiative of the family – often using the services of a marriage-broker – and requiring the approval of the household head. It was possible for a son to seek 'emancipation' from his father, and if, at marriage, he were to separate from his father's household it was likely he would obtain it. Yet such a grant depended on the will of the father and normally imposed on him the obligation of surrendering to the son something from the family patrimony. Without such a surrender 'emancipation' in fact became 'expulsion', a penalty for disobedience, formally granted by the commune, which was likely to prove extremely painful for the *exfamiliatus*. In place of the paternal blessing, he would receive in his father's will, the paternal curse:

I curse my son Benedetto: may he be accursed to the extent of my power. . . With lies, tricks, and betrayals he has continually disobeyed and vituperated me, my Commune, and my family and relatives. . . May he be accursed by God, amen! And if he survives me, and I have not chastised him as he deserves, may the just sentence of God punish him according to his deserts as a vile traitor.[10]

Daughters too, of course, lay under the same authority, and were emancipated from it only when at marriage they came under the *mundeburdium* and power of their husband. To the problems of inheritance and property within that marriage the lawyers of the north-Italian communes had addressed themselves in a long series of legislation stretching from the twelfth century, whose final effect was powerfully to reinforce the agnatic principle. In particular they concentrated upon the *Morgengabe*. These were those gifts made to a wife by her husband before marriage, consisting of, for those who lived under Langobard law, a *quarta* or quarter of all his possessions, and for those claiming to live under Frankish law, a *tertia* or third. The *Morgengabe*, together with the similar *Donatio propter nuptias* (Donation due to marriage) made by those claiming to live under Roman law, were now subsumed under the one, newly-coined word, *antifactum*, and came under two centuries of prolonged attack.

It was the age of 'the hatred to the *quarta*'. By the thirteenth century wedding gifts to wives had been notably restricted at Genoa (1143), and played little part in or had wholly disappeared from the customs of Siena, Lucca, Bologna, and Padua. In the first decades of the thirteenth century they were abolished at Pistoia and Volterra. At Milan, in the Constitutions of 1216, it was decreed that: 'By hatred to the *quarta*, the *quarta* will not be given.' By the 1230s the donations had been attacked in Trentino and the Alto-Adige, by 1255 at Florence. They disappeared at Como between 1231 and 1281, were being legislated against at Ferrara in 1287, and at Brescia in 1298.

It was a long and uneven process. Milan and Brescia, and the statutes of Bergamo of as late as 1374, prohibited the giving of the *antifactum* only in so far as it comprised fiefs and long-leases. In many cities, indeed, these donations continued, and the authors of notarial formularies were still compelled to include them in their works. Like Martino da Fano they might grit their teeth at the thought ('this evil custom ought to be abolished since it should be neither valid in law nor in justice have any effect. Do it this way . . .') or, like Rolandino Passagieri, simply shrug their shoulders ('in the city of Bologna this instrument is deemed in the custom of our time to have been abolished. Still, when in Rome you must do like the Romans'). The *antifactum* often remained.

This was notably so in the south of Italy. The *dotarium* (called also *tertiaria*, though it could consist of less than a third of the husband's property) was normally constituted 'on the day of the wedding before the doors of the church'. Frederick II's *Constitutiones Augustales* even permitted the nobility, under certain conditions, to use a third of their feudal possessions in making the gift. By the fourteenth century, it is true – despite the efforts of Charles II, who had insisted that the *tertiaria* should be made 'whether a dowry be given or not' – it was becoming frequent for the size of the *dotarium* to be calculated as the equal of the dowry the wife brought to her husband. None the less here the wife's rights in family property seem to have been much stronger than in the North, and nuptial donations seem to have had a more tenacious hold. Moreover, in Sardinia and in the island of Sicily there grew up, or is documented for the first time, the custom of a communion of matrimonial goods in which the husband, wife, and children could each claim a right to a third. Aragonese influence has been suspected here. But it may be that this was in fact a long-existing practice adopted by spouses who at marriage possessed nothing. For the *condominium* began not at marriage but after the birth of a child and the cohabitation of the spouses for a year (as at Palermo) or for a year, a month, and a day (as at Caltagirone, Corleone, and Piazza). The system was still enjoying an admittedly very limited life in the seventeenth century.

To look at Italy as a whole, however, the rights of women in property seem to be declining in this period, and a new emphasis upon the *privilegium* or *favor masculinitatis* increasingly hindered their inheritance of land at the expense of any male kinsman, however distant. At the same time, as their claim to a share in the wealth of their husband came under attack, so did the importance of their dowries increase.

The maxim smuggled into canon law: *Nullum sine dote fiat coniugium* ('no one without a dowry shall be a spouse'), though received into the *Decretum* (*c.* 1141) of the most authoritative of all canon lawyers, Gratian, had, it is true, as legists came increasingly to emphasise the consensual rather than formal aspects of marriage, been set aside; and in the statute law of the communes the condition of wives without dowries was taken into careful consideration. None the less, as the *antifactum* declined the dowry loomed ever larger in the practical business of everyday life and became more and more necessary as a guarantee of the economic subsistence of a married women should her husband predecease her. Again and again the statutes insisted that all who could should dower their daughters in conformity with the status of their family, and for the élite classes of the commune (and for many below those classes) the dowry became an essential element in marriage. Salimbene, for example, tells how he had persuaded the lord Guido da Polenta and the lord Aldegherio da Fontana to provide a large dowry for the daughter of a citizen of Ferrara and how the man had thanked him on his deathbed: 'Fra Salimbene, may God repay you, for my daughter would have gone in to an inn and perhaps have become a prostitute, but for you who gave her in marriage.'

Yet as the dowry grew in importance the wife's rights in it came increasingly to be called in question. More and more it came to be thought of less as an economic guarantee of the woman's position and more as a means of supporting what were described as the *onera matrimonii*, 'the burdens of marriage' ('which', as Rolandino put it, 'are generally heavy'). The jurists debated, indeed, whether, if the wife's dowry were too small to support the *onera matrimonii*, the husband had any duty to support her (reaching the conclusion: 'Yes, because she is in the husband's service . . .'). As a result men came to look for the constitution of the dowry in a particular form. Turning against that composed of the specific lands or goods which the wife had brought with her to marriage (the *dos inaestimata*), they sought more often one constituted as the money-equivalent (*dos aestimata*) of such lands or goods. From the husband's point of view the *dos aestimata* had the merit of weakening the idea that the wife herself might have *dominium* or property rights in her dowry, and allowed him a much freer exploitation of it.

Again, when a husband predeceased his wife, both the university legists and the communes agreed that, whether there were children of the marriage or not, the dowry should be restored to the wife (though the complaints of the statutes show that relatives very frequently tried to prevent this). The overwhelming majority of the legists also taught that if the wife predeceased the husband and there were no children of the marriage, the dowry should be returned to her family. Against this the communes decreed that in these circumstances the widower should be allowed to keep either a third (Siena) or a half (Pisa, Arezzo, Modena) or all (Brescia and Piacenza) for himself. Only in a few cities (such as Bologna) was the dowry returned in full. At the same time the wife's authority over the *parapherna* (that is to say those goods and lands which she owned or inherited, which were outside her dowry) was weakened. Among the glossators, Placentinus and Azzone had seen these as the exclusive property of the wife; Accursius, however, had argued that while the wife had dominion over them the husband enjoyed the right to their fruits. It was a judgment wholly acceptable to the lawyers of the communes. At Ravenna (early thirteenth century), Venice, Bologna (1250), Verona (1276), Florence (1325) and Modena (1327), it was decreed that all goods of the wife not contained within her dowry should be treated as if they were, while the marriage was in being.

In all, over these three centuries, the attack upon the *antifactum*, the rise of the dowry, and the diminution of the wife's property right within it, implied for much of central and northern Italy a powerful strengthening of the patrilineal family. This development is significantly parallelled by the decline of the matronymic, which had been quite common in earlier centuries (Dante, for instance, tells us that his surname, Alighieri or Aldighieri, had been derived from the name of his great-great grandfather's wife) but which was rare, outside the lower class, by the mid-thirteenth. The reasons for this reorganisation of the family have been much discussed. The twelfth-century renaissance of Roman law, in that it recalled to life new authorities to challenge the rule of custom, can be thought of as creating a climate in which women's customary rights could be easily over-ruled. Yet the contention that the process represented a 'national' victory of Roman over 'barbarian' law is obviously misplaced, since it necessitated the frequent and flagrant over-riding of the *Ius Comune* taught in the universities. In seeking to resolve the question it is significant that the South felt less compulsion than the North to follow in this direction. Given this, it has been suggested that it was the exigencies of the commercial revolution in northern and central Italy between the eleventh and fourteenth centuries which provoked the change. In the rapid expansion of mercantile operations, it has been argued, it was seen as necessary that, in his daily business, the merchant should have at his command all the capital available from the members of his household.

There is, probably, some truth in this and it is certainly suggestive that the great port of Genoa should have been the first commune to proceed to the abolition of the *Morgengabe*. Yet in those Lombard towns, such as Milan and Brescia and Bergamo, where the attack upon the *antifactum* related only to feudal and leasehold property, some other explanation seems to be called for. In these circumstances the most convincing hypothesis is that offered by Bellomo, who sees the coming of the new family as the result of the struggle for power developing within and between the communes. In order not simply to gain pre-eminence but to survive within the world of government it was necessary for the great families of the town that a new power should be given to the father-husband. This interpretation gains powerful support from, for example, the wording of the statutes of Parma of 1255, which, decreeing that the usufruct of an estate willed to a daughter should pass to her husband, then adds the significant words: 'which husband should be held to serve the Commune with horses and arms according to his resources and that of the estate'. Again the same commune in 1300 gave rights in the *parapherna* of wives only to those husbands who were adherents of the Guelf party: 'that they may be better able to serve the commune and party'.

II

Outside questions of property and inheritance women were subject to a variety of mutually-reinforcing economic, legal, and social disadvantages. They were sometimes able, it is true, to invest money derived from inheritance (or to invest on behalf of their husbands and others) in commercial activities, and in some communes, as those of Piacenza and Perugia, they had in matters of business (which meant, in effect, small retail business) full juridical capacity. Yet, on grounds of their presumed instability, their testimony was held unacceptable in criminal cases; they were excluded from public office; and though, occasionally, found as (poorly-paid) elementary teachers, they had no access to the world of professional learning. Normally they could earn money in such posts as Francesco da Barberino details in his *Del reggimento e costumi di donna*[11] (1348), a didactic poem which offers advice (mostly relating to sexual matters) to all women in society. He mentions the Lady's maid ('Don't praise your mistress's beauty too extravagantly, hold to the mean'; 'don't spy on what she and her husband do in the bedchamber'), the serving girl ('don't let the husband seduce you, the wife will never forgive it'), the washer-woman, the market women ('don't buy food from servants who've stolen it'), the baker, mill-girl, chicken-seller, pedlar ('don't act as a bawd to young virgins'), the waitresses in taverns ('don't serve heated-up meals; sell food, not yourself'), and the beggar-girl ('don't swear at those who won't give you bread'). In considering female employment, mention should also be made of peasant women, 'who carry out work in the fields like men',[12] the wives of townsmen who formed a pool of casual labour at times of harvest, and those weavers, stretchers, and spinners who were probably more numerous than men in the textile industries.

The general economic dependence of women went hand in hand with the status they were assigned – in Italy as in all Europe – by the Church. Theologians and canon lawyers, divided between views of women as Eve or Mary (and between Mary as perfect virgin and perfect mother), played an ambiguous rôle. The Church asserted the equality of women and men before God. It honoured the nun, and though it has been calculated that only 23.65 per cent of Italians canonised in the thirteenth and fourteenth centuries were women, its enthusiastic espousal of those like St. Clare, St. Catherine of Siena, St. Angela of Foligno, who were renowned for sanctity, provided women with their best opportunity for public fame. The comparatively novel insistence of canon law upon the validity of a woman's marriage, when made without her father's consent, and (though in practice the ruling may have been difficult to enforce) upon the need for her consent to marriage, may have done something to protect her interests. So too, perhaps, did its assertion of the indissolubility of marriage. Such an assertion, it should be added, did not preclude the strong-minded from obtaining annulments. Since common agreement between spouses wishing to separate made it difficult for any alleged canonical impediment to be disproved, and since such impediments were very numerous, the rich, at least, were in a position to obtain what was, in fact if not in theory, divorce by mutual consent. The remarriage of those whose unions had been annulled was the object of ecclesiastical disapproval though not prohibition.

On the other hand the rise in canon law, whose pronouncements on *connubium* took as their starting point the Pauline conviction (1 Corinthians, 11, 3) that 'the head of the woman is the man', probably served to lower the general esteem of women in society. So too did the theologians' espousal of newly-translated Greek learning. St. Thomas Aquinas, for instance, took over from Aristotle the view that women were the result of some imperfection and deformity in nature, the fruit, possibly, of unfavourable meteorological conditions at the moment of conception, and declared in consequence that they were by nature subject to men who possessed greater abundance of reason. They were one of those many things provided for man's use, in this case the reproduction and conservation of the human species. In the climate of such opinions they were excluded, 'being not perfect', from the grades of the ecclesiastical order, and were prohibited by Innocent III from touching the altar, linen, and sacred vessels. At the same time the ecclesiastical exaltation of celibacy, which led men like St. Bonaventura to see marriage as necessary, but a necessary ill, a *medicina preservativa* against extra-marital sex, and which, again, disapproved of the re-marriage of widows, tended to depreciate their rôle as wives. The learned described marriage as a sacrament, yet disputed whether as such it were merely a figurative sign or could indeed give grace, nor did they ever claim that the participation of a priest was (as with other sacraments) essential for its validity.

In practice the Church, while emphasising the dominance of the male, sought to protect women from grosser male brutality. So at Genoa in 1222, an archdeacon orders one Pietro di Ortoxeto:

> to take back Druda [his wife] in the house of his father and treat her with marital affection, that is to say to lie with her in the same bed, and to pay there his conjugal debt, and to eat with her at table from the one trencher . . . Item, he orders him that he shall not hold any concubine publicly in the place where he is living, nor lead any concubine into his father's house, and that he shall treat the said Druda, his wife, in all those ways in which a good husband ought to treat his good wife.[13]

The same attitude was taken by civil governments. Much of the legislation protecting women — as, for example, Frederick II's decrees against bride-rape (rape carried out in order to compel subsequent marriage) — was, to judge by the later persistence of the crimes, probably ineffective. Yet, on certain occasions, the communes would force husbands to support their wives, exact maintenance expenses from husbands whose cruelty had forced their wives to return to their fathers, intervene to prevent the 'immoderate' corporal chastisement of wives, or again stop husbands from wasting the family substance on drink or gambling. Moreover secular law was flexible enough to come to all manner of private arrangements outside the conventional matrimonial patterns. So, in Genoa, towards the end of our period, a document was drawn up in the church of S. Maria de Servi, on behalf of a wool-worker, Antonio di Venozza, and his wife, Sancia. She has, it says, committed adultery many times, sometimes for money, both in and outside his house. Now, in return for 40 florins, her husband absolves her from those acts, and both agree in future that they may take lovers or mistresses without penalty.[14]

Many communes, in fact, prescribed penalties for adultery, penalties which were, occasionally, disproportionate between the sexes (at Belluno, for instance, the man was fined £200; the woman burnt). It is probable that these were rarely invoked. Yet in practice the murder of adulterous wives was condoned, and the *Constitutiones* of Frederick II specifically allowed a husband to kill his wife if found in *flagrante delicto*. On the other hand, though it is not a subject on which one can easily generalise, one gains at times the impression that, outside the official world, illicit sexuality provoked no strong hostility. One recalls the sympathy shown by Dante to the adulterous Paolo and Francesca and his hostility to their cuckolded murderer, and then again (though sodomy was occasionally punished by burning) of his moving tribute to the damned homosexual, Brunetto Latino. Or one thinks of Salimbene's friendship with the lord Guido da Monte, whose attempt to seduce his first cousin's wife he mentions quite casually, and of his affection for the lord Nazaro Ghirardini ('a handsome knight, and very rich, my acquaintance and friend') who had acquired his wife ('a beautiful lady, fat, and fleshy') by taking her from a husband in Treviso by whom she had already two daughters.

Significant too, perhaps, was the matrimonial career of the lady Nicoletta of Venice. On the death of her first husband, a count of Ossero, she had taken a vow of chastity. Around 1219, putting aside this vow, on the grounds that she was insane when taking it, she married Enrico Dandolo, nephew of the doge of the same name. She then became the mistress of one Manfredo de' Ricchi, who already possessed a wife and child. In order to dispose of Dandolo she declared to an ecclesiastical court that her claim to have been insane in making her vow of chastity was untrue and asked, therefore, that her marriage to him should be dissolved. This done she bigamously married Manfredo, had sons by him, and lived with him until, tiring of her, he resolved to rejoin his legitimate wife. These vicissitudes led the ecclesiastical order eventually to make some protest, but lay society seems simply to have courteously averted its eyes from them. The principal inhibition against sexual freedom seems to have come not from law but from the possibility of vengeance from a family which might consider itself dishonoured. So Paolo Sassetti of Florence groaned in spirit at the news that his kinswoman Letta Sassetti had died as the mistress of Giovanni Porcellini, but confided to his *ricordanze*: 'We are contemplating a vendetta which will bring some balm to our feelings'.[15]

In the literature of the age the familiar medieval genre of misogynist satire features most prominently. Ecclesiastics vowed to a painful celibacy, laymen who must frequently have had difficulty in accommodating the reality of a known woman to the theory of her inferiority combined to give it immense popularity. It had its mirror-image in a frequent and no less extravagant idealisation of individual women which in fact served the sex as a whole poorly. To Dante's wife, the living Gemma Donati, to all wives, the glory of the dead Beatrice stood as a constant reproach. And what was seen as women's essential weakness was feared all the more in that it was held to be united to an immense strength in ill-doing; Sacchetti writes of them as 'having much more subtle and quick intellects than men in doing and speaking ill'. Constant vigilance was necessary lest family honour be besmirched. Hence Paolo da Certaldo's advice:

The female is an empty thing and easily swayed; she runs great risks when she is away from her husband. Therefore keep females in the house, keep them as close to yourself as you can, and come home often to keep an eye on your affairs and to keep them in fear and trembling. Make sure they always have work to do in the house and never allow them to be idle.[16]

Within this general climate of contempt and subordination the inequalities between men and women became stark and painful at only the higher end of the social spectrum. Among the poor the lot of peasant women, who bore and raised children, in addition to performing hard manual labour in the fields, merged easily with that of their husbands in a common struggle for survival. Among the urban working class, the importance of the wider family was small and marriage could be a matter of free choice and affection. In this respect it is perhaps significant that, in defiance of the law, a large number of artisans of Genoa in the thirteenth century were giving their wives at marriage an *antifactum* which equalled or exceeded her dowry and that here too men are sometimes identified by both their father's and mother's names.

At the level of the artisanate, this freedom diminished. The higher the social class the greater became the importance of the family, and the more the inequalities between the sexes were made explicit. In a middle-class family the rôle of the wife was simply to produce sons and to manage the household. It has been pointed out that in an era when even urban households were far more self-sufficient in feeding and clothing than they can easily be thought of today, such management had intrinsically more interest and importance than the work of a contemporary housewife. Moreover, though women on the whole seem to have been admired rather as mothers than as wives, the business-like character of marriage did not prohibit the growth of affection between fortunate spouses. One thinks here of the letters of Dora del Bene to her husband, filled with tenderness, jokes, simulated jealousy, or even of Donato Velluti's tribute, albeit characteristically egoist and acquisitive, to his Bice:

She was small and not beautiful, but wise, good, pleasing, lovable, well-mannered and full of and perfect in every virtue, and she made herself liked and loved by everyone. And I have much to praise myself in her, for she loved and desired me with all her heart. She was most good in her soul; and one should believe that our Lord Jesus Christ has received her in his arms, for she did very good works, almsgiving, praying, and visiting the church. She lived with me in holy peace and increased my substance with much grace, honour, and goods. . . She died in July 1357, so that she lived with me seventeen years. May God have mercy upon her soul.[17]

One must not discount, either, the power of conscious or unconscious repudiation of authority which is characteristic of subject peoples, and which is brought out in Fra Salimbene's account of his mother:

She was called Inmelda, a humble woman and devoted to God, often fasting, and liberally giving alms to the poor. She never seemed angry, never struck any maid-servant with her hand. For the love of God she always liked to have some poor little woman from the mountains to stay the winter with her and she gave her food and clothing. This, despite the fact that she had maids to do the work of the house. On her behalf Pope Innocent gave me letters at Lyons that she might enter the order of St. Clare.

So far the paragon. But earlier the good friar has let fall a story whose memory endears her to him less:

My mother would often tell me that at the time of this great earthquake [Christmas Day, 1222] I was lying in the cradle, and she picked up my two sisters, one under each arm (for they were small) and leaving me in the cradle, she ran to the house of her father and mother and brothers. For she was afraid, so she said, that the Baptistery would fall on her, because it stood next to my house. And for this I loved her less brightly, for she should have cared more for me, a male, than for daughters. But she would say that they were easier for her to carry since they were more fully grown.[18]

Not the least interesting aspect of this tale are the words: 'my mother would often tell me'. At a subliminal level one catches the accents of passive resistance to the world as it has been established by others.

None the less, for women of independent character the daily experience of wives of this class – who normally surrendered even the suckling of their children to country wet-nurses – must often have been considerably tedious. The

73

behaviour expected of the good woman is well brought-out in the fourteenth century *Avvertimenti di maritaggio*,[19] wherein a mother is assumed to be instructing her daughter in the 'Ten Commandments of Marriage' (a misleading phrase, since there are many, many more). These, if followed, will ensure that she becomes her future husband's companion and 'obedient servant'. Follow his moods, the mother advises, study his taste in food rather than your own, take the utmost care in looking after his property, don't try to know his business, don't do anything without his consent, don't say: 'My opinion is better than yours', even when it is ('for it may be that this will bring him into great dislike and hatred of you'). Don't, she continues, ask him to do anything which he dislikes doing; keep yourself clean and beautiful; don't be familiar with the servants (a certain pride and lordliness is better); don't wander about too much outside the house, a wife who goes out little is her husband's joy; don't chat too much ('small speech, saintly lady'). Be modest; don't try to know too much; don't give credence to spells and incantations; give him a good welcome when he comes home; honour his relatives more warmly than your own (as he should do yours). Finally, the greatest commandment, avoid anything which might make him jealous. So will you become the golden crown of your husband.

What distinguishes the life offered in this treatise from the lives of bourgeoises of later centuries is perhaps marginal, for the neglect of any emphasis on religious duties is interesting but exceptional. Yet it was accompanied by a stronger element of seclusion than is to be found in more modern societies. Upper-class women rarely left their houses, save to go to church or to family gatherings. It is this element in women's life which Boccaccio, who at times was admittedly to express himself in the bitterest misogyny (the *Corbaccio*), brings out very clearly in the *Decameron*, a work remarkable both for its continual emphasis upon the conflicting claims of nature and society within which women lived, and for its continuous sympathy for the reality of women's lives. Written, ostensibly at least, for 'the ladies with time on their hands' its preface dwells strongly on the cloistered aspect of women's life: 'cooped up within the narrow confines of their rooms, where they sit in apparent idleness, wishing one thing and at the same time wishing its opposite, and reflecting on various matters, which cannot possibly, always, be pleasant to contemplate'. It is a work which continually reflects the low quality of their everyday lives. Confined to their needles, reels, spindles, their silk-embroidery, they pass their days chewing upon idle and concealed dreams of love or upon the words of the friars. So the week passes until Saturday comes again, the Saturday when they 'wash their hair, fast in honour of the Virgin, and do nothing else in honour of the coming sabbath'.

Against this background, what better entertainment than the *Decameron* itself, the creation of an ideal world outside the *città*, the city of ordered social values? Here young men and women of intelligence, youth, and beauty, in complete equality and freedom, and yet without harm to their honour, tell stories which avenge society's affronts against nature, which avenge the jealousy or sexual incapacity of husbands and the dual standard of morality; fictions in which the woman, strong, vigorous and witty, triumphs with the words: 'I shall simply be breaking the laws of marriage, whereas he is breaking those of Nature as well'.

They are dreams which come the brighter, faced with reality:

After all, what the devil are we women fit for in our old age except to sit around the fire and stare at the ashes? . . . When we're old neither our husbands or any other man can bear the sight of us, and they bundle us off into the kitchen to tell stories to the cat, and count the pots and pans. . . .

They remain dreams. At the end comes the recall to real life and everyday reality, to the recognition, in the words of Emilia, that:

if the order of things is impartially considered, it will quickly be apparent that the vast majority of women are through Nature and custom, as well as in law, subservient to men, by whose opinions their conduct and actions are bound to be governed. It therefore behoves any woman who seeks a calm, contented and untroubled life with her menfolk, to be humble, patient and obedient, besides being virtuous, a quality that every judicious woman considers her especial and most valued possession.[20]

So, she continues: 'law, directed to the common good, and custom too, instruct'. Nature shows it in 'having made us soft and fragile of body, timid and fearful of heart, compassionate and benign of disposition'. On then, the book moves, finally, to the story of the ideal woman of real life, the masochistic, patient Griselda.

At least there remained the pleasures of reading; it could be the *Decameron* itself or some such work as Filippo Ceffi's translation of Ovid's *Heroides*, written for Lisa Peruzzi and appearing under the title, *Libro delle donne*. Paolo of Certaldo characteristically disapproved of teaching a girl to read, 'unless she is going to be a nun', but one gains the impression that a high proportion could read and write in Italian. Beyond that their education was confined to what Paolo recommends: 'to make bread, clean capons, sift, cook, launder, make beds, weave French purses, embroider, cut wool and linen clothes, put new feet into socks, and so forth, so that when you marry her off she won't seem a fool, freshly arrived from the wilds.'[21]

A woman of this class was at her freest either when her husband was abroad on business, in which case she might direct the administration of his estates, or, again, when widowed. At the husband's death, she was supposed to receive her dowry from his estate, and might, in these circumstances, establish herself in comparative independence. Yet the return of the dowry proved often difficult, sometimes impossible to secure. Many husbands willed a provision for maintenance of their wives in the home after their death, on condition that the dowry should remain in the family estate: a condition which served both to preserve the family patrimony and to prevent, through lack of a dowry, his widow's remarriage. While it was expected of widowers that they should remarry in order to provide a mother for his children, there was strong prejudice against the remarriage of widows, partly as a result of the dislike expressed by the religious, partly through fears for the rights of children of the first husband.

Daughters who, through lack of dowry, remained unmarried, presented a problem. Among the upper classes they could be sent to a nunnery, where a dowry was still necessary for admittance though one normally much smaller than that required for a patrician marriage. Among the lower orders in the towns all that remained to them was that variety of ill-paid posts already considered, prostitution, or some relationship of concubinage.

III

Most of those alive were young; yet their youth was immensely precarious. It is probable that of those who survived the most dangerous first year of life only one half reached the age of 21. There was nothing unusual in the experience of Giovanni di Durante, merchant of Florence, who between 1323 and 1343 had 15 children, 9 girls and 6 boys. Of these Niccolosa died at 8 months in 1334; Bianca at over a month in 1336; another Bianca at 4 months in 1336; Jacopo after 2 months in 1340; Lionardo, aged 18, in 1346, and Bettina, aged 3, in 1347. Between May and August 1348, when the Black Death was at its height, there died Margherita, aged 24; Durantozzo, aged 22; Andrea, aged 19; Costanza, aged 15; and a third Bianca, aged 6. In 1351 died Simone, aged 13. At the end of 1351 there were still living only Francesco (born 1323), Tommasa (born 1330), and Filippa (born 1331).[22]

Examining the high infant and child mortality rates in roughly comparable pre-industrial French and English societies, some sociological historians have postulated there an emotional world in which parents, faced with the all too likely prospect of their children's death, either detached their emotions from them and refused to accept that childhood existed as a separate and unique status, or, alternatively, treated their children with casual brutality.

One would not linger on these largely speculative hypotheses but for their influence upon certain historians of the Italian *Quattrocento*, who, finding there recognition, respect, and love for children, have portrayed their century as representing a breach with the past, as witnessing, almost, the birth of a 'modern' ideal of the child. The truth is that, in so far as the generalisations of these writers suggest that these things were absent in the thirteenth and fourteenth centuries, they find no correspondence with reality.

One has only to open Dante's *Comedia* to discover a close and tender observation of young children. Here one finds the *fante* or *fantino* or *fantolino*, waking suddenly and turning instantly to the source of his milk, or 'bathing his tongue at the breast', or holding out his arms to his mother when he has drunk from her, or again, dying from hunger and yet driving away his nurse. *Fantolini* are teased when they beg for something: they begin to speak in childish language, using 'pappo' and 'bindi' to mean 'bread' and 'money': 'that speech which *infantes* use to those with them'. They are in a tremulous dependence upon their parents. When Dante first meets Beatrice in the Earthly Paradise, he turns to Virgil, his *dolcissimo patre*:

> col rispitto
> con quale il fantolino corre alla mamma quando
> ha paura o quando elli è afflitto.

> 'In the way in which the *fantolino* runs to his
> mummy when afraid or when in distress.'

Slightly older children too, the *fanciullo* and *fanciulla* who have not yet attained puberty, are the subject of close scrutiny. The soul issues from the hand of God:

like a *fanciulla* that plays, crying and laughing, the simple little soul, that knows nothing, except that, moved by her joyful Maker, she turns eagerly to what amuses her. She does not know at first the savour of a trifling good, is deceived by it, and runs off to it, if guide or curb do not turn her love away.[23]

The same association with motion is conveyed in the image of the circle of the sun, 'that ever like a *fanciullo* plays'. Again Virgil smiles at Dante, as does one who smiles when a *fanciullo* is won over by the gift of an apple, and in another particularly striking metaphor, Dante receives the reproaches of Beatrice:

> Quale i fanciulli, vergognando, muti
> con li occhi a terra stannosi ascoltando
> e sè riconoscendo e ripentuti[23]
>
> 'As children, ashamed, silent, standing
> with their eyes upon the ground, listening,
> acknowledging and repentant.'

These are no isolated examples. In the *Four Times of Ages of Man*, by the thirteenth-century Lombard jurist, Filippo da Novara, one comes upon these words:

Our lord God who knows and can do and governs all, gives of his grace and pity three ways of knowledge and of natural love to little children, of which two are in them, and the third in those who nurse them as well as in them. The first is that the infant loves and knows at once the woman who nourishes him with her milk, whether mother or nurse. And often it falls out that he will not take any other breast than hers. The second is that he knows and makes a show of joy and love to those who play with him and carry him from one place to another. The third is in those who nurse children and in the children themselves: it is in the great love that they have given them in nature, feeling, and nurture.[24]

In the association between the grace and pity of God to *petiz aufanz*, as in Dante's comparison of the newly-born soul, moved by her joyful Maker, to a little girl, one has something of the Wordsworthian message that: 'heaven lies about us in our infancy'. One recalls again the lullabies that have survived, or Donato Velluti's memory of his daughter, Selvaggia ('a dear little child; she had the best speech that you've seen in a girl, mocking and intelligent; she died before the mortality of 1348, being in age less than six years old'), or Boccaccio's letter, telling Petrarch how he has met his grand-daughter:

With more modest step than is customary in one of her age, came your Eletta, my darling. And before she knew who I was she looked at me laughing. I took her in my arms not just joyfully but avidly for at first sight I had the illusion that she was the little girl I had lost. What to say? If you don't believe me, ask the doctor, Guglielmo da Ravenna, and our Donato, who were there. Your Eletta resembled my baby girl so much; she had the same smile, the same joy in the eyes, the same gestures and movement, and the same carriage of the whole little person, though mine was a little bigger through being older, since she was five and a half when for the last time I saw her. If beyond that she'd spoken the same dialect she would have said the same words with the same simplicity. The only difference you could tell is that yours is blonde, mine had chestnut hair. Alas! As I held her and delighted in her prattle, how many times did the memory of the little girl taken from me bring tears to my eyes which I tried to change to a sigh that no one might see them. But you, now, can understand how I could cry over your Eletta, how sad I was.[25]

It is obvious that, as in every society, some parents would treat their children with indifference or cruelty. Rudimentary birth-control was practised, but it was unreliable; abortions were attempted, but they were dangerous. In their default the children of the poor were particularly vulnerable to infanticide, a situation obliquely revealed by the constant ecclesiastical warnings to parishioners against 'over-laying' in bed. Yet this is to touch on a rather different issue. Among the higher classes of the commune, again, immediately after baptism, it might be when three days old, children were normally sent to a wet-nurse in the country, with whom they stayed for some two years. Were the wet-nurse to die or become pregnant, the child would be transferred to another, and might, for these reasons, have three or four substitute mothers in its first two years of life. At best, the Italian middle- and upper-class child was normally exposed to one deep trauma in its early life: in the separation from its foster-mother towards the end of its second year. It could be too – though the volatile race of paediatricians may soon tell us otherwise – that the close-swaddling, commonly adopted, adversely affected the child's development. Yet both these practices were followed on the advice of the most prominent medical authorities, and there survive very careful instructions for choice of suitable wet-nurses, which preclude the possibility that their employment was due to indifference. (Parents are warned for instance, against those with overlarge breasts, which might, it was thought, cause the child to grow up snub-nosed.)

Pre-adolescents, it is true, feature less in the literature of the age. It was well for them if they matured young. As everywhere in Europe, peasant children would begin to help their fathers in the fields when physically capable. In towns boys would start school between the ages of 8 and 11; could be at university by 15. They might be apprenticed from 10 to 12 (the contracts often ask the master to treat the apprentice 'as a good father treats a good son'); take up work in commercial firms at 13 or 14. Girls were often betrothed in infancy ('in the cradle', contemporaries complained) and were given in marriage from puberty. Probably a very high proportion were married by the age of 17. In law, it has been seen, the young were subject to the monarchical – it could be despotic – control of the household-head. Yet, as ever, views on the rearing of children varied from individual to individual. Bellino Bissolo, like many others, urged beatings ('who spares the rod, loves not his child') and instructive visits to public executions. Filippo da Novara warned against an excessive display of affection, against allowing them to do whatever they wished, and recommended correction, first verbally, then by beating, finally by locking them up. In a gentler spirit, Aldobrandino of Siena told parents that up to the age of seven they should give the child what it wanted and take away what it disliked, which would, he believed, cause it to grow up a good-humoured adult. From seven he should be forced into good habits, but the process should be gradual and designed to keep him biddable. He should be found a master who taught without beating and who would encourage him to stay willingly at school.

How can one generalise from such material or from the so many varieties of individual experiences of the young that there must have been? Let us choose one, as recorded in his *Memories* by the Sienese notary, Ser Cristofano di Gano di Guidino,[26] and, quite arbitrarily, form our conclusions from that. His mother, who was a Piccolomini, had brought a dowry of 100 florins to her marriage, but was not able to retain it as a widow. They lived, when he was a child, in the village of Rigomagno in the Valdichiana, with his grandfather: 'I never knew any father but him'. His mother 'with great care and in great poverty brought me up': the grandfather taught him reading, writing, and the elements of Latin. Then his mother sent him to stay with an uncle at Siena, where she paid for his board that he might go to school. His teacher there was Master Petro dell' Occhio, 'who since I was poor, bore me great love, and gave me many advantages'. Going on to study to become a notary, he gained his livelihood by acting as a *repetitore* or tutor to the children of two families. With the first, with whom he stayed for three years, he was paid his expenses. With the second, for another three years, he was given his expenses and 'pocket-money' of six florins a year. And our conclusion? what else but that it was a harsh life in which the child participated, but one too in which he was surrounded often by love and loving kindness.

Illegitimate children were another case on whose fortunes it is difficult to generalise. 'Natural children' in the strict sense, born of concubinage and living with their parents in a stable household, suffered few disadvantages and were easily legitimised upon their parents' marriage. The lot of the 'adulterine' child or *spurius*, born of an adulterous or casual union, was more problematic. At the lower end of society many were killed at birth; and it was specifically to limit this practice that many hospitals took in and fostered illegitimate and other unwanted children. It was Innocent III's horror at their 'countless' bodies afloat in the Tiber which caused him to secure the establishment of the foundling-hospitals of Santo Spirito and S. Maria in Saxia at Rome. Even in such refuges there could be problems of survival. Salimbene tells a story, a fiction, but one illustrating a social reality, in which the rector of a hospital returns to his confessor after death to announce that he had been damned. Asked why, he replies that, 'moved by a certain indignation', he had allowed children, born of secret-sin, and left at the hospital, to die without baptism, since the maintenance of foundlings involved such trouble and expense.[27] The problem was made more acute in that adoption, common in the early Middle Ages, seems, for reasons which are not clear, to have declined from the thirteenth century.

Among the more prosperous classes illegitimate children seem often to have been accepted on terms nearer to equality with the legitimate. It seems likely, one should add, that there were many of them; among 152 Genoese notaries in 1382 at least 54 (35.5 per cent) had between them a total of at least 64 natural sons.[28] In their different ways the lives of those two illustrious Florentine bastards (and school companions) Giovanni Boccaccio and Niccolò Acciaiuoli, Grand Seneschal of Naples, suggest that such children suffered few disadvantages. Yet a certain slur attached to their status – the minstrels never forgot that the mother of the Marquis Obizzo d'Este was a washerwoman – and this, even when they had been legitimised, as they could be, through the offices of an emperor, pope, or count palatine. Although they had no right to any part of the family property, illegitimate sons or daughters were often mentioned in wills, though generally treated there less generously than their half-brothers and sisters. And even the legitimised child could not inherit fiefs and entails at the expense of a legitimate. In a world where the family meant so much the person whose membership of it was in some way defective, had, with whatever tolerance he were treated, certain penalties to pay.

NOTES

On legal aspects of the family see A. Pertile, *Storia del diritto italiano*, iii, ch. 2, Turin, 1894; E. Besta, *Le persone nella storia del diritto italiano*, Padua, 1931; *idem, La famiglia nella storia del diritto italiano*, Padua, 1933; F. Brandileone, 'Studi preliminari sullo svolgimento storico dei rapporti patrimoniali fra coniugi in Italia' in his *Scritti di Storia del diritto privato italiano*, ed. G. Ermini, Bologna, 1931; and two important contributions by M. Bellomo, *Problemi di diritto familiare nell' età dei communi. Beni paterni e 'pars Filii'*, Milan, 1968; and *Ricerche sui rapporti patrimoniali tra coniugi: contributo alla storia della famiglia medievale*, Rome, 1961. For wider considerations, see D. Herlihy, 'Family solidarity in medieval Italian history' in *Economy, Society and Government: Essays in Memory of R. L. Reynolds*, ed. D. Herlihy, R. S. Lopez, and V. Slessarev, Kent, Ohio, 1969; Diane O. Hughes, 'Urban growth and family structure in medieval Genoa', *Past and Present*, 66, 1975; *idem*, 'Domestic ideals and Social Behavior: Evidence from Medieval Genoa' in *The Family in History*, ed. C. E. Rosenberg, Pennsylvania, 1975; *idem*, 'Kinsmen and neighbours in Medieval Genoa', in *The Medieval City*, ed. H. A. Mismikin, D. Herlihy, A. L. Udovich, London, 1977; J. Heers, *Le clan familial au moyen âge*, Paris, 1974; and Part iii of *Famille et Parenté dans L'Occident Médiéval*, ed. G. Duby and J. Le Goff, Rome, 1977. Three works which deal with different periods in the history of the Italian family also provide valuable insights: P. Toubert, *Les structures du Latium médiéval*, i, Rome, 1973 (ch. vii 'Les structures familiales'); N. Tamassia, *La famiglia italiana nei secoli decimoquinto e decimosesto*, Milan, 1910; and F. W. Kent, *Household and Lineage in Renaissance Florence*, Princeton, 1977.

On canon law aspects, G. le Bras, 'Le mariage dans la théologie et le droit canonique de l'église du XIe au XIIIe siècle', *Cahiers de civilisation médiévale*, xi, 1968; *idem*, 'Mariage' in *Dictionnaire de théologie catholique*, Paris, 1927, ix, pt. ii, 2123 ff. 'Empêchements de mariage du XIIe au XVIe siècle' in *Dictionnaire de Droit Canonique*, directed R. Naz, vol. v, Paris, 1953 (and see 'Mariage', vol. vi, 1957); G. H. Joyce, *Christian Marriage: An Historical and Doctrinal Study*, London, 1933; A. Esmein, *Le mariage en droit canonique*, 2nd edn, ed. R. Génestal, Paris, 1929–35.

On women there is something in I. del Lungo, *La donna fiorentina del buon tempo antico*, 2nd edn, Florence, 1926, and in L. Chiappelli, *La donna pistoiese del tempo antico*, Pistoia, 1914. See too G. Jehel, 'Le rôle des femmes et du milieu familial à Gênes dans les activités commerciales au cours de la première moitié de XIIIe siècle', *Revue d'histoire économique et sociale*, 53, 1975; A. Briganti, 'La donna e il diritto statutario in Perugia: la donna commerciante', *Annali della Facoltà di giurisprudenza di Perugia*, xxvi, 1911; R. Metz, 'Le statut de la femme en droit canonique médiéval' and G. Rossi, 'Statut juridique de la femme dans l'histoire du droit italien' in *La Femme* (Recueils de la Société Jean Bodin, xi), pt. 2 (1962); S. Chojnacki, 'Patrician women in early Renaissance Venice', *Studies in the Renaissance*, xxi, 1974; *idem*, 'Dowries and kinsmen in early Renaissance Venice', *Journal of Interdisciplinary History*, v, 1975. There are stimulating pointers to material in *Not in God's Image*, ed. J. O'Faolain and L. Martines, London, 1973.

On children see Mary M. McLaughlin, 'Survivors and Surrogates: Children and Parents from the Ninth to the Thirteenth Centuries' and J. B. Ross, 'The Middle-class Child in Urban Italy, Fourteenth to Early Sixteenth Century', in *The History of Childhood*, ed. L. deMause, N.Y., 1975.

1. For the 'Ages' discussed here, see Geza de Francovich, *Benedetto Antelami*, Milan-Florence, 1952, ii, nos. 248, 250 (for illustration), i, pp. 207–10 (for discussion); Dante, *Il Convivio*, ed. G. Busnelli and G. Vandelli, Florence, 1954, iv, 23–4 (on which, particularly valuable is B. Nardi, 'L'arco della vita' in his *Saggi di filosofia dantesca*, 2nd edn, Florence, 1967, ch. vi); Petrus Abanus, *Conciliator differentiarum philosophorum et precipue medicorum*, Mantua, 1472, *differentia*, 26; Orlandini Rodulphini [sic], *In artem notarie*, Venice, 1565, p. 135–6.
2. Orlandini Rodulphini, *cit.*, p. 70 r.
3. P. Torelli, *Un commune cittadino in territorio ed economia agricola II. Uomini e classe al potere*, Mantua, 1952, pp. 54–93.
4. Cf. B. Migliorini, 'Dal nome proprio al nome comune', *Biblioteca dell' Archivium Romanicum*, s. ii, 13, Geneva, 1927, p. 40; P. Aebischer, 'Les origines de la finale i des noms de familles italiens', *Onomastica*, i, 1947 (who convincingly argues against Gaudenzi's claims that the final i derives from a nominative plural).
5. *Liber Grossus Antiquus Comunis Regii*, ed. F. S. Gatta, Reggio Emilia, 1944–62, iv, pp. 156–85.
6. G. de' Mussi, 'Placentinae urbis ac nobilium tum in ea' in *RIS*, xvi, cols. 565–6; A. Castiglioni, 'Il salasso nell' arma gentilizia dei Manfredi' in *Essays in the History of Medicine presented to Professor K. Sudhoff*, ed. C. Singer and H. Sigerist, London, 1925.
7. F. Cognasso, *Il Piemonte nell' età sveva*, Turin, 1968, p. 158; F. Nicolai, 'I consorzi nobiliari ed il comune nell' alta e media Italia', *Rivista storica del diritto italiano*, xiii, 1940, p. 294, n. 1; *Cronica di Giovanni Villani*, ed. F. G. Dragomanni, Florence, ii, 1845, pp. 42–3 [Lib. viii, 39].
8. Donato Velluti, *La Cronaca domestica*, ed. I. del Lungo and G. Volpi, Florence, 1914; and see, now, C. M. de la Roncière, 'Une famille florentine au XIVᵉ siècle: Les Velluti', in *Famille et Parenté, cit.*
9. For this and all this section see the works of Bellomo, *cit.*
10. In the translation of G. Brucker, *The Society of Renaissance Florence: A documentary study*, London, 1971, p. 63.
11. Bologna, 1875.
12. 'quae exercent opera rusticalia sicut masculi', C. Fumagalli, *Il diritto di Fraterna nella giurisprudenza da Accursio alla Codificazione*, Turin, 1912, p. 135.
13. L. T. Belgrano, *Della vita privata dei Genovesi*, Genoa, 1875, p. 315.
14. *Ibid.*, p. 319.
15. Salimbene de Adam, *cit.*, pp. 95, 899–900, 929; G. Biscaro, 'Le vicende matrimoniali di una gentildonna veneziana nel Dugento', *Studi medievali*, 1930, pp. 121–9; G. Brucker, *The Society of Renaissance Florence, cit.*, p. 42. See, too, Cecilia da Albano, below, pp. 129–30

81

16. Paolo da Certaldo, *Libro di buoni costumi*, ed. A. Schiaffini, Florence, 1948, pp. 105–6 in the translation of O'Faolain and Martines, *cit*., p. 169

17. *La cronaca domestica, cit*., pp. 290–1; for Dora del Bene, see *Alcune lettere familiari del secolo XIV*, ed. P. Dozzi (fasc. xl of *Curiosità lettararie*), Bologna, 1868, pp. 46–55.

18. Salimbene, *cit*., pp. 76–7, 48.

19. in *Strenne nuziali del secolo XIV*, ed. O. Targioni Tozzetti, Livorno, 1873.

20. I quote from the translation in the Penguin Classics by G. H. McWilliam, Boccaccio, *The Decameron*, Harmondsworth, 1972, pp. 46, 471–2, 721–2.

21. *Libro di buoni costumi, cit*., p. 128, in the translation of O'Faolain and Martines, *cit*., p. 169.

22. A. Sapori, 'La cultura del mercante italiano' in his *Studi di storia economica*, 3rd edn, Florence, 1955, i, 67 n. 1.

23. *Paradiso*, xxx, 82–3; xxxiii, 188, xxiii, 121–2, xxx, 139–41; *Purgatorio*, xxiv, 108–11, xi, 106; *De vulgari eloquentia*, i, 1, 22; *Purgatorio*, xxx, 40–50; xvi, 87–94; xv, 3; xxvii, 44–5; xxxi, 65–6.

24. Philippe de Navarre (sic), *Des iiii tenz d'aage d'ome*, ed. M. de Fréville, Paris, 1888, p. 2.

25. *La cronaca domestica, cit*., p. 47; G. Boccaccio, *Opere in versi . . . Epistole*, ed. P. G. Ricci, Milan-Naples, 1965, p. 1198.

26. In G. Cherubino, 'Dal libro di ricordi di un notaio senese del trecento' in his *Signori, Contadini, Borghesi*, Florence, 1974, pp. 397–8.

27. Salimbene, *cit*., pp. 104–5.

28. B. Z. Kedar, 'The Genoese notaries of 1382: The anatomy of an urban occupational group' in *The Medieval City*, ed. H. A. Miskimin, D. Herlihy, A. L. Udovitch, London, 1977, pp. 92–4.

CHAPTER FIVE

The nobility

I

Certain families were described or described themselves as 'noble'. The term had no clear meaning. It was merely an extension of the word 'notable' from which it derived, and was used of a wide variety of men among whom there were great disparities of wealth, status, and manner of life. Some were powerful landowners from dynasties of counts and marquesses, with titles, that is, which originated in an imperial grant of office. Below these were men who were or whose ancestors had once been their *valvassores* (*arrière*-vassals; those enfeoffed by *capitanei* or tenants-in-chief). Of these many originated from and dwelt in towns and owed their prominence to their rôle as administrators of episcopal lands or to wealth derived from trade. Then again there was a host of little lords living in fortified villages or towns or remote countryside towers who, either by violence or prescription, claimed rights over the men of their 'court'. Finally comes a twilight world of poor nobles declining to the condition of peasants, of *popolares* moving up in the world: men like 'the noble knight Tolosano', son of a serf at Passignano, or that Spata, 'tavern keeper', who in 1229 was enfeoffed with the *castello* (i.e. fortified village) of S. Pietro by the bishop of Mantua. All that was common to the men drawn from this wide spectrum was either a general claim to exercise an hereditable jurisdiction over other men or an assertion of their right to bear arms or, perhaps, an aspiration to a certain unifying culture or life-style.

There were no typical nobles and so there was no typical noble estate. Yet as an example of what was characteristic of a large family holding one can consider the estates of the da Romano, one of the four most powerful dynasties of the Trevisan March. In 1223, the year of their father's retirement to a monastery, his sons, Ezzelino III and Alberico, divided between them the rights and properties which he had ceded to them *pro indiviso*. (See Map 2.) The documents describing this and other transactions of the family[1] give a fairly clear indication of what was involved. In the towns of Vicenza and Treviso they owned palaces, and leased out houses and shops to the citizens. In the countryside, their lands grouped around Bassano and the left bank of the Brenta consisted of allods and of enfeoffments from seven bishoprics and other ecclesiastical institutions. Here they held

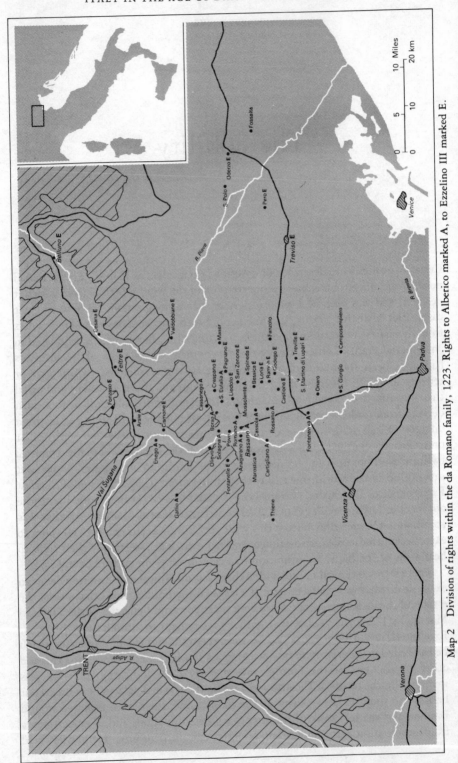

Map 2 Division of rights within the da Romano family, 1223. Rights to Alberico marked A, to Ezzelino III marked E.

pastoral and agricultural land, woods, and mills, administered by a numerous variety of officials: *visconti, vicedomini*, judges, and *gastaldi* (i.e. reeves). As was normal in northern and central Italy, at this period, these properties formed no compact unity. Often within each village their possessions were very tightly interwoven with the allods and fiefs of other men. In strict territorial terms our map is deceptive. To attempt to draw a true map would require detailed investigation, field by field, of each rural commune, and the final result would resemble a fall of confetti, or rather, since the position was ever changing, a series of glimpses through a kaleidoscope.

Nor were the rights of the family uniform from place to place. Here men held land from them by lease, for money or food, here by service as *homines de masnada* or *fideles*: that is as men bound to their lord by an oath of servile status. Again, each rural commune had reached its own agreement with the lord upon the service to be rendered to him. So at Solagno the family possessed the right of jurisdiction, the tax upon goods entering and leaving the gates, the right of appointing officials, and a right to a third of the fines levied by agrarian police. By contrast at Bassano (where towards the end of the thirteenth century there were over 800 male inhabitants between fourteen and seventy years old) the powers of the da Romano were formally much more restricted. Yet it would be wrong to consider the noble's position in terms simply of proprietary or abstract judicial rights. At Bassano, for instance, the da Romano *homines de masnada* took part both in the parliament of the commune and in its 'Council of the Forty', and it was they, as the 'free-men' of the commune were to complain, who dictated which decrees were passed and which officials elected. In some ways one could look upon a family estate more as a political than an economic entity. Often the size of plots of lands the family leased, like the rents they received from them, were miniscule, and probably had a very largely symbolic significance, representing an acknowledgment of service in return for protection.

Together with those other lands which they administered and exploited as 'Advocates' of the bishop of Belluno, the patriarch of Aquileia, and the monastery of Pero, the da Romano properties gave the family a social and political dominance within their region which could be contested by few other noble houses. Yet it is significant that the division of property in 1223 had very little effect upon the respective careers of the brothers who benefited from it. Ezzelino's base of operation was to be Verona, where before his political intervention in 1225 he held no land, and Alberico's was Treviso, which, in terms of property rights, was in Ezzelino's field of influence. The truth is that broad estates as such were very frequently the result as much as the cause of political dominance. (And thanks to this dominance, both Alberico and Ezzelino were to increase their territorial rights to an immense extent during their lifetimes.) Land gave prestige, it gave rents, but, of much greater importance, it gave *homines de masnada*, those *fideles* whom the lord, according to his ambitions and abilities, could use to further or to retain, if he could, his power. It is doubtful if the *masnade* were gathered together in great numbers at any one particular time, yet their rôle was important. In the countryside they could intimidate; in the town as a small band of tough streetfighters, they could exercise, amidst the general indifference of the population as a whole, a preponderating influence upon party struggles.

Very few nobles possessed the power of the da Romano. Most might own rights in half a village, a village, a handful of villages. If their families were weak or disunited (or if they were rich and powerful and their family tradition dictated that they should do so) they might come together with other nobles, sometimes related to them, sometimes not, to form an artificial clan, a *consorteria*. From the mid-thirteenth century the *consorteria* – or as it was here called the *albergo* – was particularly prominent in Genoa. By the fourteenth century when the lineages composing an *albergo* were tending to become less close in blood than previously, there were some thirty-five of these groups, each linked to a district in the city and each with its own tower and private church. But the institution was by no means confined to Liguria and through all the peninsula, in towns and in countryside, often embracing both town and countryside, *consorterie* were frequent.

Among the peasantry where *consorterie* were also found the primary purpose of the union was to secure a unit capable of working efficiently land which a small conjugal family would have had insufficient numbers to farm and in these circumstances the *consortes* generally shared the same household. Among the nobility the *consorteria* had a more ambitious function. Dwelling in their own houses, its members came together in a sworn union of self-defence and frequently built a fortified house or tower, sometimes assigned certain lands to be held in common. Sometimes it was led by an elected member, sometimes by the eldest member, sometimes by an impartial outsider. Often there would be an elected chamberlain with responsibilities for finances. Generally members adopted the same coat of arms and the same banner and spoke of brotherhood between them. Occasionally the union was exogamous, both men and women being forbidden to marry within the *consorteria*. Frequently the group claimed all rights of justice, with the right of imprisonment, over its members.

Some idea of the bond is given by the oath of the twenty-two lords of the *consorteria* of Ripafratta (a village some sixteen miles to the north-east of Pisa)[2]:

> In the name of the living God for ever and ever, amen, I, from the consorts and lords of Ripafratta, swear on the holy gospels, and to the honour of God and the city of Pisa, that from today forth I will defend and help to defend all my consorts of Ripafratta who take this oath with me, and the whole territory which I hold in common with them, and which is common to us, together with all that which was once common and which is now divided between them and me, and all which belongs or can belong in any manner or by any law to me or them, whether held in freehold, lease, or fief. That is to say, what I or my consorts hold up to the walls of the city of Lucca, and in the valley of the Sarno, and in particular the common territory I hold with them in Castel Vicipisano and its boundaries, and in S. Giovanni di Vena and in the lands and open and fortified villages of Collina, wherein the consorts have their common territory. . . .

The oath goes on to specify other rights and duties. The member will defend his consort's children up to the age of eighteen when they too will be obliged to take the oath. He will be compensated by the consorts for losses which he may suffer in defending common interests, but he is not obliged to defend any of the consorts against a man outside the *consorteria*, with whom he holds a tower in common. Should one of the consorts injure him or his men he will not declare a vendetta against him without first asking for compensation. If the offending party agrees the compensation shall be decided by the consuls of the *consorteria*. He reserves, however, the right to take vengeance on any of his own *fideles*, should they offend him, without reference to the consorts. He will not receive the *fidelis* of another lord into his service without the lord's consent. If he sells any of his property he will give the consorts the right of pre-emption. All disputes between members or between the dependants of different members will be settled by the consuls, after taking the advice of the councillors, within sixty days. One or more consuls are to be elected every year. If a consul wishes to journey across sea or land either to serve God or in a spirit of gain (*animo lucrativo*) and the oath-taker is elected in his place he will not refuse the office. The consul or consuls will give an account of the incoming and outgoing revenues of the group within fifteen days of their laying down of office, and will present three audits a year, in May, September, and January, of the profits from tolls in passage through Ripafratta. They will not spend more than £5 a year without the consent of the councillors. Every year, at Easter, they will receive a lamb from each of the consorts.

There is much which this document reveals. Vendetta is a commonplace within the countryside, and a primary function of the *consorteria* is to strengthen its members in this situation, both by offering protection and aid and by neutralising its development within its member's own circle. The system is flexible – one-time common lands have been divided out among individuals, and yet its very flexibility must in some ways have made it difficult to operate. The problems of a man joined with a friend in a *societas turris* (an agreement to share a tower) against whom the *societas consortium* declared a vendetta must have been considerable. *Fideles* within the countryside are abandoning their lords and seeking new masters under more attractive terms. The more enterprising among the consorts are abandoning the countryside and, moved by their *animi lucrativi*, are making for the town. Not the least significant element of the Ripafratta oath is that it is made to the honour not only of God but of the city of Pisa.

New money was flowing in to the rural *consorterie*. The wealth they acquired often went to the building of churches and the endowment of religious foundations; the lords of Ripafratta established their own monastery of San Paolo in Pignino. So too links with the town were growing ever stronger. In 1284 the *consorteria* fought for Pisa in the disastrous sea-battle of Meloria. By 1290 it was already firmly established in the city, and began to play a part in urban politics. In the 1330s, the consul of the nobles of Ripafratta and their *fideles* were still holding their own court, yet now always within the city-walls.

II

In their involvement with the city the consorts of Ripafratta were typical of the nobles of northern and central Italy. By 1200 *comitatinanza*, the process by which the nobility of the *contado* became citizens of the town, was already well advanced and throughout the thirteenth century it continued. In *comitatinanza* the communes of the towns and nobles of the countryside came to a perpetual treaty of alliance. The two parties normally agreed to hold the other's friends as friends, enemies as enemies, and promised to wage war and make peace together. Sometimes these were the sole stipulations, particularly where the towns were dealing with nobles on the borders of the *contado*, who might be tempted to give their allegiance to a neighbouring commune. More often the treaties had wider terms, hammered out according to the relative strengths of the individual nobles or groups of nobles and the commune of the town at the particular moment the treaty was signed. The lords could promise to buy a house within the town; or they could be given one; or could be given money to aid in its purchase. Often they promised to dwell in the city in time of war, sometimes with their families (presumably as half-hostages), sometimes without. Sometimes they promised, or were absolved from promising, that they would live three or six months during each year in the city in time of peace. They could engage to hold their lands under the full legal jurisdiction of the city's *podestà* or arrangements could be made for the settlement of contrasting jurisdictions of lord and commune in cases affecting both their subjects. In certain circumstances the commune was granted the right to impose hearth-taxes or *corvées* upon the lord's *fideles*; in others the subject is ignored and the lord himself is exempted from all taxation and gabelles. The lord could agree to exact no tolls upon men of the commune on his lands; the commune could promise to compensate him for damages suffered in war on its behalf or stipulate that war was to be carried on at its expense. And so on. Often the lord's own subjects were expressly excluded from the commune's jurisdiction; often the commune promised that the town would receive no serf within it, fleeing from his lord.

Though the commune doubtless wished for them, simple surrenders to the town were very rare, particularly before the mid-fourteenth century. The contracts of *comitatinanza* were brought about in some cases by force or threat of force, but much more often by a mingling of this with hopes of alliance, mutual benefit, and by simple bribery. The nobles of the countryside who became citizens of the commune either came as equals or enjoyed a position of privilege within it. They lost little. What they gained was of much greater importance: an opportunity to take part in the political and economic life of the communes.

These communes, whether they existed in cities which had a large stake in commerce or in towns which served simply as market-centres for the products of the countryside, were, at the beginning of the thirteenth century, dominated by comparatively narrow oligarchies of noble families. The simplest and yet in some ways archetypal form of communal life is found at Belluno, where four noble *consorterie* named all the councillors and officials of the city. Normally the oligarchy controlled government through the influence it exercised over a small council and a larger 'council of the commune' presided over by an executive official, appointed for a limited period and generally a foreigner to the town, called the *podestà*. So, for instance, at Mantua in 1199, some eighty of the 100 councillors of the commune can be identified as land-owning nobles, drawn from the circle of the vassals of the church of Mantua and the holders of 'Matildine' land (lands given to the Papacy by the Countess Matilda in the eleventh century). Among the remaining twenty only three can be identified as non-nobles: two butchers and a moneychanger. Yet true power did not lie here, but with certain élite families, some old, such as the Avvocati, the counts of Casalodo, the Poltroni, Calorosi, Visconti, and Vicedomini, some of them incorporated within the commune at the end of the twelfth century, such as the Savioli, Riva, Rivalto, and Pizari. These were the men who held true authority, who dominated the councils and determined their composition.

This type of oligarchy appears in all towns. In Siena, power lay largely with men descended from, or related to, old feudal houses. Here the Piccolomini, the Tolomei, the Rinaldini, and Salvini families all claimed descent from the counts of Cacciaconti. The Urgurgieri, Malavolti, Cerretani, and Bandinelli boasted of their descent from the Berardenghi. Other leading families sprang from the ancient Ardenghesca and Alberti clans. Generally the origins of the oligarchy were more varied. In Florence there were, perhaps, a 100 families of *maiores* or *milites* (knights), of which, during the first half of the century, some thirteen effectively monopolised power. They had diverse roots. The Uberti, with their houses on the site of what is today Palazzo Vecchio and Piazza Signoria, were feudal nobility who had settled in the town even before the foundation of the commune. The Adimari held large landed properties in the twelfth century, acquired more in the thirteenth, and married then into the ancient and powerful house of the Guidi, Counts Palatine. The Buondelmonti were 'ancient noblemen of the countryside'. Others, as the Chiermontesi, owed their nobility to wealth acquired as merchants. The Cavalcanti, for example, had acquired riches through usury, had been knighted, and by the 1260s were to acquire towers and lands in the *contado*.

Whether becoming members of the oligarchy, whether remaining outside it, very many of the nobles of the countryside who had assumed citizenship assimilated with little difficulty to the nobles of the town. The urban nobility, with their liveried retainers, served as mounted knights in the military leadership of their communities. Like the lords of the countryside they often came together in *consorterie* or in 'tower-societies': sworn agreements by two, three, or more men to hold a fortified tower in common. These towers, constructed for reasons both of defence and prestige, rose above the towns, as Fazio degli Uberti described those of Lucca, 'like a little wood'. There were perhaps over 180 at Bologna and, it is said, by the mid-thirteenth century 300 at Florence, each with their own expressive name: 'the Chestnut', 'Lance', 'See the Dead', and 'Kiss-cat'. Finally, too, the various lineages and *consorterie* within a town would come together to form a *societas militum*, a guild of all nobles designed to defend the local interests of their class as a whole.

The overwhelming majority of these men had some connection with commerce. Not all. The ancient houses of Counts Palatine, like the Conti Guidi, and some old families like the Este, though they often invested in trade or were content to marry their children to those who took part in it, avoided direct participation. In the southern kingdoms, as is illustrated by a story from 1319, the rôle of the noble-merchant was ambiguous. In that year the twenty nobles of Alfedena, possessors of very small fiefs who payed tribute to the lord of the village of Alfedena, are found appealing to King Robert. They lived, they explained, under Langobard Law, and in consequence have divided their goods and are unable to live without devoting themselves to trade. As a result the local *popolani* have affected to consider them merchants and have forced them to pay taxes which as nobles they should not pay, since their entry into trade has come about only to keep them from dying of hunger.[3] In this society commerce (of which there was little enough) was seen as the only alternative to starvation. It was otherwise in northern and central Italy. Here there was no *dérogeance*. Trade was not a specifically 'middle-class' activity and the distinction between being a noble and (in so far as one was not a mere shopkeeper) a merchant did not exist.

It was something strange and disturbing to the rest of Europe. A chronicle of the Holy Land, *L'Estoire de Eracles*, describes how in 1187 the count of Tripoli was accused of having betrothed his daughter to a villein: a certain 'rich man of Pisa'. 'For those of France,' the author explains, 'hold those of Italy in contempt: for however rich or impetuously brave (*prous*) they are, they hold them as vile, for most of those of Italy are usurers, or corsairs, or merchants; and because they are knights they hold them in contempt.'[4] It is not too much to say, in fact, that the Italian empire of overseas trade had been founded by its old noble families: the Spinola, Doria, and Fieschi at Genoa who had set out on buccaneering expeditions against the Saracen; the *contado* nobility of Pisa with its *animus lucrativus*; the Venetian patriciate who held the monopoly of long-distance commerce within their city. So too at Asti, Milan, Siena, and Piacenza, nobles played a leading part in the establishment of the great banking firms while at Florence 'the knight' was normally a merchant.

Not all the rural nobility were interested in commerce or felt a commitment to town life. As a result of *comitatinanza* many of them indeed came to live within the city's walls, to play a full part in city life, and to stake their futures upon the chances, good or ill, of urban politics. Yet very many others yielded to the town, fulfilled, when necessary, their statutory obligation to dwell within it for limited periods, yet, without desire for power, held themselves aloof from its politics and commerce, and passed most of their lives in traditional style upon their estates. These were the men whom the communes categorised as *cives silvestres*, 'citizens of the wilds'. There were many of them. Of forty-eight nobles at Orvieto in 1322, twenty-one were resident in the *contado*. Of the 150 families placed among the *grandi* at Florence in 1293, only seventy-three dwelt in the city. These were only the most powerful of their class. In the mountains of Bologna, at the beginning of the thirteenth century, it has been estimated, lived no less than 3,500 people who claimed some grade of nobility.

Other families presented a consistently hostile bearing before the commune, defied its decrees, robbed its merchants in transit through their territories: great lords like the Ubaldini of the Mugello, the Pazzi and Ubertini of Valdarno, lesser nobles like Rinier da Corneto and Rinier da Pozzo, 'who made so great a war upon the roads'. Upper-class brigandage was endemic. The towns struggled with men like these for over a century before securing their passive allegiance. So, at the beginning of the fourteenth century Florence created the *terre nuove* (or *bastides*) at S. Giovanni and Castello di Sopra in Valdarno and at Firenzuola on the Apennine watershed in order to lure away their *fideles* and to exercise continuous pressure against them in the *montagna*.[5] But the work of assimilation was slow; until the 1380s they remained a danger to the commune, ever-ready to foment rebellion and to ally with its enemies.

Despite *comitatinanza*, the *cives silvestres*, whether hostile or reconciled to the commune, remained, collectively, an important element in, and gave a characteristic tone to, large areas of north and central Italy within the thirteenth and fourteenth centuries. Looking at their families it is easy to point to some spectacular failures (just as it is easy to see them among those who became full citizens of the towns). Giovanni Villani tells of 'men of noble stock, now workers upon the land'. Then again there is the oft-told tale of the counts of Tintinanno, begging for the gift of a tunic from the Commune of Siena.[6] And they were subject, of course, to normal extinction rates. They could produce too few descendants or too many. Yet one cannot generalise from incidents to the virtual extinction of a whole group. Many still held substantial landed properties, and from the end of the thirteenth century were to reconcentrate them into effective economic units. Many were to continue in substantial prosperity, and like the Gherardesca, Donoratico, Ponzano, and Ricasoli in the Tuscan countryside, are still to be found today living upon the estates of their ancestors. Among them many, at some later stage in Italian history, whether as a *Barone di Ferro*, whether as the husband of a film-star, were, after centuries of fortunate obscurity, to emerge again into public fame.

The power and fortunes which these men could bear are well illustrated by the Counts Palatine Aldobrandeschi, and their heirs.[7] At the beginning of the thirteenth century, Count Ildebrandino VIII (an uncle of Pope Honorius III) was the owner of properties in Pisa, Viterbo, and Orvieto, rights of taxation upon the transhumant flocks passing up the Serchio from Lucca through the Garfagnana valley, and, by imperial grant, lands in Apulia. Above all, at the centre of his power, were his rights in 'the Aldobrandine' county, extending from the shore along the Maremma and Grosseto to the Anti-Apennines and the Val d'Elsa, an area in all, 100 kilometres north to south, and 60 east to west. These rights derived from papal, ecclesiastical, and imperial enfeoffment; and above all, by emphyteutic grants (that is to say, renewable leases, generally at a nominal rent, given for three generations) from monastic houses. (Common enough in central Italy, these were often made by abbeys whose land had been usurped, who acknowledged the *de facto* situation, and who, none the less, sought to maintain their ultimate proprietorial claim.)

This was poor territory; the coastal plain was notorious for 'the ill vapours' of malaria; inland the arid climate allowed only stock-raising and could support few men. Yet the Aldobrandini, with their eleven castles, enjoyed great wealth from it. Part of their lands was re-enfeoffed to some seventeen powerful noble families, and other lesser *valvassores* (often related to them by blood or marriage). Batignano and its tower 'with all its men and lands and tenants' went to Manto di Guglielmo; Monteguidi and Montelivranti to Rinaldo da Colle 'as his father had held it before'; to the count's Captain-at-Arms went Piancastagnaio and the wood of Pignatello *in rectum et purum feudum*; and so on. To the count went the lion's share. It was as though, to deny the existence of a universal poverty, all on that land had come together to contract that one family among them should be rich. To Ildebrandino, almost to him alone, flowed its fruits: 'the right of sailing and fishing' in the sea around the island of Giglio, the profits of the silver-lead mines at Batignano, Silvena, and Ravi, the transit-taxes over the herds of cattle which set out under armed guard from Orvieto and the Apennines to pasture on its moors, the gabelles upon corn and salt passing to Siena, the revenues of the salt-works at Grosseto and Montegemali. In the village communes of the hill-top hamlets the peasants assumed the titles of Rector and Chamberlain and held council among themselves. But they were obliged to attendance at the lord's *parliamento* and here gave a purely formal assent to the dues he imposed upon them, dues payed in silver pennies which bore his name.

During the thirteenth century, the family divided its properties. By 1274 the line of Bonifazio d'Ildebrandino established themselves as counts of Santafiora, and took the lands and rights to the north of the river Albegna; while the line of Guglielmo d'Ildebrandino, calling themselves counts of Sovano and Pitigliano, assumed those to the south. The subsequent story of the counts of Santafiora, taken by itself, might indeed lead to the conclusion that the nobility of the *contado* were ultimately crushed by the communes. The author of the *Ottimo Commento*, writing in the 1330s, declared: 'The Counts of Santafiora had and have and will almost always have war with the Sienese; and the cause is that the Counts wish to maintain their jurisdiction, and the Sienese want to take it from them, as is customary in the Italian communities.' The years in which he was writing saw in fact the decisive advances of Siena against its feudal neighbours, and here the divisions of inheritance between the ten sons of Ildebrandino Novello and the five sons of his brother, Enrico, no doubt played a part. Santafiora itself was lost to them in 1382. Inexorably the pressure continued against their house until all their lands had fallen to the commune, until that day in 1443 when a former lord of Santafiora sent his humble petition to the council of Siena asking for assistance in dowering of his daughters. (With a niggard generosity they granted him ten cartloads of salt from Orbetello, that Orbetello which, with all men and lands within it, his ancestors had once owned.)

Individual families fell; yet this does not represent the future of a class. The cadet line of the Aldobrandini, the line of the counts of Sovana and Pitigliano, in one sense came to an end in 1284 on the death without male heirs of Ildebrandino 'il Rosso'. Yet the county of Pitigliano remained, passing through Ildebrandino's daughter to Guy de Montfort, and eventually to the Orsini. With the French and Spanish invasions of Italy from 1494, there was still a count of Pitigliano, with Aldobrandini blood, to lead the Italians against them. More than this, long after Siena had lost its independence, Pitigliano remained an imperial fief. Obviously to defy the greater communes *à l'outrance* was to steer a dangerous course (just as to take part in urban politics was very often perilous), but few families of the *contado* did; and among even these several survived and maintained something of their state. Comparatively, if not always in real terms, the great aristocratic houses of the countryside in the north were less powerful by 1400 than they had been in the twelfth century: yet still, very often, they were names to conjure with.

Away from central and northern Italy, within the Mezzogiorno, the nobility as a class retained and frequently increased their traditional powers. In Rome and Latium were the Prefects of Vico, the da Ceccano who could raise 400 horses to follow their banner, the Savelli, the Colonna, the Annibaldi, and numerous other powerful houses. Through their landed strength they dominated the *curia*, and through their access to the highest offices of the Church they increased their own territorial holdings: a dual development only partly checked by the occasional urban insurrection against them and by the growth of French control over the Papacy. At the same time, in the southern kingdoms the affirmation of noble authority was, as has been seen, still more striking.

III

The world of the rural seigneury, of the *civis silvestris*, is easier to imagine than to document. Yet the state kept by powerful rural magnates often comes to life in their last testaments. One thinks here, for instance, of the will of Ildebrandino 'il Rosso' Aldobrandini, Count of Pitigliano, drawn up in his chamber in the castle of Sovana, where he lay dying, in May 1284.[8] He asks to be buried in the church of San Francesco (to whom he professes a special devotion) at Orvieto, and fixes the expense of his funeral at £500. To this church he left from his own chapel his silver thurible, chalice, crosses, candelabra, ampula, and basins, its vestments, altar-cloths, and liturgical books, together with half his 'silver tablets' to go towards the making of chalices and the restoration of the fabric of the church. His bed, with its bedclothes, all his mounts — destriers, palfreys, mules, and nags — with their trappings, were to be sold and the proceeds given to the same friars. The annual tax upon the rural commune of Sovana (£50) was to be assigned to them for the saying of masses on the anniversary of his death, and they were to be allowed to take wood from his forests for their building work. The other half of the silver tablets was to be sold and the money from them distributed at the will of the bishop of Sovana as recompense for all his insufficient offerings in the past.

He then distributed what he believed to be another £3,000 (in fact, however, the sum amounts to £3,300) in gifts to various ecclesiastics, churches and others: money to the bishop and canons of Sovana; a silver chalice to the same canons; £200 to the monastery of S. Galgano for the decoration of their altar; £100 towards the building of a church in Piancastognoio (to be given from the tax on the rural commune there); and so on. Fifteen other Franciscan convents and one house of Poor Clares benefit, together with numerous churches within the area of the count's properties. There follow gifts for the poor: £450 for a hospital to be built at Sovana or Saturnia; £25 to the lepers of S. Lazaro at Sovana, together with all the clothes in wool-cloth on his person at the moment of death. Then further to these sums, £500 for the poor, 'especially at Ischia' and £500 to provide dowries for poor girls in the county.

In addition Ildebrandino stipulated that if he were to die without male heirs (as in fact he did) a further £7000 was to be given away. £4,000 was to be spent in the county; £1,000 towards the fabric of ruined churches; £1,000 on the decoration of churches; £1,000 towards dowries and the needs of the poor. (On the fourth £1000 the will is silent.) The other £3,000 was to be spent on churches outside the county.

The dowry of his first wife, Francesca degli Conti Uberti, was to be returned to Florence. That of his present wife, Francesca dei Baschi, in sum 4,000 florins, was to be restored to her, with a further 1,000 florins, and all her jewels, garlands, and clothes. To make up the sum she should sell the cattle, sheep, and pigs he had assigned to her. Ildebrandino's sister, Gemma, widow of Uguccione, Lord of Pereta and Montemerano, was to be assigned the castle of Pereta by its castellan; she and her two sons were to receive £1,000. Another sister, Beatrice, wife of the Lord of Montiano, also received £1,000, while a third, Ildebrandesa, was to be assured of her rights in Rochetta. The Lord Ranuccio dei Ranucci and his son receive each £1,000 for unspecified services. Then the count's followers are remembered. His knights and servants receive 'the house and farm they have' and the horses and arms conceded to their use. The executors are instructed to reward servants according to their length of service, its character, and their devotion to him. His notary, Giovanni of Sovana, is to be freed and given an annuity of £10. All his *fideles* south of the River Ombrone were to be freed from every burden for four years, those to the north for three years. Each of his castellans was to receive £25, and Ildebrandino, castellan of Sovana, was to get £100 and to be given his freedom.

Finally it is declared that were the count unable to go personally on crusade, provision was to be made for the expenses and pay of one knight to go to the Holy Land as a crusader in accordance with the mandate of the Council of Lyons. Eight years was set as the term for carrying out the will. The executors were named and their legacies declared. Pope Martin IV (1,100 florins); two cardinals (500 and 300 florins); two bishops (300 and 100 florins); the Lord Ermanno Monaldeschi of Orvieto (200 florins): the Minister of the Roman province of the Franciscans (50 florins); and two other Franciscan friars (50 florins each). The residue of his estate, *mobiles* and *immobiles*, rights and jurisdictions, went to his daughter, Margherita, and all his castellans, viscounts, gastalds, officials, and *fideles*, were admonished to secure her rights.

The Homeric scale of gift-giving evokes a certain remote barbaric splendour. There is great wealth here. The count is an expensive man to bury; he is a very expensive man to marry; his very *largesse* makes him an expensive man to have as lord. Apart from the annuities and the very considerable donations in kind whose value cannot be estimated, he was giving away about £14,500 and 3,250 florins (about 11,500 florins in all). In his life the one rich man among multitudes of the poor, he redistributed at death an immense part of his substance. Of the money actually assigned, which can be calculated, he left 19.5 per cent to executors (presumably as a stimulus towards their zeal in actually carrying out his wishes); 1.4 per cent to his servants; 24.4 per cent to his family and friends, and 41.2 per cent to the Church. What went to religion (and with it too went most of the gifts in kind) was bequeathed, no doubt, in the hope of winning divine favour and of obtaining pardon for having acted against God's servants. (There were considerable gifts 'for restitution of his debts and insufficient offerings', a grant to the church of Albaresio 'for damage done to the said church by him or his predecessors'; permission given to the prior of S. Quirico of Vitozzo to rebuild his mill and the payment of compensation 'for damage done to him'; which all hint at something of this.) Yet perhaps too what is found there is a belief that it is by this means that the poor (who otherwise receive only 13 per cent and merely paltry goods in kind) would best be served.

With the riches goes a cavalier attitude to money itself, apparent in many things, in the defective accounting and arithmetic of the document; in the failure in the returning of the first wife's dowry (carelessness or canniness?); above all perhaps in the way his wealth is kept in those silver bars rather than in the share-capital of some house of merchant adventurers. Unlike so many nobles of lesser rank, he is far from the world of merchandise, familiar more with the cattle, sheep and pigs he has assigned to his wife. Despite the wider world which appears in the names of his executors, despite the request for burial in, and the friendship with the friars of, the town of Orvieto, the centre of his life is his county, 'especially in those lands' as he says in assigning money to the poor, 'where the Lord Count was wont to stay, and especially in Sovana'; and 'especially in Ischia'. His sisters are all married to local nobles who hold fiefs from him. His second marriage is to a lady of the Lords Baschi from the same part of Tuscany. It is here, in the countryside, that he is at home, surrounded by men, whether notaries or castellans or peasants, who are his *fideles*, and by his four chamberlains, his vavassors, and his men-at-arms. The cities were remote.

Yet he belongs to a wider society. He is a Christian knight. His ancestors, the counts Guglielmo and Bonifaccio, had been on crusade (admittedly the somewhat inglorious crusade of Frederick II). If he has failed in this he yet acknowledges where his family traditions direct him. Family pride here, one imagines, must have been a way of life. It is the count's brother, Omberto, who in the eleventh canto of the *Purgatorio* speaks of how the arrogance of ancient blood and the memory of ancestral deeds had induced in him, 'unmindful of our common mother', a contempt for all other human beings.

The world of the Aldobrandini was, of course, representative of only the highest and most ancient nobility. There were many other nobles in the peninsula; men who were urban usurers; sophisticated bankers; sea merchants and pirates; villagers possessing one-hundredth *pro indiviso* of a marquisate. Within this varied class can one point with any confidence to a shared system of values which were peculiar to it? This is no easy question in that many of the ideals of an upper class were inevitably diffused, to a greater or lesser extent, throughout the whole community. Yet some answer is to be found in 'the literature of nobility', the stories of Arthur and Charlemagne which were so popular at the time, and above all in the culture of the Provençal lyric whose troubadours (generally native Italians) were present at most of the courts of the greater families. It was a literature bound up with the ideals and rites of knighthood, the blessing of the spurs, shield, and sword of the newly-dubbed knight, found in the thirteenth-century *ordo* of St Peter's at Rome,[9] and with all the ceremonies described in the *Ordene de Chevalerie de Hues de Tabarye* which was well known in the peninsula. It was linked too with the feasts so eagerly described in the chronicles, above all with the *corte*, the entertainment held, sometimes for its own sake, sometimes to celebrate dubbings, weddings, or victories. Normally this consisted of several days' round of banquets, with perhaps pageants and tournaments, which were likely to attract jesters, mimes, minstrels, and troubadours from all over Italy. In all these was ever-present the dream of that *cortesia* found in the Provençal poems.

The full meaning of *cortesia* was expressed in certain key words whose force is more easily felt in their contexts than easily translated. Three extracts from poems written by Aimeric de Peguilhan[10] may give some idea of them. The first is from a lament for the death of Azzo VI d'Este:

> Qu'elh fon savis, conoyssens, e saup far
> A mezura, tan qu'era sa valors
> El plus alt gra pojad' e sos pretz sors,
> E sostener que no·s pogues baiscar
> La saup ab sen, pueys fo larcs e cortes. . .

('He was *savis* (wise), *conoyssens* (understanding)
and could act with *meaura* (restraint) so that his
valor (fame) mounted to the highest grade,
and his *pretz* (honour) rose up. By his *sen*
(intelligence) he was able to sustain it so
that it could not fall, for he was *larcs* (generous)
and *cortes* (courtly)'.)

The second is from a panegyric written in 1220, of the Emperor Frederick II, seen here as a physician, coming from Salerno, to cure the world's evils:

> Anc hom no vi metge de son joven
> Tan belh, tam bo, tan larc, tan conoissen,
> Tan coratgos, tan ferm, tan conqueren,
> Tam be parlan ni tam benentenden. . . .

('Never was seen a doctor of his *joven* (youth),
so *belh* (handsome), so good, so *larc*, so *conoissen*,
so *coratgos* (brave), so firm, so conquering,
so skilled in speaking and in listening.')

The final lines are taken from Aimeric's elegy for the Marquess Guglielmo Malaspina:

> Era par ben que Valors se desfai
> E podetz o conoisser e saber,
> Quar selh que plus volia mantener
> Solatz, Domney, Larguez', ab cor veray,
> Mezur' e Sen, Conoissens' e Paria,
> Humilitat, Orguelh ses vilania,
> E·ls bos mestiers totz ses menhs e ses mai,

Es mortz! Guillems Malespina marques,
Que fo miralhs e mayestre dels bes.

('Now it is clear that *Valor* is undone,
and you may know and understand it,
for he who most wished to uphold
Solatz (joy), *Domney* (service of ladies),
Larguesa (generosity), with an upright heart,
Mezura and *Sen, Conoissens* and *Paria* (friendliness),
humilty, *Orguelh* (pride) without *vilania* (baseness),
and all good deeds without minus or plus,
is dead, Guglielmo Malaspina, the marquess,
who was mirror and master of all good things.')

In these three passages one finds most of the key concepts which inform the knightly ethic, and most of the key words which run through poem after poem in this genre. A nobleman is preferably *belh* or handsome. He is *coratgos*, possessing like Oliver *pro* or impetuous courage, and yet like Roland *savis*; he balances his pursuit of danger with his *sen* or intelligence, to produce *mezura* or balance. This is combined with a gracious worldliness; he has *joi* or delight in life, and what is of great importance *solatz:* he presents a cheerful, convivial face to the world. He is *larcs, franc* (free handed), he has *larguesa* which implies munificence and contempt for wealth as such. These are qualities most likely to be found in *joven*, youth and youthful feelings, and go together to make up his *pretz, valor, proeza* (prowess), and the whole doctrine of *cortesia*. This word is contrasted with *vilania*, the behaviour of a villein who is both cowardly and simple; *orguelh* which can be a virtue but which may degenerate into presumption and arrogance; *cobeitatz* or meaness and attachment to wealth; *enoi*, the failure of joy and commitment (in Latin, *accidia*); *folatge*, folly leading to behaviour which is *descortes*. At the same time *saber* assumes often the meaning 'one knowledgeable in poetry and music' and *mezura*, the sobriety of good taste. To possess these was to be *conoissens* and *ben ensenhaz* (well brought-up, well educated).

With *cortesia* too went *Domney*, the service and celebration of noble ladies, expressed above all in those poems to the wives of the great lords of Liguria, Lombardy, Emilia, and the Trevisan March – Adelasia of Viadana, Giovanna d'Este, Emilia Traversari, and Cunizza da Romano. One thinks here of the opening of Lamberto Buvallelli's melodious poem to Beatrice d'Este:[11]

Eu sai la flor plus bella d'autra flor
E plus plazen als dichs dels conoissens,
En cui es mais pretz e valors e sens
E deu per dreich portar major lauzor
C'autra del mon, que hom saubes eslire;
Car no·il faill res de ben c'om puosca dire
Qu'en lieis es sens, honors e cortesia,
Gens acuillirs, ab tant bella paria
C'om no la ve que non si' envejos
Del sieu ric pretz pojat sobrels plus pros.

('I know the flower, fairer than other flowers,
And pleasing more, as say the *conoissens*,
In which is greatest *pretz, valor*, and *sen*
And which by right should greater praise enjoy
Than any other men can choose.
For she lacks nothing of the good that could be asked
For she has *sen, honors*, and *cortesia*,
Noble welcome with such fine *paria*
That but to see her is to love and know
Her *pretz* that's richer than the highest *pro*.')

Here is a doctrine of *fin amor*, a mode of loving beyond the capacity of ordinary mortals, open only to the *conoissens*, in that the loved one is loved for her own chivalric qualities.

Despite the fact that clerics are often spoken of in these terms (an anonymous poet, for instance, writes of Cardinal Gregorio da Montelungo as 'so *pro*, so *franc*, so *larc* in giving. . .'), the ideal preserved here has little formal contact with what most ages have thought of as the leading ideals of Christianity. (And after the 1240s even the standard poems appealing for a Crusade disappear.) This is a starkly secular ethic, though one which often blended harmoniously with the everyday ethic of the Church. Some, of course, have portrayed *cortesia* as a purely literary construct, having no connection with behaviour or attitudes in the world outside the poems. It is true that one can find any number of examples of violation of its principles. (One hardly imagines, for example, that the principle of *larguesa* was embraced with any notable enthusiasm by the magnate bankers of the *Calimala*.) It is true too that just as the literature of Christianity of the period is filled with laments at the failure of its ideal, so too this is a commonplace in Provençal poetry. One sees a typical example in Falchetto di Romans' *consehl* to Frederick II:[12]

Far vuelh un nou sirventes
    Que razon n'ai granda
E dirai de Pretz on es,
    S'om tot nol demanda:
Pretz sojorn' ab los cortes
    E noi quier liuranda
    Mas joi e valor,
E ten celui per senhor
    Quil da tal vianda.

Pretz vol ome conoissen
    Ab fina largueza,
Franc e umil e plazen
    E ses avoleza;
A celui se don' es ren
    Ei a s'amor meza;
    Mas pauc n'a conques,
Qu'en cen baros non a tres
    Complitz de proeza.

98

('I wish to make a new sirventes and I have great cause. *Pretz* dwells with the *cortes*, and asks no other aid than *joi* and *valor*, and holds for lord he who gives such food.

Pretz requires a man to be *conoissen*, of fine *largueza*, *franc*, modest, and pleasant, and without baseness; to such a one does it give and yield itself, and loves him. Yet few have conquered it, for in a hundred barons there are only three, provided with *proeza*.')

Dante's dream of a society in which a whole class pursued chivalric values, the world of:

> le donne e' cavalier, li affani e li agi
> che ne' nvogliava amore e cortesia
>
> ('the ladies and the knights, the trials and the feasts
> which bound our hearts in love and *cortesia*'),

the world he makes Guido del Duca evoke in Romagna and Marco Lombardo in Lombardy, could necessarily exist only in an imagined past. Yet the point at issue here, whether considering the effects of chivalric or Christian rhetoric or teaching, is not how far it was followed, but rather how far it constituted the final framework of values to which assent was given or rejected, how far it constituted an ideal which, followed or not, men acted consciously with or against.

One finds some answer in the chronicle written in the early 1280s by the Franciscan friar, Salimbene de Adam, himself from a family of new men but deeply imbued with the ethic of the nobility of his native Emilia.[13] Written in Latin, its vocabulary constantly seems to demand translation into the key-terms of Provençal *cortesia*-lore. One has, certainly, only to look at his accounts of what he calls 'the great barons' of Parma to recognise, had one ever doubted it, how very varied the noble class was. There is Guidolino da Enzola, who turns to religion, comes to reside by the cathedral where he attends the offices each day, spends his time in good works – speaking of God, frightening off the children who throw stones at the windows and statues – and who still finds time to dub personally his sons as knights. There is his daughter, Richeldina, who married Jacobino da Beneceto (a convicted murderer, though Salimbene does not tell us so): 'a handsome knight and very rich in possessions and houses and treasure, but who consumed and dissipated it all on *corti* and minstrels and his acts of *cortesia*' so that his sons had nothing to live on. There are Guidolino's grandsons, Jacopo, who makes a wealthy marriage, puts the dowry out at usury, and so becomes very rich, and Bernardo, 'a knight and a valiant man'. Jacopo's son, Ghirardino, fined for leading a gang of youths which severely wounded two Modenesi ambassadors who had insulted his father's memory, was: 'a young man (i.e. *joven*), generous (*larcs*) and free handed (*franc*), and courteous (*cortes*) and one who lived in honour (*pretz*)'.

There is the da Gente family, which received its name from Giliolo, who, when overseas, kept on saying: 'our family (*gens*) acts in this way'. His son, Ghiberto, became Lord of Parma, but was a man guilty of *vilania*. Ghiberto's son, Jacopino, who was killed by his cousins, had, Salimbene believes, ordered the murder of his first wife. 'He was a handsome man (*belh*) and of magnificent heart, brave and confident, and in the manner of the men of Parma immensely proud.' Or there is the famous Pelavicini family. Pelavicino Pelavicini of Castel Pellegrino was 'a handsome man and *solatiosus* (full of *solatz*) and a maker of songs'. His brother, Manfredo, was a handsome man, married to Chiara da Lomello: 'a beautiful lady and most *saber* and full of *solatz*'. Among their sons was Enrico who 'if he had lived, I believe, would have subjugated all Lombardy' but who was killed at Benevento, fighting bravely in war against King Charles.

What unites these very different characters is the vocabulary in which Fra Salimbene describes them. This follower of St. Francis (that saint, who had himself called his brothers 'knights of the Round Table' and who had praised Charlemagne, Roland, Oliver, and the paladins as warriors for the faith, who dying in battle for Christ had won martyrdom)[14] saw his contemporaries – as they must have seen themselves – in terms of their physical grace and those adjectives which constantly come to his pen: *solatiosus, curialis, pulcher, avarus* and *rusticus*. The vision of life enshrined in these words coexists for him side by side with a Christianity with which it cannot always be easily reconciled. The force of chivalric legend works upon him more insidiously but almost as potently as the bible to which he has given so much study. So, of Bernardo de' Rossi (whose father, significantly, had borne the name Rolando), he writes:

I've never seen a man who better represented the person of a great prince. He had the appearance and the reality. For when he came to war and struck at his enemies with his iron mace, they turned and fled from him as from the face of the devil. And when I try to bring him to mind, the Emperor Charlemagne comes to me, what I've read about the one, what I've seen with my own eyes of the other'.

It is rhetoric; it is literature; but Salimbene shows that for many it was a way of life:

In this army Pagano di Alberto di Egidio de' Pagani of Parma, who was *podestà* of the Modenesi, made his son, Enrico, a knight, and said to him: 'Go, attack the enemy and fight like a man!' He did as commanded and was immediately pierced by a lance. And the blood drained from his body like unfermented wine from the jar when the stopper is taken out, and a little after he died. His father was told and said: 'I care not. For my son was made a knight, and died fighting like a man.' I have heard of this from one who was there.

Such an attitude is not confined to the pages of the friar's chronicle. Even in the *Cronica* of Rolandino of Padua, who, in a civic-humanist vein, is consciously looking to a different tradition, one finds a lingering over the great *corte* and the pause to illustrate the *valor* of courtly honour. He tells, for instance, of the death of Tisolino da Camposanpiero, who was fighting for the Este on their expulsion from Ferrara in 1222. He was surrounded by men of the village of Girzola, who called upon him to surrender. 'But, great of soul, he refused to yield save to one of knightly blood. And when none was found there, they killed his good destrier, and then alas!, he himself was slain'.[15]

This rhetoric, whether of Provençal origin or deriving from the traditions of Carolingian or courtly epic in the *langue d'oeil*, had a potent influence among all classes. Its popularity may have been reinforced by the establishment of the

Angevin kings in the south and the coming to their court of such French poets as Adam de la Halle and Perrin d'Agincourt, but long before them it was firmly rooted in the north of Italy. Its power among the nobility is testified to by the prevalence of such Carolingian and Arthurian personal names as Galeazzo (Galahad), Guglielmo (from Guillaume d'Orange), and Rolando, and by the surviving *manuscrits de luxe* written in French, Franco-Italian, and Italian, which preserved the epic tales. These same tales street-singers chanted in Franco-Italian to the people in the market-place. Men like the Paduan judge, Giovanni da Nono (died *c*. 1346), drew up genealogies which related their enemies to such villains as Ganelon and traced their own descent from Roland; notaries, like the Paduan author of the *Entrée d'Espagne* (*c*. 1320) or Niccolo' da Casola with his *Attila* (*c*. 1350), elaborated the old themes in new ways in Franco-Italian speech.

The educated mind of the thirteenth and early fourteenth centuries had an infinite capacity for transmuting everyday reality into epic forms. The first Italian chronicle which was composed in a vulgar tongue, the *Estoires de Venise* (written 1267–75), portrays contemporary life as a feudal pageant in which jousting and chivalric prowess stand at the centre of attention. In this climate of feeling the Venetian republic found it natural enough to employ the dreams of the Arthurian world as an instrument of government propaganda. A work, purporting to have been transcribed by one 'Master Richard of Ireland' at the court of Frederick II (in fact composed by a Venetian citizen in the late 1270s), intersperses stories of Lancelot and Tristan and Palamède with a series of 'prophecies of Merlin' which exalt the future greatness and political morality of *les bons mariniers* who live on the *grant ille de mer*. Within this context the Venetians are shown as battling against an evil emperor, uncourtly Pisans, Mohammedan infidels, and 'an evil dragon' who turns out to be Ezzelino da Romano of Verona. (The contemporary epic, *Chevalerie Ogier*, represents this same Ezzelino as meeting his death at the hands of a hero from the *Chanson de Roland*.)

Yet perhaps the most remarkable re-writing of experience in terms of chivalric literature is to be found in the *Milione* of Marco Polo. In the prisons of Genoa Marco told his story to Rustichello of Pisa, author of various compilations of chivalric prose romances. Rustichello, in so far as lay within him, wrote it down in the style which he brought to his other works. Thus the reception of the Polos at the court of Kubla Khan mirrors the coming of Tristan to the court of Camelot. The wars of the Mongol Barka and Alau are preceded by the same courtly embassies which feature in the world of Celtic chivalry. Seven battles in Asia are described in seven identical ways, that is in all the remorseless clichés used to describe battles in chivalric literature. The Asia of Marco Polo has become the Britain of Arthur or the enchanted far-off island from which, after long years of captivity, the hero returns to his home. Little wonder that in the fourteenth-century romance of *Baudouin de Sébourg* the *Milione* should serve in its turn as a source-book for new chivalric fantasies. What was Marco doing in those long years in the East? Was he a merchant or an administrator or a court-curiosity? Rustichello does not tell us because whatever it was was incompatible with the lives of Guiron le Courtois and Meliadus and the *chevaliers errants* of romance.[16]

Yet, in another sense, the prevalence of this genre did not distort contemporary reality so much as give it heightened expression. For it was not those earnest, prudent virtues, that homely everyday wisdom, which Weber detected in 'the bourgeois ethic' which characterised Italian society in the first age of commercial capitalism. A society with such values would have created nothing. Rather was it those ideals of impetuous courage combined with *mezura*, of contempt for wealth as such, which gave the Italian nobility its dynamic. For these men a commercial venture was as much a test of nerve and judgment as a joust; trading with strange peoples in Astrakhan or Zaitun the equivalent of a meeting with legendary monsters; the lending of money to a northern king the expression of a willingness to put all to the touch in search of greatness. The authoritative accents of Europe's first capitalists are heard not in the moralisings of men like Paolo da Certaldo but from the mouth of the Genoese Perceval Doria:

> Pero bem platz qel temps francs
>   Fai los brancs
> Dels arbres vermeils blancs;
> E am guerra qils estancs
> D'aver fan remaner mancs;
> Em plaz can vei sobrels bancs
> Aur et argen co fos fancs,
> Per dar als pros ses cors rancs
> C'amor suffrir colps els flancs.[17]

> 'So I like it when fair weather makes
> red and white the branches of the trees.
> And I love war which strips the weak of
> their riches. And I like it when I see
> on the counters silver and gold, ready
> to be thrown like mud to the men
> with *pro* of firm heart who love
> to take blows on their bodies.'

IV

Side by side with the traditions of chivalric *pretz* and intertwined with it, there existed another tradition, one found in all classes of society, yet in that it was inevitably bound up with their claim to exercise public justice, particularly characteristic of the nobility, namely belief or rather joy in vendetta and the blood feud. Reading the commentators upon the *Comedia* (where Dante confesses shame at his own failure to avenge the murder of a cousin), one becomes aware of the ease with which blood-feuds could be provoked and the immense sensitivity of these men to the claims of honour. A blow on the face leads Alberigo Manfredi to a mass murder of his relatives some years later; a careless joke causes Tebaldello Zambrasi to betray his town to the enemy: 'from so slight a cause such hateful vengeance'.[18] In these crimes any other interest is subordinated to a love of glory and an obsessive concern for one's personal esteem in the eyes of one's fellows. Yet the thought of a lineage bent upon vengeance was enough to alarm all, for its effects could be so widespread. In December 1287 Aldo Rangone of Modena was married to the Marquess Aldobrandino d'Este. After a few weeks it was discovered that they were within the prohibited degrees of kindred. In the case brought before the pope to legitimise the marriage, witness after witness deposed one sole testimony: that the uncle and father of the bride and the Rangone family as a whole were so powerful in Modena and had so many friends and followers that if the couple were forced to separate they feared the last desolation and ruin, both of Modena and its neighbouring cities. The Rangoni, it was said, would do anything and use any means to attain vengeance: 'even if they have to associate with Saracens' or, as another witness puts it, 'even if they have to ally with the devils of Hell'. Faced with such arguments, Nicholas IV was prudently persuaded to a swift recognition of the union.[19]

Many discussed the issues involved: vengeance was indeed the highest *solatz*: 'the greatest joy in the world'.[20] Yet it offended the Lord, who would repay, and was, they explain, difficult to achieve satisfactorily: a slight revenge was an object of scorn, too great brought contumely. After the killing of Tisolino da Camposampiero, for instance, his brother Jacopo replied by attacking the village of Fratta, occupied by the friends and *fideles* of his enemies. It fell easily, and all inside, men, women, and children, were slain. Jacopo, Rolandino tells us, rejoiced particularly in this vengeance, for he himself had there slain many, yet the writer's own belief is that this was unjust 'for the sins of Titus should not be visited on Sempronius'. Again, the fact that so many killings were carried out by relatives against relatives necessarily diminished the kin-character of revenge taken for them. It was a thought which worried Fra Salimbene, who, despite his order, normally looked quite cheerfully on the process ('the men of Parma, of whom I am one, have the saying that thirty years is time enough for vengeance'). Telling of how Pinotto da Gente had been killed by his nephews after years of conflict over a small tongue of land adjoining a mill, he goes on to observe: 'if outsiders had killed Pinotto then they, for the honour of their family and following the custom and vainglory of the world, would have had to kill them'.[21] The truth was that since the blood-feud was directed so often against relatives its satisfaction had very frequently to be based not upon kinship but upon a 'political' party, composed of men, themselves weakly linked by blood, frequently related to members of an opposing party, having often, each, their own separate objects of vengeance. Thus party was coming to take the place of kin, and, more and more, men were turning to non-familial groups for the achievement of their own household security.

Given the claims of everyday life, however, vengeance had to be taken. The moralists advised on how it should be done: with silent preparation and without haste. So counsels the notary, Grazioli de' Bambaglioli, in his *Trattato sopra le virtù morali*:

> Somm' allegrezza è fare sua vendetta
> perché lontan dolore

si muta in nuovo onore
ma faccia sí che, scarsa in fretta
nuovo danno non gravi il suo stato
ché peggiorando, é l'uom mal vendicato.

'The highest joy is vengeance once to taste,
So lengthy pain
Is turned to honour's gain,
But then beware that over-haste
Brings no new burdens to your state
For then but ill-avenged will be your hate.'

Such subtlety or discrimination was, in reality, rarely practised; by the mid-thirteenth century the traditions of the *vendetta* were tearing the stability of the communes apart.

NOTES

There are few general studies of the nobility. See, however, Gina Fasoli, 'Feudo e castello' in the Einaudi *Storia d'Italia*, vol. v, pt. i, *cit.; idem, Momenti di storia e storiografia feudale italiana*, Bologna, 1957; *idem*, 'Signoria feudale ed autonomie locali' in *Studi ezzeliniani*, Rome, 1963. There are however, some studies of the consortorie: eg. F. Nicolai, 'I consorzi nobiliari ed il commune nell' alta e media Italia', *RSDI*, xiii, 1940; P. Santini, 'Le società delle torri in Firenze', *ASI*, s. 7, xx, 1887; G. Gozzadini, *Delle torri gentilizie in Bologna e delle famiglie alle quali prima appartennero*, Bologna, 1880; E. Grendi, 'Profilo storico degli alberghi genovesi', *Mélanges de l'Ecole Française de Rome, Moyen Age – Temps Modernes*, 87, 1975.

For cives silvestres see W. Bowsky, 'Medieval citizenship, the individual and the state in the commune of Siena, 1287–1355', *Studies in Medieval and Renaissance History*, iv, 1967; G. Marchetti-Longhi, 'La carta feudale del Lazio', *QF*, xxxvi, 1956; G. Cecchini, 'Ghino di Tacco', *ASI*, 1957; E. Sestan, 'I conti Guidi e il Casentino' in his *Italia Medievale*, Naples, 1966.

On comitatinanza, see G. Luzzatto, 'Le sottomissioni dei feudatari e le classi sociali in alcuni comuni marchigiani (Secoli XIII e XIV)' in his *Dai servi della gleba agli albori del Capitalismo*, Bari, 1966; G. de Vergottini, 'I presupposti storici del rapporto di comitatinanza e la diplomatica comunale con particolare riguardo al territorio senese', *Bollettino senese di storia patria*, lx, 1953; *idem*, 'Il papato e la comitatinanza nello stato della chiesa', *Atti e Memorie per la Romagna*, n.s. 3, 1952–3.

On chivalric literature in Italy there are two collections of Provençal poetry, G. Bertoni, *I trovatori in Italia*, Modena, 1915, and *Poesie provenzali storiche relative all' Italia*, ed. V. Bartholomaeis, Rome, 1931. For works in the *langue d'oeil*, Franco-Italian, and Italian see A. Viscardi, *La Letteratura franco-italiana*, Modena, 1941; R. Ciampoli, *I codici francesi della R. Biblioteca Nazionale di San Marco in Venezia*, Venice, 1897; D. Delcorno Branca, *Il romanzo cavalleresco medievale*, Florence, 1974; and E. G. Gardner, *The Arthurian Legend in Italian Literature*, London, 1930. Its values have been little studied though A. Vallone, *La cortesia dai provenzali a Dante*, Palumbo, 1950, and R. M. Ruggieri, *L'umanesimo cavalleresco italiano da Dante al Pulci*, Rome, 1963, give some help.

On the **vendetta** are U. Dorini, 'La vendetta privata ai tempi di Dante', *Giornale Dantesco*, xix, 1926; and A. M. Enriques, 'La vendetta nella vita e nella legislazione fiorentina', *ASI*, s. 7, xix, 1933.

1. See the documents in volume iii of G. B. Verci, *Storia degli Eccelini*, Bassano, 1779, particularly for 1223, pp. 200–5.
2. 'Breve consortum et dominorum de Riprafracta', ed. F. Bonaini, *ASI*, vi, pt. ii, 1845, pp. 805–12; see too M. Lupo Gentile, 'Sulla consorteria feudale dei nobili di Ripafratta'; *Giornale storico e letterario della Liguria*, vi, 1905; and E. Cristiani, *Nobiltà e popolo nel comune di Pisa*, Naples, 1962, pp. 124–7, 426–9.
3. R. Caggese, *Roberto d'Angiò*, Florence, 1922–31, i, p. 224.
4. *In Recueil des Historiens des croisades*, ii, Paris, 1859, pp. 51–2.
5. C. Higounet, 'Les "Terre nuove" florentines du XIVᵉ siècle', *Studi in onore di Amintore Fanfani*, iii, Milan, 1962.
6. Giovanni Villani, *Cronica*, Trieste, 1857, iv, p. 10–13; xii, p. 23.
7. See G. Ciacci, *Gli Aldobrandeschi nella storia e nella 'Divina Comedia'*, Rome, 1935, ii, pp. 22–9, 246–7.
8. Ciacci, *cit.*, ii, pp. 261–6.
9. M. Andrieu, *Le Pontifical romain au moyen âge*, Vatican, 1938–41, i, p. 302; ii, pp. 579–81; iii, pp. 447–50.
10. *The poems of Aimeric de Peguilhan*, ed. W. P. Shepard and F. M. Chambers, Illinois, 1950, pp. 161, 146, 81.
11. G. Bertoni, *I trovatori d'Italia*, Modena, 1915, i, p. 223.
12. *Poesie provenzali storiche, cit.*, ii, pp. 3–4. For similar complaints, pp. 24–27, 49–50, 95–6.
13. On which C. Violante, 'Motivi e caratteri della Cronica di Salimbene', *Annali della Scuola normale de Pisa*, 1953. My illustrations are taken from Salimbene, *cit.*, pp. 886–90 (descendents of Guidolino), 650, 98–9, 884 (Da Gente), 543–5 (Pelavicini), 290 (Rossi), 85 (Pagani).
14. *Scripta Leonis, Rufini et Angeli*, ed. Rosalind Brooke, Oxford, 1970, pp. 210–15.
15. Rolandino da Padova, *Cronica in factis et circa facta Marchie Trivixane*, ed. A. Bonardi, *RIS*, viii, pt. 2, p. 30.
16. See *Les Estoires de Venise*, ed. A. Limentani, Florence, 1972; *Les Prophecies de Merlin*, ed. L. A. Paton, London, 1926–7; H. Krauss, 'Ezzelino da Romano-Maximo Çudé', *Cultura neolatina*, xxx, 1970; L. F. Benedetto, *La tradizione manoscritta del 'Milione' di Marco Polo*, Florence, 1926, ch. 1.
17. *Poesie provenzali storiche, cit.*, ii, p. 190.
18. Benvenuto de' Rambaldi da Imola, *Commentum super Dantis Aldigherii Comoediam*, Florence, 1887, ii, pp. 514–15 (on Tebaldello in *Inferno*, xxxii, 122–3).
19. G. Tiraboschi, *Memorie storiche modenese* in A. Namias, *Storia di Modena*, 1894, pp. 177–8.
20. 'la prima allegrizia del mondo', Paolo di Pace da Certaldo, *Libro di buone costumi*, ed. Morpurgo, Florence, 1921, nos. 119 and 276.
21. Salimbene, *cit.*, p. 930.

CHAPTER SIX

Party conflict and the *popolo*

I

By the 1240s the traditions of the vendetta had already destroyed any unity which might once have existed within the societies of the knights. In each town two leading parties had arisen which, when not at war, dealt cautiously with each other in a state of armed truce. In Brescia were the Rivola and the Coglioni; in Mantua the Poltroni and Calorosi; in Vicenza the Vivaresi and the Counts of Vicenza; in Cremona the Barbarasi (or 'clean-shaven') and the Capelleti ('hairy'); in Reggio the Palude and Correggio; and so on, throughout the peninsula. These parties were, of course, in the first place, alliances of men seeking control over government. Yet the climate of murderous hatred in which they fought out their differences had other origins; the parties were not simply political groups, they were also the coming-together of men united in blood feud.

It is interesting to look at that celebrated myth, current by the 1240s, which sought to explain the origins of party conflict in Florence. In 1216, the tale runs, there was a drunken quarrel at a banquet to celebrate the dubbing of a knight, in which Buondelmonte Buondelmonti wounded Oddo Arrighi with a knife. At home Oddo took counsel with his consorts, among whom were the Amidei family. They advised not vengeance but peace, and suggested that hatred should be dissolved by arranging a marriage between Buondelmonte and a daughter of the Amidei. So it was done; a treaty was made and the marriage contract drawn up. But the Lady Gualdrada Donati sent to Buondelmonte, urged upon him the shame that would be his were he to marry through fear, and suggested that he should instead marry her daughter. Moved by her words, Buondelmonte reneged on his bond to the Amidei and accepted Gualdrada's offer. At this all the friends and relatives of the Arrighi met in the church of S. Maria sopra Porta (an important touch; they were engaged on a sacred task) to plan revenge. Their decision reached, they ambushed Buondelmonte on his wedding day and killed him at the foot of the statue of Mars: an appropriate site in that this incident, the chronicler claims, was the cause of the war between parties in Florence and the divisions found still between the nobles of the city.[1]

In this story there are many obvious mythopoeic elements (notably in the Eve role fulfilled by the Lady Gualdrada, a characteristic thirteenth-century theme), and it is quite clear that faction conflict was already alive in Florence some thirty years before 1216. Yet the form the tale takes is instructive. The chronicler does not say that the origins of faction lay in who should be *podestà* or who should control the distribution of taxation, let alone in what way public policy should be directed. What was at stake was a simple question of affronted aristocratic honour. It is this theme which looms largest in all contemporaries' explanation of civil strife. There are very occasional references as well to 'competition for office', yet it features as a primary cause only in the writings of Marchionne Stefani in the second half of the fourteenth century.[2] It was not the way in which men of the thirteenth century habitually expressed what they were fighting for. Their silence here is misleading; they were indeed struggling for real power in government. Yet it would be equally misleading to define party conflicts simply in terms of what is most easily comprehensible today. In origin they were often contests for political advantage but they were also – and it was this which gave them their particularly unpolitical, that is to say, unconciliatory and irrational character – tournaments of honour.

Virulent already by the 1230s, these conflicts intensified and expanded thenceforth with the great war of Papacy and Empire. As this developed it was inevitable that in each town the factions should choose different sides and draw from their professed allegiance both new allies and some higher justification and sanction for their personal quarrels. In origin these loyalties to pope or emperor were dictated primarily by calculations of advantage against domestic enemies; often they were very lightly worn. Frequently, as the years passed, as the troubadours sang their songs of the defence of Faenza or the death of Conradin, they might come to be accompanied by deep sentiments or even combined with some ideological yearning for an effective universal order. But whether these allegiances were idealistic or born of political calculation – and such calculations were rarely absent – their effect was the same: to unite the feuds of any one town to those of all the other towns in the peninsula. Marriage links between noble families in adjacent cities had already had this effect; now the process was reinforced. In each town the imperialist party (later to be known as the Ghibellines) looked to the imperialists among its neighbours as an ally against the party of the Church (to be known as Guelfs). Party conflict thus came inextricably to be bound up with the foreign policy of the communes. If a Florence, dominated by a Guelf party, were at war with a Siena, dominated by Ghibellines, then the Ghibellines of Florence, the Guelfs of Siena, would fight for the victory of the alien commune. Hence to oppose the dominant party in the commune became synonymous with treachery; members of the opposing party were stripped of their citizenship, their houses were destroyed; their goods confiscated. Expelled from their cities, the *extrinseci* would continue the conflict by waging war from their castles in the countryside upon the *intrinseci*. Meanwhile the parties everywhere sharpened their structure, gave stronger constitutional form to their councils and offices, and developed their own statutes, finances, and common properties.

Neither the death of Frederick II nor the end of imperial–papal conflict with the triumph of Charles of Anjou could halt the struggles. By 1270, when so many of the old imperialist parties had been annihilated, an outsider might have assumed that with the triumph of one party and the destruction of its opponents peace would come. But the factions had not been in conflict primarily for the sake of empire or Church; 'imperialist' and 'ecclesiastical' had been principally labels to identify themselves to their allies throughout Italy. What they had been fighting for, quite independently of any wider issues and prior to them, were the fruits of office and the satisfaction of their blood feuds, and these still remained and grew. Hence, everywhere, once one party had exterminated its opponents and was supreme, it began to split into two new parties. So by the early 1280s the old 'party of the Church' in Parma was divided between 'the party of the Bishops' and 'the Rossi and Correggio'; in Reggio between 'the Uppers' and 'the Lowers'; at Modena between 'the Savignano' and 'the Guidotti'; in Imola between the Alidosi and Nordigli; in Piacenza between the Bordellina and the Scotti; and so on. Similar changes were coming to the Guelfs of Pistoia, Lucca, and Florence, who reformed as 'Blacks' and 'Whites'. At the same time the triumphant Ghibellines at Arezzo were split between the Verdi and Secchi.

There were positive reasons for the continuation of the party struggles and there were negative ones as well. The very violence with which they had been fought made them difficult to end, even when victors magnanimously offered terms to the vanquished. Salimbene de Adam describes how in 1250 the imperial party of his native Parma, then in exile at Borgo San Donnino and Cremona from where they were waging war upon the city, asked 'the party of the Church', 'for the love of God and the glorious Virgin' that they should be admitted into the town with which they now desired peace. This was speedily agreed, and they were received with honour. The first thing that the *extrinseci* saw on readmittance, however, was the burnt-out ruins of their houses. The first thing that they asked – and the chronicler seems to see their request as preposterous – was that they should be treated as equals. Hence they quickly turned to plotting against the regime in favour of the imperialist Uberto Pelavicini, who, they hoped, 'would expel and completely destroy the party of the Church, so that for all eternity, they should not return to Parma'. The same thing, Salimbene says, has happened at Bologna, Modena, Reggio, and Cremona. It was extremely difficult for any party to acknowledge defeat when it could look to the aid of a dominant faction in a neighbouring town. You could not expect peace, explains Salimbene, because these people were playing the children's game of cover-hand: 'once one boy has his hand on top and thinks he's won, the other takes his hand from the bottom and puts it on top again'.[3]

Again, the inadequacy of communal justice provoked conflict. Salimbene again gives us an illustrative vignette here from the party conflicts of 1286 in Reggio Emilia.[4] On 5 April of that year, Guido da Bianello and his brother of the Upper party, riding to their castle, ill-mounted and without escort, were killed in the wood at the foot of Montefalcone by an armed band. This was led by the Lord Scarabello da Canossa, who belonged to the Lower party and had been expelled from Reggio, and Brother Azzolino, monk (and brother of the abbot) of Canossa. Guido had been the chronicler's friend, he speaks of him as handsome, one who knew Latin, a good speaker, and full of *solatz* (and he held the view, the friar adds, that he was predestined to heaven or hell whether he sinned or not). The city authorities were unable to reach the real criminals, esconced in the *contado*, but they called Scarabello's first cousin, Rolandino da Canossa, to answer the charge of being involved with them. Rolandino appeared, surrounded, wisely, by a great retinue of armed men, and was acquitted of guilt. The 'Upper' party bayed all the more for vengeance, and insisted that the *podestà* should arrest and question the Lord Guido da Albareto, father of Brother Azzolino, the assassin monk. Two rumours were current about what happened next. According to the first the *podestà* pointed out to Guido that he was forced, against his will, to torture him and asked him to bear it patiently for the love of God. At this, Guido, formerly bitter, realising that this had to be for the honour (significant word) of them both, bore the torture patiently and indeed with a jocund spirit. According to the second tale, the Abbot of Canossa bribed the *podestà* and captain of the people with £100 each, that his father might not be tortured. The *podestà* had gone into the chamber alone, had sat down on the machine for weighing flour that stood there, and had simply had a friendly conversation with Guido about what had happened. Although he had, apparently, to be assisted in leaving the Palace of the Commune, Guido spent the rest of the day in *solatz*, eating, drinking, and living blithely. Whatever the truth of the matter – and, of course, quite independently of any bribes it was dangerous to torture a man of power – Reggio began to prepare for the civil war, which was indeed shortly upon it.

Mistrust of public justice appears here as a major cause of conflict. At the same time, when the essential element in the detection of crime was the torture-chamber, one sees why with the best will in the world the nobility had very good reason for being chary of submitting themselves to it. The only sanction against the willingness to kill one's private enemies (which was always accompanied by the psychologically maiming recognition that they were prepared to kill you) remained that of religion. Yet the upper clergy of the town very largely consisted of the brothers of the lay nobility; so that disputes among laymen either drew the clergy into secular quarrels or were fuelled by disputes within the secular world. The party-bishop was a common phenomenon, the party-monk, the party parish priest. These quarrels infected even the nunnery. During the election of the Abbess of the Benedictine house of S. Pier Maggiore at Florence in 1294, two of the nuns had asked, in fact without success, that they might consult with their fathers and others of their families before casting their vote. As events transpired the community chose an avid supporter of the White Guelfs. When, five years later, Lisa, daughter of Guidolino da Calestano, a partisan of the Blacks, asked to be received as a nun, she was told that there was no vacancy. At this she produced a letter, commanding her acceptance from none other than the arch-patron of the Blacks, Pope Boniface VIII. Suor Margherita's reply was as forceful as her brothers might have wished: 'Who are you calling pope? What most holy father? Boniface is not pope, but the devil on earth and bane of all Christians. And the Lord God will give such power to the Colonna at Rome that they will do to him and his relatives what he's doing to them against right and justice'.[5]

What in the final analysis made civil conflict inevitable was the conviction of all that it could not be avoided, that it was a natural concomitant of upper-class life. Two years before the murder of Guido da Bianello, the commune of Parma, acting as honest broker, had sought to bring permanent peace between the 'Uppers' and 'Lowers' of Reggio. Ambassadors from the two parties had gone to Parma, had there agreed upon the maintenance of peace, had arranged marriages between rival families, and obtained a promise that Parma should assist either party if it were expelled by the other. A prospect of harmony dawned. At this point the emissaries sought a greater guarantee. Staying in the inn at Borgo Santa Cristina they learnt that the city possessed a local shoemaker-prophet, one Asdente, much patronised by the bishop of Parma (though to be consigned to the *Inferno* by Dante). Calling him to them they asked whether peace would in fact be maintained. Asdente's answer was discouraging. At this both parties left for Reggio, abandoned their marriage plans, and began to prepare for war.[6] For these men, in reality, the call to Asdente was a moment of cool reason after an interlude of deceptive dreams. For the prophecy of any shoemaker, with or without mystic gifts, would have been that peace would not, could not, last; that if there were two parties in a town violence must follow and that any spark might ignite it.

One speaks of the extreme violence of these civil conflicts, yet the assertion may raise doubts. For looking at the development of the towns in the thirteenth century, what strikes at once, amidst all the faction conflict, is the strongest evidence for what seems to be an immensely resolute collective will. Reading the chronicles one meets it on every page. The communes were continually engaging in local hydraulic works, systematising rivers, draining waste land; they were active in constructing government buildings, *palazzi comunali, palazzi della ragione*, in rebuilding their cathedrals, in ordering their towns with new paved streets, in replacing wooden by stone bridges, in building town walls. Above all the machinery of government was growing all the time. It is curious to find all this co-existing with the divisions in the ruling class. In these circumstances one is tempted to ask did these conflicts really represent anarchy? Is it not a question rather of occasional street fights, the equivalent of election-riots in eighteenth-century England; a means of testing opinion which brings, perhaps momentary but hardly permanent chaos? There are blood-feuds certainly, but are they not simply functional, self-regulating mechanisms for obtaining justice in defect of public order? Do they really represent the tearing apart of the oligarchies as a whole?

The more laconic the chronicle evidence the easier it is to accept some thesis along these lines. Reading the *Annals of Bergamo* and coming to this passage –

1226. Around the middle of the month of May there was *civile bellum*, and most foul, from the hour (number missing in chronicle here) to the beginning of the night, and this was on the 19th of May.[7]

one is tempted to translate *civile bellum* as 'extensive street brawls'. The great merit, yet once again, of Salimbene's *Cronica* is that the laconicism disappears and the reality of what lies behind these words is made explicit in great detail. His account of, for example, the faction conflicts of 'Uppers' and 'Lowers' in Reggio

Emilia in the 1280s makes manifest the progressive degradation wrought by violence.[8] At the driving out of the Lowers by the Uppers in April 1287, the prisons were opened, a band of criminals attacked the Franciscan Convent, the house of Rolandino da Canossa was given to the flames, and four or five other houses of those who had fled were destroyed. Then Matteo da Fogliano, leader of the triumphant Uppers, built a new house, which he called 'Altabella', from the stone and wood taken from that of the exiles. War continued, however, in the *contado*. During the next eighteen months the exiles established themselves in the mountains above the Crostolo valley and, hiring mercenary knights and footsoldiers, ravaged the lands of their enemies. There was destruction of crops, burning of houses, uprooting of the high-quality *vernaccia* vines, seizure of animals, killing and kidnapping of peasants. Anyone seized, 'men who had harmed no-one', would be tortured in the hope of exacting ransom. Salimbene, who describes these tortures in some detail – 'these things are written that it may be known that some men are crueller than beasts' – drew from knowledge of them a recognition of the justice of hell in which the men who did such things would themselves be tormented by demons. The *intrinseci* hit back, tortured in turn those suspected of assisting their enemies, and marched out with 3,000 men, mangonels and trébuchets, to attack their enemies at the castle of Rochetta. A peace, or a truce of exhaustion, followed in September 1288, when the *extrinseci* were re-admitted to the town. But peace was an illusion. Within a year the parties came to blows again, and Matteo da Fogliano's 'Altabella' in its turn went up in flames. All that was permanent was an enduring legacy of hatred.

These conflicts were enough to destroy the unity of any comparatively small oligarchy. It needs only a handful of violent men to infect all of society with their violence. As Rolandino remarked of the Trevisan March in the 1230s: 'All hoped to remain and continue in good peace, but the whole mass was corrupted by a slight ferment'.[9] The atmosphere of treachery and suspicion involved all. The *fideles* and tenants of the Lords in the countryside, their clients in the city, were all drawn in. The traditions of the blood-feud made the killing of enemies normal. The destruction of houses – and one thinks here particularly of the hubristic and provocative building of 'Altabella' from the ruins – guaranteed the continuance of bitterness, the impossibility of any lasting reconciliation.

If this be so, if faction-conflicts were so violent, had this anarchy always existed or was it particular to the thirteenth century? In the 1260s men looked back to a *buon tempo antico* when life was much less violent. Rolandino of Padua tells of how in 1208 Azzo VI of Este had taken Verona and there captured Ezzelino II da Romano, how Ezzelino was honoured by all his captor's ladies and knights, freed, and accompanied by his knights to Bassano, where they in turn were honoured by the knights and ladies of Bassano. It reads like a chivalric pageant; to its author it brings a bitter and nostalgic outburst. '*Ha Deus! tunc erant werre, si licitam est dicere, bone werre*'. 'Ah God, at that time wars were, if one is allowed to say it, good wars. One man, struggling manfully with another, though he were captured, was not sentenced to a living death, nor put in chains; no terrible mutilation was decreed against him; he was released rather with *pretz* and *valor* to go where he wished.'[10] Obviously this type of reflection is in large part simply an idealisation of the past at the expense of the present. Yet, in the last analysis, it must be conceded that the conflict of Hohenstaufen and Papacy in the twelfth century was fought out with less general violence than in the thirteenth. In seeking for an explanation contemporaries blamed the emperor. Indeed it could be supposed that the wars of Frederick II brought with them a greater partisan bitterness than those of Frederick I. Later enquirers may play with the idea that the removal of an external enemy through the Peace of Constance and the imperial interregnum permitted the growth of internal discord; or alternatively that an old ruling-class solidarity had been broken by the acceleration of *comitatinanza* and the introduction of a new nobility within the towns.

Yet a much more basic cause is that the very growth of the collective will, the very expansion of the powers and pretensions of the communes, which came about as a result of their triumph over Barbarossa, made the powers much more worth contending for. The commune of the late twelfth century was marked by a curious unsubstantiality. It was a chaotic, haphazard mingling of conflicting interests and resistent franchises, which never claimed to compose the city in which it was found. It was simply one of other parties found within it. Its powers were very limited. Few at that time were going to struggle fiercely with their neighbours to be known as a consul when all that office gave was the possibility of being branded a traitor by the emperor. Yet as the pretension of the commune grew, as its legislative claims expanded, as its statutes increased in volume, as it acquired a formidable bureaucratic machine; when what was at stake was the allocation of an ever-expanding taxation and the control of the marketing of food in the *contado*, then many men might think it worth their while to stake their lives upon the gaining of a great prize. Significant here is the remark of the anonymous chronicler of Reggio on the eight 'Rectors' appointed by the Uppers after the expulsion of the Lowers in 1287. All these men, he remarks, 'were the greatest robbers of the goods of the commune'.[11] The facts were that there was much more now to be robbed, much more to be fought for. One could say that most communes began to fail only when they put aside their weakness and insubstantiality, or, again, that it was the attempt of the communes to turn themselves into states which brought into existence those forces which everywhere threatened to destroy them. The transmutation of commune into *signoria* in our period had nothing in common with, say, the fall of the Florentine Republic and the coming of the Medici Dukes in 1530. The *signoria* was not replacing or destroying a fully formed and well articulated system of republican government. The elaboration and articulation of government were part of the process which produced in some towns *signoria*, in others a reconstituted commune. For from the 1230s one thing seems clear in the towns of the North. An anarchic struggle for power in which violence was ever present was rendering existing governmental institutions incapable of exercising those functions which men, more and more, were demanding of them. In these circumstances the ground was prepared for the movement of the *popolo*.

II

That same expansion and sophistication of the rôle of government, which had brought a new bitterness to the conflict within the nobility, had at the same time given the non-noble class within the communes a new and more pressing concern with the control of power. Hence from the end of the twelfth and beginning of the thirteenth centuries, a new organisation came into being within the communes. This was the *popolo*: an association of non-nobles (often called *pedites* or men who fought on foot), bound together by oath, and seeking a variety of concessions from the nobles (*milites*). By the end of the 1230s it was rare to find any town in North and Central Italy where some form, however rudimentary, of this alliance did not exist.

Within the ranks of the *popolo* two categories of membership can be distinguished. First were those men made wealthy by trade, banking, usury, land-holding, or exercise of a profession, who were denied admission to the ruling oligarchies. Often wealthier than the oligarchs, often closely akin to or indistinguishable from them in their life-style, they sought admission to the privileges of the *nobili cittadini*. They looked for access to the lucrative benefits of secular office and required that members of their families should be eligible for election to the chapters of local cathedrals, whose posts were generally monopolised by the ruling class. This latter was an important issue, in that the canons of the major churches, in addition to enjoying lives of great comfort and status, often had a decisive say in determining to whom perpetual lease of ecclesiastical property should be granted.

A second group within the *popolo* consisted of prosperous members of the artisan and shop-keeping class. These men, rarely seeking office as such for themselves, required a more equitable distribution of taxation (from which nobles were frequently exempt), a better administration of the finances of the commune, and some say in matters such as the export of food, which directly concerned their lives. In particular they looked for the impartial administration of justice – one might say the establishment of justice – between noble and non-noble: some system which would guarantee freedom from assault and oppression by the retainers of those claiming to exercise private justice. Finally, all of the *popolo* and many of the nobility themselves had an interest in the establishment of a form of public order which would end faction conflicts and minimise as far as possible the effects of blood-feuds between noble houses. Only from the mid-thirteenth century, and then only in a few cities, did the *popolares* as a whole seek parity or preponderance or the permanent control of political power. Yet most, in the course of the century, came to look for an institutional reorganisation of the commune, some system of representation and control, which would secure order: 'the tranquil and peaceful state of the city'.

Although, occasionally, charismatic figures from quite humble circumstances were to be found among its leaders, the urban poor and agricultural labourers were normally excluded from the *popolo*. Adventurers, demagogues, or idealists from the ranks of the nobility frequently joined its ranks. But broadly speaking membership was confined to the two classes already mentioned. At Milan they were gathered in two separate organisations. Here the *Motta* consisted of the rich seeking admission to the privileges of the ruling group while the *Credenza di Sant' Ambrogio*, in origin at least, was composed of small masters and shopkeepers. Normally, however, the two elements united in one association. Indeed, at Milan, the *Credenza* came, like the *popolo* organisations elsewhere, to be dominated by the rich and powerful.

In the formation of the institutions of the *popolo* three local associations already in existence provided the organisational nucleus. These were the *vicinanza* or neighbourhood ward; (often undistinguishable from it) the *populus* or parish which administered the goods of the local church and elected its priest; and the *arti* or guilds which represented the employers (not the employees) of the trades of the town. Frequently, from the men attached to these groups were also formed 'societies of arms' (*società delle armi*): groups of men pledged to take part, if necessary, in street-fighting. As these groups came together the *popolo* gradually developed its own broader organisation forming itself into a sort of commune, existing side by side with the 'official' commune. It came to have its own statutes, its own elected officials called priors or *anziani* (elders), and, from the 1240s, its 'Captain', often a noble from outside the city, elected for a limited period of office, and corresponding in many other ways to the *podestà* of the commune. Thus constituted, many of the unions of the *popolo* secured between the 1230s and 1270s, if only temporarily, some acknowledged position within the government of their towns. Occasionally, if rarely, the affirmation of their power came about, as at Piacenza in 1250, through some sharp outbreak of revolutionary violence in which the mass of the nobility was confronted by the mass of the people. More normally the *popolo* inserted itself within the organisation of the commune by alliance with a noble faction seeking aid against its rivals.

Typical in this is the case of Parma. In 1244, following an attack upon the house of a prominent noble by a 'society of arms', it had been agreed that 'the consuls' of the ward-associations and of the trades should be called to council. 'Whatsoever the *popolo* wished,' writes the chronicler, 'it had in full'. The events of this year did not at all overthrow the noble monopoly of power in the commune – the Captain of the People at that time was in fact the lord Ugo di San Vitale from one of the oldest houses of the city – but it gave some element of representation to those outside the oligarchy and provided a legitimised precedent for violent action by the *popolo* at time of stress. This was to bear fruit at the end of 1250 when (see p. 108) the imperialist *extrinseci* were readmitted to Parma, and began to plot with Pelavicini in neighbouring Cremona against their rivals in the party of the Church. Warfare between the town nobility seemed inevitable. Yet at this point the threat was dramatically averted by the appearance of one Giovanni Barisello, a tailor, and son of a farmworker in the service of the Tebaldi Lords:

He took a cross in his hands and the Gospels and went through Parma to the houses of those of the imperial party whom he suspected of wishing to betray Parma to Pelavicini and he made them swear to the articles of the lord pope and the party of the Church. And he had a full 500 armed men with him who had him as their captain and followed him almost as their general and prince. And many swore allegiance to the party of the Church and to the precepts of the high and Roman pontiff, some willingly, some through fear, because they saw the armed men. Those who refused to swear left Parma as unwanted guests and went to Borgo San Donnino and lived there.

'A man', wrote Salimbene, savouring his biblical learning, 'poor and wise, had been found in Parma, who freed the city through his wisdom'. Barisello is a surprising phenomenon in this hierarchical world where most of the effective leaders of the people were nobles. Contemporary society responded by trying to turn him into a noble. He was given wealth and a noble wife from the family of the Cornazano. He was admitted to the Council (where 'he had a natural sense and grace in speech') on all occasions without election, and for the next fourteen years was allowed to take his company with him wherever he went. Yet he remained a commoner. In 1264, the *podestà*, the lord Manfredino da Sassuolo of Modena, decided 'for the good name of the men of Parma' that such a man should enjoy influence no more, and ordered him to dismiss his society and put aside his pomp. Barisello, significantly enough, made no objection, went off to his shop, took up needle and thread, and began to sew again.[12]

None the less an armed company of the people, 'the Company of the Crusaders', working in co-operation with the party of the Church and aiming to suppress noble violence by violent measures remained in force. It did not by any means have any full success in this, and yet on certain occasions it gave the *popolo* a base from which to halt threatening conflict. So, in 1291, for instance, the anonymous chronicler, writes, with enigmatic concision:

There was a certain disturbance in Parma, and so four trades, that is, the butchers, the smiths, the shoemakers, and furriers, together with the judges and notaries and the other trades of the city, took oath together to maintain themselves, and, having made certain provisions, all disturbance immediately stopped.[13]

More important than this the societies of arms launched frequent attacks – the *cursus populi* – upon nobles guilty of violence. At Parma the *podestà*, together with the *anziani*, the leaders of the companies, with the 1,000 foot deputed to the task 'with trumpets and banners, to the sound of the bells of the commune in the accustomed way', would march within the city walls or outside to destroy the house of a man held responsible for the murder of or attack upon a *popolano*. Between 1278 and 1298, there are only four years when the chronicler of Parma does not refer to one more of these incursions.

These assaults by the *popolo* no doubt did something to restrain noble violence against lesser men. Yet their very frequency shows that they by no means eliminated it. In their turn they were often little more than exercises in that sectional 'self-help' in law which the nobility claimed. So, for example, in March 1294, a notary of Parma was killed and buried at Olmo in the *contado* by certain men from that village. When, a month later, suspicion of murder came to a head, the notaries of the city suspended all business, closed the doors of the Old Palace of the Commune, and, one hundred in number, went, together with the *anziani*, to the village where they seized two suspects. Brought back to the city, one confessed and was hanged; the other, who, despite severe torture, refused to acknowledge his guilt, was imprisoned for life. The notaries then returned to

Olmo, pronounced a sentence of banishment upon many of the inhabitants, and destroyed the houses, trees, vines, and all possessions, of those banished. It is an incident which underlines the fact that the justice of the *popolo* was extremely rough and ready and often little different in character from the anarchic justice of the nobility.

Nevertheless the aggressive attacks of the Societies of Arms constituted a principal means by which the *popolo* could find its place in the world of the communes. Without violence or the threat of violence nothing would have been achieved. Yet the real test for the *popolo* was not whether it could show its strength by organised, if spasmodic, attacks upon unpopular members of society but whether it could insert itself as a permanent and significant element within the political structure of government. In some towns, on certain occasions, it sought to achieve this by the creation of a temporary dictatorship favourable to its interests. So at Piacenza in 1250, after a revolt against the nobility concerned with the export of grain from the town, Uberto dell' Iniquità was appointed *podestà* of the *popolo* and ruler, for five years, with the understanding that, should he die within that period, the succession should go to his son. (In fact he was deposed in 1252.) Normally such arrangements were made in alliance with members of the noble class. So, at Genoa in 1257, the *popolo* and 'some of the most powerful men in the city' appointed Guglielmo Boccanegra as Captain of the *popolo* and ruler of the city for ten years, with the succession passing to his brother at the event of his death. (He held power until 1262.) The virtue of these arrangements was that they allowed the nominee of the *popolo* to pass legislation in its favour, which, even after the dictator's fall, was easier to leave upon the statute-book than to repeal.

In Parma the role of champion of the *popolo* was filled by Ghiberto de Gente.[14] A knight, he had been captain and standard bearer of those exiles of the party of the Church who had taken the city from the Imperialists in 1247. At that time, though neither wealthy nor of great lineage, he was clearly one who by his personal abilities had become a leader within the oligarchy. Yet five years later, amidst tensions produced by the attempted reconciliation of Church and Imperial partisans, he was given the lordship of Parma, first for ten years, then for life. He had, we are told, 'the aid of the butchers', and, no doubt, of Barisello's society of arms as well. Taking to himself the styles of *podestà, podestà of the merchants*, and *podestà of the popolo*, he ruled the city for six years and eight months (1252–59), and held sway too, though briefly, in Reggio (1253–5). Unfortunately we can view his government only through the eyes of a bitter critic. Salimbene, who normally had very little time for most supporters of *popolani* pretensions, had tried to persuade Ghiberto to join the Franciscan order and on his failure complained bitterly of his *'vilania*, avarice, and crappiness'. As might be expected his account of Ghiberto's government is jaundiced. He accused him of paying himself too much, much more than any *podestà* normally received. (There may be something in this; an initial salary of £I[mperiales] 500 was soon raised to £I.200.) 'Although, before, he was a poor knight', he was said to have 'built two great high palaces from the riches of his fellow-citizens', one in the city, one in his lands in the countryside at Campegine. 'Wishing to magnify his splendour and lordship', he is said to have attempted to make his brother, the Abbot of San Benedetto da Leno, bishop of the city, and to have created a society of 500 men who accompanied him, armed, whenever he wished. 'I've seen these men, armed, on the vigil of the Assumption of the Blessed Virgin, attending him in the interests of his ambition and pomp, honour and boastfulness, as well as for a guard, when he went, as the custom is in Parma, with wax candles to the cathedral'. He is said to have given bad justice, sometimes through personal spite, sometimes simply for money. He spared ill-doers who paid him; he threatened with the law those who failed to do so. He debased the coinage; he established a communal monopoly in the sale of food. These charges may, of course, be justified. But many of them sound like the complaints of nobles at a man who is carrying out the will of the *popolo*. If, for instance, during the great famine of 1258, Ghiberto forbad the private marketing of corn, he was, undoubtedly, striking a blow at the great landlords of the *contado*. Yet at the same time he was saving a lot of commoners from starvation. And one virtue in his rule, even Salimbene had to admit: 'he reduced the citizens of Parma to peace'.

Yet, of course, in one respect Salimbene was undoubtedly correct: it was predictable that any dictator of the *popolo* was going to end up as a tyrant. The alternative to a dictator was that the *popolani* should attempt to work with the commune, to establish their own institutions side by side with those of the commune in a more gradual and peaceable manner. To some this attempt could seem a monstrosity, a reversal of the order of nature. The principle that the noble should be under the rule of law was accepted slowly and with difficulty. Everyone was able to understand why the Marquess Marchesopolo, uncle of Uberto Pelavicini, had gone off to the East to fight the Greeks. 'Since he was noble and of a magnificent heart he disclaimed and could scarce bear that any man of the people, whether from town or country, should, sending a messenger with a red wand, compel him to go to the Palace of the Commune, there to be arraigned in judgment.' In writing of the Bolognesi decrees of 1287 against violent magnates Salimbene, deeply shocked, warned that the *popolo* should be aware of God's anger. '*Populares* and *rustici* destroy the world; knights and nobles preserve it.' It is, he points out, extremely unpleasant when an inferior man rises up, more, a sin which will (see *Deuteronomy*, 28) be punished by God. He recalls two butchers of Cremona. One of them had a great big dog, which was continually tormented by the other's little dog. One day, however, provoked beyond endurance, the big dog had drowned the smaller in the Po. That sort of thing happened in this life to a lot of people who (see *Ecclesiasticus*, 7) if they lived peacefully and didn't busy themselves looking for a quarrel wouldn't get hurt. Divine scripture too defines the worst government as that exercised by women, children, slaves, the stupid, one's enemies, and, finally, the common people.[15]

These sentiments were doubtless common, and probably found some measure of assent among the lower orders themselves. (It is interesting, for instance, that when executing their enemies, the *popolo* hanged commoners but beheaded nobles.) Yet in a few towns during the passing of the century, the *popolo* did succeed in making constitutional gains. In some cities where the nobility did not monopolise all wealth, where trade, finance, industry, or even the presence of a powerful university, produced a complex social structure, the oligarchy was persuaded or compelled to come to terms. No faction could ignore the support which could be offered by an effective and well-organised society of arms of some 500–1,000 men. Provided they were organised, butchers and smiths had in the tools of their trade frightening weapons. Faced by such societies the nobility could discover where its interests lay, and, to a certain extent at least, could find that its own interests blended with those of its inferiors. In foreign war, in war against the *extrinseci*, there was every advantage in having the mass of the population on one's own side. More than this, the governments of the Italian towns, like all governments in contemporary Europe, were deeply concerned with the problem of public order. Though each individual wished to be free from its constraints, most believed that some general system of public justice, which the *popolo* seemed to promise, should be established. As a result – generally against the background of some particularly striking failure in the rule of the oligarchy such as defeat in war or catastrophic blood feud – a council of the *popolo* under its captain would be established side by side with the old 'council of the commune' under its *podestà* as one of the consultative elements in the rule of the towns. Government would then be exercised no longer simply in the name of the commune but by 'the commune and *popolo*'. Sometimes a proportion of offices in the communes was specifically allotted to *popolares*. In some cities the *anziani*, elected by the *popolo*, came to be consulted on all policies undertaken by the government; in others, they were considered to be the supreme authority and decision-making body within it.

In towns where the *popolo* achieved such control the problem of noble violence was frequently attacked in a much more radical manner than hitherto. Certain men were declared to be 'magnates' and severe discriminatory legal and political penalties were decreed against them. How a magnate was defined was extremely imprecise. The Statutes of Bologna, for example, characteristically dissolve into incoherence on this point; he was:

any noble, tenant-in-chief (*capitaneus*), or vavassor, or of noble family, or the family of a knight, *or of a family from which there may or will be any knight*, or anyone in the highest positions of any land or village in the *contado*.

In fact, many nobles were exempt from magnate status and several men who were not noble were assigned to it. In their own minds the legislators knew at whom they were aiming: men who were both powerful and violent, families with a reputation for violence. In practice public fame created the magnate; the *popolo* resolved any legal question by drawing up lists of those families they considered to be magnates. So, following the insurrection of the *popolo* at Modena in 1306 (a revolt to be sustained in fact for only a brief period) the names of men from eighty families were recorded as 'those who are not worthy to be in the present *popolo*, and they are written in the present book not as nobles and powerful men but because they are not worthy to be in the present *popolo*'.[16] Families designated as magnates were then generally required to produce bail for good behaviour, were subject to discriminatory penalties for violence against *popolani*, and were excluded from public office.

III

The *popolo* took different forms and experienced different fortunes in each commune. Florence provides one example of a city in which it enjoyed considerable success.

Here, by the middle of the thirteenth century, the dominant element within the *popolo* was an elite class drawn from the guilds. To be a guildsman was already to be in some measure privileged since membership was confined to fully-fledged masters of trades and professions; all other workers were simply *sottoposti*, subject to, but not members of, the association. Not all guilds again were equal. Those of the artisans whose masters enjoyed only modest wealth carried little weight. Real power lay with the seven major arts (*Arti maggiori*). These were the judges and notaries (*Giudici e notai*), men whose training gave them expertise in government; the *Calimala*, whose members specialised in foreign cloth-trade, the import of wool from France and England, and banking; the *Arte di Cambio* of the moneychangers; and the *Arte di Por S. Maria* of those who dealt in local silk and traded overseas in silk, cotton and linens. Behind these came the *Arte dei medici e speziali*, of doctors and apothecaries; the *Arte della Lana* with some international traders in wool; and the *Arte di vaia e Pellicciai* of the fur-dealers.

Even in these major guilds, only a small minority of guildsmen enjoyed any significant position. In the first place each was a composite organisation, incorporating a wide variety of other, often very humble, trades, whose members had little to say in the policy of the guild as a whole. In the *Medici e speziali*, for example, were included not only doctors and apothecaries (who themselves were often overseas merchants in spices) but saddlers, packdealers, hatters, nail makers, painters of pictures, and dealers in small goods. Looking at the Florentine *popolo* and guild system as a whole the men who dominated above all were such wealthy banking and cloth-exporting families of the *Calimala* as the Mozzo, Spini, Frescobaldi, Bardi, Cerchi, Acciaiuoli, and Falconieri. These, the *popolani grassi*, did indeed from time to time put forward the demands of lesser guild members. Yet what they sought above all was the satisfaction of their own ambitions vis-à-vis the oligarchy.

That oligarchy was divided between the party of the Church (the *parte guelfa*), dominated by the Donati, Adimari, Visdomini, Tosinghi, Tornaquinci, Buondelmonti, Chiermontesi, and Cavalcanti clans, and the party of the Empire, composed by the Uberti, Fifanti, Amidei, Caponsacchi, and Lamberti. It was this division which first opened the way to the power of the *popolo*. In 1244, the Ghibelline Uberti and their allies, threatened by the Guelf party, sought to gain the support of the *popolo* by incorporating the priors, or leaders of the seven major guilds, within the councils of the city. This was merely a temporary expedient and soon abandoned. But six years later, in September 1250, when the Ghibellines marched out to engage the Guelf *extrinseci* in battle at Figline, the *popolo*, organised in twenty local companies, seized control. When the Guelf nobility, triumphant in battle, re-entered Florence, they were forced to come to terms with the new power. The *podestà* still presided over the old Council of the Commune but, side by side with this, a new General Council was established,

119

presided over by a Captain of the People. Membership of this council was based upon representation from the six local divisions (*sesti*) of the city.

This constitution, the rule of the *primo popolo*, lasted for only some ten to thirteen years. The Guelf nobility and the leaders of the *popolo* who had come to ally closely with them were defeated in battle at Montaperti in 1260, and the Ghibelline nobles who then reassumed power reverted to oligarchical government. Although the guilds rose against the Ghibellines in 1266 and were then instrumental in securing the return of the Guelfs, they played no formal part in government between 1267 and 1282. Charles of Anjou, who ruled the city as *signore*, made no effort to revive a constitution with *popolani* councils. Yet within these years the nobility itself was undergoing a profound transformation. The powerful *popolani* banking families of the *Calimala*, in return for their aid to King Charles, received from him economic privileges, were given political office in the commune and the *parte guelfa*, were dubbed knights; were in short assimilated to the ruling class. At the same time certain among the old oligarchical families, notably the Abbati, Tornaquinci, Adimari, Lamberti, Chiermontesi, and Caponsacchi, took to banking and themselves became members of the Calimala.

At this point it might have seemed that the aspirations of the majority of the *popolo* were to be thwarted. The old Guelf nobility, following the classic strategy of admitting the leaders of the opposition to their ranks, had seemed to triumph. What prevented this was the outbreak of new feuds within the reconstituted oligarchy. Guelfs still fought Ghibellines, now, too, Guelfs fought Guelfs, as the Donati came into conflict with the Adimari and the Pazzi. These rivalries, once again, gave the *popolo* its opportunity. A section among the Guelfs turned for aid to the *Arti Maggiori*; the Ghibellines sought to redress the balance by looking to the lower guilds. Out of this contest for support the *popolo* was re-established in September 1282, not simply as an equal power alongside the commune, but as the arbiter of government. The seven major guilds, together with five of lesser importance (the *Arti Medie* or middle guilds: the Butchers, Shoemakers, Smiths, Stone-masons, and Second-hand Dealers), were empowered to elect every two months from their members six priors who would rule the city as supreme magistrates. At the same time the General Council and the Captaincy of the People were revived.

Such were the constitutional arrangements. Yet in the years which followed the re-establishment of the *popolo* can have seemed to have brought very little change in the character of government and very little amelioration of noble violence. The guilds came to be dominated by nobles who enrolled in them in large numbers; and the new Priors were almost exclusively the agents of the Guelf–Calimala oligarchy. Again, noble blood-feuds intensified. To meet this, in 1281 and again in 1286 the experiment had been tried of requiring 'magnates' to raise bail as security for their good behaviour. It was a move which had little effect. 'Citizens carried out many murders and killings and outrages, one against the other', Villani writes, 'and in particular the nobles called *grandi* and powerful used force and violence against the persons of those without power and seized their goods both in the *contado* and the city'.[17]

It was in these circumstances, and against the background of financial crisis precipitated by a ten-year-long war against Arezzo and Pisa, that Giano della Bella, a noble from an old family of the Calimala, re-mobilised the *popolo* against the ruling class. Although he held the office of Prior for only one two-month period, yet for two years (February 1293–March 1295) he was the moving spirit behind the *popolo* and virtual dictator of the city. This was the period, a notary remarked, 'when Giano della Bella was held almost as lord of the city of Florence, and commonly did what he wished with it'. His power-base rested almost wholly upon lower elements in the *popolo*. In the period of his rule the offices of the city were largely in the hands of the middle guilds. The representatives of the upper guilds and the Calimala were virtually excluded. He allied with nine lesser guilds (the *Arti minori*: Bakers, Tanners, Innkeepers, and so on) and incorporated them into the guild militia. With this support he moved to an attack upon the nobility.

This attack took two forms. In the field of administration Giano sought to eliminate frauds in the accounting of government funds, to recover communal property appropriated by noble families, and to confiscate the goods of the *parte guelfa* to the commune. Second, following Siennese and Bolognesi precedents, he worked to exclude the violent from government and to place them under the rule of law. By the *Ordinances of Justice* of January 1293, the members of 152 families were declared to be magnates. No magnate, it was decreed, could be elected as prior, could sit in the council of the captain, or could be consul or rector of a guild. Each magnate was forced to swear a special oath of obedience and to give a bond of £2,000 that he would keep the peace. If a magnate wounded a *popolano*, he or – if he could not be apprehended – his kin could be fined up to £2,000. If he killed a *popolano* he would be sentenced to death, the confiscation of his goods, and the destruction of his house. In evidence the word of a *popolano* was to be accepted as true against the word of any magnate. To enforce the sentences a militia of 1,000 men was created under an elected 'Standard-bearer of Justice' (*Gonfaloniere*) who now sat side by side with the priors in their two-month period of office. Later in August 1294, a special prison, 'La Pagliazza', was built to house guilty magnates. Not all men defined at this time as magnates were noble. Some noble families, such as the Albizzi, Peruzzi, Medici, della Scala, and Chiermontesi, to whom belonged members not backward in violence were not included among the lists of magnates, either because they were popular with the people, or were allied personally to Giano della Bella. But, these apart, virtually the whole of the old oligarchy was subject to these particular political and legal penalties.

Giano's power ended at the beginning of March 1295. The magnates struck back, the lower guilds were too confused to come to his aid, and he was forced into exile. Of his personality and motives we know little. He pursued in office his own vendetta against the Abbati family, and doubtless he was no unstained hero. Yet for a future generation he was to be 'the loyalest and most upright *popolano* and lover of the common good of any man in Florence, and one who gave to the commonwealth, and took nothing from it'; or as Giovanni Villani, again, was to put it, he was one of those, like Farinata Uberti and Dante Alighieri, who, ill-treated by the city, were yet 'leaders and sustainers of the people'.[18]

These are remarkable judgments for at first sight Giano's dictatorship seems a transitory phenomenon. Personal factions within the nobility continued. 'The Whites' under Vieri Cerchi waged war with 'the Blacks' under Corso Donati; and when the Whites were finally expelled, the Blacks turned, in the customary pattern, to fighting among themselves. More than this, the regime which came to power in 1295 emended the Ordinances of Justice to allow magnates to enroll in the guilds, as such to enter many of the councils of the city, and so to hold a measure of political power. Yet in two respects Giano's work was decisive. In the first place magnates, the violent nobles and their families were marked with a deep stigma. However little proceeded against in everyday life, they were condemned by law and public opinion; were seen as hostile to the city, and penalised accordingly. More than this Giano's brief political career ensured the continuance of a system in which supreme power rested and was acknowledged to rest with priors who were elected predominantly by the *popolo*.

IV

The experience of Florence was not typical. The number of towns where, in fact, effective *popolo* control existed for any significant period of time was small. In the Veneto one singles out Padua; in Lombardy, Cremona and Brescia; in Liguria, Genoa; in Emilia, Parma and Bologna; in Umbria, Perugia. The movement was most effective in Tuscany, where one can point to Florence, Prato, Pistoia, Lucca, and Siena. It should be added that by the 1380s most of these towns were either ruled by *signori* (Padua, Cremona, Brescia, Parma) or threatened by signorial rule (Bologna, Genoa) or absorbed by another commune (Prato, Pistoia).

While they survived, however, they were capable of broadening the base of government. One must be careful to delimit what this implied. It is true that in fourteenth-century Florence, for instance, a large number of citizens, perhaps one in five adult males, were eligible to take part in some form of political activity, had the right to vote for councillors, and the right to be elected to office. Yet this did not imply any general participation by them in political life. From the time of Giano della Bella, as Villani pointed out, 'the artisans and little people had little power in the commune'. Henceforth the overwhelming majority of the major offices in the city were to be held by the *popolani grassi*, the leaders of the upper guilds, and their clients. So, too, at Siena in the same period a mere sixty families out of a total town population of perhaps 50,000 genuinely affected political decision. None the less, in these centres individual access to the oligarchy did not depend merely upon wealth. Political ability and ambition could, as in Dante's day, and for men like Dante who came from families which enjoyed no particularly impressive status, open the way to the highest offices. During the fourteenth century 'New Men' are to be found within the oligarchies and continued to provoke (quite misleadingly, for they were always in a minority) complaints that, 'we are ruled now by the dregs'. A certain socio-political mobility did exist.

Moreover, within these towns, the creation of a specific magnate class, excluded from formal participation in supreme power and assigned to a position of judicial inferiority, was a repudiation of that violence in social life associated with the old nobility. That a noble who achieved office in Genoa had to resign his nobility, that in fourteenth-century Florence many magnate houses secured permission to change their names, renounce their nobility, and be enrolled within the *popolo*, might seem, at first sight, of little significance. When the Tornaquinci began to call themselves Tornabuoni or the Cavalcanti Cavallereschi, they remained the same men and possessed the same wealth and power. Yet the symbolic significance of the change was important; it implied their identification with public order and a social ethos in which noble violence was checked and punished. Describing Florence in the years around 1338 Giovanni Villani remarks that there were 1,500 'noble and powerful citizens' who, under the Ordinances of Justice, gave bail for their good behaviour. He goes on to observe that the number of fully-dubbed knights had fallen from 250 before 1293 to seventy-five and explains this by saying that with the establishment of *popolo* government few became knights, since 'the *grandi* had neither state nor Lordship as before'. It was now the violent noble who assimilated to the wealthy *popolano*; not, as in the 1260s, the reverse. Effective access to power rested now with a patriciate consisting of wealthy merchants and non-magnate nobles who gave an at least formal adherence to the idea that government should be in the interest of all citizens who were members of the guilds (i.e. moderately prosperous). Hence the *popolo* represented an extension of the power of government, not only because it gave, if only formally, a broader basis of representation and consent, but also because it provided a focus for all those who sought to establish a unified and coherent social order against the individualist, often anarchic, noble factions of the earlier commune.

This did not, by any means, imply the total extinction of violence. In the *Statutes of the Podestà* at Florence of 1325 (repeated in 1356 and 1415, and found in substance in all towns) both judges and Executors of the Ordinances of Justice were expressly forbidden to proceed against men making 'lawful' vendetta. Vengeance became 'lawful' when the offence was manifest, when the vengeance was *condecens* or appropriate, when taken against the offender's children only when the offender was dead, and when carried out by the offended man's family within the degree of fourth-cousinship. In the middle of the fourteenth century the blood-feud could still on occasions be almost a spectator sport, as a diary-entry of Luca di Totto da Panzano makes clear:

Memorial, how I went to Prato to kill Carlo di Baldovinetto Gherardini. Sunday, after the sounding of nones, on the 13th day of June 1350, I heard from some trusted friends how Carlo di Baldovinetto Gherardini . . . was in the church of S. Margherita at Mintisci, of which he was patron . . . many people, my friends, went there immediately to my aid . . . and we laid siege to it . . . we put fire under the campanile and burnt two large parts of it and destroyed all the roofing . . . and the battle lasted until sunset . . . and more than 5,000 people from Florence and the *contado* came to watch, and there came all the officials of messer Andrease Rossi of Parma, who was *podestà,* and all the officials of Guadagno di ser Lando of Gubbio, his assessor, and there came Ser Nuto from Città di

Castello, a proud constable, with many troops. And when he came he gave orders that we should go away and that we should leave him to fight Carlo (who had been outlawed by the commune) and the other group there . . . But we were so strong that we just laughed at him . . . and they, willingly and with much courtesy, left us to our business.[19]

Again, studies in Florence suggest that the administration of the Ordinances of Justice, in so far as they touched upon noble violence against *popolani*, was weakened by a judicial system in which continual dispensations of sentences were offered and some 15 per cent of regular condemnations were pardoned outright. Hence, particularly in the *contado*, noble brigandage was endemic, and the continual usurpation of lay and ecclesiastical property was difficult to prevent. None the less, as the century continued, one senses in those communes where the *popolo* had achieved real success, a distinct strengthening of public order.

Meanwhile, though forbidden to accede to the highest offices, the magnates of these communes still enjoyed great influence. They became partners with *popolani* in business enterprises. They filled important posts in embassies, as judges, as captains of the *contado* and as captains of the *popolo* (a post which, characteristically, was virtually monopolised by nobles) and *podestà* in neighbouring communes. They remained the military leaders of the communes even in the heigh-day of the *condottieri*; and their social glamour never failed.

'The triumph of the *popolo*', that is, was a limited phenomenon, even in those few towns where true *popolo* control endured. In some towns, like Ferrara and – above all Venice – the *popolo* never came into being. Elsewhere, in, that is, the majority of the towns, its role was severely restricted. As characteristic one might take Modena, where in the 1220s the pressure of a Society of Arms was able to establish the admission of the rectors of the guilds and the consuls of the Society of Arms themselves to the Council of the Commune. Later indeed there were two brief and unstable periods of *popolo* rule (1249–64 and 1271–87). But in a town such as this, where there was no large-scale trade, banking, or industry, where such shops or artisan business as there were had been often established and maintained by noble capital, it was inevitable that all patronage and social control should remain with the oligarchy, and that any prominent *popolano* could be either assimilated into the noble class or terrorised or bribed into acquiescence in full noble control. Hence, from an early date, members of the oligarchy came to dominate the organisations of the *popolo*. In towns such as these the power of the lower orders, at best, was henceforth manifested, as at Modena in 1306, only by some sudden revolution which might establish a temporary regime, might pronounce severe penalties against magnates, but which, within a year, its original impetus lost, would surrender again to the rule of the party-leaders.

This is not to say that the movement was wholly insignificant. During the fourteenth century most governments claimed to rule 'on behalf of the commune and *popolo*'. Everywhere the ranks of the governing class had been enlarged by the arrival of newly-enriched families, a process perhaps inevitable, yet probably speeded-up by pressure of the societies and guilds. In most towns, the fiscal privileges of nobles were abolished or diminished. At Verona, for example, it had been decreed in 1228 that both knights who held arms and horses for the defence of the commune and, too, 'those noblemen who through poverty do not maintain horses and arms' should be free from the hearth-tax. By the 1270s, however, it was laid down that in respect of taxation, 'no-one shall in future be held to be a noble'.[20] In general, the rise of the *libra* or property-tax in the thirteenth century made for a tax system which was more equitable between classes. Almost everywhere captains of the *popolo* and priors or *anziani* and general councils gave legal authentication to the acts of the commune. Almost everywhere a large number of middling citizens, prosperous masters of trades and shopkeepers, had now some claim to give their votes for those who would speak in councils, and might, at times, be able to speak in council themselves.

One would not, of course, make too much of these changes. Burdened with earning a living, most *popolani* of small towns could not, and rarely wished to, concern themselves continuously with political life, and they had real cause to beware of making enemies of powerful men. Those powerful men remained in control. Again, as the functions of government extended, it was perhaps inevitable that the machinery of consultation of the governed should have extended, whether or not there had been a *popolo* revolution. It is instructive, in this respect, to consider the government of the towns of the Neapolitan kingdom in the fourteenth century.[21] In the city of Naples itself the two *piazze* or administrative divisions of Capuano and Nido, in which were gathered those members of the nobility established in the city before the coming of the Angevins, held a third of the offices. The nobles of more recent settlement, assigned to the *piazze* of Montagnana, Portanuova, and Porto, together with the *popolo* in the other forty-three *piazze*, held the remaining two-thirds. By *popolano*, King Robert explained in this context: 'we understand those normally called *grasso* and not the *popolo minuto* and artisans who are not accustomed, and for whom it would not be becoming, to be involved in unwonted burdens and honours'. In the other towns there were similar divisions of power between *nobiliores, mediocres* (i.e. *popolo grasso*, jurists, notaries, and doctors), and *minores* (*popolo minuto*). Decisions on the division of taxation here were normally taken by a committee consisting of two *nobiliores*, two *mediocres*, and two *minores*. Again, although the Neapolitan nobility was exempt from taxation on their feudal possessions, they were liable for payment on non-feudal properties.

In the kingdom, that is to say, the non-noble classes enjoyed most of the benefits brought by the *popolo* to the majority of the towns of the North. The real virtue of the movement perhaps was, outside centres like Florence, mainly symbolic. It gave to the independent communes the traditional theoretical role of a king in his kingdom; it caused them to acknowledge, or at least to give lip-service to, the idea that they ruled in the interest of the governed classes. Be that as it may, in one respect the movement of the *popolo* in most towns failed. It was unable to bring about that 'peaceful and tranquil state' in society which had been so prominent a feature in its original formation. This failure was crucial.

NOTES

On **conflict between nobles** see J. K. Hyde, 'Contemporary views on faction and civil strife in Thirteenth and Fourteenth century Italy'; R. Brentano, 'Violence, Disorder and Order in Thirteenth-century Rome'; L. Martines, 'Political violence in the Thirteenth Century', all in *Violence and Disorder in the Italian Cities 1200–1500*, ed. L. Martines, Los Angeles, 1972; and G. Masi, 'Sull 'origine dei Bianchi e dei Neri', *Giornale dantesco*, 30, 1927.

On **the popolo** there is no overall study. See, however, G. de Vergottini, *Arti e popolo nella prima metà del secolo XIII*, Milan, 1943; I. Ghiron, 'La Credenza di S. Ambrogio; *Archivio storico lombardo*, 3s. iv, 1876; and E. Cristiani, *Nobiltà e popolo nel comune de Pisa dalle origini del podestariato alla signoria di Donoratico*, Naples, 1962. For **the popolo in Florence**, B. Stahl, *Adel und Volk im Florentiner Dugento*, Cologne, 1965, gives a more satisfactory account than either G. Salvemini, *Magnati e popolani in Firenze*, Florence, 1899, or N. Ottokar, *Il comune di Firenze alla fine del dugento*, Florence, 1926, though both works still have their value.

On **magnates** there is G. Fasoli, 'La legislazione antimagnatizia a Bologna', *Rivista di storia e diritto italiano*, vi, 1933; *idem*, 'Ricerche sulla legislazione antimagnatizia nei comuni dell' alta e media Italia', *ibid.*, xii, 1939; N. Rubinstein, *La lotta contra i magnati a Firenze*, Florence, 1939; G. Pampaloni, 'I magnati a Firenze alla fine del dugento', *ASI*, 1972; M. B. Becker, 'A study in political failure: The Florentine Magnates 1280–1343', *Medieval Studies*, xxvii, 1965.

1. *Quellen und Forschungen zur ältesten Geschichte der Stadt Florenz*, Marburg 1875, ii, 221ff. Cf. G. Villani, *Cronica, cit.*, V, 38; *Paradiso*, xvi, 140–7; *Inferno*, xxviii, 103–11.
2. See Hyde, 'Contemporary views', *cit.* I exclude here the views found in the chronicle of Dino Compagni, for whom see note 8 to chapter 1.
3. Salimbene, *cit.*, p. 857.
4. For these events, Salimbene (who was in Reggio at the time, and leans to the Upper party), *cit.*, pp. 772–9, 895–9, 917–47 and *Continuatio regina libri de temporibus* (*MGH. SS*, xxxi), pp. 572–7 (whose author gives greater sympathy to the Lower).
5. D. Moreni, *Notizie istoriche dei contorni di Firenze*, Florence, 1795, vi, pp. 77–81.
6. Salimbene, *cit.*, pp. 776–7; Dante, *Convivio* iv, xvi, 6; *Inferno*, xx, 118–20.
7. *Annales Bergomates* (*MGH. SS*, xxxi) ed. O. Holder-Egger, pp. 331–2.
8. See note 4.
9. Rolandino, *cit.*, p. 47.
10. *idem*, p. 22.
11. *Continuatio regina, cit.*, p. 573.
12. *Chronicon Parmense*, ed. G. Bonazzi (*RIS*. ix, 9) p. 13; Salimbene, *cit.*, pp. 538–42.
13. *Chronicon Parmense, cit.*, p. 62.
14. Salimbene, *cit.*, pp. 649–54. The *Chronicon Parmense, cit.*, pp. 20–1 is disappointingly laconic on him. See, however, *Statuta Communis Parmae digesta MCCLV* (Mon. Hist. ad provincias Parmensem et Placentinam pertinentia), Parma, 1855, pp. 211–26. I. Affò, *Storia della città di Parma*, vol. iii, Parma, 1793, adds something, *Appendice*, lxxiv, lxxx vi–vii.
15. Salimbene, *cit.*, pp. 547, 937–9, 942.
16. E. P. Vicini, 'Il "Liber nobilium et potentum" della città di Modena del 1306', *R. Dept. di st. pat. per l'Emilia e Romagna; Studi e Documenti*, Modena, 1939, pp. 166–88.

17. G. Villani, *cit.*, viii, 1.
18. G. Villani, *cit.*, viii, 8; xii, 44.
19. 'Frammenti della cronaca di messer Luca di Totto da Panzano', *Giornale storico degli archivi toscani*, v, 1861, pp. 62, 64–5.
20. E. Salzer, *Uber die Anfänge der Signorie in Oberitalien*, Berlin, 1900, p. 12, n. 26.
21. Caggese, *Roberto d'Angiò, cit.*, i, p. 275.

CHAPTER SEVEN

Party-leaders and *signori*

How could public order be restored within the commune? The answer which almost everyone seized upon was the establishment of a dictatorship in the Roman sense, a temporary grant of sole power to one man who would bring peace between rivals and, this achieved, retire into an honoured private life. It has been seen how the *popolo* at Piacenza and Parma had sought this solution in their election to supreme power of Uberto dell' Iniquità and Ghiberto da Gente respectively. Clerics, too, thought along the same lines. In the revivalist 'Alleluia' peace movement of 1233, when Fra Gherardo of Modena arrived at Parma or Fra Giovanni da Vicenza came to the cities of the Veneto, their first request was that such absolute authority might be bestowed upon them. Sometimes again the oligarchy would call in powerful outsiders to bring stability – men like Manfredo II Lancia, appointed as 'Lord' of Milan for three years in 1252, or Charles of Anjou who assumed the virtual lordship of Florence and Lucca for six years in 1267.

King Charles was himself, of course, a party-leader on a grand scale. With whatever intentions such men first came to power, it was soon borne in upon them that they could fight faction only by the contradictory process of allying with a faction. It was so much easier for them to become party-leaders than to seek to maintain the ideals of the commune. And for most party-leaders, peace was to be achieved only by war. Their aims were to seize power, drive out rivals, and establish themselves as *de facto* heads of their towns in the name of their own parties, not for a limited time, not under the constraints of any constitutional formula, but simply for as long as their power endured.

There were two notable examples of this phenomenon in the first half of the century: the Traversari family, who ruled Ravenna from *c.* 1210 to 1240; and Salinguerra Torelli, who dominated Ferrara from 1222 to 1240. From the late 1230s single-person rule, often arising from the grant or conquest of power in the name or under the pretence of the general imperial or ecclesiastical interest, became more frequent. It was, for instance, in large part as a nominee of pro-ecclesiastical parties that Azzo VII d'Este was imposed as ruler of Ferrara in 1240. Azzo d'Este, again, in alliance with Count Sambonifaccio of Verona, held Mantua against the imperialists from 1253 to 1269. Men such as these worked

128

through the traditional machinery of the commune. Sometimes they appointed themselves to be *podestà*, sometimes to be Captains of the *popolo* (as, bizarrely, the most noble Azzo VII did at Mantua). At other times they simply left the office to nominees or relied upon their clients in the councils to secure the decisions they required. The true basis of their power was not institutional but rested upon their own strength, upon their ability to crush or intimidate rivals.

The treaty drawn up against Ezzelino in June 1259 spells out, albeit unconsciously, what had happened. Agreement here was made between:

the illustrious man, the lord Uberto Pelavicini, lord and *podestà* of Cremona, and the distinguished man the Lord Buoso da Doara, and the Commune of Cremona, *that is to say the party of the Barbarasi, which now is the commune of Cremona and rules Cremona* . . . on the one hand . . . and the illustrious man lord Azzo, by grace of God and the apostolic see, Marquess of Este and Ancona, and the magnificent man Lodovico, Count of Verona, and the communes of Mantua, Ferrara, and Padua, *that is to say the Party of the said lord Marquess and Lord Count, and those who now rule the same cities and communes* . . . on the other.[1]

The commune was now identified with the party, and the party was identified with the party-leader. Historians have frequently defined such men as 'the first signori'. But the character of their government was different from that of the signori of the fourteenth century, and it is more helpful in some ways to consider them as the last rulers of the communes, as men who, normally working within, though contemptuously transcending the old institutional frameworks, revealed the final bankruptcy of the communal system.

II

Most famous or most notorious among them was Ezzelino III da Romano. His family had entered Italy with the Ottonians in the tenth century and by the beginning of the thirteenth was (see Map I and pp. 83–6) one of the four most important landed houses of the Trevisan March. In that area (the cities and *contadi* of Treviso, Verona, Vicenza, and Padua) political life was, by the 1220s, dominated, above all else, by a blood-feud between the da Romano and Camposampiero families. The origins of this division, it was said, lay in the tender aspirations of Gerardo da Camposampiero of Padua to the hand of the wealthy heiress, Cecilia da Albano. In pressing his suit the ingenuous Gerardo had invoked the aid of his uncle, Ezzelino II, and was understandably disconcerted when Ezzelino himself succeeded in marrying her. Distraught at this offence to his affections, his honour, and his purse, the young Camposampiero brooded on revenge. Meeting by chance one day with his erstwhile love, now aunt, he was able to satisfy his resentment by, as some have it, seducing or, as others prefer, raping the object of his onetime lawful passion. Pausing only to repudiate the spouse who had exposed herself to this insult to his honour, Ezzelino demanded from the commune of Padua that it should avenge him upon its vassal. But the indifferent or timorous citizens refused to act.

Though Ezzelino soothed in some part the angry wounds to his sensitivity by taking as concubine Maria, of the Camposampiero family, his wrath against the city and his nephew was unabated. Such at least was the story as contemporaries believed it and, if it be not true, this tale with its intermingling of rivalry for property, feud through affronted honour, its noble violence, its communal impotence, encapsulates at least a symbolic truth. (And suggests, too, that the *domney* of the Provençal poets was not wholly platonic nor some mere expression of wish-fulfilments, wholly unrelated to life.) However this may be, as a result of some quarrel between the two families the nobility of the March between the Alps and the Po, between Treviso and Verona was divided. With the da Romano stood the Torelli of Ferrara; the Count of Vicenza, Uguccione Maltraversi; the Count of Tyrol; the Poltroni and Calorosi in Mantua; the Montecchi and 'the party of the Eighty' in Verona. Against this faction stood 'the party of the Marquess d'Este' to which Camposampiero belonged; the Count of Sambonifaccio and his clients; the Crescenzii and Turisendi in Verona; the Zanicali and Gaffari in Mantua; the Vivaro and Pilii in Vicenza. This is only to mention a few names. By bonds of marriage, clientage, self-interest, the whole of the nobility was by 1225 interlocked in an ever-expanding struggle. Though at any moment the allegiance of individuals might, through new offences or new hopes of gain, be transferred, the conflict itself was to continue for the next thirty years.

Such was the inheritance of Ezzelino III, a central position in a vast chain of local hatreds, a commitment to a continuous struggle for pre-eminence, waged now in one city, now in another, now in the *castelli* of the countryside. From 1225, with the aid of the Montecchi and 'the party of the Eighty', he had established control over Verona, and made it the centre of his power. When the Second Lombard League decided that it was more advantageous to retain the allegiance of 'the party of the Marquess' than that of his own faction, he abandoned their alliance and enrolled in the imperial cause. His reward came in May 1236 when Gebhard von Arnstein arrived at Verona, bringing to his aid 500 German knights and 100 crossbowmen. With this support Vicenza and Padua fell into Ezzelino's hands. For the following twenty years he was the dominant power in the March.

During this period there was no distinct office which he exercised within the imperial administration. It was only from 1242 that he actually assumed the title of 'Vicar of the March', and it is not clear what this implied. It was characteristic of him to be uninterested in titles. His role was simply exercised as 'captain and councillor of the imperial party' and as one who, married to the emperor's illegitimate daughter, Selvaggia (March 1238), was supposed to enjoy imperial confidence. In each town (in Padua to 1256; in Vicenza, Verona, and, by alliance with the Counts of Tyrol and Gorizia, in Trent until his death in 1259), he acted simply as a party leader, refusing office himself, yet intimidating the councils into electing his chosen officials and following his commands. At no time, that is to say, did he repudiate the formal mechanism of the communal system. In all the March, Rolandino tells us, through reverence, love, or fear, men called him simply 'the Lord'. Yet he asked for no legal acknowledgment of lordship. He was wholly indifferent to institutions, had no wish to be anything more than a party-leader, which is to say that he had no interest in building for the future, no interest in anything outside the gaining and retention of power for its own sake.

His enemies asserted that he ruled solely through terror:

He was feared more than the devil, for he held it as nothing to kill men, women and children, and he exercised unheard of cruelties . . . long would it be to speak of his cruelties, for they require a great book. I certainly believe that as the son of God wished to have one special friend whom he made like himself, that is to say, the blessed Francis, so did the devil create Ezzelino.

Can one believe such judgments or are they simply a part of history as written by the victors? It is curious, after an outburst such as this, to find Salimbene writing of Fra Bonaventura de Iseo that he was 'a friar, old in age and in the order, most wise and of a holy life and loved by Ezzelino'. (And one recalls a fourteenth-century Lombard tradition of him: 'fierce against enemies, sweet to his friends, firm in his promises, soft in his words, far-seeing in counsel, in every matter he seemed a distinguished knight'.)[2] On balance one concludes that the propaganda campaign launched against him by the Papacy at the time of the north-Italian crusade was likely to have been highly coloured yet not too far from the truth. The terror he inspired appears most strongly in men's asides: in the astrologer Guido Bonatti's references to the evidence of his cruelty or in Salimbene's remark on a jester who had mocked Frederick II: 'If he'd made a joke like that to Ezzelino he'd have had his eyes gouged out or been hanged.' Even though some element of hidden propaganda may not be absent, one senses again the atmosphere of his rule in a letter written by the Priors of S. Agata and S. Maria of Padua to the council of Lübeck. The councillors had asked them to engage an Italian canon and civil lawyer for their town; the priors reply that they had indeed found two men prepared to consider the offer:

but they were unable to obtain a licence from the Lord Ezzelino da Romano, who has been appointed vicar of King Conrad in the March of Treviso and Lombardy. They would like to go, but it is the custom of the Lord Ezzelino that when anyone disobeys his commands he executes vengeance both upon the culprit and his families. He imprisons them, confiscates all their goods, and delivers them to a captivity from which they are never freed.[3]

There seems a supreme pointlessness in his life: for what, in all those years, was he fighting and killing? Not for the empire, to whom his allegiance was barely half-given, nor for the sake of his children, for he had none. (Rolandino hints at a bastard, but almost all the other chroniclers remark on his freedom from lust and indifference to women; significant material for the psycho-analyst, perhaps, might be the remark of the *cronaca* of Brescia that 'it was believed that he had never lain with a woman'.) In accusing him of heresy the Papacy flattered, for the heretic must have some form of inner life outside the egotism of aristocratic honour and drive for power. He appears simply as a sterile force, the brand of fire, as Dante saw him, that had wasted the Trevisan March, doomed to an eternity in the river of boiling blood in the seventh circle of the *Inferno*.

It would, of course, be preposterous to equate all the rulers of the communes with Ezzelino. Yet in most towns the reality of what the thirteenth-century commune had come to mean – rule by an unstable tyrant – was symbolised by him. The character of what the commune's political life had come to mean is encapsulated too, in, the story of the end of the da Romano family: the massacre of San Zenone. Ezzelino's brother, Alberico da Romano, had not joined with him in the imperial alliance. Instead he had seized Treviso and from there had fought on the side of 'the party of the Marquess d'Este' for twenty-three years. Finally, however, in 1257 he had sought reconciliation with Ezzelino. As a result, two years later he was banned with his brother as an enemy of the North-Italian crusade. Cardinal Ottaviano preached the holy war against him with all the publicity resources of the age. At Venice he had led on to piazza Santa Maria, naked, the ladies Alberico was said to have dishonoured, and in their presence had told the citizens of his lust and cruelty; so that they, appalled, cried out: 'Burn him alive, with his wife, and wipe out all his line'. And the cardinal had agreed. The crusaders caught up with Alberico at the ancient da Romano castle at San Zenone. There are many descriptions of what happened when it surrendered. We may follow that which turns the stomach least, the account given by Rolandino, whose words seem borne out by a fresco then triumphantly painted within Treviso's Palazzo del Consiglio. First, one by one, Alberico's male children were beheaded and torn to pieces. Then his wife and two daughters were burnt alive. Finally the father, having been forced to witness the death agonies of his family, was dragged at the tail of a horse until he died.

What is one to make of this incident? The particular refinements of cruelty were gratuitous, merely symbols of a good vendetta. But the deaths of the whole family were strictly necessary as acts of policy. No one could be left alive from the da Romano family to make vendetta or to bear a child who might make vendetta. This consideration is strongly emphasised by Rolandino in the speech, clearly designed as an *apologia* for the crusaders, which in his chronicle he puts in the mouth of Alberico before his final surrender. Here Alberico is made to tell his family of the great party they still have in Lombardy, in the castles of the Altopiano d'Asiago and with the Counts of Mangona in Tuscany. Accordingly:

You dearest loved children of this noble house, live and be my heirs. If any of you should happen to escape the hands of your enemies, may you manfully preserve yourself and your goods, and may you for the unjust death of your parents, take a worthy and deserved vengeance.[4]

Order could come to the communes only by the total extirpation of those who opposed at any one moment the dominant faction within them. It was from the barbarities of this system that the institutions of the *signorie*, of government by single families, were to deliver the Italian towns of the North.

The original function of the communes had been to unite the secular nobility of each town against the claims of jurisdiction made upon it by the officials of a distant emperor: the communal movement had been the form that the *diffidatio* (or formal repudiation of feudal authority) of northern Europe had taken in Italy. Once, however, it had established its local regimen in *de facto* independence from the empire, the difficulties inherent in its constitution revealed themselves nakedly. A government by committee of hereditary notables could survive only if composed of men who were willing to strive continually to maintain unity among themselves – more than this, to recognise that a majority within the oligarchy should rule in the interests not simply of the majority but of the minority as well. Yet in most Italian towns these conditions never existed. The belief in the right or rather the glory of private justice and the traditions of the vendetta allied to the lack of any conception of 'a loyal opposition' meant that the ruling class was bound to be divided. In the 1220s men were still looking to the office of *podestà* as some alleviation of the situation. It was hoped that the appointment of some important outsider as a temporary president of the Council of the Commune would still internal conflict. As events proved it was a false dream. All that resulted was that conflict came to centre upon who should appoint the *podestà*, upon securing a man favourable to one's own party.

It is curious, in its own way, perhaps moving, to read the words of those who, in these circumstances, still sought to maintain the spirit of the commune. When they analysed what was happening they saw justly that party had taken the place of the commune. Their response to this situation was a continual rhetorical appeal to men to rule 'in common' and not 'by party'. Sometimes, as at Modena in 1306, they enacted statutes forbidding the continuance or establishment of parties. Reading the chronicle of Rolandino of Padua, a work specifically designed 'as a mirror and lamp against future plagues', to make propaganda for the idea of the commune, one seeks in vain for any other solution. These men could not ask for a real good: that parties should live side by side; and so they held to a greater dream: that in political life there should be no parties, basically, if one considers it, that all should think alike and have the same interests. It was not something which could have ever existed in the real world. Yet only this, Rolandino assures his readers, could deliver the communes 'from the hands of the impious, from the wickedness of an infernal tyrant, and, one might say, from the clutches of an Antichrist, that is to say, from an Ezzelino'.

III

What was to take the place of the commune? The first to confront this problem, the first to attempt to give any institutional form to the government of a party leader, was the Marquess Uberto Pelavicini (otherwise, Pallavicini).[5] He was the first to require of towns subjected to him a specific grant of lordship and office for life. A powerful landowner from the borders of Parma and Piacenza, Uberto held many fortresses and territories between the Taro and Chiavenna valleys. They stretched from within the Liguarian Apennines down to the Po, where stood his principal castle of Busseto, set amidst the waters of a lake surrounded by woods, and long believed impregnable. From the 1230s he had been a constant imperial partisan, had held podestaships for the empire, and in 1243 was created Imperial Vicar of Versilia, Lunigiana, and Garfagna. With the death of Frederick II he became the leader of all those local parties looking for shelter against the force of the ecclesiastical victories. Such was the material basis of his power; any juridical support deemed necessary was provided by King Conrad's appointment of him as

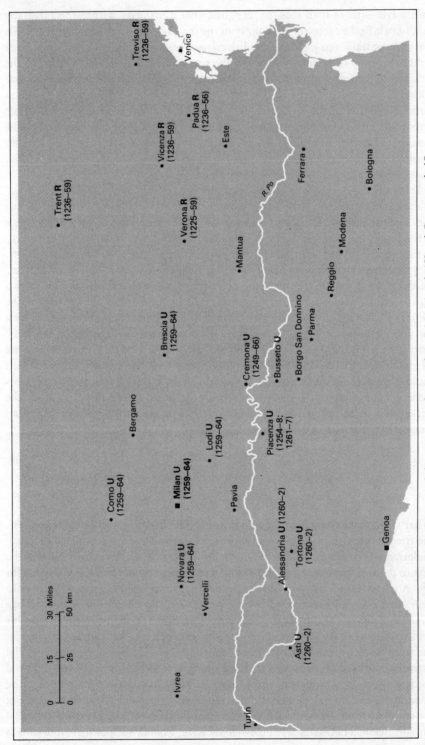

Map 3   Northern Italy 1236–67. Communes subject to Uberto Pelavicini marked U; to da Romano marked R

Captain General and Vicar of the Empire in Lombardy 'below the Lambro' in 1251.

The central bulwark of his power (See Map 3) rested upon Cremona, where he was appointed *podestà* in 1249, where by 1254 he was designated as 'perpetual lord and *podestà*', and which he held right up to 1266. During the 1250s, his influence broadened from this base; in 1254 he was made life-*podestà* of Piacenza, Pavia, and Vercelli. In 1257–8, the years of the threatening North-Italian crusade, his power waned and he was driven from Pavia and Piacenza. But his skill in turning the crusade to his own ends allowed him to build a newer and stronger domain at the end of the decade. Brescia was his from 1259 to 1264; he was associated in the rule of Milan by the della Torre party from November 1259 to 1264 (which brought him control over Lodi, Novara, and Como); he returned to Piacenza – though merely with a grant of lordship for four years – in 1261, and, in Piedmont, gained a brief supremacy over Asti, Tortona, and Alessandria from 1260 to 1262. Elsewhere his influence had to be taken into account. In Parma, of which he was a citizen and where he had a palace, he had many partisans; we read of him seeking to intimidate Ghiberto da Gente there, hurling his sword to the ground and calling out: 'By God, why shouldn't I rule this city?'. Ghiberto was too strong a personality to bow out before threats, and he had the support of the companies of the *popolo*. None the less he and his successors deemed appeasement necessary. 'Realising that everything had its time', they paid him an annual danegeld of £I[mperiali]. 1,200, and, on occasions, sent knights and foot in his support.

Uberto's power was at times immensely strong but was always insecurely based. Its incoherence derived from the impossibility, at that stage, of creating any overarching institutions which could give a unity to the different communities which he ruled, and which he ruled, sometimes, from widely differing power bases. The titles he used: 'Vicar-General of the Empire in Lombardy and perpetual lord of Parma, Piacenza, and Vercelli'; 'Vicar General of the Holy Empire in Lombardy, Lord and *podestà* of Cremona, Piacenza, and Pavia'; and so on, varied from place to place and from time to time according to the whims of the notaries drawing up the documents. (One of them ascribes to him the words: 'the communes of the towns, over which, with the favour of God, we preside'.)[6] Within his domains as a whole he sought no unifying elements outside his own person. The treaty of Lombard monetary union of May 1254, often cited to suggest that he did, included some cities which he never ruled, others which he did not rule at the time, and would doubtless have been drawn up if he had never existed.

One would not want, that is, to overemphasise his interest in institutions as such. In each town over which he ruled the institutions themselves were almost unchanged. What marks him out as original was his simple decision that the government of Cremona (if possible, elsewhere) should not rest with temporary dictatorships but should be placed, and – it was this which represented the decisive break with the idea of the communes – should be explicitly acknowledged to be placed, in the hands of one ruler for life. This willingness to strip the masks of the past from the commune argues the practical realism of a

135

good politician. So, too, does his constant readiness to co-operate with the *popolo*. His uncle, the Marquess Marchesopolo, had gone off to the East rather than live in an Italy where he might be called to justice by a *popolano*. Uberto, by contrast, like Ghiberto da Gente in Parma, made the *popolo* a principal instrument of his purpose. Indeed it might be that for contemporaries his particular gift was seen as the ability to reconcile and harmonise nobles and *popolani*. So, in Cremona, he preserved the formal institutions of both commune and *popolo*. His lieutenant there, Buoso da Doara, was from an ancient Lombard house, and among his ancestors was a captain of the First Lombard League. Yet this lustre did not prevent him from being 'Perpetual Captain of the Merchants' in the city, and 'Captain of the *popolo*' in 'the new city' of Cremona. And it was, in fact, in 1256 that the Society of the *popolo* erected its palace and tower in the new city. Again, in Piacenza, where the marquess' lieutenant was Uberto di Lando, the affairs of the *popolo*, following upon the dictatorship of Uberto dell' Iniquità, had assumed very great importance, and here it is probable that his assumption of power was owed to his ability in reconciling *milites* and *pedites*. In this respect it is perhaps significant that the immediate cause of his expulsion from Pavia in May 1257 was the breakdown in his efforts to bring the two classes together.

Ultimately, however, whatever his influence with the *popolo*, Uberto's power rested on the alliance of the pro-imperial parties. When the Papacy and Charles of Anjou began their preparations for the attack upon the remaining Hohenstaufen his influence waned. Milan and Brescia fell away in 1264. In 1265 his attempt to deny the pass to the Angevin army under Guy de Monfort and the Count of Flanders was defeated. In 1266 Cremona, in 1267 Piacenza, were lost to him. The men of Parma seized the opportunity to destroy his palace in the city, and through 1268 attacked his castles in the countryside. He was perhaps lucky, the following year, to die in his bed, 'in the mountains, denying any remorse to his confessors'.

In many ways the Marquess Uberto was a characteristic politician of the time. 'He had the appetite for dominating all men . . . he expelled many from Cremona, and tortured many and killed many.' Yet he was of a different calibre to Ezzelino. There was at the last something which contemporaries could admire in him: perhaps that he was a gentleman of the old style. One feels it in reading his will where he recommends his heirs to various great lords and then to all his *fideles* 'and especially those of the Val di Mozzola whom among all others we hold most dear'. The author of the *Annals of Piacenza*, his partisan, speaks of him as 'most *sapiens* (*saber*) in the business of the world, more so than any Lombard of Lombardy, *largus* (*larcs*), *curialis* (*cortes*), *probus* (*pro*), and *sagax* (*conoissens*) in war'. Even Salimbene describes him as old, thin, weak, one-eyed (men believed that a crow had pecked at him in his cradle), but of great heart and filled with the spirit of *larguesa*. What money he received he gave away, so that he had none for himself, and would ride through the streets, accompanied by a mere two squires on lean horses: 'as I have seen with my own eyes and still known then that he was a great man'.[7]

But, of course, ultimately a failure; and there were several others in this age who failed as he had done. Ghiberto da Gente, whose lordship of Parma had been based much more explicitly on the support of the *popolo*, fell from power in 1259. In Piedmont, where the movement of the *popolo* was weaker, Guglielmo VII of Monferrato, from one of the most famous feudal families of Europe, followed a rather different course. First in the early 1260s, and then later from the end of the 1270s, he subjected Alessandria (split by factions between the Trotti and Lanzavecchia), Asti, Tortona, Ivrea, and other communes to himself, by a feudal oath of loyalty, and in return left them with some measure of self-determination in taxation and legislation. It was a promising approach to the problem of the communes and was to bear fruit in the region during the fourteenth century. Guglielmo himself, however, ending his days in the prisons of Alessandria, was to see his own hopes of it frustrated.

Others were to have greater success. From the 1260s men came more often to assume and retain lordship over their cities for life, to give their rule explicit institutional form, and then to pass on the power they had achieved to their sons. It was in this age that the *signoria*, permanent legal rule by a single family, came into existence.

IV

The success of the *signori* was owed in the first place to their virtues as party-leaders: their skill in dominating their own faction and in securing its triumph over their adversaries, their ability to inspire respect or fear, their intelligence and brutality, their wealth, the size of their retinues, their external alliances. They came to power through the exercise of superior force in the midst of party violence; what they offered their fellow-citizens was the exercise of superior force in eliminating that violence. Where they went beyond the party-leaders was in giving their rule those juridical trappings which, in the course of time, were to make their government appear normal and legitimate. From a cowed and intimidated communal council they would secure the title of lord, the right which went with this to control the commune at their will, and to pass on this grant to their heirs. At some later date, in the course of the fourteenth century, they would seek the legitimisation of their *de facto* power by securing a grant of vicariate from the emperor, or, in the Papal State, from the pope. Henceforth, as imperial or papal 'vicars', they were transformed into those hereditary lordships or principalities which, by the fifteenth century, seemed to constitute the natural order in large areas of northern Italy.

It was in the Trevisan March, Lombardy, Emilia, and the Marche that the *signorie* were to be most strongly developed. The Trevisan March, which had experienced the rule of the da Romano, had particular cause to fear the passing of the commune, and in April 1262, Verona, Padua, Treviso, and Vicenza had made an alliance to prevent the domination of any one person in their cities. Yet Verona fell, almost immediately afterwards, to Mastino della Scala, and the della Scala (or 'Scaligeri') family came from 1311 to rule Vicenza too. Treviso gave itself to the da Camino (1283–1312) and then to the counts of Gorizia. Only

Padua, where loyalty to the commune lasted longer, put up a stronger resistence. Yet ultimately this city, too, was forced to resign itself to the rule of the da Carrara (or 'Carraresi') family (1328–1425).

In Lombardy the *signoria* of the Visconti came from 1300 to extend over a very large number of subordinate towns. At Milan during the thirteenth century, the Visconti, in origin *capitanei* of the Archbishops, had led the opposition to the faction of the landowning della Torre (or 'Torriani') family. Between 1263 and 1281 the della Torre had exercised lordship. They were replaced then by Ottone Visconti, who had succeeded in obtaining the position of archbishop, with its great landed wealth and followers, and who ruled until his death in 1295. From then the conflict between the two families continued indecisively until, finally, in 1311, Henry VII proscribed the Torriani, and made Matteo Visconti his vicar. In the next thirty-five years members of the family were to become lords of Cremona (1322–7, and then, continually, from 1334), Piacenza (1314, continually from 1337), Pavia, Lodi, Bergamo (1332), Como (1335), Tortona, and Parma (1346).

To the south the d'Este had already begun to create a *signoria*, which, though much smaller, extended over more than one city. Here we know something of the immediate circumstances of its foundation. At Ferrara, Azzo VII, who had ruled, informally, as a party leader, died in 1264. At this the partisans of the Church party in Northern Italy met in the city, and decided that his (illegitimate) grandson, Obizzo II, should be established as lord. The citizens were called to the piazza and urged in a series of speeches to vote for their subjection to him. A Ferrarese chronicler, present at the event, sardonically describes the final speech and its sequel:

'The friends of our party need not fear, our enemies should neither rejoice nor take heart from the funeral of the marquess Azzo. For he still survives for us in a youth of good character, from whom much can be hoped. And if there were no branch of the house of Este suitable to govern, we would create one to rule us out of straw.' And the crowd standing there cries, 'so be it, so be it', and especially those that hold the goods of the exiles and have or hoped to have office in government. When silence falls a representative is elected to confer the dominion of the city and district of Ferrara on Obizzo, then seventeen years old. The representative hands over the fullest dominion to that Obizzo so that he may do everything, just or unjust, by the power of his will. The new ruler has more power than God eternal, who is not able to do unjust things.[8]

The words express something of the feelings of those who had come to fear the *signore* more than they had disliked the commune. The 'youth of good character' was, according to Salimbene, who knew Ferrara well in these years, 'the worst type of man, of Ezzelinian morals . . . of great heart, but not a good man, because he did many evil things'. He clothed himself in chivalric trappings, lost an eye in a joust to the honour of his lady, and held a great 'court' for the marriage of a son to the niece of Pope Nicholas III. But absolute power, perhaps, too, the jeers of the minstrels at his bastardy, worked their effects on him, and his rule was 'beyond measure long and hard'. He sold out any commercial privileges Ferrara might have attained from the Po trade in return for Venetian support. He abolished the guilds and caused the statutes to decree that the *podestà* should execute his orders whether legal or illegal. He dishonoured the wives of both nobles (it is, of course, Salimbene who draws the distinction) and non-nobles in the city.[9]

Popular gossip hit back; it was all that was left to his subjects. It was whispered that he had murdered his mother, a noble lady of Naples, through shame at that fall from virtue by which he had been conceived; that he had slept with his sisters and his wife's sister; that finally he had been murdered by his own sons. The Fontana family, his principal supporters at the time of his 'election', came to regret their choice, and were expelled from the city. Yet this man 'of Ezzelinian morals' offered something to contemporaries. In 1288 the nobility of Modena, in 1290 that of Reggio, offered him the lordship of their towns on the same terms that he held it in Ferrara. It seemed to them that the rule of a tyrant was preferable to the continuance of faction more particularly, perhaps, if it were combined with the extinction of any remaining vestiges of *popolo* power.

Elsewhere *signoria* took different forms. In Piedmont the towns were split by the same factions that were found in those of the Veneto, Emilia, and Lombardy. Here however the beneficiaries were not faction leaders, native to the towns, but the five principal feudal houses of the region. These normally succeeded in securing their submission by the explicit acknowledgment of 'vasselage'. (The rôle of the Este in Modena and Reggio, of the Visconti in Lombardy had been somewhat similar.) The position here fluctuated constantly as first one, then another, lord grew powerful and then declined. But at the beginning of the fourteenth century, the counts of Savoy, from Chambéry, with lands in France, on Lake Leman, and in the Susa and Aosta valleys, held Ivrea; while their sub-vassals, the counts of Acaia-Savoy, from Pinerolo, held Turin and most of the area north of the Po. The Marquess of Saluzzo held the upper Po and Varaita valleys and lands extending south of the Po to Carmagnola; the Marquess of Monferrato, from Chiavasso, held Alba and Casale. Finally, the Angevins of Naples and Provence controlled Asti and Alessandria.

In the Papal State, where most of the towns were almost exclusively dominated by landowning nobles, one might have expected to find, even more strongly, that same pattern of development characteristic of the North. But here the officials of the pope's secular power represented a third element between commune and *signore*, as the emperor had never done, and strove, however weakly, to impose upon the towns the *signoria* of the Church. Hence, though everywhere faction conflict was intense from an early period, and though by the 1280s one finds the emergence of men who ruled as party-leaders and who passed on *de facto* supremacy to their sons, the full grant of authority by vicariate came later than might otherwise have been forecast. In Romagna, for example, the first attempts at the formalisation of lordship in the legal institutions of the towns were probably made by the Ordelaffi at Forlì in 1315, by the Manfredi at Faenza in 1320; by the da Polenta at Ravenna in 1322; by the Malatesti at Rimini in 1334; and by the Alidosi at Imola in 1342. In the Marche in the same period the Montefeltro came to dominate at Urbino and Cagli (and also at Gubbio in Umbria), the Brancaleoni at Castel Durante, the Chiavelli at Fabriano; the da Varano at Tolentino and Camerino. But these developments were resisted by the

Church. Only gradually, with Albornoz's failure to dominate the Papal State (1353–7; 1358–63), and the collapse of papal power in the War of the Eight Saints and the Schism, did the popes throw in their hand and allow local conditions to take their course. By the grant of papal vicariates they came to allow that unfettered growth of the principate which had taken place in northern Italy. It was a gradual development. Vicariates were at first offered for ten years; only from the 1390s were they granted for the life of the recipient or for the life of the recipient and his heir. And in the more important cities the Papacy was able, either, as at Rome, Perugia, and Ancona, to resist the movement altogether, or, as at Bologna, hinder its growth. In these centres the communes might survive with considerable autonomous powers, or might be ruled, with a greater or lesser degree of subjection, as a papal *signoria*.

The development of the principates then was an uneven process. One can point, too, to certain differences between them. A distinction could be drawn between those *signori*, such as the Este, who sprang originally from the ranks of the ancient nobility, and, what was much more common, those, like the Alidosi and Varano, who by birth were lesser vassals. In some places again the *signoria* arose from an alliance with the *popolo*, and was even – though the della Scala in Verona are a unique case – exercised by a family of *popolano* origins. In others – Modena could be an example – it may be that a strong element in the formation of the *signoria* was noble reaction to *popolano* power. In fact these are not very significant differences since, within a generation, *signori* of whatever origins came to resemble one other. Much more basic is the contrast between those who, like the della Scala in Verona, the da Carrara in Padua, the Manfredi in Faenza, were native-born to the towns over which they ruled and so provided some focus for local loyalty, and those, like the Visconti, whose *signoria* embraced many different cities and had, therefore, something of the character of conquest by a foreign power. Yet, ultimately, what they had in common was more significant: the idea of the unquestioned legitimacy of single-person government, their status as rulers whose rule could not simply be dismissed by their enemies as 'tyranny'.

V

A characteristic example of the institutionalisation of princely power is provided by the establishment of the *signoria* of the Bonacolsi and Gonzaga at Mantua. Set amidst the melancholy fens of the Mincio, it was a typical small city of the North. There was some slight export trade, a little cloth manufacture, but basically the wealth of its citizens came from land. It had the usual violent faction conflicts, a rather weak movement of the *popolo* in the 1240s, and then between 1253 and 1269 fell under the rule of two party-leaders of the Trevisan March in opposition to Ezzelino. These were Azzo VII d'Este (followed by his grandson, Obizzo) and Ludovico di Ricciardo da Vinciguerra da Sambonifaccio, titular count of Verona. In March 1269 Obizzo's party seems to have tried to seize sole control of the city, but were themselves driven out, leaving Count Ludovico as its ruler. He was a man who excited Salimbene's admiration, both as a noble and as an exemplar of Christian virtue, 'wise and brave, skilled in arms and learned in war' and so chaste that he averted his eyes from women as he passed through the streets. Yet this was not a world where good men flourished. In June 1272, with his local partisans, the counts of Casoldo, he was driven from the town by two of its citizens, Federico, count of Macaria, and Pinamonte Bonacolsi. Dante refers obscurely to the event in the *Inferno* (xx, 94–6), and early commentators upon the passage embroidered his words in their imagination, but no real picture of the immediate circumstances comes through. It remains yet another of those tedious laconically-narrated stories of treachery and violence which go to make up so much of the history of the towns in these years. In the following year it was rounded off by Pinamonte Bonacolsi's expulsion of his erstwhile ally, Count Federico, apparently on the pretext that he was in a secret league plotting to give the city to Obizzo d'Este. During the next four years Pinamonte, employing the title 'Captain of the Party', built up his *de facto* control over the city.

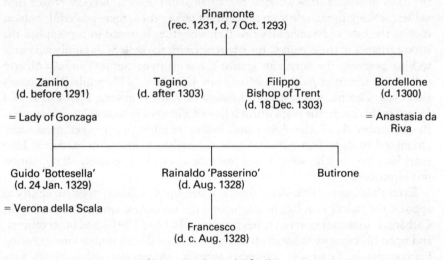

Table 1   The Bonacolsi family

The Bonacolsi family was hardly to be compared with that of the Este or Sambonifaccio. We know the name of Pinamonte's great grandfather, but nothing more about him. His grandfather had been a consul of the commune in 1200; his father was a lesser vassal of the Mantuan church with fiefs at Carzedole. It was not until its seizure of power that the family became a large landowner. (In April 1282 the Abbot of St. Zeno was protesting that by harsh threats and against his will he had been forced to infeudate properties to Pinamonte and the Scaligeri.) What raised him to eminence was his personal quality, that supreme confidence and ruthlessness suggested in Salimbene's anecdotes:

He usurped the lordship of his city and expelled his fellow-citizens and occupied their property and destroyed the houses and towers of those whom he thought were his enemies. And he was feared like the devil. . . . 'Thus and thus', he used to say, 'I do in my domain'. . . . He used to boast that in that domain of his he never experienced any misfortune, but that all things went according to his will. That was great folly for as the wise man says in *Proverbs*, xxvii: 'Boast not thyself of tomorrow; for thou knowest not what a day may bring forth.'[10]

Yet the friar does not portray a complete thug. He tells us how, in 1283, white-haired, surrounded by his children, he received 'with *cortesia*' a Franciscan colleague who bore letters to him from a Cardinal Legate. Their import was that he should bring back peace to his neighbours and fellow-citizens, and that they should enjoy a quiet and peaceful life. Pinamonte's answer was to decree that anyone who brought another letter should be beheaded; yet at the same time he and his family sent gifts to the Franciscan's house and to the cardinal.

One must be chary about assigning to factions any interests outside clan-loyalties, inter-family alliances, and personal hatreds. None the less, the suspicion remains that the party led by Pinamonte, often simply called 'the Party', but in 1279 'the Party of Mantua', was precisely that: that it represented the party of *campanilismo* (or local patriotism), of the local interests of Mantuan nobles, seeking to exclude from the fruits of power alien, more powerful, nobles, such as the Este and Sambonifaccio. If this be true, it would in part explain the strong alliance in these years of the Bonacolsi with the della Scala family who were seeking precisely the same aim against the same dynasties in Verona. (Alberto della Scala served as *podestà* at Mantua in 1275 and 1277, while Pinamonte's eldest son, Zanino, was seven times *podestà* of Verona between 1274 and 1288.) However this be, in the years which followed Pinamonte consolidated his power. In November 1277 the Arloti and Pizoni families 'with other great men' attempted to drive him out, and were themselves banished or executed. Four years later the da Riva were driven from the town. Progressively all opposition was eliminated.

So far Pinamonte's rule was *de facto*; it rested upon violence, upon his ability to appoint the *podestà* – in fact he nominated the Bolognese Ghibelline, Pietro de' Carbonari, to the office seven times between 1280 and 1291 – and other officers, and upon his capacity to intimidate the councils of the commune into accepting his commands. Gradually, however, various institutional arrangements were devised to give his government legal form. First came a title. By 1279 he was 'captain of Mantua', as well as 'of the party of Mantua', and by 1282 'captain general'. In January 1285 the General Council, called 'by the officers of the party, and all there gathered from the greater and lesser councils of the Lord Captain and party of Mantua' gave commands to the *podestà* 'by the will of the Lord Captain', and henceforth the council always met and deliberated '*de voluntate domini Capitani*'.

The triumph of one family and the final crushing of rival families within the commune was often the prelude to the outbreak of rivalries within the dominant family. So, too, it proved with the Bonacolsi. After the death of his eldest son, Zanino, the old Pinamonte had associated his second son, Tagino, in his government. For the third son, Filippo, this was an acceptable arrangement. 'A good man, and chaste, and a reader in theology', according to Salimbene, he had entered the Franciscan order and had become Inquisitor General in the Trevisan

March in 1275. In this office he burnt 166 heretics from Sirmione, and received his reward in 1289 on being elevated to the see of Trent. But a fourth child, Bordellone, had no similar opportunity to expend his aggressive energies. Moreover, his wife's family, the Riva, had been expelled from Mantua in 1281. Perhaps through this, perhaps through other resentments, in circumstances which are obscure, he threw off the loyalties to his family, and in September 1291 seized control of the city from his father and brother.

Pinamonte died, an old man – he was probably well into his eighties – two years later, having had time to reflect upon the *stultitia magna* which Salimbene had detected in his histrionic utterances, and also, no doubt, having had sufficient opportunity to stoke up indignation against his unworthy son, Bordellone. Perhaps, for this reason, Bordellone's rule seems marked by an uncharacteristic atmosphere of conciliation. He recalled most of the exiles in 1295, and in 1298 admitted his dispossessed brother, Tagino, to the city. Either for this spirit of clemency, or for his unfilial treatment of his father, he experienced difficulties within his own family. In February 1299 he was forced to expel his nephew, Guido 'Bottesella', and his followers. This triumph was temporary. In the following July Guido returned with the aid of Alberto della Scala. Bordellone was forced to renounce the captaincy, and died in exile within a year. In the words of the Mantuan-Veronese treaty 'the Lord Guido, called Bottesella, captain of Mantua and his friends, now rule the commune of Mantua and are the commune of Mantua'.

Between 1272 and 1299 the Bonacolsi had held continuous power in the commune. Despite Bordellone's usurpation of power and his cousin's counter-stroke, the rule of the one family was coming to be accepted as the norm, and the legal formulas of the commune were slowly adapted to the new situation. Bordellone had had himself appointed 'captain and perpetual lord'. What this implied was spelt out in the statute which the General Council of the city was induced to pass with the triumph of Guido Bottesella in 1299:

We order and decree that the distinguished Lord Guido Bottesella should, and ought to, be perpetually, captain general of the city and district of Mantua and the commune of Mantua, and should rule and govern that city and district and commune of Mantua at his undiluted, pure and free and general determination and will, as shall best and most usefully seem agreeable to him, with council or without council, and he shall have . . . undiluted and pure power and jurisdiction, decision, power, lordship, and free determination over the commune, *universitas*, and men of the city and district of Mantua.

He was given, specifically, the right to make war, truce, concord, and peace. He might make alliances, contract agreements, recall exiles at his will. He was awarded the power to convene councils of *savii*, boards and committees, and 'with their council or without' make reformations, establish decrees, interpret ordinances, and declare statutes. He was empowered to name all communal officials and 'with council or without council, at his undiluted, pure and general determination and will, paying no attention to any solemnity of law, custom, reformation, decree or statute' ordain everything in respect of Mantua.[11]

In 1294 Bordellone had appointed twelve *anziani*, three from each 'quarter' of the city. These, we are told, had in full council solemnly assigned to him a new flag (in vermilion, with a figure of St. Peter in white) called 'the flag of Justice', as a sign that 'he could and should maintain securely each citizen of the town and bishopric of Mantua in good justice and good law'. What we have here is the establishment of a small signorial council in which the business of the commune will be discussed under the *signore*'s presidency. It constitutes moreover the recognition in a formal ceremony – one of those ceremonies in which the new rulers are to seek to give the aura of the prince to their deeds – that the council itself meets in a purely advisory capacity, that it claims no rights against the lord's undiluted determination and will. Both this council and the councils of the *savii* (*sapientes*, the wise ones) meet now in his palace. To the old councils of the commune will be left henceforth only the formal role of confirming those decisions taken by the *signore*. They have solely a sort of legitimising function, and constitute in this a residual element from the old commune.

In the law of the city the head of the Bonacolsi family now possessed almost absolute power. All that was lacking was recognition of his right to transmit that power by inheritance. Some measure of this was secured in 1308 when Guido associated his brother, Rainaldo, with him as vicar and declared him to be his successor, a decision confirmed *nemine discrepante* in full council. In December of the same year another signorial privilege was authenticated. On his deathbed Guido explained to the *anziani* that he was worried by the thought that he had taken money from the commune and used it for the construction of his palace. In reply they declared that he was perfectly justified in what he had done and that in future he should use all his communal finances as he thought fit. Six days later their decision was put to the General Council which prudently concurred. Councillor after councillor rose to his feet to compose some rhetorical exercise on the theme: 'by the custom and vigour of the statutes of the commune of Mantua, he is and has been able to dispense and dispose and expend and donate the money and property of the commune of Mantua and to convert it to his own use'.

On his accession to power at his brother's death Rainaldo must certainly have obtained a grant of the life-captaincy from the General Council on the same terms granted to Guido Bottesella. With the coming of the Emperor Henry VII to Italy, an imperial *podestà* was appointed, the exiles were restored, and his control of power temporarily threatened. But Rainaldo triumphed over the difficulties, brought aid to the emperor in his siege of Brescia, and received his reward. Some time between May and December of 1311, jointly with his brother, Butirone, he was invested with the imperial vicariate. In return he promised a payment of 20,000 florins (of which it is probable the emperor in fact received some 1,200).

The commune's grant of captaincy was now reinforced by the supreme juridical authority of the empire. After the emperor's death this imperial grant was then submitted to the communal council for confirmation, a proceeding which, however legally bizarre, had a sound psychological basis. The confirmation to the two brothers of 'the vicariate of the Holy Roman Emperor', reaffirmed the rights given to the captain in 1299, and added too those financial rights awarded in 1308. They were to have authority:

to conserve, guard, rule, govern, dispose, spend, give, and also receive to themselves, have, and retain the property, money, revenues, and goods of the commune of Mantua, and the possessions and goods of exiles, and whatever pertains to the commune of Mantua; and to do, in whatever manner they shall please, and as shall best and most conveniently seem and appear convenient, each and every thing, at their pure, undiluted, and free will and decision.

Finally the vicars were freed from any obligation to render accounts, or to stand to sindication (i.e. enquiry into the performance of their office).

Behind these *de jure* formulations lay the growth in the same period of a genuine signorial ethos, which was given outward form by the building of the magnificent Bonacolsi palaces. The Bonacolsi became princes who required courtly flattery and who, in return, would give their patronage to learning and the arts. The Paduan student of the natural sciences, Pietro d'Abano, dedicated his *De physiognomia* to Bordellone. Vivaldo Belcalzer (who had been chosen by Bordellone as one of his *anziani* and who had then witnessed his deed of abdication) presented Guido Bonacolsi with his translation into Mantuan dialect of Bartholomew the Englishman's *De proprietatibus rerum*. The style fawns in the manner of the accustomed courtier:

Praise and honour to Guido Bonacolsi, that lord, so noble and magnificent, captain and perpetual lord of Mantua, and to his brothers, the sons born to messer Zanino of sweet memory. To him, his Vivaldo Belcalzer recommends himself, in true and whole obedience to his commandments . . .

So it goes on. Belcalzer has not minded the vigils and fatigues of his labour, because in truth he is bound to consume all the days of his life in that which may give glory and honour to Guido's greatness, and so on.[12]

The formulations of law, the stabilising of signorial power, the growth of the mentality of subservience, all went together. Rule by the arbitrary whim of one man came to be thought of as the lawful state of things as they were and ought to be. Hence when in 1328 the Bonacolsi fell from power, to be replaced by the Gonzaga family, there was, apparently, no general feeling at the time that the system of the old commune should be restored, merely consideration of the question: who should be *signore*? The details of the change of power are complex and obscure. Apart from noting that the incident had something of the character of an inter-family conflict (for Rainaldo's mother was a Gonzaga) it need not be discussed here. In November 1329 Luigi Gonzaga obtained the imperial vicariate from Lewis IV. Thenceforward the long rule of his family came to be unquestioned. All that was lacking to make of it a virtual monarchy was the establishment of the principle of full hereditary right in succession to the vicariate. Something of this was already present in the 1329 grant, where it had been agreed that were Luigi to die before the emperor, his vicariate should pass to his sons. But the complete recognition of what the family sought was delayed until June 1383. In that month the Emperor Wenceslas was explicitly to invest the vicariate in Francesco Gonzaga 'and his legitimate male heirs and successors'. Over the course of some hundred and ten years Mantua had become a true principality.

VI

Grants by communes and conferments of vicariates were, of course, purely legal forms enshrining *de facto* situations, and hence there is much justification in the complaints, often heard, against any exclusively juridical approach to the story of the coming of the *signorie*. Yet the power of law to shape and define what is normal and expected cannot be neglected, if only, and at least, as a symbol of what changes have occurred. The rule of a party-leader, the rule of an Ezzelino, was very different in character from the rule of a Francesco Gonzaga. In a large area of northern Italy some seventy years had seen a profound transformation in political life and social attitudes. Government of the commune by one man was no longer conceived of as unnatural, a bizarre, temporary, and revocable expedient, but as a fact of life. Under the new regimes, the councils of the commune normally, of the *popolo* sometimes, remained; but their functions were limited either to discussion of minor administrative arrangements or to such tasks as giving legal ratification to treaties with foreign governments or approval of the *signore*'s choice of successor. In practice all that was left of the old system was, basically, what had always been its most valuable element, its administration, its staff of experienced notaries who, behind the interminable changes of regime and the intolerable strife of faction, had sought to keep the political structure in being.

The movement from commune to principality was not something which men of the time sought to justify. Perhaps they were silent because in legal terms they believed it unjustifiable. The very need felt for the ratification of the *signore*'s most important acts of state in general councils suggests a mentality which held fast to the principle that 'what touches all, should be approved by all'. But the acceptance of *signoria* had its own justification in the world of everyday life. As Dante in the *Monarchia* looked to a world monarch as the sole force able to bring peace to mankind, so contemporaries came, though often with pain, to see in the *signore* the sole force able to end the factions and blood feuds of the past hundred years. 'The philosopher [Aristotle] saw this argument when he said: "Things hate to be in disorder, but a plurality of authorities is disorder, therefore authority is single." '

The weaknesses of oligarchic government have frequently been underlined: the lack of continuity in policies, discussion and decisions in councils as the fruit of divided and selfish interests. In themselves these should not be unduly stressed for they are the weaknesses of all liberal elective regimes. What made them of particular importance here, however, was that they were present in a context where 'the state' did not exist, where the commune as a point of reference and identity was weak, where men did not give any instinctive loyalty to government. In an underdeveloped society it is much easier to give allegiance to a person than to an abstraction. This is not to say that there was any collective will to substitute *signoria* for communal government. The commonplace of much discussion of this issue in which the citizens, wearying of conflict, hand over power to a single ruler, is clearly an over-simplification. It was something – one thinks of Modena and Reggio – which happened on occasion. But, more often, power was snatched rather than bestowed. Few can have consciously preferred a signorial system to a regime of commune and *popolo* which worked effectively. The difficulty lay in making the commune work. As it normally existed, it was not anything to fight for, to die for. It offered nothing to one not enrolled in the noble factions, to men of peace who simply echoed the words of Emmanuele Ebreo: *'Viva chi vince, ch'io so' di sua parte'* – 'Long live the winner, I'm of his party'.

The *signoria*, that is, did not come about as the answer to the question: how can one obtain a reasonable fabric of social life? It came through the successful ambitions of violent men. Yet it remained and became rooted in much of Italian society because it did, to a certain degree, answer that question. The Hobbesian 'war of all against all', the interminable play of faction did not end altogether. It was no easy task to suppress it. In Parma, split for years between the rivalries of the Correggio, San Vitale, and Rossi families, the Lord Ridolfo Visconti, as late as 1366, was threatening death to anyone calling himself 'Guelf' or 'Ghibelline' or referring to himself as belonging to any party 'save that of the Visconti'. The parties often continued, yet above them remained a principle of permanency. On balance it seems impossible to resist the conclusion that life within the cities, though still very violent, was under a fourteenth century *signore* more peaceful than under a thirteenth century commune. Again, while it is true of course, that, for instance, the individual cities composing their domain were inevitably drawn into the Visconti wars against other powers, the establishment of the large territorial *signorie* did bring external peace to neighbouring towns which had long been engaged in war with one other.

By and large it was the nobility who most benefited from the changes from commune to *signoria*. Provided they were not irreparably compromised in their relations with the new ruler, nobles found it sensible to abandon a naked conflict for power and to enter instead upon a competition for the favours of a court. Hence, by virtue of his absolute power, the *signore* was able to reconstitute, perhaps it would be truer to say, to constitute for the first time, a harmony between the upper classes of the commune which allowed the continuance of social life. At the same time he could reconcile the interests of nobles and *popolo*, or, if need be, suppress the pretensions of the *popolo* altogether. Decrees against magnates were allowed to fall into desuetude or were used only in a partisan spirit against families hostile to the regime. Yet in so far as a principle aim of the *popolo* had been to establish that public order which the *signore* brought, this was not wholly a ground for complaint.

For the non-nobles of the towns it is difficult to see whether the coming of *signoria* brought, outside the greater internal peace within the oligarchy, advantages or disadvantages. No more than the commune did the *signoria* seek any form of social revolution. Whether justice thereafter was more or less corrupt is unknowable. Claims for the greater efficiency of signorial rule – through greater speediness of decision, secrecy, and so on – seem on reflection *a priori* doubtful. An oligarchy, after all, is in a much better position to check vicious or stupid policies than a monarchy. The greatest danger in the *signoria* arose from the psychological pressures upon the *signore*, the threat of madness springing from the possession of sole power, leading to a Caligulan violence, only to be countered by assassination and conspiracy. In the fourteenth century, however, such conspiracies were normally undertaken by and became the duty or prerogative of the signorial families themselves. With them rested the burden of faction, once undertaken by the whole of the oligarchy.

VII

The emergence of those *signorie* which developed into principates was merely one element in the constitutional history of the north-Italian towns in the fourteenth century. By and large it was a phenomenon confined to the Veneto, Lombardy, Emilia, the Marche, and, in a somewhat different form, Piedmont. In most towns of Umbria and Latium (as too in Bologna in Emilia) the fluctuating balance of power between the local nobility and the Papacy permitted the frequent temporary assumption of sole power by individual lords, but allowed only a few families (such as the Montefeltro in Gubbio, the Trinci in Foligno) to take permanent root as the sole leaders of the communes. In Tuscany too the movement towards a principate was, though with some exceptions (as with the Casali in Cortona), resisted. Pisa had a succession of alternating 'foreign' and native families as rulers, though none was able to establish a dynasty. Lucca underwent the same development, though witnessing a remarkable revival of communal government from 1369 to 1392. For Florence, the Lordships of King Robert of Naples (1313–21), of Carlo, Duke of Calabria (1325–8), and Walter, Duke of Athens (1342), were merely incidental to a period of continuous oligarchical rule. Several neighbours of Florence, Prato, Pistoia, Volterra, Sangimignano, in which *signorie* might have developed, were conquered by her before the process might have taken place. In Liguria, Genoa alternated between *signorie* (King Robert, 1317–35; Giovanni Visconti, 1353–6), and a series of Ghibelline, anti-magnate dictatorships. Two communes, Siena and Venice, rejected *signoria* altogether.

It follows that to speak *tout simple* of the fourteenth century as 'the age of *signoria*' is, if we use that term in a strict sense to mean a principate, misleading. Large areas of central Italy were either still subject to the government of alternating party-captains, to the rule of papal legates (generally alternating with party captains), of other communes (whose rule, admittedly, had something of the character of non-native *signorie*), or of – and among these were some of the most powerful cities – their own native oligarchies.

In the past, historians have written of 'the problem' of the origins of the *signorie*, almost as if oligarchy were to be considered – in defiance of the whole tradition of medieval European history – as a more natural form of government than monarchy. Considering the instability of the thirteenth-century communes it would seem more legitimate to identify as a problem the survival, notably at Florence, Venice, and Siena, of the oligarchies. Why was it that these cities preserved communal rule until the fifteenth century or even later? One could not argue that the existence of a strong *popolo* was an essential factor – though often it helped – for Venice, most powerful of the communes, knew nothing of the *popolo* movement. Could it be then that in towns of great mercantile wealth the needs of commerce produced among the nobility a greater need and instinct for compromise and peace, a new spirit transcending the old chivalric ideal of the vendetta? There may be something in this, though commerce, of course, throws up its own rivalries, and the supposed new spirit is difficult to discern among the noble bankers of thirteenth-century Florence. It is, of course, true that a single family required much greater power if it were to dominate an oligarchy of noble bankers and patrician merchants than an oligarchy of noble landowners, precisely because the power of its subjects was so much greater. It was much easier for, say, the Malatesti in Rimini to rule over landowners, small artisans, and peasants than it was for the lords of Pisa or Lucca to claim pre-eminence in a world in which their power could be outweighed by extremely wealthy men. The very complexity of societies of high economic development, as the Duke of Athens was to discover in his brief *signoria* over Florence, made it less amenable to autocratic *Diktats*. Something of the answer to the problem of communal survival is to be found here too. Yet Perugia under communal government, for example, hardly compared in importance as a banking centre, with, say, Asti or Piacenza under signorial rule. And Milan, though we know very little about its social and economic composition, had, it is clear, complex mercantile interests, was a great and populous city, and, none the less, produced the most powerful of the *signori*.

For a complete answer one would have to look at each city in which communal rule survived in its own uniqueness. As our exemplar, we might take Venice, though in this Italy which was already a world of special cases, Venice was, as contemporaries were constantly pointing out, a particularly special case. 'O happy commune of the Venetians!' declared Rolandino of Padua in this vein, 'whose citizens in all their actions, consider only the community, so that they hold the name of Venice as the divine will, and almost take oath upon their reverence and honour for Venice!' These Venetians, lacking in all the self-interest of other mortal men, were of course a myth, and yet a myth which, because of the element of truth within it – namely that self-interest and public interest often coincided – was destined to have a long history. Though there were times in the city, as in the 1260s. when there seems to be evidence of widespread lower-class discontent, or, as in the Tiepolo–Querini–Badoer conspiracy of 1310, when factional treachery threatened the existing order, these disturbances were never the constant *leit–motif* of the city's history as they were in so many of the cities of the mainland.

In seeking to explain the constitutional success of Venice historians have pointed to a variety of factors. There was, it has been suggested, though one instinctively distrusts such generalisations, a Byzantine inheritance of ruler worship. There was an ideal, and one it would seem translated into reality, of equal justice between rich and poor. Offices were held for brief periods and filled by a system of election in which lot featured prominently, so that the plans of faction were moderated by chance. Throughout the thirteenth century entrance to the ruling class was opened to wealthy and powerful non-nobles without those clamours which had accompanied the movement of the *popolo* on the mainland. 'New men' were able to reach even the office of Doge. This widening of the ranks of the nobility culminated in 1297 with the expansion of 'the Great Council', the repository of sovereignty, responsible for the election of all officials, to over 1,000 members.

Yet to say these things still fails to explain why Venice, but not its neighbours, was able to engender such a civic pride and such a constitution. After 1297, in particular after the 1320s, access to the Great Council became much more difficult. It is true that up to the 1390s *popolares* were sometimes rewarded with grants of nobility for their services to government and that each extinction of a patrician family, it seems probable, led to an ennoblement of a commoner in order to maintain the council's numbers. It could be said, that is, that the celebrated 'Closing (*Serrata*) of the Great Council', which created a fixed hereditary class, did not occur in 1297, but was a slow process extending for some eighty to ninety years from the end of the thirteenth century. The fact remains, when all reservations have been made, that the ruling class was, in the fourteenth century, hardening itself into a caste; and yet managing to preserve political harmony. Ultimately, perhaps, to explain the secrets of Venetian political success, we are driven back on geography. The *contado* was exiguous, merely the coastlands of the Dogado, and hence the nobility had for long no large pool of rural peasantry from whom *masnade* could be recruited. Within the city the pattern of canals made the streetfights, characteristic of the mainland, difficult. More than all this – one compares the Venetian situation with that of Milan, set amidst the wide and fertile agricultural hinterland – the huge island population was doomed to starvation were the fabric of government to collapse and the galleys fail to set out, and this consideration imposed a stimulus to social discipline. The critical problem of food supply was common to all cities, particularly the largest (at Florence too starvation would follow without provisioning by sea), yet here it was dramatised and given a sharper intensity through the physical sense of the surrounding waters.

In both Florence and Siena one can discern elements common to the Venetian situation: an extension of the oligarchy in the thirteenth century, an over-riding concern with trade, an economy which would be menaced by internal disunity. Here too was a ruling class deeply involved in a pursuit of commercial advantage which offered new satisfactions beyond either claims to rule over other men or the pursuit of aristocratic honour. In every case there was some powerful stimulus at work to preserve that public order which was the key issue in the continued existence of the communes.

NOTES

On the **party leaders**, see, For Ezzelino, *Studi ezzeliniani*, by G. Fasoli, R. Mansuelli, *et alii*, Rome, 1963; M. Rapisarda, *La signoria di Ezzelino da Romano*, Udine, 1965. On Uberto Pelavicini there is the old work of Z. Schiffer, *Markgraf Hubert Pallavicini·Ein Signore Oberitaliens im 13. Jahrhundert*, Leipzig, 1910; L. Astegiano, 'Ricerche sulla storia civile del comune di Cremona' in *MHP*, s. ii, t. xxii, chs. xv and xvi; and E. Nasalli

1. The sick, maimed and blind appeal to Death: 'Since prosperity has abandoned us, O Death, medicine of every pain, come give us now the last supper.' Their plea is ignored; Death moves instead to strike down the young, healthy and prosperous. From the 'Triumph of Death', frescoed in the Campo Santo of Pisa in the mid-fourteenth century by an unknown artist, perhaps Francesco Traini, perhaps Buffalmacco.

2. Pope Boniface VIII, portrayed, while still living, as a slim, youthful symbol. Statue of bronze plates nailed to wood from the Museo Civico of Bologna.

3. (*right*) Clement IV (d. 1268). The first 'portrait' representation of a pope to survive. Tomb statue in S. Francesco, Viterbo.

4. (*top left*) Gregory X (d. 1276). Tomb statue in the Cathedral of Arezzo, carved *c.* 1300.

5. (*bottom left*) Nicholas III (d. 1280). Tomb statue in the Vatican Grottoes, carved 1281.

6. (*above*) Honorius IV (d. 1287). Tomb statue in S. Maria in Aracoeli, Rome, from the workshop of Arnolfo di Cambio.

In death the popes were portrayed as enjoying no peaceful sleep but ravaged still by the pressures of their lives.

7 and 8. (*following pages*) The expulsion of the poor from Siena in the famine of 1328 (*left*); feeding the poor outside the walls of Florence (*right*). According to the Florentine corn-official, Domenico Lenzi, the Sienese expelled the poor from their city in the famine. Though the assertion may merely reflect Florentine–Sienese hostility, the illustrator of his chronicle eagerly seized the opportunity to portray the rival commune's brutality. (*Libro del Biadaiolo*, Florence, Biblioteca Laurenziana, Tempiano 3, c. 57v.)

9. (*top left*) Knight on horseback. Perhaps from a Paduan funeral monument, mid-fourteenth century. (London, Victoria and Albert Museum.)

10. (*bottom left*) Scenes of war. Drawing on paper, late fourteenth century, in the style of Altichiero. (London, British Museum.)

11. (*above*) Palazzo Comunale of Buggiano Alto. Even small communities, such as Buggiano (in the Val di Nievole between Prato and Pistoia), come in this period to have their own *Palazzi Comunali*.

12–15. (*following pages*) Four scenes from the Commune at Work from the Statutes of Pisa: 12. (*top left*) Election of Anziani (*Breve Populi et Compagniarum Pisani Communis 1303–8*, A.S. Pisa, Com. A.N.5, c. 43v.); 13. (*bottom left*) The Capitano del Popolo takes the oath (*Breve del Popolo et delle Compagnie del Comune*, A.S. Pisa, Com. A.N.6, c. 7r.); 14. (*top right*) Road-builders (*Breve Pisani Comunis, 1303*, A.S. Pisa, Com. A.N.4, c. 394r.); 15. (*bottom right*) Official dictating to a notary (*Breve Pisani Comunis, 1303*, A.N.4, c. 9v.)

De electione antianozum.

DIOXILIAQADIRIFOR
saerai vinis menabus et sincere ho
minum consaentie precordi delet.
Et in elecmonibus antianozum et
cozum notariozum ad quas in ex
saeram pro salute rei pub pris civi
tatis precedendum est et precord

D. Di mantenere le cōpagne del populo di pisa ꞇ de
del giuramento di mess lo capitano.

O. CAPITA
di pisa ꞇlla cita ꞇ
uro alle sācte dio u
fendero ꞇ māterro l
et difendro ꞇ māter
li honori ꞇ le ragione
pisa ꞇ dell universita
del populo di pisa ꞇ d
che lo daro aiuto ꞇ f
ni ꞇ alle cōpagne
ꞇ del distrecto sop
tenere ꞇ difendere

Quartus liber de opibus incipit
De uia buryi ecalus

BAPtin ubicum que necesse fuit ficam
et shalter ab ecclia sancti michaelis
usqs ad pontem ueterem. et ast de
pontis ueteris usqs ad turrim de
quarris. de tegulis siue lapioibus
et isin alsan et impodian sicut o

16 and 17.   Sienese country dwellers bringing produce to the city-market. From the fresco
of 'Justice and the Common Good', painted 1338–40 by Ambrogio Lorenzetti in the
Communal Palace of Siena. (See also 18 and 19. on the following pages.)

18 and 19.   Two further scenes of country dwellers going to market in the city, from Ambrogio Lorenzetti's 'Justice and the Common Good' in the Communal Palace of Siena. (See 16 and 17.)

20.   (*following page*) The Triumph of Saint Thomas Aquinas. By Francesco Traini, in S. Caterina, Pisa.

Rocca, 'La signoria di Oberto Pallavicino', *Archivio storico lombardo*, lxxxiii, 1957. For Guglielmo VII of Monferrato, A. Bozzola, 'Un capitano di guerra e signore subalpino', *Miscellanea di storia italiana della R. Deputazione per le antiche provincie e la Lombardia*, s. iii, xix, 1922.

On the emergence of the signorie, E. Salzer, *Über die Anjänge der Signorie in Oberitalien*, Berlin, 1900, is still useful. F. Ercole, *Dal comune al principato*, Florence, 1929 approaches the theme from a juridical point of view. Studies of particular aspects are: L. Simeone, 'La formazione della signoria scaligera', *A.M., dell' Accademia di Agricoltura, Scienze e Lettere di Verona*, cviii, 1926; F. Cognasso, 'Le origini della signoria lombarda', *Archivio storico lombardo*, lxxxii, 1956; L. Simeoni, 'L'elezione di Obizzo d'Este a signore di Ferrara', *ASI*, 1953, pt. i; W. Montorsi, 'Considerazioni intorno al sorgere della signoria estense', *A. M. della Deputazione di Storia Patria per le provincie modenese*, s. 8. x, 1958; J. K. Laurent, 'The signory and its supporters: the Este of Ferrara', *Journal of Modern History*, 3, 1977; J. K. Hyde, *Padua in the age of Dante*, Manchester, 1966; A. Torre, *I Polentani fino al tempo di Dante*, Florence, 1966. There are general discussions in E. Sestan, 'Le origine delle signorie cittadine un problema storico esaurito?', *BISI*, lxxii, 1962 (and in his *Italia medievale*, Naples, 1968); F. Diaz, 'Di alcuni aspetti istituzionali dell' affermarsi delle signorie', *Nuova rivista storica*, 1, 1969; and G. Chittolini, 'La crisi della libertà comunale', *RSI*, 1970.

For the coming of the signoria at Mantua see P. Torelli, 'Capitanato del Popolo e vicariato imperiale come elementi costitutivi della signoria bonacolsiana', *A.M. della R. Accademia Virgiliana di Mantova*, ns., xiv–xvi, 1921–3; *Mantova: La storia*, I *Dalle origini a Gianfrancesco primo marchese*, ed. G. Coniglio, Mantua, 1958. Useful too is the annotated edition of the *Breve chronicon mantuanum* (1095–1309), edited by E. Marani, Mantua, 1968.

On the signorie in general P. J. Jones, 'Communes and Despots: the city-state in Late Medieval Italy', *Transactions of the Royal Historical Society*, 1965 and D. M. Bueno de Mesquita, 'The place of Despotism in Italian Politics' in *Europe and the Late Middle Ages*, ed. J. R. Hale, J. R. L. Highfield, B. Smalley, London, 1965. On individual signorie: A. Vasina, *I romagnoli fra autonomie cittadine e accentramento papale nell' età di Dante*, Florence, 1965; P. J. Jones, *The Malatesta of Rimini and the Papal State*, London, 1974; J. Larner, *The Lords of Romagna*, London, 1965; W. L. Gundersheimer, *Ferrara: the style of a Renaissance Despotism*, Princeton, 1973; G. Franceschini, *I Montefeltro*, Varese, 1970; E. Cardini, 'Una signoria cittadina "minore" in Toscana; i Casali di Cortona', *ASI*, 1973.

On the government of Venice see F. C. Lane, *Venice: A Maritime Republic*, London, 1973, chs. 8 and 9. See too his 'The Enlargement of the Great Council of Venice' in *Florilegium Historiale: Essays presented to Wallace K. Ferguson*, ed. J. G. Rowe and W. H. Stockdale, Toronto, 1971; S. Chojnacki, 'In search of the Venetian patriciate: Families and factions in the Fourteenth Century' in *Renaissance Venice*, ed. J. R. Hale, London, 1975; and *idem.*, 'Crime, punishment and the Trecento Venetian State' in *Violence and Civil Disorder, cit.* G. Cracco's *Società e stato nel medioevo veneziano (Secoli XII–XIV)*, Florence, 1967, is stimulating but has been much criticised.

1. J. C. Lünig, *Codex Italiae Diplomaticus*, Frankfort, 1735, i, 1583.
2. Salimbene, *cit.*, pp. 281, 805; G. de' Mussi, *Chronicon Placentinum, cit.*, p. 596.
3. Thorndike, *A History of Magic, cit.*, ii, 827; Salimbene, *cit.*, p. 516; E. Jordan, *Les origines de la domination angevine en Italie, cit.*, i, 59, n. 1.
4. Rolandino da Padova, *Cronica in factis et circa facta Marchie Trivixane*, ed. A. Bonardi, *RIS*, viii, pt. 1, p. 171.

5. Salzer, Fuiano (*Carlo d'Angiò, cit.*), and many others have given preeminence here to Pelavicini's lieutenant, Buoso da Doara, on the strength of concessions of lordship made to him by Sabbionetta (March 1247) and Soncino (July 1248). But these are minor communes and the character and circumstances of the grants are obscure.
6. Astegiano, *cit.*, i, p. 291 (no. 643).
7. *Annales Placentini Gibellini, MGH*, xviii, p. 531; Salimbene, *cit.*, especially pp. 501–4, 695–6, and 880.
8. *Chronica parva ferrarienses, RIS*, viii, cols, 487–8.
9. Salimbene, *cit.*, pp. 244–5, 528, 748.
10. *Idem*, 632–3, 729.
11. Salzer, *cit.*, pp. 203, 302–3.
12. V. Cian, 'Vivaldo Belcalzer e l'enciclopedismo italiano delle origini', *Giornale storico della letteratura italiana*, Supplemento no. 5, Turin, 1902, pp. 145–7.

CHAPTER EIGHT

The countryside

I

The political struggles continued; ultimately everything depended, not on them, but on the weather. It was a subject which loomed large in the pages of the chroniclers. There was the expected cold of January and February when in many years the Po froze over, and horses, carts, and sledges were driven across the ice. A knightly 'court' might be held upon it, with great fires blazing, sometimes even a tournament of arms; it evokes a vignette as if from the pages of Folgore da Sangimignano. At such times, it was said, one could walk upon rivers from Ferrara to Treviso. Then there was the sudden unexpected cold, as in 1330, when men and women went in scanty clothes to the wine-harvest and were attacked by rain and snow so as to be 'in danger of death'. The grapes were so frozen they could not be touched and fires of straw and vine-tendrils had to be lit under the vats before they could be trodden. In winter the snow might lie in ten feet drifts in the Apennines, and wild-boar, men believed, would multiply but pigs and cattle die of hunger. Wolves from the mountains, weak and starving, would enter the towns of the plain at night, be hunted to death next morning, and hung up around the cathedral square. Wine would freeze in the bottles; bread would freeze. If the snow lay too long the pulses could not be sown, the sown corn would die, and so too almost all the animals, 'and many men freeze and die from the cold'. In March one feared the hailstorm that might destroy the unripe almonds, figs, and other fruits. In April, or even the beginning of May, might come a sudden hoar frost out of a blue sky to kill the vines and olives, so that in that year, as the chroniclers complained in 1234, 'weddings were celebrated more with water than wine'.

But the main preoccupation was rain. Sometimes too little of it, so that the earth was rock-hard and the mill wheels could not turn in the dried-up river beds, and the wells inside the cities dried up. At which the *podestà*, the commune and people, would follow their bishop and clergy in procession around the town, appealing to a cloudless heaven for mercy. But worse, worst of all in areas of Mediterranean climate where even a slight increase in normal rainfall can bring disaster, was too much rain: the September deluge which could destroy the

153

grapes; the continuous downpour from cloudy skies between September and Christmas which could prevent sowing; the great May and June rains which brought floods to the Arno and (very much more frequently) the Po valleys. The chronicles at such times expand, describing crops submerged, stooks of gathered corn floating on the waters, gravel swept from the roads, bridges broken, houses destroyed, men from tree-tops or the roofs of houses seeing their fellows drowned.

It was a capricious climate. There were years 'of great abundance', many of them; and years when corn was dear. There were times when the harvest was poor at Bologna, Ravenna, and Siena, but rich at Florence and Arezzo, who would come to their help (and the next year, it might be, the favour would be repaid). Scarcely a year passed when some town, somewhere, was not coping with the problem of starvation. But there were also some years, years which no one who had lived through them would forget (from the harvest of 1226 to that of 1227, of 1258–60, 1271–2, 1276–7, 1281–2, 1285–6, 1311–12, 1328–30, 1339–40, 1346–7, 1352–3, 1374–5), when almost everywhere the seeds had been flooded out or the crops of April and May had been lashed down by storms or shrivelled up at the onset of a great heat and when, until the next summer, there followed sometimes painful shortages, sometimes a universal famine.

The towns then witnessed harrowing scenes as starving peasants abandoned the countryside and begged for bread through the streets or at the church doors, children dying as their mothers held them: 'and a great scum played about their mouths' (presumably a result of *cancrum oris* or gangrene of the mouth, particularly associated with famine diarrhoea in children). 'The poor were begging in infinite numbers; you heard their cries and groans through the squares, in the suburbs, and churches, and an infinite number of them died of hunger both in the city and the diocese.' The weaker, or more ruthless communes, as in 1329, Perugia, Siena, Lucca, and Pistoia, responded by expelling the poor, so that 'at this bitter time' Florence then, as Giovanni Villani records with a certain rueful pride, 'supported in God's pity all the beggars of Tuscany.' As the famine deepened it would begin to strike the more prosperous. There would be murmurings among the citizens when the commune began to mix millet and barley in the wheaten loaves; the officials would respond by placing a chopping block and an axe outside the corn market and cutting off a few limbs as a warning to troublemakers. Yet there would be riots if the commune were unable to draw corn from outside. Misery too. By the following June many citizens would be eating loaves of flax seed as good bread, would be selling their furniture, their very houses, for a little corn or a little money. In June, July, and August the famine plagues would begin, dysentry, typhus, typhoid.

In contrast to northern Europe Italy in this age can be thought of as the seat of 'an urban economy' as a world of towns. Yet – indeed until our own day – the majority of Italians have passed their lives outside the towns, and the fate of the towns was always intimately bound up with the *contado*, the countryside over which they ruled or claimed to rule. Life depended ultimately upon the men of the villages: those settlements distinguished as *ville* (unfortified villages) or as *castelli* (villages 'fortified', though not necessarily with a wall, often simply by a ditch or even a hedge). The cities themselves, where fields of corn and vineyards were normally to be found within the walls, where the law courts closed at harvest time, where life depended upon the business of the corn and cattle markets, had a strongly rural flavour. Most of the men who ruled them were landowners; quite modest town dwellers held property in the countryside; many peasants went off each morning through their town gates to their holdings; and the wives of the urban poor provided a pool of casual labour at harvest time. The livelihood of most men depended upon agriculture, not upon commerce.

That livelihood had to be won from a soil, and in face of climatic conditions, which varied very widely, not merely from region to region but also within regions. Though in general the South, the world of mountainous Basilicata, rocky Calabria, the wasted Terra d'Otranto, the malarial lowlands of Latium and lower Tuscany, had a malign climate and harsh terrain, there were some areas within it, such as the coastal plains of Sicily and the corn-lands of Apulia and Campania, which were immensely fertile. If the lands of the North, in particular the plain of the Po, presented a picture of prosperity, they were by no means uniformly rich – one thinks particularly of the central Apennine mass, or of the still undrained regions of northern Tuscany and the Veneto – and contained the sharpest contrasts in landscape and vegetation and in successful and unsuccessful farming. These differences went hand in hand with wide differences in food-gathering techniques, so that in this age Italy could be seen almost as a museum illustrating the historical stages in their development. Hunting was represented by those areas in the South where the nobility, for love of the chase, still preserved their lands from the encroachment of agriculture. The age of nomadic herdsmen is recalled by the seasonal passing of huge transhumant flocks which grazed upon the mountains from the spring and returned to the plains in autumn, moving from Apulia to the Abruzzi, from Tuscany and the Romagna to the Apennines, from Lombardy and Piedmont to the Alps. In some mountainous areas the earliest form of farming was still practised, 'slash and burn', where woodlands were cleared by fire and a single crop taken from the land fertilised by the ashes. In the dry fields of Latium and the south the 'fallow' system was frequent: after harvesting the land was grazed over and fallowed for three to five years before being resown. In other areas, in much of Tuscany and Emilia, intensive agriculture was common. Vines and olives were planted between the corn, and three or more field systems were common. Finally in the vicinity of certain towns agricultural production was often determined by export requirements, often to an international market; here one found stock-raising, the market-gardening of fruit, and the cultivation of industrial crops such as flax and hemp.

Diversity was the key-note. Despite this three general aspects of change in rural life can be identified in the thirteenth and fourteenth centuries: first a decay in personal, feudal bonds of dependence and the rise of new economic bonds between lords and men; second, a large increase in agricultural production; and third, the slow emergence of the land-settlement patterns of modern Italy. These developments were often muted or appeared tardily, sometimes not at all, in the South; but in the North they went to make up a real, if not uniform, movement.

II

In Italy the manorial economy (*sistema curtense*) had never had any absolute dominion. By 1200 it was in full decline. Tenurial serfdom, the exaction of agricultural services and the working of demesne land (the lord's own fields) by serfs had passed or was passing away and by 1300 survived only in isolated and remote areas. Everywhere men variously described as *villani, coloni, manentes, inquilini, adscripticii* – terms which on different estates, sometimes on the same estates, implied different burdens and degrees of dependence – were becoming landowners or landless men, free from any obligation to work for their lord.

Yet the disappearance of tenurial villeinage did not mean the disappearance of all forms of feudal dependence. Indeed the decline of economic feudalism in the twelfth century had been accompanied by a certain increase in the incidence of personal bonds. At the beginning of the thirteenth century most men in the countryside were still *homines alterius*: juridical dependants, that is to say men who often answered for various obligations to their lord rather than to any commune, and who could be sold or pledged as security for loans by him. The system of demesne service had frequently been replaced by one where land was leased in return for both rent and an oath of 'fidelity' which emphasised the lessee's servile status. The obligations upon the *fideles* (or *homines de masnada* as they were frequently called) who took these oaths could vary widely. Sometimes they promised to stand to their lord's jurisdiction, sometimes to pay taxation, to contribute 'aids' at the marriage or knighting of the lord or the members of his family, to perform military service, to carry out *corvées*, to give hospitality to the lord or his guests, and so on. On other occasions the obligations sought from them were so slight as to be insignificant. Not infrequently they obtained licences from their lords to go to the cities and to engage in trade or the professions.

At the *castello* of Passignano, for example, in the Pesa valley in Tuscany, all but five of seventy-eight males from sixty-nine families were expressly recorded in 1233 as being dependants of the abbey.[1] Among these can be noted the family of Gianello the Smith (see Table 2), all of whose sons and grandsons had been temporarily pledged by the abbot against a loan in 1193. Yet it was a family which enjoyed considerable prosperity. In 1204 its members did homage to the abbot for twenty-one pieces of land which they held as *fideles*, while around the same time Gianni di Gianello is found selling freehold land to other men. Their status did not prevent members of the family from becoming knights. It did not forbid their emigration to Florence, nor their entry into the legal profession. In fact the Judge Ridolfo, recorded between 1231 and 1282, was still registered as a dependant of the abbey while exercising his office. Another judge from the same village, the son of one Massese di Jollarino, recorded in the document of 1233 as 'a knight for the commune of Florence' only obtained a charter of freedom from the Abbey in 1257.

It can be seen that often the relation of *fidelis* to lord was more an irritant than something involving major hardship, a largely residual element of the feudal system, likely to die away simply with the passing of time. Looking at these

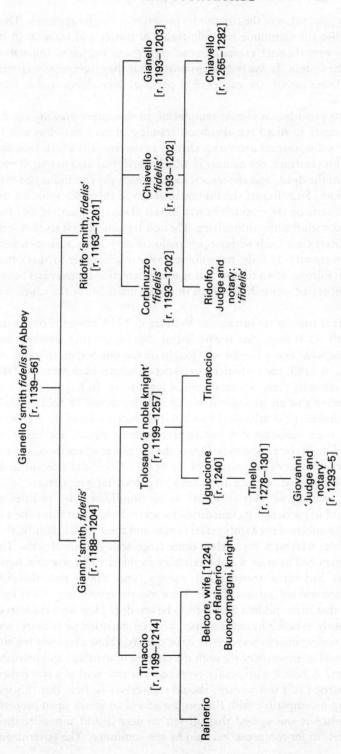

Table 2 The family of Gianello 'fidelis' of the Abbey of Passignano

From J. Plesner, *L'émigration de la campagne à la ville libre de Florence au XIIᵉ siècle*, Copenhagen, 1934. (r = recorded at this time)

bonds of fidelity, the rulers of the communes preserved a neutral approach. They often claimed that the commune had sole rights of justice and taxation in its *contado*. Yet they were themselves often the owners of *fideles* and felt no imperative call to change the system. It was only occasionally that they intervened to limit, to a greater or lesser extent, the existence of personal dependence within their territories.

Such occasions provided an instant temptation to the notary drawing up the necessary documents to recall the rhetorical training of his schooldays and to break forth into a disquisition upon such themes as the free will which God had bestowed upon his creatures, the manner in which Christ had died to free all men from servitude to the devil, and the tenacity with which the commune had ever fought for freedom. Such flights should not be taken at their face value for the emancipation of serfs by the communes was in fact always limited, *ad hoc*, and designed to deal with specific difficulties. Though legislation reveals that serfs did sometimes leave their lands without permission of their lords, such men were not welcomed in the city. In Italy 'town air' was very much slower to 'make free' than in northern Europe; often the serf had to evade detection for ten years before being deemed liberated, something which in the intimate life of the towns was not easy.

Sometimes, it is true, as for instance at Volterra in 1213 when the commune was at war with its bishop, the towns issued decrees offering freedom and citizenship to the *fideles* of any knight who fought on the side of their enemies. At Florence, again, in 1289, the authorities freed dependants sold to enemies of the commune. Occasionally there was more radical legislation. In Reggio Emilia in 1242 it was enacted that all possessions within the city should be held as allods (i.e. freehold), and in 1258 all feudal bonds within half a mile of the city were dissolved. But such incidents did not imply, by any means, the universal abolition of serfdom in their territories. One of the few places where this did occur was Bologna, where a series of measures of the years 1256–7 did attempt to do away with the institution, at least in so far as regarded lay proprietors.

It is worth pausing on this incident[2] as it illuminates the realities of emancipation and in particular its unradical character. Bologna at this time was dominated by the nobles of the Lambertazzi faction and the d'Andalò family, that is to say by nobles who were themselves quite large-scale owners of serfs. The problem these men had to meet was the existence in the city of a powerful *popolo* whose members had often married serf women, and whose sons therefore inherited the stain and obligations of serfs. How was the resentment of free men who discovered that their children were serfs to be avoided? How were the fears of re-enserfment likely to be felt by any free man, who, on statistical probability, was likely to have a serf-woman in his ancestry to be quelled? How again was the city to be spared a total re-enserfment through the chances of marriage and breeding with serf women? A solution originally proposed was that sons of a free father, even though married to a serf woman, should themselves be free. But this was rejected as being incompatible with Roman law and as an attack upon property rights. In its place it was agreed that all serf owners should surrender their dependants in return for compensation paid by the commune. The government indemnified each owner with £B[olognesi] 10 for each male or female serf over fourteen, and with £B. 8 for each under. In addition he was allowed to confiscate within six months all property belonging to the serf.

The book in which the names of the 379 serf-owners and their 5,791 serfs were inscribed in order to meet the claims for compensation was called the *Liber Paradisus*. For serfs who had been allowed to leave their lord's lands and dwell in the city it did indeed bring some relief, though often, if the confiscations were in fact carried out, rather expensive relief, from fears of recall to the countryside and from trying legal complications. But the Paradise to which the unfree in the countryside were now admitted was one rather remote from the dreams of the religious. Deprived of all their property, if their lord wished it so, their first act as free men was to register themselves upon the commune's tax rolls, a duty which they were commanded to follow upon pain of the penalties for homicide. For these men, threatened with the loss of their lands, the first instinct must have been to seek from their lords a re-establishment of the old servile bond. In fact, they were prohibited from doing this under pain of amputation of 'the tongue, a hand, and a foot'. Despite these threats it is clear that many did seek to reinserf themselves in the years that followed. In 1282 and then in 1304 the commune was legislating again in an attempt to abolish the serfdom it had thought to annul in the 1250s.

To release serfs from their bondage was considered a work of Christian piety, and it is possible to find occasional examples of emancipation which came about through that motive. The Lady Cunizza da Romano (who appears in canto ix of the *Paradiso*), for instance, freed all her dependants in 1265 in the hope of benefiting the souls of her brothers Alberico and Ezzelino (who appears in canto xii of the *Inferno*). But in general the decline of personal serfdom was not the fruit of any generalised sentiments of legal or religious good will, nor, save indirectly, the work of the city-communes. In the mobile society of the age it was difficult for the lord to secure his rights from the system, and so often he drew little profit from it. Normally he was willing, either through individual manumissions or through charters of freedom granted to village communities, to dissolve the bonds of his serfs in return for a money payment. The most important rôle that the city communes played here was in abolishing those privileges hitherto enjoyed by *fideles* against free men. In the Florentine *contado*, during the first half of the thirteenth century, for instance, most men must have preferred to be considered as serfs than as freemen, for while *homines alterius* paid only 2s. 2d. in taxation levies, free men were charged at 12s.: a distinction which caused the commune to pass laws against those who claimed the status of serfs when they were in fact free. In these circumstances the change in the Florentine tax system in 1250, whereby property became the basis for assessment, irrespective of the status of the man upon it, removed a powerful stimulus to claim to be 'unfree'.

From that time, both in Florence and elsewhere the number of *fideles* and others unfree in their persons declined very rapidly, There were still, of course, some who looked with distaste at the coming of the new order and who struggled against it as best they could. One sees this sentiment in the will of the Lord Ramberto Ramberti of Ferrara, drawn up in 1312. It is a document filled with nostalgia for former comrades in arms and old battle-fields ('the Lord Giovanni Soranzo of Venice who was in the army at Trieste' and 'the Lord Taddeo of the Counts of Montefeltro at the time San Leo and the country of Montefeltro were fighting with the said Lord Taddeo and there stood Count Bono, son of the late Guido da Montefeltro, and at that time Mercatello and Predappio were burnt and Uguccione della Faggiuola was in that *chevauchée* . . .'). Here is a bluff old gentleman who hardly surprises us with his last – and for his heirs no doubt highly awkward – stipulation:

Item he has willed and disposed that neither his heirs nor their heirs nor their successors can or may in any way, on any pretext, for any price or reward, manumit or free his serfs, and always shall they be and remain serfs and in servitude as they are at present. And if his heirs or their successors shall act otherwise, either now or in future, they shall be eliminated and removed from and deprived of the inheritance of the testator.[3]

One of the pleasures of drawing up a will is the illusion of being able to shape the future. But, it is, of course, an illusion. At the beginning of the thirteenth century most men who lived in the countryside were unfree. By the end, one may guess, most were legally their own men. None the less, in some areas, notably in the Apennines, the holding of land by *fideles* continued throughout the fourteenth and fifteenth centuries; while in the Alpine regions, Piedmont, Friuli, and the South, the process of enfranchisement was much slower than in northern and central Italy. Feudalism, which, after all, was only abolished by Napoleon (and which continued in Sardinia until 1838), has been perhaps an under-rated factor in early modern Italian history.

However, tenurial serfdom, feudalism as an economic system, was dead. In its collapse four principal forms of land-ownership came to dominate. In the first, the large landowner held on to his land and farmed the old demesne by hired labour. This was much more characteristic of the South than the North. Second, all over Italy some individual peasants continued to work their own freeholds, as indeed they had done even when the manorial system had been most widely diffused. Third, large amounts of land, especially that owned by the Church, were let at perpetual hereditary lease in return for a purely formal fealty and low rents in money or kind. In this case the tenancies might sometimes be burdened with high re-entry fines; frequently they were not; and very often in the course of the fourteenth century they came to be converted into allods. A common effect of the introduction of this lease, in northern Italy in particular, was to dispossess ecclesiastical proprietors in favour of laymen. (By the middle of the sixteenth century the Church in the north and centre of the peninsula owned only 10–15 per cent of the land, whereas in the south it still retained 65–75 per cent). Sometimes the holders of these hereditary tenancies (*fittaiuoli perpetui, livellari*) were peasants working their own land; more generally – and particularly in flat, fertile, well-drained regions – they were mesne tenants, town dwellers or members of a rural middle class, who sublet in their turn to others.

But from 1200 the most marked innovation in tenurial practice was the ever-increasing establishment of short-term leases in return for heavy rents either in money, or, more frequently, in kind. Among these leases, sharecropping, especially *mezzadria*, began to assume a prominent place, in particular on developed land in central and northern Italy. In contracts of *mezzadria* land was leased to the tenant on condition that he should pay each year half the fruits of the land which he worked to the landlord. An early example may be cited from the formulary of a notary of Arezzo,[4] drawn up between 1240 and 1254:

Ubertino, son of the late P., has taken on lease and received in order to work, for the following three years, from Ugo, son of the late Bono, a piece of land placed in such and such a place, next to such and such, which land the aforesaid Ugo has leased to Ubertino, and has promised, for himself and his heirs, to Ubertino, accepting for himself and his heirs, not to take nor molest but to lawfully protect that land for him, up to the aforesaid term, from every person and condition of man. And the aforesaid Ubertino for himself and his heirs, has promised to the same Ugo, receiving for himself and his heirs, in each year, from now to the aforesaid term, truly and at the appropriate time, to plough, plough again, cultivate well, and prepare that same land, and to return in due course and plough for a fourth time with seed; all at the expense and cost of that same labourer. And he has promised that he will in each year, at the appropriate time, cause to be carried, sent, and borne to that same land, 40 measures of good dung, at the cost of the same worker. And that he will not uproot from that land any tree nor fruit-trees but will duly preserve it. And that half of each and every one of the fruits which he shall receive from that earth he will each year, through the whole month of August, bear and bestow at the house of the aforesaid Ugo in the city of Arezzo, or, when the lessor shall wish it, at another house standing in the same city or at the threshing floor of the said Ugo; and this shall be at the choice of the lessor. And each and everyone of these aforesaid things, the aforesaid lessor and lessee have promised for themselves and their heirs . . .

Similar contracts govern the lease of other types of land. From the Arezzo formulary may be cited the lease of a vineyard for four years or for another term which was agreed in common. The lessee here promises:

to prune, hoe, harrow, plough for a second time, and to prepare well all posts, poles, withies, all at the expense of the labourer, and to stake out and plant each and every part of the vineyard, and to drain and hold drained that vineyard, to make ditches and hedges around it, and to extend the same hedges, and to do each and every thing necessary for the vineyard to remain in good condition. And he promises, each year, to bring and to bear in the city of Arezzo at the house of the aforesaid lessor or where he should wish, one half of the grapes, figs, nuts, pears, and of each and every fruit in the same vineyard, at the total expense and risk of that labourer . . .

Though the essence of the system is here, everywhere there were local variations in contract. Often it was renewable, not, as here, every three years, but every year, a stipulation implying great insecurity for the lessee, who was obliged, if the landlord wished it, to vacate his land at the term. Normally the landlord promised explicitly to provide half the seed. Often, what is implicit, namely that the peasant should live on the land with his family, is spelt out in the document; the assumption was that the fields would be farmed both by the contractor and his wife and children. With time it was customary for much more detailed conditions governing the use of the land to be added: on rotation of crops, digging, manuring, ploughing; all of which were designed to ensure that the landlord received a full return from his lease.

One can see something of this, and something of the mutual recrimination which the system engendered, in a notarial minute drawn up at the end of our

161

period, preparatory to the renewal at *mezzadria* of a farm near Settimo.[5] Here Bellozzo di Lorenzo Bartoli, from the parish of San Lorenzo in Florence, grants the land for five years to Piro 'called Capello' and his sons, Pipo and Giovanni. They should plough it 'in good ploughman fashion, and give me half of what they harvest'. They should dig and hoe the vineyards as best they can, and they should keep ditches trimmed, levelled, and in good order: 'as they have not done so far'. They should reinforce the vines in season: 'and I will give them for this a *staio* of grain, if they really raise the vine shoots from the stem. Even if the *staio* of grain costs a florin, I ought to give them this as aid'. They should repair the shed by the side of the house, 'which is broken and it's not my fault but theirs', at their own expense with some fifty to sixty faggots of cane. Each party is to have half of the wine which has been made:

I mean I want to have one *cognio*, the first that comes from the spout. I don't want to happen what happened last year when Pipo said he wanted to fill his barrel before I filled mine, so that I wanted to overturn it for the fury I felt.

Half of the fruits should be sent to Florence. They should see that the canes are staked out in the vineyard 'as they haven't done yet for this year I found good stakes not used'. And they should bring to Florence every year a brace of fat capons and a pair of fat chickens and eight-dozen eggs. If they beat the flax they're to be paid 6 *solidi* per *mazzo*. If they keep a pig, Bellozzo will have half of it and will provide them with three staia of bran. 'And they're to put my share of brushwood on one side, for I've no wish to feel I want to kill or say obscenities to myself any more'. Because they owe Bellozzo a lot of money they must repay him four florins at the grain or grape harvest: 'for the money I've lost is worth more than the harvest on this farm'. They should close the dyke at the garden gate, even though the garden's small, 'so that it doesn't seem a waste land as Capello's kept it'. Half of the straw and the pigeon-dung is to be put among the wines. 'If news comes that he's pruned in a damp season, he's to be fined a *cognio* of wine'.

This type of contract in land came increasingly to be accompanied by leases of livestock on similar lines. In agreements *in soccidia*, cows, goats, and sheep were leased to the peasant who pastured them at his own expense and in return paid half the progeny of the beasts, together with half their wool or cheeses to the lessor. Oxen and horses could be hired by two systems. In contracts *ad laborandum* the beast was valued (say at £15 *modenesi*) and leased in return for a fixed payment (say 15 *staia* of grain). If it were lost through ill custody, war, hunger or thirst, theft, or through any fault of the lessee or his family, restitution of its value had to be made, together with interest, to the proprietor. In leases *ad quartem partem lucri et damni* the lessee returned the beast he had hired, together with a quarter of the profits he had made from ploughing with the animal. Such contracts, in which the investment was always protected against loss at the expense of the peasant hiring the animal, brought very large profits to urban speculators.

III

In effect *mezzadria* was more a contract to hire labour than to let land, and its diffusion in the thirteenth and fourteenth centuries represents the reduction of many customary tenants to the role of landless agricultural workers. Perhaps its coming could, in the first place at least, be explained as the effect of a surplus of men and consequent shortage of land, brought about by the immense increase in population from the tenth century. So too could the rise in the population be seen both as effect and cause of the continued expansion of agricultural production which took place in northern and central Italy up to the early fourteenth century.

This expansion is revealed above all in efforts made to increase the area of arable land.[6] *Bonifiche* (or drainage works), designed to capture more land from water, continued. The evidence of documents and of place-names (in, for example, the common Ronco from *runcus* = newly cleared land, or the frequent Cortenuova = new village) shows the work of assarting still going forward through the thirteenth century. In Piedmont the establishment of new communities amidst waste land, in Umbria the terracing of hill slopes, in Lombardy the embankment of rivers and construction of dykes and canals, tell the same story. Along the Po the statutes of neighbouring communes, as those of Ferrara in 1287, show an intense concern for the maintenance of hydraulic works designed to channel the river, and a wide range of officials: Judges of the Dykes, Notaries of the Dykes, Labourers and Guards, appointed to protect the system. In the Tuscan hill-country, with the increasing drainage of the valley bottoms, hill-top villages were abandoned for settlements in the plains. Here, too, roads which had run along the watersheds or middle terraces of hills were given up for new routes on recently drained flat lands, a development too gradual to be described as a 'road revolution' but a movement which slowly changed the face of the countryside.

In general *bonifica* was an immensely slow and sporadic process. At the end of the fourteenth century large areas of the plains were still undrained. In the Lucchese, Pisano, in the Senese Maremma and the Veronese, vast lakes and marshes still gave a distinctive character to countryside. In the Ravennate in our period, the waters were progressively expanding at the expense of land. The effects of 'the agricultural revolution' must not be overemphasised, for the defects of the system are obvious: undercapitalisation, particularly in respect of farm beasts (predictable enough, since in times of famine, animals died before men); inadequate provision of manure; primitive crop-rotations; and the predominance of corn cultivation. Though it is difficult to generalise here from individual examples, it is doubtful if there were any overall increase in crop yield. In the royal farms of Apulia in 1282, officials were set targets of a 10–1 return on wheat, 12–1 on barley, 18–1 on broad beans, and 13–1 on chickpeas. Yet in 1309, in the same region, the royal officials were hoping for (though failing to get) a return on barley of 20–1, which, for that period, seems extraordinarily high. One can guess that the mean average for corn production over the whole peninsula stood somewhere in the region of 4–1; the same ratio calculated by the Roman agronomist, Columella, in the first century A.D. (and not all that far, it might be added, from what was found at the beginning of the nineteenth century). None the less, in certain regions, investment of urban landlords did something to produce a more intensive farming. Profits from commerce were sometimes devoted to the consolidation of scattered properties into large united farms, the building of homesteads, draining, planting trees, the provision of livestock, manure, and agricultural instruments. At the same time comparatively new crops such as the dye-plants, saffron and madder, rose in importance. Fruit growing was extended. Vineyards began to produce in large quantities the grapes of those particularly favoured wines, notably the *trebbiano* and *vernaccia*, which were marketed through the whole of Europe.

It was an age which could be seen as seeking a more rational ordering of agriculture. One is aware of something of this even in the South. The farms of the royal demesne of the kingdom of Naples were organised in a tight bureaucratic system, where each province had its 'master of farms' with a notary and a 'writer to the notary'. Both under the Hohenstaufen and their Angevin successors royal ordinances laid down rules for their management in great detail. In addition to crop targets one finds there very precise regulations for the payment of hands and numbers to be employed. The Master of the Farms is, for instance, instructed that fifty pigs require five swineherds and a sixth who will guard where they pasture. But in acorn-time another swineherd must be engaged. So too with stock; each plough should have six oxen, and with every plough one should sow four *salme* (15·44 kilolitres) of barley and eight *salme* of corn. Again, a wide variety of account books had to be kept; one, for example, containing a description of all animals on the farm together with their distinctive marks. Yet the cumulative force of these regulations has a final rather negative effect upon the reader. King Manfred's pronouncements on the laying habits of hens, the normal ratio of heiffers to calves likely to be bred from a herd, his insistence that 'each dove ought to have its own cot', suggest ultimately not so much a sensitive understanding of the land as hints to a harassed town-bred official on how to avoid being cheated by countrymen. And some incidents in the history of the royal farms, in fact, suggest that the grossest mismanagement in their everyday operations was all too possible. At Ordona in 1317, for example, 164 men were taken on as day labourers for harvest time at a wage of ten *grani* a day. Before setting to work – and this itself hints at an extraordinary situation – the men insisted that the local deputy of the Master of the Farms should present pledges guaranteeing the payment of their wages at the end of the harvest. In fact when the corn had been gathered in it was discovered that no money could be found with which to pay them. Hence the deputy's pledge, which consisted of nothing less than thirty-eight cattle from the royal herd, was handed over to the no doubt jubilant harvesters.[7]

In the same way one remains sceptical about the beneficent influence which, it has been claimed,[8] was exercised on the development of agriculture by the provisions in the statutes of the north Italian towns. Decrees, ordering, for instance, that land for corn be ploughed four times (as at Bologna and Reggio) or three times (as at Modena and Parma) before sowing, regulations on the number of times vines should be pruned, were merely attempts to support proprietors against peasants in the maintenance of share-cropping contracts. (The fixing of wages for day-labourers at harvest time has something of the same character.) The general declarations of obligations upon farmers to plant so many trees or vines each year, the demand, as at Modena, that each owner of a pair of oxen should sow a *mina* of hemp or flax and a *biolca* of sorghum, appear clumsily indifferent to local variations in soil and circumstances. Some statutes were perhaps useful. The setting of the earliest date for the *vendemmia* or wine-harvest worked against the production of immature wine by men seeking to be first upon the market. But in general one suspects that these measures had only the most marginal effect upon production.

The regulations for the royal farms of Apulia, the decrees of the northern communes, are both illustrations in their way of that contemporary passion for categorising and laying down precise legal rules, however inappropriate, for all the awkward irregularities of everyday life. Very much more valuable is the treatment accorded the farmer's livelihood in the *Liber ruralium commodorum*[9] of Pietro de'Crescenzi. Pietro, a Bolognese judge, was one of many in the thirteenth century (one thinks of the rhetoricians and the civil lawyers) who sought in their own specialised studies to apply the learning of the ancient world in a systematic way to modern problems. 'I have read many books of ancient and modern *savants*,' he writes, 'and I have examined myself the various methods used in cultivating our fields': words which recall Machiavelli's claim to attention in his preface to *The Prince*, and which fairly summarise his method. A close reading of classical writers on agriculture – Varro, Columella, Cato, and the Virgil of the Georgics – is combined with a knowledge of medieval treatises, such as those of Albertus Magnus and Giovanni of Salerno on plants and Burgundio of Pisa's translation of a Greek work on the vine. These are given contemporary relevance by the author's own observation of agricultural practice, and by knowledge gleaned from discussions with landlords of his own day, among whom he mentions particularly the Dominicans of Bologna, of whose house his brother was a member. Though the work was dedicated to Charles II of Naples it could have had little relevance for the *latifundia* of the South. Crescenzi's ideal was the new compact estate, organised round the *cascina* or enclosed 'fortress' farmhouse, and administered by an intelligent owner, informed by knowledge and love of the land. In many ways it still seems a remarkably valuable book. It discusses the character of plants, vegetables, and soils in general; trees and fruit trees (the author is aware of all today's forms of graft save the modern 'English graft'); gardening; uses of meadow and wood; stock raising, fishing, and bee-keeping. Particular attention is paid to the prevention of soil erosion, and careful consideration given to crop rotation, green manure (explaining the different methods used in Tuscany, Romagna, and the Milanese), the sowing of clover, and careful use of fertilisers. There is a long and useful section on the herbal properties of plants. Throughout the attention to detail is remarkable, from warnings against the danger to pure water supplies from lead piping to the recommendation that the feet of those treading the vine should previously have been washed.

'The virtues of the soil should be studied. When they are discovered they are as some priceless treasure to be conserved with humility and patience.' Crescenzi, who had given so much to that ideal he expounds, died in 1321, the year of

Dante's death. His book was destined to have a long-enduring influence. Translated into Italian and French in the fourteenth century, into German later, it ran into twenty-five printed editions before 1500, and was still being reissued in the eighteenth century. If 'the Renaissance' be a phrase to have any meaning outside the literary and artistic worlds, the *Liber ruralium commodorum* should be recognised as one of the most influential and, in its method, most representative works within it.

Certainly it marks an important stage in the history of the Italian countryside. The rise of that intensive farming for which Crescenzi was the propagandist, taken together with the extension of short-term leasing, laid the foundations for the gradual but decisive transformation of the Italian landscape to its modern aspect. In 1200 a normal pattern of settlement was a countryside in which men dwelling in *castelli* and *ville* went out each day to work a number of small separated fields dispersed widely throughout the territory of their village. In large parts of the South, it is true, this settlement in villages continued, and, though in decline, common field agriculture on unenclosed fields together with common rotation, pasture, and gleaning was still practised. In the North however landlords often used capital raised from the sale of remote lands and manumissions of serfs towards the consolidation of their estates. Before 1260 homogeneous and extensive estates were a rarity, and it was exceptional for any one proprietor to own a half or more of a parish. From the second half of the thirteenth century, however, portions of land scattered in various parts of the village territory were more and more brought together into consolidated farms: the *poderi* of modern Tuscany. Here the common field system was beginning to disappear; individual properties were increasingly hedged; and common pasture, too, declined. The men who worked the soil came to live on the farm, while the villages came to house merely a reserve pool of casual labour. Often by the end of the fourteenth century the old *castello* with its *fideles* holding dispersed lands had been transformed into the *casa da signore*, a country house or *villa* (in its modern meaning) where an urban landlord relaxed at the centre of an estate composed of broad, unified lands. Yet this process was nowhere yet complete. Where *bonifica* had been unsuccessful or untried, the land, its produce, and its tenures, remained unchanged. Even in the Emilian plain and in Tuscany, where the phenomenon was most marked, there were areas untouched by the new developments, and still, everywhere, many different varieties of land occupation could be discerned.

IV

At any one time rural society in this age could present wide contrasts in economic status. At the beginning of the thirteenth century the wretched *fidelis* who owned no land, for that matter the poor free-holder holding a small piece of land, enjoyed a greatly inferior standard of living to that of the family of Gianello the Smith in Passignano. There were *contadini grassi* in the countryside, as there were *popolani grassi* in the towns.

Yet such men were a small minority. It is true that a very large number of peasants owned land outright, but the area they held was generally miniscule and constantly fractioned between heirs. Small proprietors were very often, by necessity, at the same time both day-labourers and *mezzadristi*. Over central Italy as a whole it seems probable that it was a small and diminishing minority who farmed their own fields as an exclusive occupation. Already in the thirteenth century only 20 per cent of the land held from the chapter of the cathedral of Cremona was leased directly to peasants. The remaining 80 per cent was taken by the urban and rural middle class and farmed by dependants. There are areas where the position seems at first sight more favourable. At Siena in 1316, for instance, of 15,000 pieces of land, 8,500 were cultivated directly by proprietors and only 6,500 at short-term lease (of which 5,000 at *mezzadria*). But these figures are misleading. The peasant proprietor here was confined largely to the more difficult and unrewarding soils, and in the flat and fertile lands, *mezzadria* and ownership by the middle class were normal. Most peasants who farmed their own land, that is to say, lived close to subsistence; most by the end of the fourteenth century had become, to all intents and purposes, landless. By the early fifteenth century, in the Valdipesa slightly over 4 per cent owned their own land; in Valdignieve 12·8 per cent; in Valdimerina 12 per cent.

Subsistence was the common lot of most peasants. Looking ahead to the Florentine catasto of 1427, it can be seen that, for instance, in the rural district of Santo Spirito, which incorporated 309 villages, there dwelt over 7,000 families, Of these some 30 per cent were said to own nothing. Around 40 per cent held mobile and immobile goods of a value from 1 to 50 florins, and can be considered as poor. These two classes include labourers and almost all dependent cultivators. Twenty per cent possessed goods from 51 to 200 florins and could be considered as enjoying modest prosperity. A wealthy 10 per cent were assessed as having goods of over 200 florins in value. These last two classes were made up from owners of land and prosperous artisans. Several indications suggest that already by 1300 most areas of northern and central Italy would show similar patterns in the distribution of wealth.

Given the inadequacies of early technology it was inevitable that most workers upon the land lived close to the poverty line. But the quality of their lives was additionally depressed by the demands made upon them by the ecclesiastical and political authorities. In return for the payments of tithes to the Church, which to the middle of the thirteenth century constituted the largest single burden upon the peasant, they perhaps received something in return, an explanation of their life, spiritual comfort, and, if their lives displayed obedience and submission, the promise of a happy immortality. The relations of the town commune with the peasant, however, seem very largely parasitic. From the thirteenth century the cities exacted considerable taxation and the execution of *corvées* in road and bridge repair from the *contado*, and in return gave little. Sometimes, we have seen, urban landlords invested in improvement to their lands which at the same time brought benefits to their tenants. If the town had large-scale manufacturers, it could provide work for rural weavers and spinners under the putting-out system. The towns, too, provided the countryside with legal institutions and urban judges.

Yet as a consequence of the town's paramount need to secure as far as possible its food supplies, these institutions were primarily designed to ensure the subjection of the worker to his landlord, to ensure as the statutes of Bobbio put it: 'that he should work in good faith, without fraud from the rise of the sun to its setting'. It is a formula repeated, with minor variations, from Sicily to Piedmont. So too the statutes guaranteed compensation from peasants to landlords for unsatisfactory working of the land and legislated against any attempt at boycott or land-strike. It was normally laid down that the village commune should be held responsible for the working of the uncultivated properties of urban proprietors, and that if it failed to do so should be liable to pay the proprietors what the land would have been deemed to produce. In the thirteenth century the oath of the *podestà* of Parma specifically included the clause: 'I, who am ruler of the city of Parma, swear that if any man within the Bishopric of Parma shall leave the land of any citizen or man of Parma uncultivated I will distrain the commune of that hamlet or village to work the aforesaid land at the expense of that hamlet or village.'

Frequently the statutes sought – though with little success – to tie the peasant to the land. At Bologna in 1250 (and there are similar decrees in Siena, Perugia, and Parma in the second half of the thirteenth century), all 'rustics' who had come to the city during the previous five years were commanded to return to their villages. Frequently too the laws discriminated against the *contadino* in cases of criminal justice. In Parma, for example, the citizen who injured a peasant was fined 20s.; the peasant who injured a citizen 100s. At Siena in 1262 a citizen who injured a peasant was fined a quarter of what he would have paid for injuring a fellow citizen. More than this, even the most impartial administration of criminal justice in the countryside, whether exercised by commune or individual lord, cannot be seen simply as a benefit conferred. Since it gave opportunities to exact financial penalties it can equally be portrayed as another form of economic exploitation. So, for example, in Piedmont during the fourteenth century, there was, it has been suggested,[10] a clear link between periods when crime was or was not punished in the law courts and, on the one hand, the ability of the rural population to pay fines, on the other, the financial needs of the rulers. The criminal justice offered by the city, it may be concluded, was merely an irrelevance superimposed upon local self-help policing.

In the statutes of Bologna it was laid down that if a village refused payment of taxes the *podestà* should:

send horse and foot under one of his knights in an armed band to destroy the houses and possessions and goods of the men of that village, and to burn that village, its houses, and possessions. Its trees should be destroyed, and he should seize the goods of its inhabitants as those of an enemy.[11]

It is a passage which underlines the true character of the rural workers' relation to the commune: something which rested upon little else but the force exercised over a subject people. It would be misleading to describe this as the oppression of the countryside by the town, for townsmen owned most of the countryside; more accurately it could be considered as part of the familiar process in which the institutions of the rich exploit the poor.

To their landlords the *rustici* paid their work, either as day-labourers or as sharecroppers. What they were left with was the possibility of a life made up of absolute dependence upon the weather and real job insecurity. Most of their houses were made from wood, clay and pebbles, thatch, wattle, and straw. In the civil war which raged between the Uppers and Lowers in the countryside of Reggio Emilia in 1287 we hear of villagers, ravaged by both sides, simply removing their houses, bodily, to safety:

Those of Castelli carried their houses away and built them around Monte Bianello, up to the top of it. Those of Cauresano and Farneto and Comiano and Pazzola did the same around Monte Lucio, at the very top of it. Those from Cavilliano built their houses round the parish-church and dug moats and filled them with water in order to be safe 'from the face of the devastator.[12]

Normally peasants suffered a debilitating diet: thin vegetable soup, porridge; bread made from acorns, chestnut and spelt; and if they were fortunate, beans to provide protein. Much of the contempt expressed by townsmen for country-dwellers in this period sprang perhaps from the irritation felt by those on a full protein diet for those made apathetic by amino-starvation. In particular children between the ages of 9 and 30 months, were likely to have suffered from that protein deficiency (kwashiorkor) which, it seems probable, produces life-long physical and mental stunting. Finally the peasant was very frequently the victim of the money-lender, a rôle often filled by the landlord. Within the Italian countryside usury weighed heavily. Crops were frequently sold in advance of the harvest; tenancies at *mezzadria* were often accompanied by loans of seed, livestock, and farm implements from the landlord which trapped the farm-worker into an unending cycle of debt.

It is impossible to penetrate into the minds of these men, save, perhaps, by analogy. The first collections of Italian folksongs[13] date from the time of the Napoleonic administration, and reading them we are too often held up by references to rifles and compulsory military service to be able to read back with any confidence the thoughts of earlier centuries. Yet some elements in these are clearly very old. The songs to greet the May and to welcome the harvest correspond to many others from all over Europe. With them go Etruscan and Roman charms and superstitions, such practices as the lighting of fires to March – rites corresponding to the 'Beltane fires' in Scotland – which the authorities of the fourteenth century tried to stamp out as 'a custom of the heathen', but which – one recalls Pavese's *La luna e i falò* – have survived into our own day. At this time the fifteenth-century stereotype of the witch was still far from being formulated, and it has recently been shown[14] that the stories of mass persecutions of witches in Italy during the fourteenth century are the fruit of later forgeries. But peasants were at home in the world of spirits and in particular with the *tregenda*: the groups of women, it was said, who joined the society of Diana or Signora Oriente and Herodias, slayer of John the Baptist. Jacopo Passavanti, in his *Specchio della vera penitenza*, describes how in Tuscany the *tregenda* would be joined by demons, who would take on, in order to discredit them, the likeness of living men and women. Before the Inquisition of Milan in the 1380s, two women were executed for joining (and not simply for heretically imagining they had joined) Diana's band. They were accompanied, they said, by souls of the living and the dead, and by animals of every kind, save only the donkey and the wolf. They would visit the homes of the rich, rewarding those who received them well; then they would eat their animals, which, once consumed, would be restored to life by the queen. Diana had taught them knowledge of herbs and magic skill in divining. One of the women — though the story was probably suggested to her by the Inquisitor, since it is alien to the folk beliefs of the age — admitted to having had carnal communion with a devil called Lucifulus. Most of these beliefs, songs, and ceremonies are clearly a residual part of the old Indo-European fertility religions, and one wonders how often it is these rather than the official doctrines of the Church which fulfilled the peasants' true religious needs. Given the eternal presence of the tithe-collector one would assume here a bitter anti-clericalism, given their condition one might guess that religion had meaning to them only in so far as it could be assimilated to magic and the needs of social self-discipline.

One can only guess; yet the views of peasant life in contemporary writers seem often little more than guesses. Two *topoi* dominate. The first, an undiscriminating idealisation, was likely to emerge from the reading of the Latin classics. What nobility in the worker's toil, he feeds us all, he is the true support of life, etc. For obvious aesthetic reasons pasturage rather than agriculture lends itself more readily to this genre, and in the tradition of the Provençal *pastorella* there are numerous tributes in verse from this period to a variety of shepherdesses, who are not always seen, explicitly, as the object of sexual conquest. Yet looking at the high literary culture of the age one is struck above all by the remoteness of the peasant. In the *Comedia* Dante presents some remarkable images drawn from country life: the poverty-stricken worker's despair at seeing hoar frost in the fields; the villein resting on the hillside at evening and watching the fireflies in the valley where he harvests the grape and ploughs; the village woman dreaming of gleaning; the villager strengthening his thorn hedge as the grape darkens; the 'rough and savage' mountaineer who stares about him in speechless amazement when he comes to the city; the shepherd's vigil at night in the open against the wolf that threatens his flock. Yet these all feature only as part of extended similes; no labourer appears in his own right. Dante places no representative of the Italian people as a whole in Heaven, Purgatory, or even Hell. For Dante these men and women existed at the periphery of his mind; they dwelt in another world.

In 'the human comedy', Boccaccio's *Decameron*, the peasant has still a minor rôle. Griselda, the villager's daughter whom the Marquis of Monferrato marries, who drawing water at the well, clothed in a thick woollen dress, yet cannot hide her nobility of soul, obviously comes from the *topos* of idealisation. In the story of Masetto of Lamporecchio, Boccaccio reminds his readers that those who think that the spade and hoe and poor victuals and a harsh life take away farmworker's lust, let alone his intelligence and commonsense, are making a serious mistake. Yet even here he speaks of the hero as 'handsome enough for a villager'; and in the story of Ferondo, the rich villein cuckolded by an abbot, part of the entertainment is intended to lie in a *contadino grasso* being put down. Only in one story — and it is set close by the city, that of Monna Belcore, wife of Bentivegna del Mazzo at Varlungo – do we enter into any intimacy with the peasants' world, the elm tree before the church where the villagers meet. Belcore is buxom, brown, rattles a tambourine, sings 'Follow your fancy', and dances country reels with a fine little scarf in her hand. She has a pair of shoes, a plaited lanyard, and a scarf of fine wool, kept in a box under the bed. She is pleased to receive presents of fresh garlic, cloves, a basket of beans, or a bunch of chives and shallots, from the lecherous village priest who has dug them himself from his own garden. We find her sifting a heap of cabbage seeds gleaned by her husband. She spins wool which she delivers on Saturdays to a firm in nearby Florence and her spinning wheel has to be repaired there. In the city too she has pawned her deep purple skirt and the waistband she wears on feast days and needs five pounds to get them back. Her favours are wooed with a drink of must and hot chestnuts. Her friend, Biliuzza, seduced by the priest, has become a prostitute.

In addition to these works there was a popular actively anti-peasant literature: expressing above all the thought that these people are lying, treacherous animals, ignorant but cunning. There is something peculiarly bitter in these writings. They have often a strong scatological character, showing the peasant as born of the fart of an ass or describing how his fart may frighten away the very devil. They actively gloat, too, over peasant misery. So the street singer, Matazone de Calignano,[15] himself of peasant parents, sneers at the peasant for his diet –

> Lo pan de la mistura
> Con la zigola cruda
> Faxoi, ayo e alesa fava
> Pamza freda e cruda rara

> ('Coarse bread baked with rye, haricots,
> garlic and boiled beans, cold mash, and
> cooked coleseed.')

– and goes on to give a gleeful calendar of the burdens to be imposed upon him from month to month. It is part of a continuous tradition in Italian society. In the 1880s it was still possible to buy a broadsheet containing a *Villein's Alphabet*, in which for each of the letters of the alphabet there appeared a couplet attacking the peasant's coarseness and malice: those *malitie laboratorum* against which both the statutes and legal textbooks of the Middle Ages made universal complaint. Even friars, themselves dedicated to poverty, saw the rural worker at the bottom of esteem in society. The Dominican Fra Giordano da Rivalto remarks that because the *villano* works the earth he is called 'villain'; goldsmiths work the nobler gold and so are held in greater esteem; doctors work upon bodies, nobler yet. Finally, of course, the noblest in society are those who work upon souls.[16]

In urban discussions of the peasant, contempt is often coupled with a certain measure of apprehension before their collective power. The jurist Odofredo of Bologna remarked that 'rustics' knew nothing of the value of words because they used their tongues to eat and not to speak sensibly; that when they were alone they weren't worth a hen and gave citizens due honour. However, he observed, 'when they're together they perform every ill, and in union would have confounded Charlemagne.' The same note is found again in Paolo da Certaldo's

Libro di buoni costumi (*c*. 1360), a book of advice on the conduct of everyday life:

If it's necessary for you to go to the village, be careful not to go there on a holiday . . . nor on the square with the labourers, since they're all swilling and hot with wine, and have their weapons with them, and have no reason in them; in fact each one thinks himself a king . . . Also being hot they've no respect for anyone who is more important than them. . . . If you've business to do with these workers, go to them in the fields when they're working and you'll find them humble and submissive. . . . If you're making your accounts with them, that is with these workers, never do it in the village, make them come to the town, and do it there; for if you do it in the village, you'll meet lots of other workers there, and all will be advocates for your worker against you.[17]

Fear of the peasant doubtless worked in his favour, yet one can wonder whether he was feared sufficiently. There is in this period very little evidence for any wide-scale, organised, premeditated peasant revolt. Village risings were generally restricted to individual villages or clusters of villages, normally took place against individual nobles claiming feudal jurisdiction, and seem to be directed very rarely against city landowners or communal or royal government and their laws as such. Even then it would be difficult to assert that such risings were frequent. In Sicily the insurrections against the Count of Geraci in 1337, against Scaloro degli Ubertini at Asora in December 1350, and other risings at Gagliano, Piazza, and Stuera in 1356 all seem to have come about as the result of royal incitement in an attempt to bring recalcitrant feudatories to heel. So too when in 1375 the men of Avola, 'subject to multiple repressions and insupportable burdens' had 'from a certain inevitable necessity' slain their lord, Federico Aragona, King Federico IV wrote to both pardon the offence and welcome the assistance it had brought him.[18]

Within the Neapolitan kingdom certainly, in the fourteenth century, our sources reveal several examples of peasant revolt at village level: attacks by villagers on bishops, ecclesiastical orders, lay feudatories, and their officers. So, in 1310, at Baiano, a fief of the Orsini, a crowd gathered against the bailiff, cut off his hands before killing him, and then surged to his house, seeking to burn it down and kill his children. In 1318 the Lord Guglielmo di Corsano, riding one day to visit his faithful retainers at Corsano, was greeted by them, armed, in great numbers, and in hostile mood. Scarcely was he able to reach the safety of the castle where he discovered his wife already sheltering within its walls. When a poor serving woman of feudal disposition sought to remonstrate with the rebels she was killed. Stones and weapons were hurled against the fortress and on all sides rose the cry: 'Burn the castle.' At the beginning of the same year the subjects of Bernardo 'de Canependuto' in the *castello* of Cituli and other properties rose against him, and declared themselves subjects of the community of L'Aquila, calling out: 'No lord. We want Aquila!' When their representatives returned from L'Aquila with the news that the commune had offered to extend its protection to them, they lit bonfires and seized the two castles of Sambucco and Alberico. Here they discovered the one-year-old daughter of their lord and carried her around in the middle of the celebrations, calling out: 'Who wants to buy this?' A final example: in August 1327 the vassals of Capradorso, some eight miles from Città Ducale, seeking to free themselves from the monastery of S.

Salvatore di Rieti, offered two men, Fortebraccio and Jacopo 'of Romagna', sixty pairs of hams a month if they would lead them against the monks. After the two men had sworn on the bible to assist them, and the vassals had assigned a tax among themselves to pay for the hams, they united at Città Ducale, invaded the lands of the monastery, robbed, burnt, and spread terror among the monks.

All these incidents are narrated by Romolo Caggese in his book on King Roberto I,[19] and are drawn from the Angevin registers of the Neapolitan kingdom. According to Caggese such episodes are 'countless in number' and he himself refers to some thirty to forty in the period 1306–42. The difficulty here is to assess what 'countless' means, that is to say, what was the proportion of those he mentioned to those actually recorded in the royal registers (which no longer exist). It seems likely, given the character of the Neapolitan bureaucracy, that all incidents occurring did appear in the registers. If we assume that Caggese mentioned them all, we have the figure of, say, thirty-six local peasant revolts within the Regno in thirty-six years. (It is not always clear from his references whether, for instance, attacks on ecclesiastics are always purely peasant outbreaks; the cry of 'Let's kill the bishop' appears frequently to have united all classes.) Or, suppose that 'countless' means seventy-two (though Caggese was a scholar with a strong interest in radical politics) this would imply a mean average of two revolts a year in the 2,300 odd peasant communities of the Regno. If there is anything in these speculations one may consider that while revolt was always a possibility in the kingdom, it was not by any means normal. It is interesting here to reflect on the vassals of Capradorso who have to bribe two Romagnol bully-boys with hams before they can take their courage in their hands to attack monks. The truth is that it is very difficult for the under-nourished to acquire the energy to revolt. Revolt, it may be suspected, came only as the result of intolerable new impositions and injustices or as a counter to intolerable violence exercised against the peasant.

Of these again, the registers were apparently full. Caggese found there, and gave many examples of, constant complaints about usurpation of peasant lands and rights, of nobles forcing free men to be their serfs, of the refusal of justice to serfs, and concluded that here was a world of a corruption essential to and inherent in feudalism. To give one example: in the Spring of 1319 the representatives of the community of Loreto, near Sulmona, 'calling in a high voice with sad and tearful face', made a series of accusations against their lord, a member of the powerful del Balzo family. Having already extorted 10 *oncie* from them, he has then claimed more money which they had declared themselves unable to pay. On this, with the words: 'I know a fine game to play', he had confined them within the walls of the *castello* until they had produced a further 25 *oncie*. He had gone on to ask for a large 'aid' for the marriage of his sister, another 25 *oncie* for allowing his vassals to buy and sell non-feudal goods, and yet another 25 *oncie* for other rights. Those whom he hates he imprisons and tortures 'in a certain cell in his castle', and frees them only for payment of money. If he is owed money he has his ruffians seize the debtors and put them in the 'certain cell'. If his vassals want to invoke the law against him he intimidates their procurators. He has, for instance, tapped the eyes of one of these with his finger, saying: 'I'll rip these out of your head.' Women who refuse to marry his retainers he forces into convents. He will not allow the divine office to be said in the parish church, saying: 'We don't want mass at any time in the church!' He takes carpenters, masons, and smiths, and compels them to work for him for nothing in forty-day periods.

Here again the questions recur. If all indeed were as the community said, how customary was such tyranny? How normal was it, one should add, for such complaints to reach the royal registers? Enquiry into this case was entrusted to a Professor of Civil Law: did he in fact bring remedy and redress, or did he shrug his shoulders before a chronic ill of rural life, a situation where, as Caggese believed, peasants and nobles were locked in a constant civil war? All these cases, of course, come from the southern kingdom; how far were they general to the centre and north as well? In these areas one reads, now and then, in the thirteenth century, of rural communes formed against their lords. In Piedmont the federated commune of the Valsesia was born of the common resistance of subject villages to the powerful Counts of Biandrate. In 1290 again, Pope Nicholas IV could write to the Rector of the Marche, saying that it had come to his ears that 'some in the boundaries of the province, malcontents, as it were seeking scandal against their *patria*, are striving to create communities in the lands of nobles to the no little prejudice and damage of the aforesaid nobles.'[20] Yet, overall, one gains the impression that rural communes were normally either formed at the initiative of lords or were incorporated rapidly within either the feudal or city-communal order. Characteristic is the agreement between the nobles and the little village commune of Penna San Giovanni in the Marche reached on 24 May 1248. The nobles with their vassals promised to take part in the *communantia*; they promised to destroy their towers and to swear obedience to its statutes. In return it was agreed that the office of *podestà* should be reserved for them alone.[21]

In the fourteenth century other examples of revolt can be found outside the South. Romagna and Tuscany provide a few instances, and one hears of 'boycott' riots in Friuli. In the mountain valleys of Piedmont, which offered a refuge to the Waldensian heresy (though this should not be considered too strictly in class terms), one has a sense of greater conflicts, notably in the Val d'Aosta, where village insurrections took place in 1324 and 1327, and a more general movement, with the burning of six or seven castles, in 1362–3. The whole of the Canavese *montagna*, again, was the scene of a large scale insurrection in 1386.[22] Yet one constant feature of these incidents is that they take place in the *montagna*, in lands remote from the authority of the city. There is, that is to say, a predictable connection between three elements: inaccessible terrain, surviving feudalism, and violence. Here, however, the occasional struggle of peasant against lord should be seen in context against a background of a continual unchecked welter of everyday violence: of brigandage by peasant and noble; of struggles between noble and noble; between peasant communities which wage war upon each other; between individual peasants who rob neighbouring villages of their goods and (since bride-kidnapping was probably frequent) of their women. Petrarch, writing in 1337, briefly but rather movingly reveals something of this in his account of the lives of those who lived on the fiefs of the

Lords of Anguillara at Capranica, set between the Monti Cumini and Monti Sabatini. Speaking first of the beauty of the landscape and the poetic associations of Mount Soracte and Lake Ciminius, he continues by remarking on the lives of those who lived there. The shepherd watches, armed, over his flocks, the ploughman at his furrow wears a cuirass, the fowler anchors his net with a buckler, the fisherman hangs his line from a sword, the herdsman pricks on his cattle with a lance. 'Among those who live in these parts, you see nothing secure, you hear nothing peaceful, you feel nothing human; only war and hatred and every work to be expected of devils.'[23]

Outside these areas, on the plains, near the cities, violence still flourished (as it did in the cities too). Yet the scale was diminished, and peasant disorder was limited to the occasional serious riot. Typical is an incident of 30 January 1212. Here, the men of Bionde in the Veneto, some 300 in number, were said to have risen up against the Archpriest of the Chapter which owned them, after an argument between a villager and one of his squires over the possession of a cooking pot and its chain. To the cry of: 'Die! Die! let the thieves die and burn', they threw stones, picked up weapons – they are said to possess some lances, swords, shields, and helmets – and robbed the squires and minstrels attending the archpriest of their weapons. On the following day order was restored and in the following April, after due legal process, heavy fines were imposed upon individuals and the village commune as a whole.[24]

Although one cannot discount the importance of the threat of spontaneous incidents like these in persuading landlords to make minor concessions as, for instance, the formation of a village commune (and we shall see what in fact that did imply), we are a long way here from 'peasant revolt'. In the plains the first movement which can be dignified with that term, though it was a fleeting and transitory incident which even some of the native chroniclers ignore, was the attack on Parma by its peasantry in August 1385. In part, of course, this may be because, at a superficial level at least, 'land war', rick-burning, the isolated murder of unpopular individuals, must always have seemed preferable, tactically, to spectacular full-scale revolts by communities. The boycott-tactics of which Florentine landlords were complaining in January 1348 ('that certain communities, parishes, and chaples of the *contado* . . . have commended or advised that none should cultivate their possessions, should dwell in their houses or grind at their mills, and that none should do business with them or their servants . . . that everyone should waste their possessions, goods, and fruits . . .'[25]) were at first sight likely to be more effective.

Yet mass revolts (one thinks of the English rising of 1381) have their uses in terrifying the landowning class into alleviating the lot of the peasant. Italy never had – and the lack may explain the difference between peasant conditions in Italy and England in the fifteenth century – a 1381, nor a body of fables like the Robin Hood ballads which glamourised the resistance of the yeoman to authority. One reason for this was that both 1381 and the Robin Hood legend were made possible by the myth – it was, of course, no more – that there was an authority, the king, who sought justice for all men under his government. But within Italy this myth could not exist in the North and failed to take root in the southern monarchies. Two other elements were prominent here as well in explaining the failure to revolt. In the first place, since landowning by townsmen was widespread even among the artisan class, there was no substantial body within the town to whom the peasant could look for support. Second, the brighter, more energetic, enterprising, and discontented men who could lead revolt were precisely those who were likely to throw away their hoes and go off to seek their fortunes in the town.

V

In some ways it is from the statutes of the rural communes that one gains the closest insight into the routine and everyday preoccupations of village life. From the beginning of the thirteenth century the customs of individual villages came, in a manner which is not found outside Italy, to be codified in written laws. These became fairly common in the second half of the thirteenth century, though the era of their greatest development lies in the years after 1375. Sometimes the statutes were imposed by the dominant town and derive from urban codifications. Sometimes they were decreed by the local lay or ecclesiastical lord. Often, however, they are clearly the spontaneous decrees of the villagers themselves, who, while generally seeking the assent of the central authority, were in effect determining the law of their own society. Very occasionally they seem to be drawn up against such authority. It is the note struck in the prelude to the statutes of 1341 of the village of Bovegno in the Alpine Val Trompia, near Brescia, a passage in which the ostentatious learning is marred only by the notary's conspicuous deficiencies in Latin grammar:

Since, as Boethius reports from the words of Plato, happy would be Republics if they were ruled in zeal for wisdom or required their rulers to study wisdom, and since, a little after, he adds, from the words of the same man, that the strongest motive for wise men to enter in the Republic is that, if they abandon the helm, evil and wicked citizens of the towns will bring plague and perdition to the good, so, for the instruction of the officials of the land of Bovegno and of all the neighbours dwelling in the same, that they more easily be able to secure the obedience of good men and restrain the contumacious audacity of wicked lords, we, of the land of Bovegno order the aforesaid statutes to be enscribed in this volume . . .'[26]

In some circumstances the statutes are legislating for a commune composed of a federation of several villages (Valsesia in Piedmont, the commune of the *contado* of Imola in Emilia). In most cases, however, the commune consists merely of the inhabitants of one *castello*. As an example may be considered the provisions of 1322 (with additions to 1366)[27] issued by Camporotondo, a hill village, above the Fiastrone valley in the March of Ancona subject to the Lords Varano of Camerino, the ruins of whose castle can still be seen there today. Its population is not known; doubtless it was small, though probably larger than today. (In 1936 it had 330 souls in the village, and 640 in the surrounding countryside.) Camporotondo was a *castello*, with an unprotected *borgo* or group of houses outside. Its gates were closed every night and only opened in the morning when the priest rang the church bell. The local form of land tenure was either *mezzadria*, or, what was quite common in the March, holding *ad coptimum*. Under this system the tenant normally paid a rent, but if there were large scale crop failures through storms or other cause, he was considered to hold at *mezzadria* instead. The crops grown included barley, grain, and millet, and there are references in the statutes to the light wooden plough of the region, the *pertecàra*, and the heavy iron plough, the *pertecarò*, used to break the heavy soils. But particular importance is placed upon vines, olives, and fruit farming: pears, apples, mulberries, nutmegs and figs. Mention is also made of horses, oxen, cows, mules, asses, sheep, pigs, and hens.

The first part of the statutes deals with the administrative life of the commune. Every six months a vicar or rector, generally a notary, was appointed who acted as judge and administrative head. He received £R[avennati] 20 for the period of his office. (On one occasion it was laid down that anyone who proposed a higher stipend should be subject to various penalties which included having his face painted on the wall of the house of the commune.) He had to be a 'foreigner' to the village, and to ensure his impartiality it was decreed that he should not take meals with any villager. Within ten days of his entry into office he had to hold a general enquiry (or 'sindication') into the acts of his predecessor, who, if all were pronounced satisfactory, would then be paid off. To assist him he had a chamberlain (*camerario*) or treasurer, and a notary, who were again 'foreigners', and a messenger (*baiuolo*), equipped with a trumpet, who, in return for 50 shillings in a six-month period of office, served as village-crier and cited individuals to appear before the vicar when necessary.

The general council which made these appointments was, theoretically at least, the supreme arbiter of the commune. Meeting in the parish church of San Marco, it was made up of all adult males liable to taxation. From its members were elected four *massari* (or priors), one from each of the four districts into which the jurisdiction of the village was divided. These stayed in office for four months, decided when the council should meet, and what points should be put to it. Discussion in council was limited to the agenda agreed by them. Together with the *massari* the council issued laws for the village; supervised its woods and pasturage; when necessary, sent 'ambassadors' to other communes; and appointed officials. Among these was the custodian of the seal and documents of the commune, the notary whose special function was to record damage to crops, and the tax collectors.

A principal responsibility of the council lay in the allotment and collection of taxation imposed by the city commune. For this purpose it ensured that all immovable goods were noted in the *catasto* or register. Again the council appointed men each March to examine the roads, bridges, and fountains in their districts, and, when required, to assemble the men of the district to make repairs to them. On occasions the vicar would summon the whole community to perform some necessary work.

A second book in the statutes dealt with crime, and laid down the various penalties for blasphemy, insults, assault, adultery, pimping, and theft. These were normally fines graded according to the scale of offence; from 10 shillings for seizing someone by the hair to £R.200 for the cutting off of a nose. The cost of premeditated homicide was, by day £R.500, by night £R.1,000. The penalties for theft involved, first, the restoration of what had been stolen, and then in addition a fine according to its value, up to £R.500 for things of a value between £R.20 and £R.50. (It was apparently considered unnecessary to legislate for the theft of anything of greater value.) Inability to pay fines was punished with the cutting off of a limb, or, in the case of murder, beheading. Failure to pay a fine for adultery led to the public whipping of the lovers and, if the woman were married, loss of her dowry. Policing was a collective responsibility. It is specifically laid down that at any disturbance by day or night it was the duty of the men of the *castello* to separate the opponents. However, four guards were specifically appointed to denounce blasphemy (presumably particularly feared lest it invoke some divine collective punishment), and, each year, on the 25 April, the feast of St. Mark, patron saint of the *castello*, four guards were appointed from each of the four districts to stop disorders, receiving 18d. and wine for their pains.

Another book deals with what always looms large in these collections, regulations forbidding damage to crops: the *danni dati*. These include scales of compensation for damage, and regulations for the preservation of the fruits of the land. Among general provisions against wandering beasts, goats were considered particularly harmful; and it was decreed that no one might own a she-goat 'except in case of necessity' (presumably through being dependent upon its milk) and after the vicar and council had given permission. Then they might hold only one. Dogs were to be tethered or walked with a collar from August to October in order that they should not damage the vines. Hunting partridges with nets, other birds, or dogs in a neighbour's field was forbidden. There were prohibitions of damage to or alterations of boundary marks and water courses. The destruction of a neighbour's dovecote could prove as expensive as killing him in manslaughter. During the hot months of July and August the burning of stubble was forbidden against the danger of the fire spreading. Fish traps in the river Fiastrone were prohibited during the spawning season of 1 May to 31 August. Oak trees received a special protection.

Civil justice, treated in the fourth book, was simple in form. Actions for debt collection and the auction of debtor's property feature largely. In many cases, particularly between relatives, disputes were settled by the appointment of neighbours as arbiters sworn to achieve 'amicable composition'. Other regulations control trades. There are brief injunctions to bakers and weavers. Millers on the Fiastrone were restricted to a fee of one twentieth of the corn they ground. The butcher was ordered to keep his shop open at least on Thursday and Sunday. The innkeeper was to use measures sealed by the commune, not to give inferior wine to a man who had asked for one of quality, and to keep the inn open until nightfall. No one was to leave the inn without first having paid or, a significant exception perhaps, having given a pledge.

Further statutes were designed to ensure safety or promote village harmony. Torchlight processions were forbidden on the feast days of St. John the Baptist and St. Peter (24 and 29 June), presumably through the danger of fire. Straw or inflammable material was forbidden in the roofs of houses. Shooting arrows or crossbows or playing snowballs was forbidden within the *castello*. On the feast of the patron, St. Mark, and in the week before and after, dancing was permitted inside the church, though not at other times. Each year £R. 10 was to be put aside towards the building of a cemetery. On feast days, geese and ducks were to be kept inside the house from dawn to tierce (nine o'clock) so that they shouldn't wander into the piazza and disturb the priest in his celebration of mass. Every Saturday each family was to clean the street in front of its house. No one was to wash his feet in the Novello fountain. Privies in houses had to be covered.

Five men were designated by the council to ensure that one person from each family should be present at the funeral of any villager who was to be buried. Yet immoderate grief, tearing of the hair, and stripping off of clothing, particularly by women, were prohibited. And extravagance was frowned upon. Presents to bride and groom at their wedding were forbidden, and even the numbers of guests allowed to accompany and visit the pair on the wedding-day were limited. (In many parts of India today, it will be recalled, the peasant often falls into the hands of the money lender for the rest of his life at the marriage of his eldest child.) Similarly when a child was born, no one was allowed to visit the new mother with gifts, except her mother or sister or other close female relative. Again, gambling was forbidden.

Reading the statutes of Camporotondo, or of any other of the village communes with their local differences, one must recall that these are essentially legal documents and designed to give a precise static form and order to a complex and mobile reality. None the less certain impressions can be drawn from them. The first is that of a tightly-knit inward looking world. The decrees against 'foreigners', the prohibitions against their inheriting or buying land, the need to obtain the permission of the council before acquiring land within the walls; these are explicable enough when set against the need to see that all within the *castello* were assisting in its tax burdens and contributing to its life. So too the fact that homicides, assaults, and thefts committed by strangers, were punished with fines double those levied upon residents can be explained by the greater difficulty in apprehending the criminal stranger in comparison with the local ill-doer. Yet they mark off the worlds of 'them' and 'us' very strongly. These penalties were powerfully reinforced when the foreigner came from the neighbouring village of San Ginesio. It was forbidden to give refuge or shelter to anyone from this commune, to work their lands, or to sell or give its members 'anything which might be turned to their use or advantage', words which conjure up a strong atmosphere of local solidarity in hatred.

Yet it can be seen that there are admirable things here too, symbolised perhaps in the way in which the council declares itself responsible for appointing the guardians of orphans, the attempts – how effective? – to secure a clean street, the saving-up of the pathetic £R. 10 to build the communal cemetery, and the prohibition of extravagances likely to bring debt. What one senses in these laws is something which perhaps softens the harsher outlines in any portrayal of the villager's lot, a certain level of social and community organisation, or at least an aspiration towards it, which is maintained by the peasant himself.

NOTES

Among **general works** the most valuable is P. J. Jones, 'Medieval Agrarian Society in its prime: 2. Italy' in *The Cambridge Economic History of Europe*, vol. 1, 2nd edn, ed. M. M. Postan, Cambridge, 1966, pp. 340–431 (with full bibliography, pp. 795–807). See too the excellent general articles in the Einaudi *Storia d'Italia, cit.* by E. Sereni, 'Agricoltura e mondo rurale' (vol. i): Christiane Klapisch-Zuber, 'Villagi abbandonati ed emigrazioni interne' (vol. v, pt. i) and G. Giorgetti, 'Contratti agrari e rapporti sociali nelle campagne' (vol. v, pt. i); and L. A. Kotelnikova, *Mondo contadino e città in Italia dall' XI al XIV secolo*, Bologna, 1975 (translation of original, Moscow, 1967). Of particular interest are the studies of G. Cherubini, collected in his *Signori, Contadini, borghesi: Ricerche sulla società italiana del basso medioevo*, Florence, 1974.

Some **recent surveys** of the problems are E. Cristiani, 'Città e campagna nell' età comunale', *RSI*, 1963; P. J. Jones, 'Per la storia agraria italiana nel Medio Evo; lineamenti e problemi', *RSI*, lxxvi, 1964; G. Cherubini, 'Qualche considerazione sulle campagne dell' Italia centro-settentrionale tra' 1 XI e il XV secolo', *RSI*, 1967 (and now in *Signori, contadini, borghesi, cit.*); I. Imberciadori, 'Agricoltura italiana dall' XI ad XVI secolo', *Rivista di storia d'agricoltura*, XI, 1971. Older studies of the *scuola economica-giuridica*, such as R. Caggese, *Classi e comuni rurali nel medioevo italiano*, Florence, 1907–8, have often to be used with some caution; see E. Fiumi, 'Sui rapporti economici tra città e contado nell' età comunale', *ASI*, 1956.

Among **discussions of particular areas** are: P. J. Jones, 'From Manor to Mezzadria. A Tuscan Case-study in the Medieval Origins of modern agrarian society', in *Florentine Studies: Politics and Society in Renaissance Florence*, ed. N. Rubinstein, London, 1968; I. Imberciadori, *Mezzadria classica toscana con documentazione del IX al XIV secolo*, Florence, 1951; E. Conti, *La formazione della struttura-agraria moderna nel contado fiorentino* (so far published vols. 1 and iii [2a]), Rome 1965; R. Romeo, 'La signoria dell' abate di S. Ambrogio di Milano sul comune rurale di Origgio nel secolo XIII', *RSI*, 69, 1957; B. A. Kotelnikova, 'L'evoluzione dei canoni Fondiari dall' XI al XIV sec. in territorio lucchese', *Studi Medievali*, s. 3., ix, 1968; P. J. Jones, 'A Tuscan Monastic Lordship in the later Middle Ages: Camaldoli', *Journal of Ecclesiastical History* 1954; J. Plesner, *L'émigration de la campagne à la ville libre de Florence au XIII siècle*, Copenhagen, 1934 (for Passignano); D. Herlihy, 'Santa Maria Impruneta: A rural commune in the late Middle Ages' in *Florentine Studies, cit.*; G. Cherubini, *Una communità dell' Apennino dal XIII al XV secolo*, Florence, 1972; M. Tangheroni, *Politica, commercio, agricoltura a Pisa nel trecento*, Pisa, 1973, ch. v; R. Francovich, *I castelli del contado fiorentino nel secoli XII e XIII* (Quaderni 3: Atti dell' Istituto di Geografia: Geografia storica delle sedi umane), Florence, 1974; D. J. Osheim, *An Italian Lordship: The Bishopric of Lucca in the Late Middle Ages*, London, 1977; P. Torelli, *Un comune cittadino in territorio ed economia agricola. I. Distribuzione della proprietà; sviluppo agricolo; contrati agrari*, Mantua, 1930; C. Rotelli, *Una campagna medievale. Storia agraria del Piemonte fra il 1250 e il 1450*, Turin, 1973; G. Chittolini, 'I beni terrieri del capitolo della cattedrale di Cremona fra il XIII e XIV secolo', *Nuova rivista storica*, xlix, 1965; A. Menchetti, 'Su l'obbligo della coltivazione del suolo nei comuni medioevali marchigiani', *Archivio 'Vittorio Scialoja'*, ii, 1935; A. Palmieri, 'I lavoratori del contado bolognese durante la signoria', *AMR*, s. 3, xxviii, 1910; C. M. de la Roncière, *Un changeur florentin du Trecento*, Paris, 1973, chs. v–viii.

On **rural housing** see the twenty-two volumes of the *Ricerche sulle dimore rurali in Italia*, ed. Consiglio nazionale delle ricerche, 1926 ff; L. Gambi, 'Per una storia della abitazione rurale, in Italia', *RSI*, 1964; and *Guida bibliografica allo studio della abitazione rurale in Italia* ed. T. Stonai de' Rocchi, Florence, 1950.

On rural communes see: A. Sorbelli, *Il comune rurale dell' Appenino emiliano nei secoli XIV e XV*, Bologna, 1910; A. Palmieri, *La montagna bolognese nel medioevo*, Bologna, 1929; F. Briganti, *Città dominanti e comuni minori*, Perugia, 1906; P. Toubert, 'Les statuts communaux et l'histoire des campagnes lombardes du XIVₑ siècle', *Mélanges d'Archeologie et d'Histoire*, lxxii, 1960; A. Menchetti, *Storia di un comune rurale della Marca Anconetana (Montalboddo oggi Ostra)*, Fermo, 1929–1936. Several village statutes have been printed from this period; see e.g.: in the *Corpus Statutorum Italicorum*, ed. P. Sella, vols i (1912); ii (1913); vi (1914); vii 1914); viii (1915); x (1927); xviii (1932) xxi (1941).

1. Plesner, *L'émigration, cit.*, pp. 77, 87.
2. See L. Simeoni, 'La liberazione dei servi a Bologna nel 1256–7', *ASI*, 109, 1951, pp. 3–26; *Liber Paradisus con le riformagioni e gli statuti connesi*, ed. F. S. Gatta and G. Plessi, Bologna, 1956.

   Documents recording collective communal emancipations of serfs (Assisi, 1210; Vercelli, 1243; Modena, 1327; and Todi, 1337) are collected in P. Vaccari, *Le affrancazioni collettive dei servi della gleba*, Milan, 1939. Vaccari's discussion of this material both in this work and in his *L'affrancazione dei servi della gleba nell' Emilia e nella Toscana*, Bologna, 1926, reaches some different conclusions from those given here.

3. A. Luzio, *I Corradi di Gonzaga*, Milan, 1913, pp. 48–9. (Luzio reads 'Montisferati' in error; cf. on this A. Theiner, *Codex Diplomaticus Dominii Temporalis S. Sedis*, Rome, 1861–2, i, pp. 278–9.)
4. 'Summa notarie Aretii composita annis MCCXL–MCCLIIII', ed. C. Cicognario, in *Scripta anecdota glossatorum (Bibliotheca iuridica medii aevii*, ed. A. Gaudenzio), Bologna, 1901, iii, p. 305.
5. D. Catellaci, 'Tre scritte di mezeria in volgare del secolo decimoquarto', *ASI*, s. v, xi, 1893, pp. 381–3.
6. See E. Sereni, *Storia del paesaggio agrario italiano* Bari, 1961; D. Bizzari, 'Tentativi di bonifiche nel contado senese nei secoli XIII–XIV', *BSSP*, 24, 1917; M. Zucchini, *L'agricoltura ferrarese attraverso i secoli*, Rome, 1967, ch. i.
7. R. Caggese, *Roberto d'Angiò e i suoi tempi*, Florence, 1922, i, 502–3; *Acta Imperii Inedita Seculi XIII e XIV*, ed. E. Winkelmann, Innsbruck, 1885, pp. 752–4.
8. B. Rossi, 'La politica agraria dei comuni dominanti negli statuti di Bassa Lombardia', in *Scritti giuridichi in memoria di A. Arcangeli*, ii, Padua, 1939.
9. No modern but many early editions e.g. Louvain, 1474. See too, Società agraria di Bologna, *Pier de' Crescenzi (1233–1321): Studi e documenti*, Bologna, 1933.
10. Rotelli, *Una campagna, cit.* pp. 13–15.
11. *Statuti sacrati e sacratissimi del Popolo di Bologna*, ed. E. Gaudenzi, Bologna, 1888, p. 53.
12. Salimbene, *cit.*, p. 922.
13. A. Borlenghi, *La poesia popolare italiana dell' 800 e le raccolte del Tommaseo*, Milan, 1965.
14. N. Cohn, *Europe's Inner Demons*, London, 1975, pp. 138–46. For what follows, *idem*, 215–18; G. Bonomo, *Caccia delle streghe*, Palermo, 1959, pp. 19 ff.; Jacopo Passavanti, *Lo specchio della vera penitenza*, ed. F. L. Polidori, Florence, 1856, pp. 318–20; E. Verga, 'Intorno a due inediti documenti di stregheria milanese del secolo XIV', *Rendiconti del R. Istituto lombardo di scienze e lettere*, s. 2, 32, 1899; C. G. Leland, *Etruscan Roman Remains in popular traditions*, London, 1892.
15. 'Dit sur les villains par Matazone de Calignano', ed. P. Meyer, *Romania*, xii, 1883,

pp. 14–28. On this genre: D. Merlini, *Saggio e ricerche sulla satira contra il villano*, Turin, 1894.

16. Giordano da Rivalto, *Prediche inedite* [*1302–5*], ed. E. Narducci, Bologna, 1867, pp. 72–3.

17. *In primam codicis partem*, Lyons, 1552, ff. 7r, 61v. For what follows: Paolo da Certaldo, *Libro di buoni costumi*, ed. A. Schiaffini, Florence, 1945, pp. 91–3.

18. V. D'Alessandro, *Politica e società nella Sicilia aragonese*, Palermo, 1963, p. 103; Michele da Piazza, *Historia Sicula* [*1337–61*] in R. Gregorio, *Bibliotheca Scriptorum qui res in Sicilia gestas sub Aragonum imperio retulere*, Palermo, 1791, i, pp. 602–4, 744, 756–7; ii, p. 54.

19. For this and what follows, Caggese, *Roberto d'Angiò, cit.*, i, pp. 65–6, 329–32, 335, 465, 467.

20. Theiner, *Codex Diplomaticus, cit.*, i, no. 473.

21. G. Luzzatto, 'Le sottomissioni dei feudatarii e le classi sociali in alcuni comuni marchigiani (Secoli XII e XIII)' in his *Dai servi della gleba agli albori del Capitalismo*, Bari, 1966, p. 387.

22. See Rotelli, *Una campagna, cit.*, pp. 11–12. The last stand of the followers of the heretical Fra Dolcino around Monte Parete Cavallo and Monte Rebello in 1304–6 cannot be seen as a simple social conflict. The heretics' principal enemies, the Valsesiani, *homines populi et super eos insignes populi*, had recently freed themselves from the counts of Biandrate, who were probably Dolcino's principal supporters. See C. G. Mor, *Carte valsesiane fino al secolo XV*, Turin, 1933, lxv. pp. 168–76; lxvi, p. 176.

23. F. Petrarca, *Le Familiari*, ed. V. Rossi, i, Florence, 1933, pp. 99–101 (II, 12).

24. L. Simeoni, 'Il comune rurale nel territorio veronese', *Nuovo archivio veneto*, xlii, 1921, pp. 195–6.

25. N. Rodolico, *Il popolo minuto*, Bologna, 1899, pp. 114–15.

26. *Statuti rurali bresciani del sec. XIV*, ed. B. Nogara, R. Cessi, and G. Bonelli, Milan, 1927, p. 25.

27. *Statuta Castri Campirotundi*, ed. D. Cecchi, Milan, 1966.

Merchants, workers, and workless

I

If life depended upon the countryside, the direction of society centred on the towns. The vast extension of land brought into cultivation between 1100 and 1300 had been accompanied, perhaps caused, by a vast increase in population. This increase generated a long-term movement of emigration in which landless men looking for work or country proprietors in search of new opportunities moved to the towns. At the same time the enlargement of the market, the rise in urban and rural rents, the new possibilities open to money lenders, which resulted from population growth, permitted new accumulations of capital which produced an economic revolution in trade, finance, and industry, and created that distinctive urban culture which marked off Italy from the rest of Europe.

Reliable figures to chart the stages in the growth of the towns are almost wholly lacking, and the process has to be deduced rather from such things as the rise of the building trades and the extension of town-walls. None the less the broad outlines are clear. By 1300 there were four cities – Milan, Venice, Genoa, and Florence – which had perhaps reached the, by medieval standards, giant size of about 100,000 people. There were, it could be, another fifteen towns in the north (among which, particularly, Pisa, Siena, and Lucca in Tuscany: Bologna in Emilia; Perugia in Umbria; Padua, Pavia, Verona, Mantua in the Lombard plain) and three in the south (Palermo, Naples, Messina) which could claim populations of between twenty and fifty thousand. In the north, again, there were very many other communities of between five and twenty thousand souls which were able to maintain some form of independent political identity. Everywhere, outside the *Mezzogiorno*, the population in these towns grew to rival, in some cases even exceed, that of the countryside on which they were dependent and everywhere tighter links were forged between the town and its *contado*.

With these developments commerce followed. Communes, unable to provision their cities from the resources of their own countrysides, were compelled to undertake a vast marketing of consumables. Corn flowed to them from the Emilian plain, Apulia, and Sicily; salt from the flats of Cervia, cattle from the Po Valley. Ox-wagons in the plains, pack-mules in the mountains, passed in increasing numbers along roads and bridges whose maintenance became of ever greater concern to the towns, while along the rivers, above all the Po, the barges moved in quickening rhythms of trade. For a town like Florence, which in the early fourteenth century could draw from its territories only sufficient food to feed its population for five months of the year, this commerce was a matter of life and death. Driven on by the imperative need to feed their peoples, the larger communes worked by force of arms, if necessary, to compel all trade in as large a neighbouring area as possible to be channelled through their ports. Genoa sought control of all shipping between Tuscany and the Rhône. Venice, claiming 'Lordship of the Adriatic', aimed to enforce a monopolistic stranglehold on all traffic along the Po and Adige rivers and all commerce entering the ports of Romagna and Dalmatia.

Trade within Italy was matched by long-distant traffic outside. At the beginning of the thirteenth century the commerce of the Mediterranean was already in the hands of Pisa, Genoa, and Venice. In the ports of Syria and Palestine, at Constantinople and Alexandria these towns had their own quarters, furnished with consulate, church, warehouse, baths, mill, and slaughterhouse. From these centres, or journeying to the heads of the Asiatic camel caravans at Damascus and Aleppo, they had obtained a virtual monopoly of all east-west traffic. To the east they carried wood, steel, and arms: to the west 'spices', pepper, cinnamon, clover, ginger, nutmeg, silk, precious wares. Colonies followed upon trade, and trade upon colonies. With the fall of Constantinople to the Fourth Crusade in 1204, Venice, which had played a large part in the enterprise, seized a variety of Aegean islands, Crete, Durazzo in the Epirus, Modone and Corone in the Peloponnese, and other centres, as staging and commercial ports. Passing into the Black Sea, she tapped the trade flowing in the north, down the Dnieper and to the Crimea, in the south, to Trebizond. Within the east her ships carried slaves from Russia, wine, oil, and fruit from the Aegean islands to Egypt; grain, fish and salt from the Crimea to Constantinople.

With the restoration of the Greek Empire under the Palaeologi in 1261, the Genoese followed the Venetians into the Black Sea, up to the rich ports of Tana and Caffa. Within the Aegean they obtained the islands of Phocea (1264), rich in its alum mines, and Chios (1304). Soon the rival communes were at each other's throats. Genoa fought Venice in two long wars (1258–70, 1294–9). Pisa, already seriously weakened in the first half of the century by her alliance with Frederick II, underwent a disastrous defeat at the hands of the Genoese in the sea-battle of Meloria (1284) and declined to the status of a secondary power. Yet neither these conflicts nor the final fall of the crusading states to the Saracens in 1291 brought any diminution in overall Italian trade. Representatives of the ports, now more and more joined by inland rivals such as the Florentines, transferred the centres of their traffic to Cyprus and Cilicia, and struck further east. Encouraged by the establishment of the *pax Mongolica* in Asia, they journeyed onward to Kipchak in southern Russia, to Astrakhan on the Caspian, to Tabriz in Azerbajan, to central Asia, and then on, finally, to India and China. 'The road from Tana to Cathay', wrote Pegolotti in his merchant's handbook, 'is quite safe by day and by night, according to those merchants who report having followed it.' At the beginning of

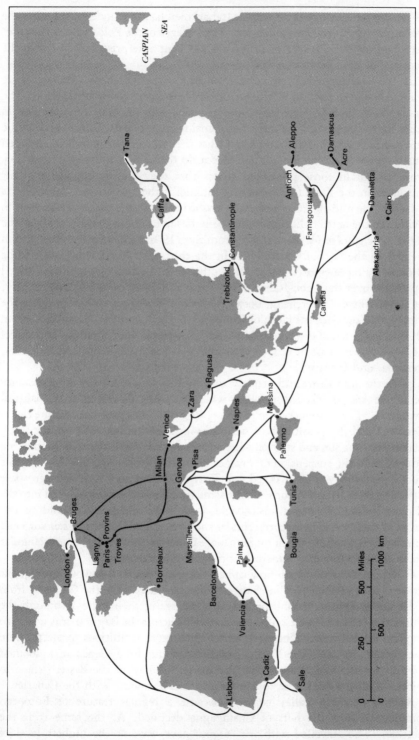

Map 4 Principal routes of Italian international trade *c.* 1320

the fourteenth century there was an Italian merchant colony established at the port of Zaytun on the Formosa strait. The voyages of the Polos were, in a sense, merely an incident, a symbol of Italian merchant enterprise and daring in the great age of their expansion.

In the western Mediterranean from the twelfth century Italians were established in the ports of North Africa, and from there crept down the Atlantic coast to Sale and Safi. Here they brought goods from the North and the East in return for the gold of Ghana carried on camel trains across the Sahara, and, in the same spirit in which they transported Christian pilgrims to Jerusalem, shipped Muslims of Morocco on the route to Mecca. In the ports of southern France they strove to obtain those privileged rights that they already enjoyed in their consulates in the East. In the Spanish kingdoms they penetrated the Balearics and, from the mid-thirteenth century, pushed through the straits of Gibraltar to Seville. To the north of Europe Italian penetration had been slower. Yet from the 1170s merchants of Milan and Asti, from the 1190s the Genoese, were found in strength at the fairs of Champagne. In the thirteenth century they were to be followed by representatives of a dozen other inland cities who rapidly attained supremacy over their non-Italian competitors and made the fairs, for a century, the major centre of interchange between northern and southern Europe. Here the principal prizes were the cloth of Flanders, the wool and tin of England. From 1200 Italians traded directly in England, and, particularly after the opening of the San Gotthard pass in 1237, in southern Germany, the Rhineland, Flanders, Bohemia, and Hungary.

From the mid-thirteenth century the rhythm and volume of long-distance commerce was quickened through what has been described as 'a nautical revolution'. The introduction of the compass gave birth to the first marine charts (*portolani*) and the possibility of sailing by dead-reckoning. The winter skies, blotting out the sun and stars on which the navigator had hitherto depended, no longer forced the suspension of voyages between October and April. With the fourteenth century ships changed too. Trireme galleys grew in size; cargo-space expanded from 50 to 150 tons. At the same time the cog was introduced into the Mediterranean. This vessel was capable, it has been calculated, of holding 150 slaves. It was steered by a central rudder and provided with a square sail with reef points which was very much more manageable than the cumbersome triangular lateen sail. To Italian commerce it brought new wealth.

Governments too, which now came to organise regular convoys throughout the year, played their part in change. From, at least, 1277 the Genoese, from 1314 the Venetians, established annual sailings of their galleys through the pillars of Hercules, thence on a compass setting across the Bay of Biscay and so to English and Flemish Channel ports. Still more ambitious projects were undertaken. In 1291 the Vivaldi brothers set out from Genoa in a doomed attempt to circumnavigate Africa and reach the head of the Eastern trade in spices. With greater success other Genoese made contact with the Canaries.

As the northern galley convoys became a regular feature of European commercial links the fairs of Champagne declined. At the same time the merchant who travelled with his cargoes gave way, at the highest level of commerce, to the resident capitalist who worked through factors and commission agents and who held his operations together by ceaseless correspondence. The development was accompanied by the invention of sophisticated mercantile techniques: account books utilising arabic numerals, double-entry book-keeping with profit and loss accounts, bills of lading, marine insurance, bills of exchange. With these there grew up a mature law of the sea and law of commerce. Meanwhile, as new mints proliferated, the coinage of the communes gained a new authority. The needs of international trade produced first the heavier silver *grosso* (at Venice *c.* 1200, Siena *c.* 1230, and shortly afterwards at Pisa, Florence, Arezzo, and Lucca), and then with the Florentine florin, Genoese *genovino* (both 1252) and the Venetian *zecchino* or ducat (1284), the first large-scale minting of gold coins in Europe.

Almost everywhere the volume and profits of trade grew. The taxed value of marine commerce passing through Genoa doubled in the first three quarters of the thirteenth century, and then quadrupled to reach by 1293 the equivalent of $5\frac{1}{2}$ million florins, double the revenues of the French Crown. In the early 1320s the equivalent of an annual 3 million florins worth of goods was being carried by Italians through French ports. This expansion of trade went hand in hand with a growth of banking and credit operations which were to make the Italian merchant-banker (merchant and banker, for here there was no specialisation of rôle, and businessmen sought as far as possible to diversify their interests) the creditor of kings, princes, and lesser men all over Europe. By the 1220s the Templars' supremacy in banking was surpassed. In the next decade Italians were acting as the principal agents of a Papacy which transferred money from all over Europe to the *curia*. Strengthened by the immense profits to be harvested from this work, the Tuscans of the inland towns, and the men of Piacenza, of Asti and Chieri, were soon established as the leading financiers of the west. By the 1290s there were fourteen branches of Italian banks at London, twenty at Paris. The capital they could command was immense. The Bonsignori company of Siena in the 1280s and 1290s, for example, boasted a share-capital of 35,000 florins, and had over 200,000 florins in deposit. Sometimes, perilously enough, Italians were tempted to expand from private banking to the realm of government finance. In France the experiment was brief. Between 1294 and 1297 'monsieur Biche' and 'monsieur Mouche', that is Albizzo and Musciatto Guidi of the Franzesi firm, acted as bankers of Philip IV, but the arrangement was soon abandoned. It was in England that the system was to be most fully exploited.

One dwells on the story as an illustration of the wealth, power, and risks amidst which the Italian capitalist moved. First in the rôle of 'merchants of the Lord King' were the Riccardi of Lucca who served Edward I from 1272 to 1294. In those years, with branches at London, York, Nîmes, Flanders, and Rome, they virtually took over the financial responsibility for the kingdom. They made regular loans, amounting in all to the equivalent of more than 3,272,000 florins over the twenty-two years, and stood surety for the king's loans from others. They provided luxury goods, jewels, and precious vessels for the court. (It was their gold which gilded the effigy of Eleanor of Castille in Westminster Abbey.) They imported miners from Lucca to prospect for silver in the Channel Isles. In return, they traded in wool free from the customary disabilities faced by alien merchants. They controlled the profitable recoinage of 1279 and lent money at court. (Among their debtors there featured five earls, two countesses, two archbishops of Canterbury, three archbishops of York, one archbishop of Dublin, six bishops, eighteen priors and abbots, as well as numerous lesser men.) It was their wealth which financed the Welsh wars and the building of those castles which were to keep Wales in permanent subjection. It was their financial expertise which stood behind the successes of the first half of Edward I's reign.

The story of the dazzling fortunes of the Riccardi was not to end happily. Their finances over-extended, they found themselves in the 1290s menaced in both their French and English branches by the rivalries of the kings, and, though fighting to the last, went down finally to bankruptcy. Bankruptcy was to be the fate of their successors too. The Florentine Frescobaldi, whose loans made possible the English attack on Scotland, were doomed by the revolt of the Ordainers in 1310. The Bardi and Peruzzi houses of Florence, without whom the Hundred Years War might never have started, crashed in 1345, in some part through the bad faith of Edward III who owed them over a million and a quarter florins.

From the standpoint of 'rational economic man' the willingness of these men to take on tasks beyond their capacities would no doubt merit condemnation. For the moment there were rewards to be won: free trade, leases of royal mines, manors all over England, rich benefices for clerical relatives. There were fleeting emotional rewards too. It must have been sweet for old Berto Frescobaldi back in Florence to have learnt that he (together with the bishop of Florence) had been made a member of Edward II's privy council; it must have been exhilarating for men who had no king to be taken by the arm and called 'brother' by a descendant of the legendary Arthur. Barone, factor of the Frescobaldi, writes of how Edward II called him to his presence:

He was in the park of Windsor, so that I went there and stayed four days. He warmly welcomed me and in the presence of his seneschal told me I could safely go and stay all over his kingdom wherever I would like, because he considered me his merchant and took myself under his protection. Besides he ordered Sir William Melton to let me have any letter I would need, sealed with the great seal, and said to me: 'Be sure you shall find me the best lord you ever found.' Consequently I was and am very merry and content . . .[1]

At that very moment the Frescobaldi in Gascony were under arrest by the king's officers. These men, playing for the highest rewards, were offering the highest stakes. Yet for many among their contemporaries who managed to maintain a sense of balance and who could avoid kings and princes, there were indeed huge rewards to be won. One thinks of Gandolfo d'Arcelli with a personal holding of 43,500 florins in the Borrini company of Piacenza, or of Giovanni Salimbene, the Sienese banker, who in 1260 offered his commune a loan of 118,000 florins from his own patrimony.

Less spectacularly profitable for individuals, although of profound social importance, was the growth of native industry. Iron, mined principally in Elba and the Val d'Aosta, was produced in only limited quantities, but there was some steel manufacture, and Brescia, Bergamo, and Milan flourished on arms production. The working of flax, leather, and hemp also had some importance. The principal source of wealth here, however, was textiles: silk, of which Lucca became the principal European producer; cotton; wool-cloths and fustians aimed at a mass-market; the making-up of imported high-quality English and other wool into cloth; or again the refining of imported wool-cloths into cloth of the highest quality for sale in the export market.

Overall this immense development of the economy was uneven. It did not touch the South. It left many towns in central and northern Italy as still little more than market centres for the agricultural products of the surrounding countryside. But for the great ports it brought a profound transformation; and it gave Tuscany a new economic predominance over the world to the north of the Apennines. During the second-half of the thirteenth century when the Tuscan cities became supreme in banking, their manufacture of textiles, hitherto of comparatively minor importance, increased until in the fourteenth century they overtook their Lombard rivals as the leading centres in the production of wool. Within Tuscany itself, Florence, with the most powerful banks, and with a third of its inhabitants dependent for their livelihood upon the wool industry, drew steadily ahead of its neighbouring rivals. Yet lesser centres too continued to flourish in their own way and all the towns quickened to new rhythms of life as the merchants of the great cities expanded their activities.

These merchants, masters of the commerce of the world, founders of European capitalism, extended their empire of trade from China to Greenland. Nothing was too great or too small for them. If the king of England wanted a war he applied to an Italian firm; when the king of Scotland required a Parisian tailor it was a Florentine company which despatched one to him. Everywhere they made their presence felt. Any one morning the good citizens of Glasgow might wake up to find that the dean of their cathedral was a Bardi, the inhabitants of Gascony to learn that their seneschal was a 'Sir Anthony' Pessagno. The seamen of Lisbon received as their admiral Sir Anthony's brother, Lionardo; the seamen of France looked to a Genoese, Benedetto Zaccaria, as the founder of their royal navy. It was the epic age of Italian history, and the merchants were its heroes. To Italy in the years up to 1340 they gave an economy which was never again to expand so fast, nor, relative to the rest of Europe, to be so powerful. It was an age of great fortunes, glittering prosperity for many, and yet too of an over-expansion which was to exact its own penalties. From the 1290s some ominous features might have suggested that the best days had passed. For the moment, however, the empire held.

II

It was, of course, the economic revolution which had enabled the towns to resist Frederick II and which had thrown up the *popolo* against the old town oligarchies. It subverted the old order. Most noticeably it had promoted, at least in the great commercial cities, a social mobility, unparallelled outside the peninsula. In many centres *popolani* who acquired riches through commerce could, in the thirteenth and fourteenth centuries, very rapidly come to be considered as nobles. One thinks of the Cerchi family in Florence, who in the twelfth century had been small proprietors in the parish of Acone in the Val di Sieve. Only in the 1250s through wealth gained from trade in France and Flanders did they rise from obscurity. Yet by the 1290s Vieri Cerchi was a magnate, a knight who had fought bravely at Campaldino, and the leader of the White Guelfs. He had married into the aristocratic Ubertini family, had bought the palace of the Conti Guidi in the city, and held fiefs and *fideles* in the countryside. He seems, at first sight, indistinguishable from his rival of ancient family, Corso Donati 'il gran barone'.

If knighthood were taken as the criterion of nobility it seemed that almost anyone could become a knight. Contemporaries were led to attempt a distinction between *cavalieri di natura*, descendants of noble families, and *cavalieri di ventura*, those who without being from noble families had attained knighthood through riches or virtue (and who were, according to the Dominican, Remigio Girolami, to be esteemed more highly than those 'di natura'). The penalties decreed in certain communes against 'magnates' (who were often identified with knights) did something, at least initially, to check the desire of *popolani* to be incorporated within the knightly order. Yet the mystique of knighthood remained. The ceremonies which surrounded it (the dubbing, the bath, the vigil, and so on), as lovingly portrayed in the poetry of Folgore da San Gimignano, struck deep chords. Within the great mercantile cities to have a knight in one's family remained a motive for pride. Consequently, as the original force of the *popolo* movement declined many non-magnate patricians aspired to the rôle. At Florence by the 1330s the commune was meeting their wishes by holding its own dubbings. Satirists might mock at the new rich who suddenly assumed coats of arms and airs of chivalry, yet provided they remained rich the mockery was soon forgotten.

Inevitably these developments led to many discussions on what the words 'noble' and 'nobility' might be supposed to mean. Among them one of the most instructive is the *Ragionamento* or 'Treatise' of the Florentine jurist, Lapo da Castiglionchio (d. 1381).[2] His brother, Francesco, was a merchant who died in England in the service of the Alberti banking house; he himself was leader of the aristocratic party of the commune in the 1360s and 1370s. Lapo's study, primarily designed to blazon forth the nobility of his own family – a normal preoccupation of the time – rejected the conclusion that this quality depended, as Dante had asserted, solely upon virtue. There were, after all, Lapo observed, many villeins who would through their virtuous lives meet with God while every day one saw examples of wicked nobles. It could again only with difficulty be seen, as the jurist Bartolo had seen it, as an hereditary office. A noble in fact must be simply 'anyone whom a prince or people accept as such'. Public fame was all.

In the course of his argument Lapo offered a striking reminiscence of his undergraduate days at Bologna. At that time he had read the various papers of his family and had maintained a virtuous and noble style of life. Among his fellow students there was one – his name he forbears to mention through natural delicacy – whose family had waxed fat in trade in Florence. One day in an argument this man had remarked that Lapo should not put on noble airs, for his own family had lived much longer in their native village of Quona than Lapo's had. 'Indeed', was the substance of Lapo's reply, 'that is most likely, for when our family bought that village no doubt they bought your ancestors with it.' Whereat his adversary had blanched and turned away. Returning to his room, Lapo tells us, he repented of his hasty rejoinder and resolved to seek out and apologise to his opponent who was in many ways a worthy fellow and with whom he had been on friendly terms. As chance had it he was forestalled by a visit from the ignoble youth in question. Lapo began his apology and promised that he would in future deny the truth of the remark he had made. But in return he was faced with only one insistent question: was it true? Seeing that the point had been reached where only frankness was possible, Lapo allowed himself to draw attention to the relevant documents. Thenceforth, he tells us, his friend was always to show an air of respect and humility before him.

In reading this story one is struck, above all, by the grossly insecure foundations upon which Lapo's apparent complacency rested. For if his fellow-student were, all unknowingly, the descendant of serfs, how immensely possible was it that Lapo's blood too was, for all his boasting of ancestors and flourishing of ancient charters, tainted with a villein strain. Again the *Ragionamento* as a whole prompts the reflection that even to think about whether one is noble or not, let alone to make a show of proving it, is at once to confess one's vulnerability It was not something one imagines which for a moment attracted the attention of the earls of Norfolk or the counts of Champagne or Aldobrandino.

This anecdote, in fact, is a monument to three centuries of development in which, as a result of the economic revolution, a new class, the patriciate, has been formed. The nobility that this patriciate claimed was of a different kind from that of northern Europe. It did not depend upon blood but upon personal achievement. If you are not noble, Lapo tells us, do not from that feel shame or sorrow of soul, but rather study 'how you may transmit nobility to your descendants'. And it is better too – the statement is all the more remarkable when one considers the author's violent opposition to 'new men' in political life – to ennoble yourself than to inherit nobility. Status is more the reward of one's own work than that of one's family. Even the despised rustic may do well. He himself may not be noble but his children and grandchildren can ascend to that state 'as we see every day'. There are descendants of serfs, Lapo tells us, who are now priors.

One would not wish to overstress the elements of social change for Italy as a whole. In most of the *signorie* the claims of blood continued to loom large. Even within the communes there was a remarkable continuity of the same élite families at the head of government. At Venice, indeed, access to the ranks of the ruling nobility was, from 1323, virtually forbidden. It remains true, however, that the upper-classes of Italy were strikingly different from those to be found elsewhere. In northern Europe in this period, at, for example, Lille, Toulouse, and Strasbourg, it is possible to find men of the upper-bourgeoisie who became fief-holders; in England there is the notorious, though unique, example of the merchant De La Pole family which made its way into the ranks of the peerage. Yet these men were assimilated into an order or system without changing it. In the commercial communes of Italy the character of nobility, already fluid, was transformed by the very ease and ubiquity of transition and fusion between noble and non-noble society.

Values changed. It is true that everywhere, and more particularly in the less developed regions, a traditional noble style of life continued and that chivalrous trappings multiplied without abatement. Amadeus, Count of Savoy, created the 'Order of the Black Swan' in 1350; King Lewis of Naples (or, more probably, his seneschal, that illegitimate offspring of a Florentine banker, Niccolò Acciaiuoli) established the 'Order of the Holy Spirit', complete with knights-errant, in 1353. Yet in the great mercantile centres the patriciate were coming to live by different lights. In Genoa, as if in recognition of the difference between their nobility and that of the north, the chroniclers came in the thirteenth century to substitute the word *bonitas* for *nobilitas* in their writings. The *popolano* knight, too, was of a different character from the noble knight, and the *popolano grasso*, however much his family had intermarried into magnate houses, however much he assumed business partnerships with magnates, was a different person from a noble magnate.

One recognises the difference at once in reading the Florentine chronicler of the *popolo grasso*, Giovanni Villani (d. 1348). He is a man who recalls 'the Breton romances' of 'the good and *cortese* king Arthur', and he dwells on jousts and *corti* with some pleasure. But his is a long way from the authentic voice of *courtoisie*. This son of a prior, merchant in Flanders, director of the Buonaccorsi company, superintendent of the mint, corn-official, whose very name forbids high-flown fantasies about his family's past, lives according to different values. Their essence is to be discerned in that inscription, or variants of it, to be found at the head of the mercantile account books: 'Al nome di Dio e di guadagno che Dio ci dia' ('In the name of God and the gain that God may give us'). A detached admiration for noble culture is subordinated to an over-riding concern for the consolidation and expansion of commercial wealth. This sentiment is combined with a complacent godliness which equates the maintenance of virtue with success in this life, and hence a certain puritan piety, a search for 'respectability', a dislike of unnecessary violence which both offends God and is likely to hurt the pocket. With these go pride in the trade of merchant, interest in whatever could reasonably be quantified, and finally civic awareness, belief in 'the greatness and state and magnificence of the commune of Florence'.

If the values of *cortesia* engendered the economic revolution, it was these that sustained it. Part of the culture of these men is to be found in the new numeracy and new literacy revealed in their account-books, letters, and diaries (one thinks of the 500 odd account-books and 120,000 letters surviving from the business of Francesco Datini, merchant of Prato). Though it would be untrue to imagine that, for most of these men, economic rationality was all, they had a practical everyday approach to the problems of life. Under their shade, particularly from the 1350s and among lesser men (among whom we must place Datini: a man whose life makes explicable the posturings of Lapo da Castiglionchio), one discerns too the growth of a sub-culture, which seeing time, friendship, and reputation as mere aspects of money, subordinates all values to prudent acquisition. Its most characteristic expression is to be found in the maxims of Paolo da Certaldo: 'Hold always to those who are richer and greater than you': 'Never cultivate the friendship of the down-and-out': 'Never expend nor undertake more than your purse can bear', etc. The spirit of this 'proto-capitalist ethic' was not the spirit of the economic revolution, but it is to be discerned often enough among the epigoni of the great pioneers.

III

The emergence of such an ethic at first sight so remote from the needs of that adventurous risk-taking which constituted medieval trade is explicable enough if one turns one's eyes away from the principal agents of the economic revolution. The great merchants and capitalists gave to their cities complex social structures, created closely-intertwined networks of relationships which bound large masses to an ultimate dependence upon them. It is, naturally enough, their careers, their spectacular triumphs and as spectacular failures, which have above all attracted the interest of historians. At the centre of their studies have stood 'the pillars of Christendom', the Acciaiuoli, the Frescobaldi, and the Bardi, or again, the rags-to-riches saga of a man such as Francesco Datini of Prato.

Yet by the side of the large companies, the great operators, were hundreds of lesser men, modest entrepreneurs, seeking to make their way in the world. Of these, there were some like Ner Picciolini in Cecco Angiolieri's sonnet, who returned to their native town from abroad 'so hot with many florins that men just seemed to him so many mice'. Yet others, perhaps much more typical, after a lifetime's struggle, had nothing to show for their labours. One thinks in this connection of Lippo di Fede di Sega (c. 1288–c. 1363) whose career has recently been brilliantly restored to life through the researches of Professor de la Roncière.[3] Lippo was a money-changer of Florence. From 1313 to 1320, his saddle-bags weighed down with coins, he visited Venice, Perugia, Siena, Arezzo, Pisa, and Bologna in hope of gain. Initial prosperity gave way to failure and a brief imprisonment for debt. Released, he embarked for Cyprus. But here too opportunities proved poor; by 1322 he was back in Florence. Still hopeful, leaving his wife and two daughters, Lippo took the road across the Alps, and established himself at Pontoise, outside Paris, on the Normandy road. He did not return until 1353 and he returned with no fortune. Over sixty now, he had nothing to show for his labours but a speech deeply gallicised; he writes 'fama' ('femme') for 'moglie' (wife), 'Noello' ('Noël') for 'Natale' (Christmas). Nothing now remained but to taste the salt of failure. His wife had died; remarriage to the widow Bernarda proved an error. Within eight months she was complaining bitterly of him in reproaches met with silence but confided to his account book: 'she said, this skinflint, this vermin, this idiot, disaster for her husbands, that Francesca [his sister] had prayed to God that I'd come back with a shirt and that I've come back quite naked . . .' Visits to his country farm dropped off.

Attempts to make ends meet by taking temporary minor offices in the commune, as for instance among the officers of the gate of the gabelles, had increasingly to be supplemented by borrowings from a nephew. A final disaster struck in January 1362, when the old man ventured a sexual assault on a serving girl. Brought before the courts, his sole excuse that she was 'of inferior status', he was fined £F.75, and with that disappears from history.

Lippo's story warns us that the triumphs of the economic revolution were not unaccompanied by casualties. Yet even from the 1340s when that revolution ceased, one would not wish to discount the elements of triumph. The merchants brought great benefits to some among their fellow citizens. They offered the possiblity of share-investment in their firms down to quite modest artisans, and above all they gave new, though, as we shall see, severely limited, opportunities for work. The cloth imported by the Calimala guild from distant Flanders, then to be reworked by native craftsmen into a luxury product; the raw silk introduced by the merchants of the Arte di Por Santa Maria; the raw wool sent from England or Spain or Morocco to the masters of the Lana, these all gave employment to large numbers of artisans and unskilled workmen who would otherwise have starved. At the same time their own wealth sustained a considerable trade in luxuries. Through them flourished the glass-blowers of Murano with their jewelled, enamelled cups, goldsmiths, the furriers dressing furs from southern Russia, builders, painters and perfume-sellers. Through them too a large number of wage-earners supported a hundred more modest trades, as those of the baker, the smith, the cobbler, on a scale unknown in northern Europe.

IV

Despite the extent of Italian industry the normal work-unit was small. There were no large industrial complexes of a modern type. The government Arsenal of Venice, which undertook the refurbishing, repair, and (from the fourteenth century) construction of all the merchant galleys of the port, was manned by gangs of independent small masters and their workmen. Even in the iron mines of Elba the normal unit seems to have been twenty-nine men. In the chemical industries of Venice, in glass-making, in soap, dye and saltpetre manufacture, where heavy equipment or large furnaces were used, firms generally had only a handful of masters and perhaps a dozen apprentices or partly-skilled workers. In 1304, when the commune ordered 20,000 steel bolts for crossbows, the contracts were given out to master ironsmiths, employing between six and seventeen workers each. Throughout Italy most businesses, those of minor retail-craftsmen, were smaller yet, and often carried on by no more than a master, journeyman, and apprentice.

Even a great industry, which required a vast network of dependants of different status and prosperity, was based upon small nuclei. In the wool-cloth trade of Florence, for instance, there were no large factories, rather a considerable number of fairly small workshops operating mainly on the 'putting-out' system. Towards

194

the end of our period there were some 279 firms in the city, each with a capital of between 2,000 and 6,000 florins, each producing something between as little as three and not more than 220 'pieces' of cloth annually. The owners of these shops, the *lanaioli*, channelled the raw wool through the twenty-six specialised processes which would ultimately produce the finished cloth. Sub-contractors took the wool to country districts to deliver to spinners and to collect their yarn. Weavers, men and women, working at home on looms which they normally owned themselves, wove the cloths. Fullers loaded the cloths on to mules and travelled out to the fast mountain streams where stood the fulling-mills they leased from noble proprietors. Other stages too were undertaken by small entrepreneurs with their own shops: men like the dyers, shearers, menders, or the tenterers who worked in large buildings furnished with the apparatus for stretching the cloth. Even the heavy unskilled labours, beating, washing, carding, combing, were often carried out away from the premises of the *lanaiolo's* shop.

Whether as part of a large industry, whether as member of a small, the skilled artisan would have begun his career at the age of between ten and twelve when he would be apprenticed to a master. Sometimes he would receive a small wage, food and accommodation; sometimes he was given nothing; sometimes his parents paid the master to take him. After perhaps seven years of training he was considered qualified in his craft and could either work for hire by the year, month, or day, or set up as a master with his own shop. For this he would need some capital for equipment (we read of a painter spending 100 florins on chests, panels, and paints) and a workshop (whose rents in the large towns might vary between 7 and 15 florins a year). He would also have to meet the expense of matriculating as a master in his guild. To meet what might be a considerable outlay, he might form a company with other men with whom he would share work, expenses, or profit. Alternatively (and very commonly) he might enter into a 'half-produce' contract with some rich man. The capitalist would provide the shop and equipment. The master would produce and sell his goods. At the end of each year, after expenses had been deducted, the profits were divided equally between them.

In most towns the artisan who became an independent master could then take his place within the ranks of his appropriate guild or *arte*. In the small retail crafts this might be governed by a rector, a chamberlain who kept the accounts, and three or more 'councillors'. All these officials were likely to be elected for six-monthly periods of rule. The greater guilds would have a more complex though similar organisation. In all the *arti* the officials would be assisted by a messenger or messengers and by a spy or spies, secretly appointed and assigned the task of reporting breaches of the guilds' statutes. Guild statutes, normally codified in a written volume, were drawn up by the vote of all the masters. Once approved, as law required, by the town-government, they were binding on all masters. Their workmen and apprentices, too, were all compelled to swear obedience to them before obtaining employment. Many provisions sought to cut down competition between masters. They prohibited work on feast-days, the luring away of other masters' workmen, the acceptance of work previously offered to another master. Many again sought to maintain standards by prohibiting the use of inferior materials. Others aimed to maintain workshop discipline by guarding against theft, abuse of masters, or inadequate workmanship by workers. Violation of statutes was met by boycott and social ostracism.

In addition the guilds of the less prosperous trades often took on a social function. They provided relief for widows and orphans of masters, or for masters who were sick, imprisoned, or otherwise fallen on hard times. All guilds emphasised a fraternal relation between their masters and it was normally the rôle of the rector to make peace between members at odds. This spirit was reinforced by joint religious observances. On the feast-day of the guild's patron saint all masters and workers would go with a candle bought at their own expense to their patron church to hear mass. When any member or close relative of any member died, one or two men from each shop were expected to attend the funeral. Sometimes – like the sub-guild of painters of Florence who founded in 1339 the company of St. Luke – the *arte* might form a confraternity, open to wives and daughters of members, for the promotion of religious devotion. For the independent master the guild stood alongside the parish as a principal centre of conviviality and social interchange.

For those who were not masters the *arte* might appear in a less attractive light. Membership and government of the guild were restricted to employers. Employees, whether apprentices or labourers, were always purely *sottoposti*, subject to the discipline of the guild, held apart from its privileges. In some towns many classes of masters too were *sottoposti* of guilds in which they had no rights. This phenomenon was particularly characteristic of Florence, where large numbers of small workshop masters were subordinate to a few large guilds. Here, for example, the painters (among whose numbers were found, in addition to artists, mattress-workers, box-makers, glass and wax workers, house-decorators, colour-grinders, etc.) came under the authority of the guild-masters of the *arte* of doctors and druggists. In the wool-guild of the same city the only masters who could matriculate in the guild were the *lanaioli*, the investor-managers who had exclusive control over the raw product. All other masters of workshops in the industry – dyers, shearers, stretchers, for example – were, though employers, treated for guild purposes simply as *sottoposti*. Such men might in fact enjoy considerable prosperity (in 1378 over 150 of them were assessed within the top 10 per cent of the tax paying population) but their subjection to the *lanaioli* was felt as a real grievance.

That sense of grievance was not unjustified for everywhere governments supported the authority of the guild-masters against their *sottoposti*, and everywhere these men exercised a forceful control over their subordinates. In the *Arte della Lana* of Florence, for example, discipline was maintained by the *officialis forestierus* or 'foreign official', so-called because always a non-native of the town and so, though appointed by the guild-masters, deemed to exercise impartial justice. Paid some 200 florins a year (in addition to taking a proportion of the fines he levied), he was served by six guards and a variable number of secret informers. He could impose fines on all *sottoposti* of the guild for work poorly done or for abuse of the masters. Against cabbaging and sabotage he had the right to beat, put to the torture, even behead workers. He was empowered to cut off the right hands of those persistently indebted to the guild who had no possibility of repayment. He was in all the *podestà* of a state within a state, taking oaths of obedience from all its subjects and enforcing the authority of its statutes.

Yet if dependent masters resented their subjection to this regime they could reflect that the alliance of guild and commune offered them considerable advantages *vis-à-vis* their own workmen. Town statutes often laid down that the master might physically beat his employees. (At Viterbo in 1251 it was stipulated that such punishment should be 'moderate, so that even though blood should flow, no limb shall be severed'.) In particular, town and guild statutes pronounced emphatically against *monopolia, posturas, ligas ac doganas ac etiam iuramenta uniquasque exationes*, against, that is, all attempts at combinations, oaths of solidarity, exaction of union-dues by working men in an attempt to raise their standard of living. As the statutes of the silk guild at Florence observed, since St. Paul has asked that all men be brothers in Christ, such divisive leagues were opposed to the spirit of religion. No doubt it was in the same spirit of Christian concern that the Florentine statutes of the *podestà* of 1325 forbade all assemblies or brotherhoods, including burial or mutual-aid societies and those formed 'under pretext of religion'.

V

In defence of the guilds it should be said that industry was intensely competitive. In particular, textile manufacturers, whose work required considerable technical expertise and administrative ability, were working on small profit margins and in the face of hazardous marketing-conditions. A high proportion of their capital (some 60 per cent it has been calculated, in the Florentine wool business) went in the payment of labour. Nor were there here any of those spectacularly great fortunes to be made in banking or commerce. Higher wages brought about by union action would have been likely to bring them to bankruptcy and their men to unemployment.

Employers and employees were caught together in a harsh economic trap, and were both bound to a severe and curiously unbalanced discipline of work. In winter in Tuscany the working-day extended from sunrise to sunset with one hour's break for lunch; in summer (1 March–1 August) when there were 16 – 18 hours of daylight there were two breaks: the first between 7 and 9 o'clock in the morning, the second between 1 and 3 in the afternoon. Yet the length of the working-day was less a burden to the employee than the fact that, in order to prevent the more extreme forms of cut-throat competition between masters, paid work was prohibited by the guilds and the town authorities for a large part of the year: at night, on Sundays, and on feast-days (of which there were some 67 at Florence, 71 at Siena). On Saturdays, too, work and wages were often reduced by a third.

Taking these Saturdays into consideration there were, perhaps, in most towns some 230–240 paid full working days a year. Labourers who could obtain work on all these days or skilled craftsmen such as weavers (who often worked on piece-rates) received a recompense which, save when the price of bread was exceptionally high, was normally sufficient to allow them to pay the rents on their accommodation and to feed and clothe a small family. Their problem – acute for the unskilled, particularly in the textile industries and particularly from the 1340s when war, plague or economic depression frequently closed down the shops – lay in securing continuous employment. For many, perhaps most, full-time work was not possible. So at Florence in the 1370s some 9,000 unskilled or semi-skilled labourers in the cloth-industry, the majority in debt (often to employers who in laying them off lent money to ensure their services when their shops reopened), eked out a precarious existence from day to day at the mercy of the trade-cycle and, above all, the price of their staple food, bread. Sharing the same quality of life amidst the stinking warrens of crowded hovels which made up the slum areas of San Frediano, San Pietro Gottolino, Sant' Ambrogio, Camaldoli, San Lorenzo, stood poor and dependent shop-owners, day-labourers in the building trades, porters, gardeners, market-women, pedlars, and messengers.

Such were the men who formed the *popolo minuto*, the little people, the poor, all over urban Italy. In his *Liber Particularis*, written in underdeveloped Sicily at the beginning of the thirteenth century, they had already been delineated by Michael the Scot. As born under Saturn, following these 'infamous' occupations 'which always pertain to poverty and make a man unhappy or unfortunate, sad, moody and miserable' stood labourers on the soil, grave diggers, porters, street-cleaners, lavatory attendants, gatherers and sellers of herbs, common criers to the *podestà*, metal workers making everyday things such as axes, crowbars, ploughshares, and mattocks. Others, herdsmen, guards, makers of tiles and bricks, monastic servants, were born under Mars. Those following lighter occupations such as cosmetic sellers, musicians, needleworkers, flower-sellers, dice-makers, servants to lords and ladies, came under Venus. To others, born under the Moon, Michael assigns a higher 'mediocre' status, though it is difficult, outside his astrological preoccupation, to see why. These included sailors and fishermen, runners, postmen, jesters, weavers, gardeners, shepherds, servants (there are certain overlaps between planets), ponces, prostitutes, and pedlars.[4]

For the energetic, the skilled, and the lucky among such people the economic revolution had opened up possibilities of raising themselves to new positions where they might enjoy, at least, a life of hard but adequately rewarded labour. But it had also allowed the birth and survival of large numbers who would otherwise have never been born or who would have died shortly after birth. In that sense it created a new world of the poor, giving the possibility of life, subsistence but not the enjoyment of life, to large masses of the towns. They had little contact with the guilds, with the parish, or its confraternities. They are that half of the city of Siena who in 1328 were described as *nullatenenti*: 'holding nothing'. They are that 60 per cent of the population of the Rota district in the slum Santa Croce quarter of Florence, which Dr. Brucker in his analysis of the tax return of 1379 had defined as indigent. They seem exceptionally rootless; of their numbers 45 per cent had not been resident in the district in the previous year. 'They moved from district to district within the city in search of lower rents and more lucrative jobs; they moved back to their native hamlets in the *contado* when the cloth factories shut down, or when seasonal fluctuations in economic activity reduced the opportunities for employment.'[5]

These men and women were the victims of an economic system whose defects were irremediable. They were also the object of an oppression which was man-made and political. It was more than anything else the development of government in this period – of government which was the spokesman of the rich and the employers – which served to depress their standards of living. To calculate with precision the relative prosperity of ordinary men and women over the thirteenth and fourteenth centuries would require a much fuller knowledge of wage and price levels – particularly of the price of corn – than we possess. None the less one has the impression that, if life could have been seen purely in terms of wages and and prices, the lot of the average worker would have improved over the two centuries, and particularly after the Black Death, when labour could be short. In relation to the value of gold the wages of oarsmen at Venice doubled during the thirteenth century and continued to rise in the fourteenth. So too the annual return of a fully-employed unskilled workman at Florence rose from the equivalent of 15 to 30 florins in the course of the fourteenth century. What intervened to nullify these gains was only in part the periodic economic depressions which struck the peninsula from the 1340s, much more an expansion of governmental financing in the course of the fourteenth century which increasingly weighed the scales of taxation against those least able to pay. The rise of forced loans (*prestanze*) led to a system where the rich were often able to receive interest on what they paid, while the small contributions of the poor were accorded no such advantage. The establishment of public debts meant too that the poor were being increasingly taxed to pay the interest that the rich received. At the same time the replacement of *estimi* (or property taxes) and hearth-taxes by the indirect taxation of the gabelles, by duties on the processing of food and retail sales of wine, vegetables, fruit, oil and salt, meant that the fiscal burden of the rich was more and more transferred to the poor.

The sacrifice of the community as a whole to the interests of the governing class which appears most sharply in the communes' taxation policies can be illustrated again in the encouragement given by that class to the import of Eastern slaves into the peninsula. During the second half of the fourteenth century large numbers of Tartar, Russian, Georgian, Alan and Circassian males and females (sometimes below seven years of age) were purchased in the slave-markets of Tana and Caffa and shipped to Italy. There, in the ports of Genoa, Pisa, Ancona, and Venice, they were auctioned as domestic servants. At Genoa in the 1380s there were 5,000 slaves, mainly female, in the city; by the end of the century no fashionable family in the peninsula was without one. Thus, precisely at a moment when periodic economic crises brought large-scale shortage of work for native unskilled labour, one opportunity of employment (however ill-rewarded) was sharply reduced. Those who could buy 'a slave-girl of Tartar race and speech' for the equivalent of a mere 17 florins were unlikely to go to the expense of employing an Italian girl.

The Church reflected, no doubt, both on the effects the trade would have upon violence within the border zones of the Eastern supply-areas and on the vulnerability of the female slave to sexual violence in Italy but concluded that these possible disadvantages were outweighed by the opportunities that slavery afforded of bringing infidels to a knowledge of Christ. Following this decision Florence, in its formal authorisation of the trade in 1363, stipulated that only non-Christians might be imported. But the possibilities of profit from the traffic were not so lightly to be set aside, and very many of the slaves were Greek-Orthodox and even Latin Christians. In human terms, it is true, the open sale of the merchandise left a disturbing impression. Hence at Venice the public auctions at the Rialto were eventually forbidden and purchase in future was confined to private contract. Of the interests of the lower classes in all this, however, nothing was said.

In large measure the principal weakness of the *popolo minuto* lay in the fact that, if fed – and all governments saw the provision of food as a first priority – its members normally presented little threat to social order. It incorporated, of course, a large sub-world of crime but the poor, after all, mainly rob the poor and for those who ventured against the rich there were quite powerful police forces and a list of severe penalties (cutting off of hands, branding, whipping, hanging) to serve as a deterrent. It has been calculated that at Siena there was one non-Sienese policeman to every 145 inhabitants (quite apart from the secret informers who received proportions of fines paid by the guilty) and that between the mid 1270s and 1290s there was an annual average of some 850 successful prosecutions for crime. Lower-class criminality, at least, the communes could to a certain extent contain. The *popolo minuto* also produced a vast network of prostitution, a white-slave traffic linking all the towns, in which, in addition to country-girls trapped into the life, it is curious to find a large number of foreign, particularly German and French, women. Yet such prostitution was to a large extent licensed, controlled, and exploited by the communes. With some surprise, indeed, we find within the Papal State the Marshall of the Holy Roman Church selling licences to hold brothels and gaming houses; while Genoa established conditions for the women which made their departure from their profession extremely difficult.

Considered as a political force the *popolo minuto*, for all its proclivity to violence, was normally powerless. As in the *popolo* movement of the thirteenth century, or in the revolution against the duke of Athens in Florence, that violence was often utilised and canalised by those more prosperous for their own ends. It is in this way, probably, that one should see the rôle of the poor in the insurrections at Perugia in 1370–1 and 1375, and at Siena in 1368–71. Again, in times of economic depressions individual patricians, like the unstable and ambitious Andrea Strozzi at Florence in November 1343 or like the Tolomei at Siena in January 1347, might, with the promise of bread, be able to raise a considerable mob (at Florence in 1343 it was said to be of some 4,000 people), who to the cry of 'Long live the *popolo minuto* and death to the gabelles and the *popolo grasso*' or 'Long live the people and death to the dogs who are starving us' would riot in favour of their attempt at *signoria*. Hunger again sometimes provoked spontaneous bread-riots without prompting from above, the high-handed action of some noble might cause a fracas, and unpopular communal officials might be assaulted.

Governments had always to be prepared for such movements, yet their very spontaneity and deficiency in organisation prevented them from bringing gains to the lower classes. Against organised economic agitation which offered a greater threat to employers, and which was particularly characteristic of Florence in the hungry 1340s, commune and guild acted with repressive firmness. At Florence one finds the execution of two men for urging defiance of their masters in October 1343, and the prosecution of sixteen wool spinners for forming an illegal union in 1346. Most celebrated is the Brandini affair of 1345. In May of that year the officials of the *podestà* seized the wool-carder Ciuto Brandini and his two sons on charges that 'moved by a diabolical spirit and by the suggestion of the enemy of humanity' he had sought to organise a brotherhood among the workers of Florence. He had held large meetings at Sante Croce and Santa Maria de' Servi, had named consuls and captains for his organisation, and had collected dues for its purposes. At Ciuto's arrest the carders and wool-combers stopped work, went to the priors, and demanded his release. Their efforts were fruitless; his subsequent execution serves as a symbol of the impotence of all working-class movements in this period.

VI

That fundamental impotence appears most clearly in the widest proletarian disturbance of the period, the so-called 'Revolt of the Ciompi' at Florence in 1378. It arose largely as a result of divisions within the ruling oligarchy. In June, Salvestro de' Medici, seeking to maintain his predominance in government, stirred up the city-poor to sack the houses of his patrician enemies. This action introduced a period of intense political activity, discussions, rumours, and conspiracies among all classes. It was a time when large numbers of disbanded soldiers had employment in the cloth industry. Experience of war had, no doubt, emboldened them to protest and action. Small masters resentful of their subordination to the wool-guild, factors whose admission to the guild as full members had recently been made more difficult, artisans and petty shopkeepers from other trades, came together with the *ciompi* (the 'muckers' or 'mates' or 'Jimmies' at the bottom of society) to air their grievances. Discontent and expectation of change grew. At the end of the third week of July, with the probable complicity of Salvestro and his patrician associates, a new upsurge of violence forced the resignation of the Priors.

The *balià* or special commission which took their place consisted of some few patricians, a predominating number of small masters who were *sottoposti* of greater guilds, and thirty-two men specificaly designated as representative of the *ciompi*. Of these last some half were poor workers; among the remainder were merchants and notaries of considerable wealth. As Gonfaloniere of Justice there emerged Michele di Lando, son of a market-woman who had sold provisions to prisoners in the gaol of the commune. Married to a woman who managed a butcher's shop, he had served in the Pisan War (1362–4) as a captain of foot-soldiers, and now worked as a foreman in a cloth-factory.

The demands of the *ciompi* represent fairly well the grievances of the working-classes. They did not, surprisingly enough, attack the gabelle system, but they identified the raising of taxation through forced loans as inequitable. Hence they sought the abolition of forced loans and the introduction of a fairer levy (the *estimo*) based upon property. Interest payments from the *monte* (or public-debt) were to be suspended, and the debt amortised over a twelve-year period. In addition – since normally paid in a silver currency which was constantly depreciating – they wanted the maintenance in value of silver coinage in respect of gold. Again they looked for a two-year moratorium on private debts and the abolition of the power of the 'foreign official' in the wool guild. Finally they sought the right to establish their own guild through which they might negotiate better wages and working conditions.

In their six-week tenure of office, the men of the *balìa* did go some way to meet these demands. Three new guilds were established: those of the dyers, the shirt-makers, and the *popolo minuto*, in which last were included, beside factors and yarn-brokers, all unskilled workers in the cloth industry. Again a new tax-system based upon the *estimo* was decreed. Yet the majority on the *balìa* had little sympathy with the *ciompi*, no desire for greater lower-class power in the political or economic world, and were offering these concessions merely as a temporary means of securing a return to law and order. Many had a stake in the *monte*. More than this, if government were to continue, finance had to be raised, and hence a new forced-loan had to be decreed. Many lower shop-keepers too were creditors of the *popolo minuto* and so the moratorium on debts was swiftly cancelled.

Disillusioned at the failure of what had perhaps been envisaged as the immediate arrival of a new social order, the *ciompi* grew restive. Their discontent was enhanced by general unemployment for despite government command the cloth-makers had closed down their shops and many wool-masters had prudently withdrawn from the city. In these circumstances the poor in the districts of S. Spirito and S. Giovanni proceeded on the 27 August to the election of 'Eight Saints of God's people'. They assembled in a crowd of 5,000 before S. Marco, and marched with new petitions on Palazzo Vecchio. At the heart of their proposals was a plan for a permanent committee of 'Eight Saints' who would, on behalf of the *ciompi*, have the right to veto or approve all communal legislation. Faced with a new phase of revolution the government temporised but determined to resist. By an opportune bribe (large enough to allow him to set up later as a *lanaiolo* in Modena) Michele di Lando was won over to its side. On 31 August it was Michele in person who led the guild-militias which drove the *ciompi* from Piazza Signoria and finally broke their power.

Within a few days, the new guild abolished, normality – the normality of a cowed lower class – had been re-established. Those tumultuous days between June and September had underlined the grievances of the *popolo minuto* but they had also emphasised their inability to redress them. Misery and malnutrition bred an apathy broken only by occasional revolt. Leadership was lacking. The economic order deprived them of all power and separated their interests from those of the artisans and shopkeepers nearest in status to them. Outside the vague conviction that they were 'the people of God', a conviction perhaps, though this is not certain, nurtured by Fraticelli heretics, they had no ideology. In these circumstances the limited horizons of their lives bound them to an unquestioning dependence upon that capitalist system of which they formed a part. They had asked not for the abolition of the guild-system, but to be incorporated within it, with banners and coats of arms like other guilds. They had asked for a moratorium not an abolition of debts. They had sought not the abolition of knighthood but that they themselves, in a bizzare ceremony, should confer knighthoods on their own representatives: a carder, a wool-beater, a baker. What had ultimately worked against their interests was their immense conservatism, their inability, inevitable given the social world in which they lived, to move to any more radical position.

VII

The troubles of the poor continued as they had always done. One would not wish to portray the harshness of their life in too extreme terms. It would be misleading to forget the alleviations of their lot, their moments of joy in domestic and social pleasures. For entertainment they had the life of the taverns, civic and ecclesiastic pageant, a back-seat view of the tournaments of the rich, dance and song on feast-days. There were the contests between town districts: races on horse or foot for the *drappo verde, palio* or flag. There was *pallone*, a sort of mass game of football; and the popular, though often brutal, mock wars, such as the Saracen's Joust at Arezzo.

There were the street-entertainers too, mimes, musicians, jugglers, tumblers, and mountebanks, travelling from town to town throughout the peninsula. And there were the *cantastorie* (singers of tales) men like Antonio Pucci, town-crier of Florence, who sang the fortunes of the commune and its leaders, or those vagrant minstrels who chanted *sirventesi* (political ballads) or retold the epics of Charlemagne and the paladins. These tales, woven from the *matière de France*, offered most of the eternal elements in popular narrative: a simple, glamorous code of behaviour, exotic adventure, romantic sex and idealised violence in an upper-class milieu, heroes and monsters, black and white characterisations devoid of psychological interest but for that very reason allowing a large measure of self-identification to the listener.

At the beginning of the thirteenth century Odofredo wrote of 'the minstrels who play in public for reward and enter the courtyard of the Commune of Bologna and sing of the Lords Roland and Oliver'. From a lawsuit in the same city, some hundred years later, we can observe these men more closely. On 11 May 1307 one Bonacosa de' Forti, a wine-seller, was indicted for abusing the Guelf party and for brawling in the via Mirasole. His defence was an alibi: that on the Sunday afternoon when the offence was alleged, he had in fact been at the crossroads by the Porta Ravennate, listening to two minstrels. These men, one of whom was lame, had performed from between 3 o'clock and vespers. Witnesses called for the defence and questioned on what the song was about replied variously and vaguely: 'something about Guillaume d'Orange', 'about, as it seemed to him, Guillaume d'Orange', 'about some Frenchman but he couldn't rememember what Frenchman', 'about a Frenchman or paladin'.[6] From these answers one has the impression of men and women strolling up to listen to part of the story, talking to their friends, and then going off on other Sunday-afternoon calls.

Yet the pleasures of the poor existed side by side with great sufferings. Very large numbers were destitute or became destitute from time to time. In September 1330 a citizen of Florence left all his goods to the poor. Among other legacies he asked that 6d. be given to all the indigent in the city. In a population of perhaps 90,000 people, 17,000 men, women, and children went to the churches – where they were kept during the morning to prevent double payments – to receive this gift. Their numbers, Giovanni Villani explains, did not include those, more than 4,000 of them, who were being tended in hospitals, nor religious mendicants, nor the *poveri vergognosi*, those ashamed to beg.

These are remarkable figures, the more remarkable in that they are drawn from before the great depression of the 1340s. At the bottom of society were huge numbers of the indigent: as well as professional beggars, the sick, the old, orphans, bankrupt artisans, the unemployed, wage-earners with insufficient wages to feed their families. If in addition agricultural workers be considered, it seems probable that the majority of the population lived at subsistence level, supporting a much higher standard of life for small numbers of nobles, merchants, superior artisans, professional men, and upper ecclesiastics. That this should have been so had not, of course, escaped the attention of contemporaries. Yet, given the basic technological level, it was, and is, difficult to see how, apart from some expropriation and redistribution of ecclesiastical wealth – which if carried out would have been unlikely in fact to have benefited anyone other than the governing classes – this inequality could in any way have been abolished. In these circumstances men concentrated either, like the Spiritual Franciscans, on urging a universal poverty, or, like the other clergy, in justifying social divisions and reconciling the unfortunate masses to their lot.

Such reconciliations could be expressed in terms of some brutality. One sees an example in the *Tractato dei mesi* of the Milanese lay-brother, Bonvesin da Riva.[7] In this poem the months in succession complain of the lordship of January. June appears in breeches and shirt, sweating through the heat and tired with his work; July with his mattock in his hand, and so on, to observe that January produces nothing, merely consumes what they produce. Can he be truly noble who merely worsens the lot of the poor? January meets their complaints forthrightly. The other months are merely 'lunatic villains', for he rules by nature and by prescriptive right. It pertains to subjects to produce, to obey, and to work well. The good poor speak no ill of him since he fills the office of God eternal. Though he suffer in this life, if he be virtuous and die in patience, the poor man will go to heaven. The sufferings of the poor indeed are a lesson teaching men to preserve themselves from the sufferings of hell. There follows the moral: the story of the months teaches us how we should live and how we should realise what madness it is to think of rebellion.

Among the friars the theme of the madness of rebellion against a God-given society was allied to the contention that the search for any improvement of status was sinful. So argues the Dominican, Giordano da Rivalto:

This world is ordered in the manner of an army. Now let's look at the ranks. Here we have one who is a king, here a count, here a knight, here a judge, here a merchant, here a cleric. The whole world is ordered in the same way; and it's for this reason there are so many diversities in the world. All this is divine dispensation in order that the world may be ruled and governed, and none should move from his rank.

In an army, he continues, the general may move you at some time to another rank but you certainly may not take the initiative. At first sight it is curious to find this emphasis in a society where, at least comparatively speaking, there were such high opportunities for social mobility. Yet it has its own logic; if the social order has been decreed by God, social mobility can be legitimate only when it is the result of his command. Hence too, of course, a new stimulus for dislike of *gente nuova* who could be seen not only as vulgar upstarts but as sacrilegious as well.

Looking at the problems of the poor, the friars joined this theory of society to the idea of a contract between its various orders. So Fra Giordano again:

God has ordained that there should be rich and poor in order that the rich should be served by the poor and the poor sustained by the rich, and this is the common rule of all people. Why are the poor so ordered? In order that the rich may gain eternal life through them.[8]

The rich control the poor for the poor's own good. In return the poor allow the rich to gain spiritual merit by exercising the virtue of charity. In that transaction too a contract is implied; the beggar who receives alms is obliged to pray for the soul of the rich man.

The spirituals argued that since poverty was a virtuous state, the state of St. Francis and, as they claimed, Christ, it seemed appropriate that there should be a levelling down of riches to make all poor. Against them the more orthodox clergy had their reply. Poverty, as a virtue they explained, was not a material condition but an attitude of mind. What it represented was a contempt for the things of this world. Hence there was no guarantee, at all, that a universal communism of the deprived would create a Franciscan or Christ-like poverty since a rich man might well enjoy the virtue of poverty whereas a poor man who failed to accept his condition might be wholly lacking in it.

To the modern sensibility which puts its faith in the future triumphs of technology or social engineering the emphasis on acceptance of poverty must grate. For those of the thirteenth and fourteenth centuries for whom such a faith would have been dismissed as the idlest of dreams it had its own justification. It was at the same time accompanied by a wide provision for the abject. Under one aspect the Church could be thought of as a vast charitable organisation. Monasteries and priories made daily distributions of food. Devout or guilty laymen founded hospitals (there were some thirty at Florence in 1339), leper-hospitals and orphanages. Pious confraternities more and more cultivated philanthropic activities. Very many left money in their wills for the benefit of the poor. Business firms often set aside a percentage of profits in their accounts to *Messer Domeneddio* ('the Lord God') and the succour of the wretched. In the great charitable institutions – the Scuole Grandi at Venice; Or San Michele, the Misericordia, the Bigallo in Florence – distinction was made between two classes of recipient. A privileged poor, issued with a card, 'their' poor, received a high rate of charity, perhaps some 5 shillings a month, plus occasional gifts of bread or clothes. In addition the other poor might be given alms of one to four pence occasionally, or of one shilling and sixpence a week and bread in time of famine.

Charity is a major key-note of the Italian church and Italian society in this period. The refusal of St. Francis to abandon the outcast expressed the greatness of that church and society, amidst all the violence in which they were shaped, in far stronger measure than their art or literature:

While I was in sin it seemed to me too bitter to look at lepers. But the Lord himself led me among them and I showed pity to them. And when I left them that which had seemed so bitter to me was turned into happiness of body and soul.[9]

Nothing can dim the radiance of those words. At the same time it must be recognised that the charity of the age had its limitations. Those whom it identified as 'the poor' were those categories to be found in the pages of the New Testament: the infirm, widows, orphans, prisoners, and the aged. This definition influenced the pattern of alms-giving. Among the 'privileged' poor of Or San Michele, for instance, 66–87 per cent of recipients of alms were women, either old, widowed, sick, or with families to raise. Such priorities were obviously reasonable enough. Yet, it has been argued,[10] the virtually exclusive concentration upon them was harmful. For other indigents, those who could not be found in the Bible, notably day-labourers with families to feed, were recognised as poor only when famine brought them to starvation. In this way Christian concern was diverted from a major social problem.

VIII

Against such criticism, one might reply that since the problem was insoluble it was perhaps as well that it could not be wholly understood. With more justice one could note the ill-effects of ecclesiastical teaching concerning money-lending. For survival in moments of crisis the poor habitually depended upon the taking of loans at interest. In these circumstances the Church's hostility to the provision of credit by pawnbroking, a transaction uniformly stigmatised as 'usury', dealt a harsh blow to their interests. Christian condemnation did not, of course, succeed in abolishing money-lending. Huge numbers of both professional and occasional usurers flourished. In addition, rather in the spirit that they licensed prostitutes, the communes licensed certain Christians to practise the trade. Money could still be borrowed. But the Church's formal condemnation of the practice made credit much more expensive. Illegal money-lenders recompensed themselves heavily at the expense of their clients both for the social disdain their activities provoked and for the possible punishment they had to fear whether at the hands of governments or of a credit-hating God. Legal moneylenders, no less sorely afflicted in their consciences, had also to recoup the heavy fees they paid to the commune in return for toleration of their sin. As a result, in small towns the communes generally permitted licensed usurers to exact up to 30 per cent interest on loans granted under full security and up to 40 per cent against a public instrument. Unlicensed usurers took much higher rewards.

The moral dilemma remained. Ecclesiastics condemned the pawnbroker in a society where his work was one of the basic necessities of life. From the late thirteenth century, however, a partial solution was increasingly applied to at least one aspect of the problems raised by the trade. Since Jews who refused conversion were held to be already committed to damnation they could be seen as eminently suitable agents for transactions involving necessary evil. Accordingly more and more communes, particularly those with lower levels of economic development, solicited the establishment of Jewish pawn-banks in their towns. It was a development which aided the poor since it gave them the possibility of securing credit and since the *condotte* or contracts which authorised establishment of the banks stabilised interest rates at lower levels than those exacted by illegal Christian money-lenders. How far it aided the Jews is less certain.

It was an age in which the Jewish faith was the object of new official assaults. Advanced theologians, repudiating the Bernardine tolerance of the twelfth century, now taught that all Jews were to be seen as participating in the guilt of Christ's death. The Papacy, claiming them as its property, rejected the use of violence against them, but none the less, in its insatiable desire to extend the area of its visible power, acted to move them further and further to the margins of society. The Fourth Lateran Council had required, amidst other restrictions, that Jews wore a distinctive badge or clothing. From the time of Nicholas III they were compelled to attend special sermons designed to promote their conversion. Under John XXII there was an attempt to commit their Talmudic learning to the flames. Against this background the expansion of their rôle as money-lenders presented dangers to a community which already suffered under the perennial suspicion which their status as outsiders attracted. Only an upper-class minority among them acted as pawnbrokers. A few others gained a living as physicians – a profession in which men of their faith were particularly esteemed. Most were artisans or small traders, 'Jews and Jewesses who go through the town and are sellers of cloth'. Yet the stigma of usury and the word 'usurer' were to come inevitably to be attached to all Jews, and indeed Christian money-lenders were often referred to as 'Jews'.

On the one hand, then, the rôle of the Jewish money-lender might intensify hatred of his religion. On the other, it could be that as one who provided a service for the poor and money for the commune he gave his co-religionists a secure niche in Italian society, that it was he who was the saviour of his people. Both effects, in fact, are to be discerned in the Italy of the day. In the South a series of pogroms, most noticeably between 1290 and 1294, virtually destroyed the old Jewish settlements. Those at the time forcibly converted to Christianity – perhaps some 6,000 in number – were in subsequent years the particular object of investigation by the Roman inquisitors, men who, as the Bishop of Trani was to complain, 'seek rather temporal gains than a work of spiritual edification'.[11]

In the North, however, the position of the Jews in the fourteenth century was still very favourable in comparison with the rest of Europe. They enjoyed the free exercise of their religion, and could bring civil cases against Christians in courts where they took oath by Mosaic law. If they provoked popular contempt they were rarely threatened by fanaticism. In particular, with the exception of the newly-established communities at Mantua and Parma, they were spared those massacres sparked off in northern Europe at the coming of the Black Death. In the towns of northern and central Italy they evolved a distinctive Italo-Hebraic culture whose most interesting representative is Emmanuele of Rome, that witty and erotic poet in Italian and Hebrew who introduced sonnet-form into Hebrew literature.

Emmanuele's marvellous spirit of insolence and panache, reminiscent in some ways of Heine, was, however, the reflection of only an aristocratic and wealthy minority among his co-religionists. Of these most were poor and followed out the strange destiny of their religion at the edges of a society which was itself dominated by poverty. The truth was that the economic revolution, with all that it meant in the extension of human potentiality through its creation of wealth for a few, was for most men a false dawn. It was incapable of developing an agricultural technology which could feed all adequately and it was unable to generate sufficient wealth to give most men a living above the level of subsistence. What it did do was to bring into being an expansion and development of governmental machines which in many ways were to impoverish their subjects and ultimately to halt the economic growth of the societies they controlled.

NOTES

On the economy see P. J. Jones, 'La storia economica. Dalla caduta dell' Impero romano al secolo XIV' in the Einaudi *Storia d'Italia, cit.*, vol. ii (1974); the articles and bibliographies by R. S. Lopez and E. Carus Wilson in vol. ii (1952) and by R. de Roover, E. B. Fryde, and M. M. Fryde in vol. iii (1963) of *The Cambridge Economic History of Europe*; G. Luzzatto, *Storia economica di Venezia dall' XI al XVI secolo*, Venice, 1961; F. C. Lane, *Venice: A Maritime Republic*, London, 1973, chs. 6, 7, 10–12; A. Sapori, *Studi di storia economica (Secoli XIII–XIV–XV)*, 3rd edn, Florence, 1956. Sources are discussed in F. Melis, *Documenti per la storia economica dei secoli XIII–XVI*, Florence, 1972. A. Sapori, *Le marchand italien au moyen âge*, Paris, 1953, has a very full bibliography.
Population has been studied in K. Beloch, *Bevölkerungsgeschichte Italiens*, Berlin, 1939–61; E. Fiumi, *Storia economica e sociale di San Gimignano*, Florence, 1961; *idem*, 'La popolazione del territorio volterrano-sangimignanese ed il problema demografico dell' età comunale' in *Studi in onore di A. Fanfani*, i, Milan, 1962; *idem, Demografia, Movimento*

urbanistico e classi sociali in Prato, Florence, 1968; *idem*, 'Il computo della popolazione di Volterra nel medioevo secondo il "sal delle bocche" ', *ASI, 1949; idem*, 'La demografia fiorentina nelle pagine di Giovanni Villani', *ASI* 1950; D. Herlihy, *Medieval and Renaissance Pistoia*, London, 1967; *idem, Pisa in the Early Renaissance*, New Haven, 1958; A. I. Pini, *La popolazione di Imola e del suo territorio nel XIII e XIV secolo*, Bologna, 1976; S. R. Blanshei, 'Perugia, 1260–1340: Conflict and change in a medieval Italian urban society', *Transactions of the American Philosophical Society*, 1976; D. Herlihy and C. Klapisch-Zuber, *Les Toscans et leurs familles: Une étude du Catasto florentin de 1427*, Paris, 1978, ch. vi. For doubts on the degree of precision which such studies can offer, J. Larner, 'Il "fuoco" e la "Descriptio Romandiole" del Cardinale Anglico Grimoardo', *Studi Romagnoli*, 1976.

Some valuable studies on money are C. M. Cipolla, *Studi di storia della moneta I. I movimenti dei cambi in Italia del secolo XIII al XV*, Pavia, 1948; R. Lopez, 'Il ritorno all' oro nell' occidente duecentesco', *RSI*, 1953; and D. Herlihy, 'Pisan coinage and the monetary history of Tuscany, 1150–1250' in *Le zecche minori toscane fino al XIV secolo*, Pistoia, 1967. I have found particularly useful Peter Spufford and Wendy Wilkinson, *Interim Listing of the Exchange Rates of Medieval Europe*, Keele, 1977.

For **Italian royal bankers** see J. R. Strayer, 'Italian Bankers and Phillip the Fair,' *Explorations in Economic History*, 7, 1969; R. W. Kaeuper, *Bankers to the Crown: The Riccardi of Lucca and Edward I*, Princeton, 1973; *idem*, 'The Frescobaldi of Florence and the English crown', *Studies in Medieval and Renaissance History*, X, 1973; A. Sapori, *La crisi delle compagnie mercantili dei Bardi e dei Peruzzi*, Florence, 1926.

Numerous statutes of the **guilds** have been published, for example, in the *Fonti sulle corporazioni medioevali*, edited by the Deputazione di storia patria per la Toscana under the direction of N. Rodolico, and in *I capitolari delle arti veneziane*, ed. G. Monticolo, Rome, 1896–1914. For guild-structure see R. Ciasca, *L'arte dei medici e speziali nella storia e nel commercio fiorentino dal secolo XII al XV*, Florence, 1927; and A. Doren, *Entwicklung und Organisation des florentiner Zunftwesens im 13. und 14. Jahrhundert*, Leipzig, 1897.

On the **patriciate** see G. Brucker, *Florentine Politics and Society 1343–1378*, Princeton, 1962; P. J. Jones, 'Florentine families and Florentine diaries of the fourteenth century', *Papers of the British School at Rome* XXIV, 1956; M. Tangheroni, *Politica, commercio e agricoltura a Pisa nel Trecento*, Pisa, 1973; R. Lopez, 'Le marchand génois: un profil collectif', and A. E. Sayous, 'Aristocratie e noblesse à Gênes', in *Annales: E.S.C.*, 1958.

On the **subordinate** classes see G. Brucker, 'The Ciompi Revolution' and R. de Roover, 'Labour conditions in Florence *c.* 1400', both in *Florentine Studies*, ed. N. Rubinstein, London, 1968; G. Brucker, 'The Florentine Popolo Minuto and its political role, 1340–1450' in *Violence and Civil Disorder in Italian Cities 1200–1500*, ed. L. Martines, London, 1972; W. Bowsky, 'The medieval commune and internal violence: Police power and public safety in Siena, 1287–1355', *American Historical Review*, 1967; V. Dorini, *Il diritto penale e la delinquenza in Firenze nel secolo XIV*, Lucca, 1923; N. Rodolico, *Il popolo minuto*, Bologna, 1899; *idem, La democrazia fiorentina nel suo tramonto*, Bologna, 1905; R. Broglio d'Ajano, 'Lotte sociali a Perugia nel secolo XIV', *Vierteljahrschrift für Sozial- und Wirtschaftsgeschichte*, 1910; F. Carabellese, 'Le condizioni dei poveri a Firenze nel secolo XIV', *RSI*, 1895; C. M. de la Roncière, 'Pauvres et pauvreté à Florence au XIVᵉ siècle', in *Etudes sur l'histoire de la pauvreté*, ed. M. Mollat, Paris, 1974, vol. ii. V. Rutenburg, *Popolo e movimenti popolari nell' Italia dal '300 e '400*, Bologna, 1971 (a translation of the original edition, Moscow–Leningrad, 1958) offers a Marxist perspective.

On the **Jews** see C. Roth, *The History of the Jews in Italy*, Philadelphia, 1946; A. Milano, *Storia degli ebrei in Italia*, Turin, 1963; L. Poliakov, *Les banchieri juifs et le*

Saint-Siège du XIII, au XVIII, siècle, Paris, 1965. On **slaves** see I. Origo, 'The Domestic Enemy: Eastern Slaves in Tuscany in the fourteenth and fifteenth centuries', *Speculum*, 1955; and C. Verlinden, 'Le recrutement des esclaves à Venise aux XIVe et XVe siècles', *Bulletin de l'Institut Historique Belge de Rome*, 1968.

1. Kaeuper, 'The Frescobaldi', *cit.*, p. 78 (translated by G. Corti).
2. *Epistola o sia ragionamento di Messer Lapo da Castiglionchio*, ed. L. Mehus, Bolgna, 1753.
3. C. M. de la Roncière, *Un changeur florentin du Trecento: Lippo di Fede del Sega*, Paris, 1973.
4. See L. Thorndike, *Michael the Scot*, London, 1965, pp. 81–4.
5. Brucker, 'The Florentine Popolo Minuto', *cit.*, p. 158.
6. E. Levi, *I cantari leggendari antichi del popolo italiano nei secoli XIV e XV*, Supplemento 16 of the *Giornale storico di letteratura italiana*, Turin, 1914, p. 6.
7. Bonvesin da Riva, *Il tractato dei mesi*, ed. E. Lidforss, Bologna, 1872.
8. Giordano da Rivalto, *Prediche inedite*, ed. E. Narducci, Bologna, 1867, pp. 51–3.
9. *Concordantiae Verbales opusculorum S. Francisci et S. Clarae Assisiensium*, ed. I. M. Boccali, Assisi, 1976, p. 67.
10. By de la Roncière in his 'Pauvres et pauvreté', *cit.*
11. Poliakov, *cit.*, p. 35.

CHAPTER TEN

Food, war, and government

I

The rich and powerful were called '*il popolo grasso*', 'the fat people'. Reading the literature of the age it seems at times that much more than religion, love, civic patriotism, let alone poetry, art, philosophy, it was eating and drinking which evoked the most powerful emotional and verbal responses. It was fat thrushes, turtle-doves, blancmanges, tortellini filled with elder-flowers, lasagne cooked in soup and served with Parmesan and morsels of hare, washed down with the sweet *vernaccia* and *greco* or the fortified wine, *vino cotto*, which called forth the most swiftly-moving prose. In verse the charm of Folgore da San Gimignano's *Sonnets of the Months* becomes ultimately indigestible through the poet's relentless emphasis on the joys of gourmandising. For March Folgore dreams of 'a fish-pool of eels, trout, lampreys, salmon, dentix, dolphins, and sturgeon'. For July there are 'full goblets of Trebbiano, the iced Vaini-wine in the taverns, and eating in company, morning and evening, one of those enormous ice-puddings, and roast partridges, young pheasants, boiled capons, sovereign kids, and, for those who like it, veal with garlic sauce.' In November he thinks of 'pheasants, partridges, doves and myrtleberry pies, hares, roebucks, roasted and boiled – and always have your appetite ready!'

The stylised Latin of Bonvesin della Riva's praises of Milan acquires its own hypnotic rhythm as he details the fruits of his native territories: chickpeas, navy beans, lentils; plums too, white, yellow, dark, damascene; wild filiberts, cornel-berries, jujubes; winter apples, and apples, and crabapples – and so on: nothing is left out. Some sober spirits protested at the reigning obsession. 'I have never liked so-called banquets,' writes Petrarch, 'those mere feasts of gluttony, enemies of sobriety and good morals.' In their sumptuary laws goverments too sought to cut down the scale of private festivals. Yet they were the first to hold, sometimes to publicise by news-letters, these garish exercises in self-indulgence.

The most famous of the period – one which Petrarch himself attended – was the feast held at Milan in June 1368 to celebrate the marriage of Violante, daughter of Galeazzo II Visconti, to Lionel, Duke of Clarence, third son of Edward III of England. In that year, from spring onward, rain had fallen continuously in the

Lombard plain and for most subjects of the Visconti it was a time of acute shortage of food. Not so, however, for the fifty guests entertained here. The meal consisted of eighteen courses. Sixteen of the courses were double: with both meat and fish dishes. Between each course gifts were given to the six principal guests. We can draw up the menu as follows:

Course I   *Meat*   Gilded sucking pigs 'with fire in their mouths'   *Fish*   Gilded sea-snails   *Gifts*   Two greyhounds with velvet collars and silken leashes; twelve pairs of foxhounds with gilt chains, leather collars, and silken leashes.

Course II   *Meat*   Gilded hares with gilt eyes   *Fish*   Gilded pike   *Gifts* Twelve pairs of greyhounds with silken collars, gilt buckles, and six silken leashes, one for each pair; six goshawks with silk creances, and silver buttons enamelled with the arms of Galeazzo and Lionel.

Course III   *Meat*   A large gilded calf   *Fish*   A gilded trout   *Gifts*   Six mastiffs and six bloodhounds with velvet collars, buckles and rings of gilded brass, on six silken leashes.

Course IV   *Meat*   Gilded quails and partridges   *Fish*   Gilded roast trout *Gifts*   Twelve sparrow-hawks with gilded brass bells and silken creances; silver buttons, gilt-enamelled with arms of Lionel and Galeazzo; twelve pairs of setters with gilded collars, twelve chains of gilded brass and six leashes of silk.

Course V   *Meat*   Gilded ducks and herons   *Fish*   Gilded carp   *Gifts*   Six peregrine falcons having pearl-topped hoods, with silver rings and buttons, enamelled with arms, with silken creances and silver buttons.

Course VI   *Meat*   Beef and fat capons with vinegar and garlic sauce   *Fish* Sturgeon   *Gifts*   Twelve steel corslets, of which the two given to the duke had buckles and bosses of silvergilt, bearing the arms of Galeazzo and Lionel. The others were of gilded brass.

Course VII   *Meat*   Capons and meat in lemon sauce   *Fish*   Tench in lemon sauce   *Gifts*   Twelve sets of jousting armour, including saddles, lances, and helmets. Those for Lionel were silver enamelled as above. The others were decorated with gilded brass.

Course VIII   *Meat*   Beef pies with cheese   *Fish*   Pies of fat eels   *Gifts* Twelve sets of war armour, decorated as above.

Course IX   *Meat*   Meat-aspic   *Fish*   Fish-aspic   *Gifts*   Twelve pieces of gold-brocade cloth, and twelve of silk.

Course X   *Meat*   Meat-gelatine   *Fish*   Gelatine of lampreys   *Gifts*   Two flasks of gilt and enamelled silver, one filled with the best *vernaccia* wine, the other with finest malmsey; six bowls of gilt and enamelled silver, and matching goblets.

Course XI   *Meat*   Roasted kids   *Fish*   Roasted garfish   *Gifts*   Six small coursers, with gilded saddles and accoutrements; six lances, six fine shields, painted and gilded; six polished steel helmets. The two helmets for Lionel had bosses and clasps of silver and enamel; the others were of gilt brass.

Course XII   *Meat*   Hares and kid in chive sauce   *Fish*   Fish in chive sauce *Gifts*   Six large coursers, with gilded saddles and accoutrements, blazoned with the arms of Lionel and Galeazzo, the two for Lionel being of silver gilt; six lances, six shields, and six gilded steel helmets.

Course XIII   *Meat* Venison and beef in moulds   *Fish* Filleted fish
Gifts Six fine small steeds with gilded head-stalls, reins and caparisons of green velvet, with crimson silk rosettes, buttons, and tassels.

Course XIV   *Meat* Capons and fowls in red and green sauce with oranges
Fish Filleted tench   *Gifts* Six large jousting steeds with gilded headstalls, reins, and caparisons of crimson velvet, decked with gilt buttons, bosses and tassels.

Course XV   *Meat* Peacocks and cabbages, with French beans and pickled
ox-tongue   *Fish* Carp   *Gifts* A doublet and ermine-lined hood of satin, with a design in pearls of a flower on the hood, a cloak lined with ermine, and covered with pearls.

Course XVI   *Meat* Roasted rabbits, peacocks, and ducklings   *Fish* Roasted
eels   *Gifts* A large fine silver basin; an emerald, a ruby, a diamond, and a large pearl set in a ring; five fine silver-gilt and enamelled belts.

Course XVII   Junkets and cheese   *Gifts* Twelve fine oxen.

Course XVIII   Fruit with cherries   *Gifts* Two fine coursers which had belonged
to Gian Galeazzo. Seventy-six horses were then given to the barons and gentlemen among Lionel's followers.

After washing their hands the guests were served with wines and sweets, and money was distributed to the minstrels, jugglers, and acrobats who had entertained them while eating. Finally further gifts of silver belts, jousting steeds, and coursers were made to five English knights.[1]

If one dwells upon this meal in such detail it is because it might serve as a symbol of so much about the Italian governing class in the fourteenth century. Here is the rich family of comparatively low ancestry buying themselves nobler blood; the massive pouring-forth of wealth in a society where the majority of men are living at subsistence; the chivalric trappings amidst which the wealth is displayed; the spirit in which food is gilded as if to boast that ostentation were preferred to palatability; the organisational skill necessary to mount successfully the whole proceedings; and with all this the humanist and moral philosopher sitting, as Petrarch did, at the top table. Equally one could see the meal in a commercial light, as a fourteenth-century trade-fair, which is designed to publicise the local manufacturers of armour and breeders of war-horses. Yet there is something more, too, one senses. The very prominence of food makes of this state occasion a sort of secular communion feast. Gluttony as a work of art was a demonstration of the power of the governing class and a symbol too of the supreme importance of food in the thought of governments.

II

What the rich ate the poor dreamt of. In the *Decameron* (VIII, 3) two painters excite the imagination of their companion by telling him of the World of Enjoy

Yourself where the vines were tied up with sausages. where a goose could be had for a penny with a gosling thrown in, and where there was a mountain made of grated Parmesan at whose summit men passed the whole day in cooking macaroni and ravioli in chicken-broth. For most living in the peninsula the world of reality was different. For the peasantry and the urban poor there was an habitual diet of soups or porridges prepared from coarse grains; for the destitute 'the great cauldrons of vegetable water' which, we learn from the *Decameron* again (I, vi), the Franciscans distributed at the gates of their convents.

With the continual expansion of the population and the continuing growth of the towns in the thirteenth century the provision of food came to assume priority in the minds of all administrators of government. From the end of the twelfth century villages of the *contado* were now subject to the *impositio blavae*, were forced, that is, to export all corn produced, outside that necessary for their own needs, to the dominant town. From the same period the north-Italian communes initiated temporary bans upon the export of food-stuffs from their *contadi* in times of crisis. These became evermore frequent as the century progressed and in many places were soon established as a permanent feature of life. Export became dependent upon the issue of *bollette* or licences. Watch-towers were built at frontiers to prevent smuggling. In Emilia statutes forbade subjects resident in the mountains adjacent to Tuscany even to possess draught animals or mules by which corn might be carried across frontiers. To prevent profiteering, charges for milling, baking bread, and, in times of famine, corn, came to be controlled by the commune. To prevent engrossment or forestalling the statutes insisted that corn should be sold only in certain markets and at certain times when knowledge of the transaction would be public and restrictions on the amount sold to any one family might be enforced.

At the same time many communes took active measures to protect standing crops and to enlarge the area of cultivation. They widened and embanked rivers in order to prevent flooding and promoted schemes of irrigation and assarting. Again, either as a temporary recourse in time of dearth or in the larger communes as a permanent feature of their existence, they began to make elaborate agreements for the import of food from well-stocked grain areas outside their jurisdiction. By the end of the 1250s, for example, Bologna was regularly drawing corn from Romagna, Ferrara, the Marche, Spoleto, and Apulia. At Florence in the 1280s the machinery for the occasional purchase of grain hitherto in existence was replaced by the *Ufficio della Biada* (or 'della Grascia'), the committee of six officials with control over all matters concerning the provision of grain to the city. By the beginning of the fourteenth century the grain of the southern kingdoms had become a major element in the calculations of the northern communes. The Bardi, Acciaiuoli, and Peruzzi companies imported into Florence from the kingdom of Naples 398,800 hectolitres in 1309, 252,000 hl. in 1310, 739,200 hl. in 1311, 470,400 hl. in 1320, and 483,800 hl. in 1322. The needs of the north were exploited by the Angevin monarchy, which enjoyed monopolistic control over corn-export, with a singular hard-headedness. In October 1323 King Robert was ordering the port officials of Apulia to send a spy to Venice in order to discover secretly at what price grain was being sold there 'and whether by delay one could hope to sell it more dearly'.[2]

Inevitably the search for food generated war and civil conflict. It has been suggested that the extension of the *popolo* movement had as one of its principal causes the wish by those excluded from government to prevent free export of foodstuff by the *milites*. It may be, too, that faction-conflicts were exacerbated by the desire of leading families to control government and so be in a position to manipulate to their own advantage the corn-markets of their towns. Externally the demand for food everywhere brought the communes into conflict at a very primitive level of need. Examples are legion. At the beginning of the thirteenth century Novara and Vercelli were at each other's throats for control of the corn-lands of Valsesia and Valdossola, When in 1221 Ivrea united with Novara, Vercelli, which was dependent upon Ivrea for millstones, retorted by making a treaty with the lords of Montestrutto, promising them all booty gained in the war apart from captured millstones. Throughout the second half of the thirteenth century Bologna and Venice fought each other for the right to export from the rich grain-producing communes of Ferrara and the towns of Romagna. Conflict here centred upon the fort of Marcabò, which was constructed at the mouth of the Po by the Venetians in the famine year of 1258 and designed to divert all ships bound for Bologna to their own city. The very construction of new canals and irrigation works provoked conflicts and in the Po valley 'hydraulic war' was a commonplace. So in 1218 the agreement between Cremona and Reggio to build a canal which would divert traffic from the loop of the Po controlled by Mantua guaranteed fierce conflicts for the next forty years.

Not all war, obviously, was fought on the issues of provisioning. Aid given to the exiled families of one commune by another, treaty obligations in a widely extended system of alliances, also played their part. Again interminable conflicts beween neighbours, between, say, Perugia and Foligno, seem often, whatever their remote cause, to have been waged through some territorial imperative (in an age when frontiers were ill-defined or non-existent) or on behalf of some satisfaction of a sense of honour or through partisanship as a relief from boredom and solace in destitution rather than from any strictly 'rational' ends. None the less the need to acquire food loomed very large in the prominent place which war occupied in the thirteenth and fourteenth centuries.

III

Because war was becoming both more professional and more expensive, its effects upon the development of the communes were intensified. Until quite late in the thirteenth century the armies of the towns were formed from militia companies of citizen horse and foot with, only occasionally and in limited numbers, the support of mercenary troops. At the battle of Montaperti in 1260 the Florentine army consisted of 1,400 native knights, 6,000 native infantry, 8,000 infantry from rural areas (likely to be armed with little more than agricultural implements), and still only 200 mercenary horse. The horsemen whose expenses in the maintenance of arms were greater and whose part in battle was more decisive than that of the of the footmen were drawn from citizen knights who in return for their services enjoyed particular privileges within their cities. Access to this class of *milites* was normally simple and anyone rich enough to own a horse and some armour could be accepted as, if not necessarily a 'noble knight', 'a knight for the commune'. In the course of the thirteenth and fourteenth centuries, however, these militia-knights were seen to be less and less satisfactory as warriors. They were in the first place generally amateurs, drawn from their country-houses and money-changers' stalls in time of crisis and called upon to engage in an activity – charging with a lance on horseback – which demanded all the skills of a trained athlete at the peak of physical fitness. Then again political factions and the coming of the *popolo* movement made the loyalty of many among them suspect. Finally their rôle was made more difficult by the diffusion of the use of the steel cross-bow.

Introduced into Italy from the East at the end of the twelfth century, the crossbow had been initially banned by the Church, at least in wars between Christians, on the grounds of its frightfulness. By the 1280s, however, its employment was becoming increasingly common. It was less accurate than the long-bow, had a slower rate of fire (one shaft to the long-bow's six a minute), and was much more expensive. The companies of crossbowmen who hired themselves out to armies expected to be paid quite highly for their initial investment in the weapon. Yet the crossbow required much less skill than the longbow, whose efficient use demanded a very long training. Above all its bolt had a greater penetrating power than an arrow and so presented a powerful new threat to the armoured knight.

To meet this development the protective clothing of the knight had to become much heavier. Leather and chain-mail gave way to plate-armour. In its turn this brought the need for a war-horse capable of bearing a much greater weight. The Lombard destrier, specifically bred for this purpose, was henceforth sought eagerly all over Europe. In addition the knight had now, ideally, to equip himself with spare horses, both for replacements for those killed and to allow rest to beasts exhausted by the weight of armour. The proliferation of spare mounts, and the increased difficulty in donning armour, in its turn, led to the need for the knight to employ a retinue of one, two, or three attendants to serve him. So was born the *lancia* or standard cavalry unit of the later Middle Ages.

As a result the militia-knight, if he were to fight efficiently, was being called upon to meet ever-growing expense. In the thirteenth century the upkeep of a war-horse had been calculated at 40 florins a year, perhaps twice the subsistence of a human being. The maintenance – and above all the purchase – of a destrier was to cost much more. At the same time ever-growing demands were made upon the knight's skill. The wearing of heavy armour was an art in itself. Moreover, as length of service in the field extended, the calls upon the amateur's time became intolerable.

In this situation there were no purely technical reasons why the communes should not have relied principally upon unmounted militia soldiers. At the beginning of the fourteenth century the Flemings at Courtrai (1302), the Scots at

Bannockburn (1314), the Swiss at Morgarten (1315), had demonstrated the ability of a mass of infantrymen to defeat the shock-charge of heavily-armed cavalry. Indeed it had been foot soldiers, armed with shields and lances, who had secured victory for the first Lombard League at the battle of Legnano (1176). Again, the most successful of the fourteenth-century companies in Italy, the English company of Sir John Hawkwood, acted as dragoons, that is to say, dismounting in order to fight. What however prevented the native foot militia from becoming the core of the communal armies was essentially a matter of morale. The majority of the *pedites* had insufficient stake in their communes to die or to stand resolutely for them.

Given this, trained professonal mercenary soldiers came increasingly to supplement the militias. Gradually the prominence of these forces became supreme. In localised wars native forces would normally be employed in short campaigns and mercenaries would be hired only if the scope and extent of the war grew. But in large conflicts and the larger political units mercenaries came increasingly to predominate. The phenomenon appeared first in the southern kingdom, which in the thirteenth century could more easily than the northern communes direct the wealth of its subjects to the ends of government. At the battle of Benevento in 1266, one third of Manfred's cavalry was drawn from the feudal levy, two-thirds consisted of German and Italian mercenaries. His footsoldiers were almost wholly mercenaries: Pisan and Genoese crossbowmen and the Saracen archers of Lucera.

In the north the change came more slowly. Yet already in the second half of the century the communes were coming to rely more and more upon mercenaries Again, increasingly they were raised not, as in the past, by hiring individuals, but by making a contract (*condotta*) with some contractor (*condottiere*) who would engage to lead a band of, sometimes it might be, several hundred soldiers, in their aid. By the 1320s and 1330s the companies of the *condottieri*, often formed from Provençal, French, and German troops disbanded after campaigns in the peninsula, were likely to boast a strength of anything between 500 and 5,000 men. It was a system which suited the communes. It was easier to recruit one military entrepreneur than thousands of individuals, and from the military point of view it seemed sensible to employ troops who were already accustomed to fighting together.

By the 1330s the communes were already giving preference to non-Italian over Italian mercenaries and that preference was to stand for the following fifty to sixty years. Italian *condottieri* were often lords of towns of regions with surplus manpower and little economic potential, men like the Malatesti in Rimini, the Ordelaffi in Forlì, the Malaspini in the Lunigiana, and the Orsini at Rome. Their followers were often bound to them in a quasi-feudal manner, their military competence was not in doubt, and they enjoyed some prominence. But governments feared that any native to the town might be tempted to employ his troops in a coup d'état and that any non-native Italian might be working in the interests of another power. (In 1364 Pandolfo Malatesti was dismissed as Captain of War at Florence under this very suspicion.) Foreigners seemed preferable. It was one possible solution to the perennial problem of political control over the military. Comparing it with that adopted in fourteenth-century England where on two occasions a native, hereditary, but still paid, military aristocracy rose up to depose their king, it seems at first sight a reasonable conclusion. What by the 1340s made the mercenary companies dangerous was not their domination by foreigners, but rather their huge size, their cohesion, and their virtual monopoly of the trade of war.

IV

Meanwhile the new developments in the art of war played their part in bringing about a profound increase in the power of the communes. In the towns of northern and central Italy at the beginning of the thirteenth century government had been weak and decentralised, administration primitive, and taxation extremely light. The vast, new expense of war was a major element in changing this situation, in bringing tighter political control, and, above all, new powers of fiscal exploitation.

By 1300 the raising of heavy, hitherto 'extraordinary' but now institutionalised revenues had become normal. To the old imperial hearth-tax was now added the *estimo*, a property-tax. This in its turn was beginning to be superseded in importance by gabelles (taxes upon contracts, sales, import and export of goods into the towns, levies upon salt, etc.). Throughout the fourteenth century the yield of the gabelles grew consistently. At Florence, where the *estimo* was abolished in the city in 1315, the gate-taxes on oil rose 500 per cent between 1328 and 1380, on pigs 700 per cent between 1333 and 1380; on wine and eggs 500 per cent between 1320 and 1380. Yet the revenues from these sources were soon eclipsed within total budgets by the rise of voluntary and forced loans (*prestanze*).

Immense administrative sophistication was brought to the raising of revenue and long-term deficit financing. In several centres state-debts were consolidated into a form of national debt; at Venice (from 1262) and at Florence (from 1345), the debtors were rewarded with securities bearing 5 per cent interest which were negotiable in the open market. Almost everywhere the extent of indebtedness tended to rise. At Florence in 1315 it stood at 50,000 florins, in 1364 at around 1,500,000 florins, in the 1370s at almost 2,000,000 florins. Total yields grew spectacularly. At Pisa, it has been calculated the average public income in the years 1227–1232 was £P[isan] 2,400. In 1288 the yield was £P.40,000 (say 23,200 florins), in 1313 £P.717,000 (say 251,600 florins). The figures here come from a discontinuous series and may in some sense be misleading, yet they symbolise the reality of what was happening. At Florence annual yields of around 130,000 florins in the second decade of the fourteenth century rose to 292,000 florins in 1325 (though this was exceptional) to an average 300,000 florins in 1336–8 and to over 400,000 florins in the 1360s.

For the people of northern and central Italy the new fiscalism had in many ways disastrous implications. It intensified injustices between classes within the communes. It diverted productive wealth into war. It allowed war to be undertaken more readily and it allowed governments to increase the scale upon which they waged war. The irresistible cycle by which taxation allowed war and war in its turn produced more taxation is perhaps a neglected factor in considering the decline of the Italian economy during the later *Trecento*.

From the point of view of men of government, however, this period could be seen as the unfolding of a success story. The inter-related demands of food-production, war, and taxation made necessary a powerful growth in institutions and bureaucracy, and, once established, bureaucracies displayed their perennial capacity to expand their functions. Local *consuetudines* or customary laws of the towns were first gathered and systematised in written form at the end of the twelfth century. Thenceforward the councils of the communes promulgated their own decrees and evolved a body of statute-law (*ius proprium*) which in each territory took precedence over the imperial law (*ius comune* or *lex*) taught in the universities. As the years passed these statutes became fuller and more all-encompassing and the smallest aspects of government and the citizen's lives (length of hair, dress and finery permitted to each social class, funeral ceremonies, etc.) came to be regulated by their control.

In the same period, around the *podestà* and captains of the people a large number of officials developed their power: the chancellor, the *massarius* or treasurer, and the judges, each with their own staffs. By the side of general committees of guild representatives in government (*anziani* or priors) and local 'wise men' (*savii*), other administrative committees proliferated: in Florence those concerned with Grain-supply, the Mint, the Prisons, Road and Bridge Maintenance, Fire Prevention, Hire of Troops. Their regular operation was reinforced by the *ad hoc* establishment of special committees (*balíe*) to deal with particular problems. Below this level of government there sprang up a large body of minor communal employees: officers of the watch, gate-guards, agrarian police, exactors of gabelles, land-surveyors, corn-officials, officers of weights and measures, police, road-sweepers, trumpeters, bell-ringers, messengers. From this general extension of institutions of the commune the *contado* was not immune. Here captaincies and vicariates, with their own officials, were increasingly established in an attempt to impose uniform systems of administration, and the village communities acquired their own statutes.

V

This growth of communal bureaucracy was made possible and was promoted by the extension and development of that revival of Roman law which had taken place in Italy in the eleventh and twelfth centuries. It was in the thirteenth century that the procedures and systems, but much more than this, the ethos and presuppositions of written law, were, for the first time since the fall of the empire, deeply rooted within the the consciousness of Italians. What was recreated in these years was the possibility of precision, subtlety, depth of thought and language in the delineation of the social world, the possibility of constructing working rules to regulate consistently daily life.

With the *Glossa Ordinaria* of Accursius (d. *c.* 1254/63) the purely academic approach of 'the Glossators' to the study of the law – an approach designed to examine each element within the *Corpus Iuris Civilis* in terms of the whole corpus – reached its peak and could go no further. Teachers of law in the era of 'the Post-Glossators' turned to other problems. How could the statute law of the communes be reconciled with Roman Law, how justified at all in the light of the supreme legislative monopoly claimed in the *Digest* by the emperor? How could the decrees of the quaestor Tribonian in the sixth century be seen as pertinent to the problems of the modern age? Men like Bartolo da Sassoferrato (1313–1357) and Baldo Ubaldi (1327–1400) wrestled with these problems in an attempt to bring the traditions of Roman law into every aspect of social life and to inform customary and statute laws (the *iura propria*) with the principles of Roman law (*ratio iuris communis*).

Parallel developments were taking place in Canon Law, a discipline which everywhere penetrated, amalgamated with, and borrowed from Civil Law, and one which, in such areas as marriage, had profound effects upon secular life. Here too the picture is one of development in sophisticated practical terms upon the pioneering work of twelfth-century predecessors. The body of ecclesiastical legislation was enlarged and with the *Liber Septimus* or Clementine constitutions, formally promulgated by John XXII, the *Corpus Iuris Canonici* was almost completed. In his *Speculm Iudiciale* Guillaume Durand (d. 1296), a French papal administrator who passed most of his life in Italy, wrote a work on the conduct of trials, the judicial *ordo* in civil and criminal cases, and the types of act relating to each process, which was to become authoritative in both civil and canon law.

The development of Roman and Canon laws was one of the most remarkable achievements of the Middle Ages, and one whose effects extended far beyond the Italian peninsula. In Italy it provided a *raison d'être* for the new universities and gave them an international renown. The schools offered an ideal corpus of law and legal principles within which the law of the communes could operate, and served as training centres in which generations of students could assimilate habits of mind appropriate to the administrator. One would not wish to idealise law as such, for law can obviously be simply one instrument of oppression among many others. Nor could one give an unqualified approval to the manner of its study in this period, for the sixteenth century was to witness a more sophisticated historical and philological approach to the texts which was to displace the work of the post-glossators from common esteem. The mighty Bartolo of Sassoferrato of the fourteenth century was by the eighteenth to have been reduced to the absurd Dr. Bartolo of *The Marriage of Figaro*. Yet reading the university legists one is struck not merely by the force and power of their work but by its purity too, by the passion for legality which runs through it.

These were not things which contemporaries despised. In December 1396 the Florentine commune resolved that the bones of four men whom they saw as vital to the making of their civilisation should be re-buried in tombs decorated with 'magnificent sculptures' within their own cathedral, for 'although they have gone from this world, they can be thought, none the less, through the glory and fame of their quality, to live still'. Of the four three were writers: Dante, Petrarch, and (as an anti-climax) Zanobi da Strada. The fourth was the Florentine jurist, Accursius. This plan for the honouring of great citizens could not be carried through. Ravenna was no more willing to surrender the body of Dante than Bologna to give up the creator of the great *Glossa Ordinaria*. Justly so. For with both men there was already a general recognition that their personalities and work transcended the boundaries of particularist governments and embraced and formed the mind of all Italy.

At a lower intellectual, but still vital, level the work of the jurists was seconded by the growth of the notarial professon, a growth of key importance in the elaboration of government and the ordering of social life. It was a widening of the legal Renaissance in which the ancient practice of the *tabellio* or scribe was allied to the new science of law. Despite the changes wrought by the economic revolution, the means of legal control of life in the twelfth century, outside some few centres, such as Genoa, had been inadequate. The old notaries, complained Salatiele, author of a thirteenth-century formulary, 'say that the art of the notary is contained in four instruments'.[3] With the thirteenth century this changed; a new complexity and diversity enters the drawing-up of legal documents, and new formulas for giving authentic legal form to wills, codicils, and matters concerning matrimony, dowry, emancipation, division of patrimony, association in partnership, leases of mobile property, procurations. Henceforth the notary sought to enclose everything within the domain of written law and legal documents acquired everyday importance,

During the first half of the thirteenth century a score of notarial formularies came into existence. But from around 1255 the *Summa totius artis notarie* of the Bolognese Rolandino Passagieri took over and swept all rivals before it. Rolandino defined the notarial art as 'the writing down in authentic form of the lawful business of men in a finished and rational document'. His treatise on the art was like Piero de' Crescenzii's work on agriculture, one of those works which by meeting the practical needs of the age was to enjoy an immense success. It was simple, yet comprehensive, and above all in a world where life seemed to be growing more complex and perilous it offered security. 'In old days', Rolandino writes, 'text-books were written about the form and order of contracts and instruments which were appropriate to the morals and customs then obtaining. Their authors were competent, and yet perhaps through the purity of their own consciences were ignorant of the subtle tricks of people today.' Against the *subtilitates modernorum* he, by contrast, offered defences which were to make the work a classic and essential text for the following three centuries.

By the mid-thirteenth century the trade of the notary to whose protocols public faith was given was coming necessarily to be closely controlled by the commune. Notarial fees (based upon a proportion of the sums referred to in the various documents) were prescribed; provision was made for the preservation of the protocol book of dead notaries, and the education and reception of the novice into the profession were supervised. At Florence in 1334 (where the regulations were in fact rather more stringent than elsewhere) the aspirant had to pass three exams. There was a preliminary test in Latin grammar and forms of contract before a board of six notaries, and then two further public exams before the consuls of the notarial guild, which, among other matters, required knowledge of law and skill in the translation of documents into Italian. On successful completion of these tests the beginner was then apprenticed to a notary for six months before being allowed to practise the trade by himself. Normally he would be formally admitted to the profession by a Count Palatine, acting in the name of the emperor or pope. In this case his documents were considered to have universal validity. Some notaries however were created by the commune itself and in these cases their office could be exercised only within the commune.

In the large commercial centres the rôle of the notary in so far as economic life was concerned was of less importance than elsewhere. Here the private contracts of merchants were received as evidence in the law-courts and as a result the testimony of the notarial protocol was less in demand. There were, too, in all communes great differences in status between notaries. Many came from comparatively humble backgrounds, were the sons of artisans or shopkeepers: bakers, smiths, papermakers, etc., and rarely moved higher than such milieux. Particularly in the countryside these were unlikely to pursue their office as an exclusive occupation; they are frequently found doubling-up as, for example, innkeepers or pharmacists. The thirteenth-century Dominican, Fra Jacopa da Cessole, in his *Book on the Game of Chess* (in fact a discussion of ranks in society), placed the notary below the smith or the worker on the land and classed him, since he worked on parchment, with skin-dressers and wool-workers. This judgment may not have been wholly malicious. Despite the exams which the notary faced his culture seems often low. At a modest level of ambition he could rub along simply by reproducing the formulas he had learnt at the notarial school, and modern scholars have indeed occasionally expressed their doubts as to whether some notaries had a precise understanding of what they were writing.

On the other hand a minority among the notaries were the sons of important judges or doctors (one was a count from the Orsini family), and, more important, a substantial minority, whatever their social origin, were skilled in the writing of Latin, had a taste for the complexities of law, and were well-equipped to take part in the business of the commune. These latter were everywhere in demand, men like Rolandino Passagieri himself, author of the notarial textbook, whose father was an innkeeper but who was a founder-member of the Bolognese *popolo's Company of the Cross* in 1274 and in 1280 became one of the 'Lords of Government' of the commune. The rise of communal bureaucracy required, above all, the skilled practice of the notarial art, and it was natural that these two things should come into existence at the same time.

In the communes the chief notary was given the title of Chancellor and exercised a general supervision over the *Notaro dettatore* (who wrote the diplomatic letters), the notaries of the Priors, of the consuls, of the *podestà*, of the captain of the people, of the gonfaloniere of justice, and of the individual guilds. Modena employed fifty-one of them in government in 1327, Perugia 108 in 1381. These men were the civil servants of commune and *signoria* alike and without them both forms of rule would have collapsed.

Much was demanded of them. In his *De regimine civitatis*, Giovanni di Viterbo sets forth the duties of the Notary to the Podestà, an office, he says, 'great in burdens and in honours'. He remarks on the need to be able to draw up minutes of conciliar discussions, interrogations, and confessions, but sees the writing of letters as requiring the highest skill:

The greatest caution should be employed for the style should be plain and brief, not swollen and obscure. Yet it should shine in wisdom and discretion so that it may be justly praised for its benevolence, grace, and gravity. Thanks to the sweetness of letters written with skill and understanding, many wraths are quietened, many matters are disposed of, which would otherwise bring heavy burdens and great trials and expenses.

But it is not technical mastery alone that Giovanni requires; the notary in government must also be a man of the highest character:

Notaries should be faithful secretaries, diligent, incorruptible, loyal, so that advantage and honour may be drawn from the office. In that way they will be acceptable to God and deservedly commended by men.[4]

These were high demands, yet not perhaps always wholly frustrated. Throughout the violent story of governments in this period one senses in the notarial class as a whole an instinct for legality, for producing order out of chaos, a search for justice, which made it one of the leading elements in medieval Italian civilisation.

VI

In response to the needs produced both by the economic revolution and the growth of government and law in this period there came a large expansion in the provision of formal education and at the same time a new type of education. By 1250 the old ecclesiastical monopoly of education – of an education which was essentially designed to meet the needs of ecclesiastics – was broken. Towards the end of the thirteenth century schools run by lay masters became common; in the fourteenth century the secular school which had been established by the local commune became general throughout the peninsula. Side by side with the old ecclesiastical establishments there grew up state-provided grammar-schools teaching Latin (with, according to Villani, 550 pupils at Florence in 1338) and such new centres of learning as 'the schools of the abacus' (or 'business schools', of which there were six in Florence in 1338) and, from 1250, the schools of the notarial art.

At the same time higher studies became both standardised and more generally diffused. It was from the end of the twelfth and beginning of the thirteenth century that the schools of law at Bologna were first brought together in institutions which one can identify as a university. To Bologna, 'mother of the laws', were added the universities of Padua (from the 1220s) and Naples which was founded by Frederick II in 1224. In the fourteenth century numerous other foundations were attempted, several of which came quickly to grief, but Perugia (from 1308), Pavia (founded by Galeazzo Visconti in 1361), and, to a lesser extent, Siena (from 1357) managed to attract many students. Their central object of study was Law. In addition Medicine, together with what were considered its attendant disciplines of Astrology and Philosophy, came to have some importance. Theology, before the 1360s, was wholly ignored. Some Latin grammar and rhetoric were taught in the faculties of Arts and it has been suggested that this instruction played some part in the development of Humanism. In general, however, the primary interests of the universities were vocational and utilitarian.

Certainly the high culture of the age, for which the Italy of the thirteenth and fourteenth century is most remembered today, largely developed outside institutionalised centres of learning. Distinguished by the great multiplicity and variety of forms it assumed in each of the arts, the style and content of this culture derived from many sources. Chivalric lyric and courtly epic, response to the new humanisation of religious feeling, the friars' vulgarisation of scholastic learning, the Spirituals' interpretation of the inspiration of St. Francis, the everyday experience of the merchant, civic pride, the Averroists' enquiries into the natural sciences, consciousness of the Roman past, all these played some part.

Of the rich final result it is not possible here to write at length. Nor could its character be easily summarised in brief space. Bare names – in the visual arts those of Giotto, Duccio, Nicola and Giovanni Pisano, Simone Martini; in literature, Dante, Boccaccio, Petrarch – must stand as its memorial. Yet a brief comment should be made upon the social forces which underlay this flowering of the arts.

The economic revolution, of course, was an essential prerequisite. It generated literacy and everything summed up by the maxim dear to merchant moralists: 'one should never stop using the pen'. It is not by chance that paper was first manufactured in Italy in the 1270s or that eye-glasses were by 1300 being marketed in Venice. Yet it was the commune's need for rhetoric as a tool of control, which, above all, served as a midwife to the birth of Italian interest in Humanism, that is to say in the intensive study of the language, history, and philosophy of the ancient world. Communal administration required skill in expression, elegant diplomatic letters and speeches, and it was this need which first drove men to a new study of the Roman classics. Again, secular administrators discovered a new fascination with the essentially secular history and literature of Rome, while the very revival of Civil Law prompted a new admiration for things Roman. It was principally judges and notaries connected with government who composed the small groups who at the end of the thirteenth century came together in Padua, Venice, and Florence to discuss the new interests. It was, too, men trained in the law, judges, jurists, and notaries (even if, like Petrarch and Boccacio, their studies were at some point abandoned), who composed the largest class of writers in both Italian and Latin in this period. Between law and government, rhetoric and literature there were essential connections.

So too in the visual arts. The economic revolution placed huge capital surpluses in a few hands. What above all served to channel part of that wealth into painting, sculpture, and building was civic pride. As governmental powers and claims grew, passionate local loyalties came to be combined in the minds of the prosperous classes with an intense ideal of citizenship. Their city – the thought continually recurs – was 'a paradise'. So writes Bonvasin della Riva in praise of Milan: 'Who shall attentively and diligently observe all that is here, though he tour the whole world, will never find a similar paradise of delights'. So, in 1313, the statutes of Brescia decreed, 'since it is said that cities are made in similitude of Paradise', that provision should be made 'for the public good and the adornment of the city'.[5] The paradise had to be preserved, the glory and fame of its government had to be blazoned to the world.

It was in this climate of patriotism and citizenship that the communes made themselves responsible for the building, interior embellishment, and maintenance of their cathedrals (of which the most famous erected in this period are Florence, Orvieto, Arezzo, and Siena) and other major churches. So too governments now came, at first often hesitantly and reluctantly, to build their own *Palazzi Comunali* or town-halls and other communal buildings. In the twelfth century these had only rarely existed; conciliar meetings were held in churches, even the prisons were sometimes leased from private proprietors. By the 1320s however it was a commonplace that:

It is delightful to the eye, joyful to the heart, and pleasing to each human sense, and also of great honour to each commune when its rulers and officials dwell in fair and splendid residences, both for their own sake, and too, for those foreigners who for many various reasons come to visit them.[6]

For the decoration of these buildings artists were now called upon to construct a new iconography in praise of civil government. At the same time the communes took over the control of town planning and through their 'Judges of the Streets' sought to establish well-paved streets, new bridges, and sanitation. A new order and a concern for beauty took the place of what had hitherto been haphazard growth. New roads and squares were constructed, fountains erected, the building and destruction of houses henceforth were normally permitted only under licence.

The involvement of government in patronage of the arts stimulated their diffusion and in some way affected their character. Given the use of art as a weapon of government propaganda, the very number of political units within the peninsula guaranteed a large measure of support for the artist. Duccio, Giotto, and Ambrogio Lorenzetti spent most of their lives in the service of states. Again, new themes: secular allegories, pictures of identifiable places and communal worthies, made new demands upon the artist, reinforced the tendency within Gothic to move towards a greater naturalism, and stimulated interest in the art of that Rome whose heirs the communes claimed to be.

The needs of government gave a new secular tone to art and literature as they had to education. The growth of secularisation in government and society in this period is of immense significance and should not be undervalued. At the same time one must be careful not to overemphasise its extent. The largest and most important buildings of the period were still cathedrals, the overwhelming mass of its surviving art and much of its greatest literature too – the 'sacred poem' of

Dante, the moral thought of Petrarch – were religious in character. Although there was now a certain tension between the way in which ecclesiastics and laymen thought of religion, it was still religion which stood at the centre of society and which ultimately defined its morale.

NOTES

On food-policies of the communes see H. C. Peyer, *Zur Getreidepolitik Oberitalienischen Städte im 13. Jahrhundert*, Vienna, 1950; G. Yver, *Le commerce et les marchands dans l'Italie méridionale au XII et au XIV siècle*, Paris, 1903, ch. vi; J. Grundman, 'Documenti umbri sulla carestia degli anni 1328–30', *ASI*, 1970; G. Pinto, *Il Libro del Biadaiolo*, Florence, 1978; J. Glénisson, 'Une administration médiévale aux prises avec la disette', *Moyen Age*, 1951.

For **warfare** there are the introductory chapters (i and ii) to M. Mallett, *Mercenaries and their Masters*, London, 1974; C. C. Bayley, *War and Society in Renaissance Florence*, Toronto, 1961, ch, i; P. Pieri, 'L'evoluzione delle milizie comunali italiane', *RSI*, s. iv, 4, 1933 (reprinted in his *Scritti vari* Turin, n.d.); and A. I. Galletti, 'La società comunale di fronte alla guerra nelle fonti perugine del 1282', *Bollettino della Deputazione di storia patria per l'Umbria*, 1974. D. P. Waley has published three important articles on the theme: 'The army of the Florentine Republic from the Twelfth to the Fourteenth Century', in *Florentine Studies*, ed. N. Rubinstein, London, 1968; 'Condotte and Condottieri in the Thirteenth Century', *Proceedings of the British Academy*, 1975; and 'Le origini della condotta nel duecento e le compagnie di ventura', *RSI*, 1976. Still useful are G. Canestrini, 'Documenti per servire alla storia della milizia italiana dal secolo XIII al XVI', *ASI*, 1851; J. Temple-Leader, *Sir John Hawkwood*, London, 1889; E. Ricotti, *Storia delle compagnie di ventura in Italia*, 2nd edn, Turin, 1893; and K. H. Schäfer, *Deutsche Ritter und Edelknechte in Italien*, Paderborn, 1914.

There is no general work on the **administrative growth of the communes** but see M. B. Becker, *Florence in Transition*, Baltimore, 1967–8; M. Bellomo, *Società e istituzioni in Italia tra Medioevo ed età moderna*, 2nd edn, Catania, 1977, ch. i; and such particular studies as N. Rodolico and G. Marchini, *I palazzi del popolo nei comuni italiani del medio evo*, Milan, 1962; K. Shimizu, *L'amministrazione del contado pisano nel Trecento attraverso un manuale notarile*, Pisa, 1975; and I. V. Bonini, *Le Comunità di valle in epoca signorile*, Milan, 1976.

A valuable study of **public finance** in this period is provided by W. Bowsky, *The Finances of the Commune of Siena 1287–1355*, Oxford, 1970, a work which should be read in conjunction with A. K. Chiancone Isaacs, 'Fisco e politica a Siena nel Trecento', *RSI*, 1973. Among other contributions are Barbadoro, *Finanze della Repubblica fiorentina*, Florence, 1929; E. Fiumi, 'L'imposta diretta nei comuni medievali della Toscana', *Studi in onore di A. Sapori*, i, Milan, 1926; *idem*, 'Fioritura e decadenza dell' economia fiorentina', *ASI*, 1959; C. de la Roncière, 'Indirect taxes or Gabelles at Florence in the Fourteenth Century' in *Florentine Studies*, ed. Rubinstein, *cit.*; D. Herlihy, 'Direct and Indirect Taxation in Tuscan Urban Finance *c.* 1200–1400' in *Finances et Comptabilité urbaines du XIII au XVI siècle: Colloque International Blankenberge Actes*, Brussels, 1964.

For areas outside Tuscany there are H. Sieveking, *Genueser Finanzwesen mit besonderer Berucksichtigung der Casa di S. Giorgio*, Freiburg-im-Bresgau, 1898–99; G. L. Basini, 'Note sulle pubbliche finanze di Reggio Emilia nell' epoca comunale (1306–26)', *Nuova rivista storica*, 1963; and G. Luzzatto, *Il debito pubblico della republica di Venezia*, Milano, 1963. The appendix by F. C. Lane to the last work has been published in English as 'The funded debt of the Venetian Republic 1262–1482' in his *Venice and History*, Baltimore, 1966.

On law there are two very full general studies – both called *Storia del diritto italiano:* by A. Pertile (Turiṇ 1894, 2nd edn, 1966) and E. Besta (Milan, 1925–7). Two useful works on a smaller scale, with the same title, are those of G. Salvioli (Turin, 1931) and A. Solmi (Padua, 1931). See too P. S. Leicht's *Storia del diritto privato italiano*, Milan, 1960 and his *Storia del diritto italiano: Il diritto pubblico*, reprint of 3rd edn, Milan, 1972. On the *Ius proprium*, see A. Lattes, *il diritto consuetudinario delle città lombarde*, Milan 1899. Good introductions to the subject are the lectures of V. P. Mortari, *I Commentatori e la scienza giuridica medievale: Lezioni universitarie anno accademico 1964–5*, Catania, n.d. and M. Bellomo, *Società e istituzioni*, *cit*. For the statute-material see L. Fontana, *Bibliografia degli statuti dei comuni dell' Italia superiore*, Turin, 1907 and (still incomplete) *Biblioteca del Senato del Regno: Catalogo della raccolta di statuti*, Rome, 1943 ff.

Among a large monograph literature on **notaries** see F. Novati, 'Il notaio nella vita e nella letterature italiana delle origini' in his *Freschi e miniature del dugento*, Milan, 1908; G. Fasoli, 'Giuristi, giudici e notai nell ordinamento communale e nella vita cittadina' and G. Orlandelli, ' "Studio" e scuola di notariato' in *Atti del Convegno internazionale di studi accursiani*, vol. i, Milan, 1968; G. Costamagna, *Il notaio a Genova tra prestigio e potere*, Roma, 1970; *Il notariato a Perugia*, ed. R. Abbondanza, Rome, 1973; C. Pecorella, *Studi sul notariato a Piacenza nel secolo XIII*, Milan, 1968; S. Calleri, *L'arte dei giudici e notai di Firenze*, Milan, 1966; B. Z. Kedar, 'The Genoese notaries of 1382' in *The Medieval City*, ed. H. A. Miskimin, D. Herlihy, A. L. Udovitch, London, 1977. For a bibliography of early notarial formulas, see *Formularium Florentinum Artis Notarie (1220–1242)*, ed. G. Masi, Milan, 1943, pp. xli–xlvii.

On **education and communal patronage** see J. Larner, *Culture and Society in Italy 1290–1420*, London, 1971, and its bibliographies. Of particular importance here are H. Wieruszowski, 'Art and the commune in the age of Dante', *Speculum*, 1941, now reprinted with other important articles in her *Politics and Culture in Medieval Spain and Italy*, Rome, 1971; and W. Braunfels, *Mittelalterliche Stadtbaukunst in der Toskana*, Berlin, 1953. Among more recent works are J. K. Hyde, 'Commune, University and Society in Early Medieval Bologna' in *Universities in Politics*, ed. J. W. Baldwin and R. A. Goldthwaite, Baltimore, 1972; N. G. Siraisi, *Arts and Science at Padua: The 'Studium' of Padua before 1350*, Toronto, 1973; G. Pampaloni, *Firenze al tempo di Dante: Documenti sull' urbanistica fiorentina*, Rome, 1973; F. Sznura, *L'espansione urbana di Firenze nel Dugento*, Florence, 1975.

1. See *Annales Mediolanenses*, *RIS*, xvi, cols. 738–40; Giovanni de' Mussi, *Chronicon Placentinum*, *ibid*, cols. 509–11; for commentary, A. S. Cook, 'The last months of Chaucer's earliest patron', *Transactions of the Connecticut Academy of Arts and Sciences*, 1916.
2. R. Caggese, *Roberto d'Angiò e i suoi tempi*, Florence, 1921–30, i, p. 507, n. 1.
3. Salatiele, *Ars Notarie*, ed. G. Orlandelli, Milan, 1961, i, p. 3.
4. Giovanni da Viterbo, *Liber de regimine civitatum*, ed. C. Salvemini, in *Scripta anecdota glossatorum*, ed. A. Gaudenzi, Bologna, 1901, iii, p. 259.
5. *Statuti di Brescia dell'anno MCCCXIII*, *HPM*, xvi, p. 1606; Bonvesin de la Riva, *De magnalibus Mediolani*, ed. M. Corti, Milan, 1974, p. 46.
6. G. Milanesi, *Documenti per la storia dell'arte senese*, Siena, 1854, i, pp. 180–1.

CHAPTER ELEVEN

Religious life

I

At all hours of the day one heard the bells. There were the bells of the commune which would have been cast by a 'famous' bellfounder, one who had come 'like a great baron' to make a chime that resounded over thirty miles.[1] The councils met 'summoned by the voice of the herald and the sound of the bell, as the custom is'. At other times they announced the pursuit of a murderer or outlaw, the dispensation of justice, the coming of daylight and of curfew and the assembly of the night-watch. Ringing backwards, they called the militia to assemble, or warned of an outbreak of fire, that fire against which many of them bore an inscription to Saint Agatha. At evening – though it did not become a general custom until the sixteenth century – it might be that already, as at Faenza, 'in honour and praise of the blessed Virgin the *podestà* must cause the great bell to sound three times so that each person of the town of Faenza and its suburbs, when he hears the said bell, shall remember to salute the blessed Virgin three times and say the "Hail Mary" to the end of the salutation'.[2]

As the bells of the commune served religion so too did those of the Church serve the society of the world. As in all aspects of life, sacred and secular here mingled. The twenty-four-hour mechanical striking clock was invented in the 1290s and by 1400 was to be found in almost every Italian town ('marking off the hours from the hours' as a Milanese chronicler puts it, 'as is supremely necessary for all classes of men'[3]). Yet for the most part time remained liturgical. Government documents were often dated by the use of such phrases as 'on the feast of the Holy Virgin in mid-August', 'the vigil of the nativity of St John the Baptist', and so on. Men continued to measure the day by ringing of the canonical hours: matins, prime, tierce, sext, nones, vespers, compline. These were the everyday events: the triumph of the bells was on the mornings of Sundays and Great Feasts; then great waves of sound, the blending of strains from harmonious and cracked metal, spread from the cathedrals (whose right to sound first was often asserted in synodical decree) out into the countryside. There they would be taken up by the parish churches and echoed and re-echoed, stage by stage, to the clapper-bells of the beasts in the high Alpine or Apennine pastures.

The building to which the bell summoned the faithful was, it was thought, the image of 'a spiritual fabrick, which is the Collection of the Faithful. . . The material typifieth the spiritual Church'. This Church was spoken of as 'the Body of Christ', as 'a Virgin' ('as the Apostle saith: That I may present you as a chaste virgin to Christ'), as 'a Bride' ('because Christ has betrothed her to himself') and, so on, as 'Mother', 'Daughter', and 'Widow'. It united the living and the dead: the 'Church Militant, expecting still the promise of heavenly rest, and called Sion' and 'the Church Triumphant, our future home, the land of peace, called Jerusalem.'[4] So much was common ground to contemporaries. Yet increasingly, as Marsiglio of Padua was to complain in the 1320s, the word was coming, 'especially among the moderns', to be more restrictively employed to designate 'the church of the city of Rome, whose ministers and overseers are the Roman pope and the cardinals'.[5]

This Church, the church of Rome, was by the thirteenth century an international organisation, bureaucratically organised, and possessing immense wealth and power. Two centuries before, its rulers had born the title of humility: 'servant of the servants of God'; to this, by now, they had added the proud boast of being 'Vicars of Christ'. From the lecture-rooms of the canon lawyers to the hill of the Vatican, one text was incessantly repeated: 'The earth is the Lords and the fullness thereof, the earth, and all they that dwell therein'. Innocent III (d. 1216), already an absolute monarch within the clerical order, declared that he had 'plenitude of power' : that he was, that is, superior to all other human beings. ('I have set thee over the nations and the kingdoms'.) 'By reason of sin', he claimed the right to intervene in any temporal matter whatsoever and intruded or sought to intrude in the affairs of secular government all over Europe. He raised taxes from the clergy of all Europe, and, claiming to be himself above human law, promulgated legislation for the Christian Church at his whim.

The fruits of these powers assumed or claimed by the Roman church were to be revealed in the first three-quarters of the thirteenth century. In earlier chapters it has been seen how in that period a succession of popes, among them men of the highest political skills, had succeeded in crushing the empire which had threatened its independence. In the same years they were to enjoy an equal success in silencing in Italy almost all those who deviated from their own fundamental beliefs about God and the spiritual life. This, in its own way, was as remarkable an achievement.

At the beginning of the thirteenth century a large variety of beliefs existed side by side in Italy. There were, for instance, the Predestinarians (or rather four types of them) who believed that there was no existence after death; and the Circumcisers who held that the sacraments of the old law should be observed equally with the new. There were the Speronists who denied the validity of the priesthood and claimed that justification came not through works or through the sacraments but through inner purity; and the Rebapisers who believed, *inter alia*, that the faithful need fast for only one Lent during their lives upon earth. So far, we are probably dealing only with localised and eccentric groups. Two other sects, however, enjoyed much greater prominence, and attracted a much wider adherence. They were the Waldensians and the Cathars.

Among the Waldensians, followers of Peter Waldo of Lyons, two particular varieties stand out. First were the Poor Leonists who professed the priesthood of all believers and who held that none who held property could be saved. Second, and claiming more adherents in Italy, were the Poor of Lombardy who had seceded from the Leonists around 1205, and who, renouncing oath-taking and hostile to capital punishment, required from their followers a life dedicated to apostolic poverty, They asserted that infants who died without baptism, far from being condemned to eternal torments, would rejoice in the pleasures of Heaven. At the same time their rude exegesis of certain notorious New Testament texts led them to declare that neither kings nor powers or the rich would be spared to enjoy those same pleasures. Pope Sylvester, whom they supposed to have been the author of the *Donation to Constantine*, was no saint, but 'at the instigation of the devil, the first founder of the Church of Rome'. Purgatory did not exist; pilgrimages, the building of churches, prayers and masses for the dead were without spiritual efficacy.

Much more radical than the Waldensians were the Cathars, who preached varieties of Dualist or Manichean faith. Cells of their followers were prominent around Verona, Vicenza, and the Trevisan March, at Mantua, Brescia, Bergamo, Rimini, and in Florence and the Vale of Spoleto. One may distinguish here three leading schools. The Cathars of Concorezzo asserted a modified dualism. Lucifer, in rebellion from God, had created the world, and, from the time of Adam had imprisoned the God-created soul within the devil-created body. Thenceforth, bodies had been created of bodies, souls of souls. Christ had come to earth to redeem the soul from the body. The followers of the church of Desenzano (or Albanenses), by contrast, held that rival good and evil principles had existed in the universe from the beginning of time. There were two Gods, two creations, utterly opposed. Christ, according to their teachings, had manifested himself, not in the good world, heaven, nor in the evil, earth, but in the third world of hell. Between these two beliefs the church of Bagnolo sought a position of compromise. Evil had not existed from all time; but souls, created before the world, had fallen into sin. For their redemption Christ had appeared on earth only in a celestial, not in a corporeal body.

Though obviously in opposition at the level of theory, Waldensian and Cathar beliefs frequently interpenetrated and their followers are often found living and working together. Both religions drew their dynamic from the same source, namely the belief that the Roman Church as an organisation could be identified with the rich and powerful in society and was thus the enemy of the material and spiritual welfare of the poor. The call for apostolic poverty was not merely an attractive ideal in itself. It was a stick with which to cudgel both the rich in the secular world and the brothers of the rich who generally monopolised the higher offices of the Church. In these circumstances what the two sects offered was doctrinally unsophisticated but no doubt powerfully-felt protests of the uneducated or semi-educated but intelligent poor against (in the case of Waldensians) the established order of society (in the case of the Cathars) the whole material order of things. Their attractions were, no doubt, less doctrinal than based upon the moral character of those who preached the doctrines when contrasted with the worldliness of so many of the Catholic clergy. To this might be added the belief of certain laymen (and laywomen too, for these enjoyed a position within the sects higher than that granted by the Catholic Church) that they themselves, laymen though they were, possessed certain spiritual insights which they had the right and duty of expounding despite the prohibition of the Roman ecclesiastical order.

How far the continued existence of 'orthodoxy' (here employed as a shorthand for that body of religious beliefs held to be true by the popes) was menaced by 'heresy' (in this context used to denote those religious beliefs considered false by the Papacy) is not clear. The number of active 'heretics' and of those in sympathy with them is unknown. It may however be assumed that the extreme asceticism demanded by the Cathar *perfecti*, the dedication and devotion required of the Waldensian preachers, must have severely limited the numbers of those active in ministry. Among their followers the coexistence of different forms of Catharism hindered the formation of a mass Dualist church. At the same time the rudimentary character of Waldensian beliefs (perhaps better considered as sentiments rather than doctrines) meant that often their followers could only with difficulty be distinguished from pious, if virulent, anticlericals. Perhaps their movements acquired momentum through the conflict of jurisdiction between bishops and communes, or, again, through local imperial sentiment. Yet although it is known that some isolated individuals from the upper classes gave them their occasional patronage, the very character of the doctrines ensured that they would make no general appeal to those powerful in the world. More important, perhaps, the expositions of belief by the 'heretics' were wholly lacking in the intellectual sophistication of 'orthodox' formulations which had been nurtured in a long tradition of theological and philosphical speculation. For this reason the sects drew little support from those educated in the schools.

In these circumstances the decision of the Papacy to embark upon the persecution and destruction of 'heretics' by violent means, with a violence which seems wholly superfluous, calls for some comment. For it was not until then that the Roman Church became a permanent fully-developed organ for the oppression of those it deemed unorthodox. Certainly, in the minds of the persecutors was predominant the notion that the work of 'heretics' would hinder men's access to the sacraments and so lead to the eternal punishment – so much more fearful than any temporal punishments – of many who would otherwise have died as good Christians. In these circumstances persecution was a duty. Yet this is not the whole story. For it is not at all clear that society as a whole accepted that premise and rejected any possibility of intellectual pluralism. There are many instances of the communes' refusal to register the anti-heretical statutes proposed by the Papacy and of their reluctance to accept the new machinery designed to eliminate 'heresy'. There is ample evidence for a widely diffused dislike of 'the rapacious wolves' (as the Inquisitors were often stigmatised) and some examples of all too human protests against their operations. So, in Parma in 1279, the burning of a citizen's wife as a 'heretic' provoked an attack by the mob against the houses of the local friars, the killing of one among them, and their expulsion from the city. At Florence, just over a hundred years later, the attempt by officials of the

Inquisition to arrest a suspected 'heretic' could arouse the neighbourhood to drive them off with the cry of 'Stone those buggering friars and the police'[6]. To be disturbed, that is to say, that 'heretics' should henceforth be classed, in the word of the day as *cruciabiles*, 'torturable', is not to transfer, anachronistically, the liberal, Western values of the twentieth century into an alien world; it is to feel what many (not least, of course, the 'heretics') felt at the time. And the very emphasis with which the Inquisitors' manuals lay down that there could be no discussion with the 'heretic' (*Non est disputandum cum hereticis, maxime in officio inquisitoris*[7]), their emphasis, that is, upon the point that all that was at issue was subjection to superior force, suggests that the persecutors themselves may, at times, have felt some disturbance before what they were doing.

The truth is that the Roman Church had now become a state-like organisation. As with all such organisations, its principal – no doubt unconscious – law of being had become the assertion of its authority over those whom it claimed as its subjects. Moreover its structure and organisation closely paralleled in many ways that of lay society. Bishops were the brothers of *podestà*, cardinals were drawn from the ranks of the nobility. To depreciate one was to threaten the other. It was a chord struck by Frederick II when he identified Milan both as 'mother of heretics' and 'a rebel to the Empire'. Now that the Roman Church was powerful and enjoyed the support of the powerful it could move to the destruction of those who rebelled against it. Just as his brother, lord of wide acres, would suffer no questioning of his commands from wretched serfs, so now the pope need brook no longer contradiction of his beliefs from a pack of uneducated and poverty-stricken laymen.

Before 1184 'the heretic' had been faced with the occasional lynching or judicial murder. Only from that year had Pope and Emperor come together in an attempt to concert a full-scale, official, attack against dissidents. In fact the attack upon the unorthodox moved forward sluggishly until the beginning of the new century. Then all changed. In 1209 Innocent III launched his crusade against the Albigenses of southern France ('the miseries of war will lead them to the truth'). In 1220 the Papacy decreed the first sentence of death against those who contradicted its doctrines; in 1233 Gregory IX established the full machinery of the papal inquisition. With Innocent IV the use of torture in cases of 'heresy' was sanctioned, and all legal safeguards to protect the accused were set aside.

The sequel to these policies was painful. The inevitable occasional incidents in which pathological sadists rose from among the ranks of the inquisitors are perhaps less chilling that the bureaucratic formulas of their account-book entries ('for expenses occurred in burning Patarines') or the means employed to encourage delation. (The property of those denounced passed to the delators; children who accused their parents were the recipients of particularly high rewards.) One senses, again, a certain embarrassment at times in the persecutors' decrees as, for instance, when in 1236, Gregory IX was compelled to forbid discussion of the faith 'in public or private', or again, in the assertion that possession of the gospels in translation was to be seen as offering a *prima facie* suspicion of 'heresy'. Yet from the papal point of view the results were remarkably successful, and everywhere in Italy acknowledgment of Roman authority in doctrine was ensured.

There were occasional burnings: at Milan, 1231–2; at Verona in 1233, at Pisa and Milan again in 1240. But probably little force needed to be used; the threat was sufficient. By 1250 the 'ex-heretic', Rainerio Sacconi, who believed that there were little over 2,300 Cathars still surviving in Italy, could remark that 'although at one time sects of heretics were numerous, by the grace of Jesus Christ they have been almost wholly destroyed'.[8] After the Guelf triumph in the 1260s, communes became more willing to admit the inquisitors, who rapidly eliminated most surviving cells (burnings at Orvieto, 1268–9; Sirmione, 1278; Florence, 1282). The last great persecution of the Cathars, at Bologna in 1299, revealed, out of a city of perhaps some 40,000 people, only 103 males and thirty seven females of the sect. They were mainly old or middle-aged, largely isolated, without a church, and with no capacity to expand their numbers.[9] From the 1280s 'heresy' was clandestine, eccentric, and of little importance. One thinks of the sect condemned by Boniface VIII for preaching the necessity of praying in the nude, or again, of the Guglielmiti. The Guglielmiti held that the woman Guglielma Bona, who had died at Milan in 1282, had been the incarnation of the Holy Spirit and was shortly to rise from the dead. At that point her companion, Manfreda (who was, perhaps, a cousin of Matteo Visconti), would become pope in a church whose cardinals would all be women. The sect has a particular interest in revealing the close connection between social disadvantage and the forms taken by 'heretical' belief, but the very character of the society in which it led its brief life forbade its wide diffusion. Only the disturbing but submerged current of Joachite and 'Spiritual' teachings within the Franciscan order, which must be considered shortly, disturbed the even waters of orthodoxy. In general it was true, as Fra Giordano da Pisa, preaching in Florence in 1304 asserted, that the opponents of orthodoxy 'did not dare to show their faces in public' and that 'through God's grace all heresy has ended'. The 'conquistores', as many documents call the inquisitors, had indeed conquered.

The victory of the Papacy, however, led neither to the dismantlement of the instruments of repression nor to the cessation of persecution. In a curious manner persecution not only suppressed but created 'heresy'. If no 'heretics' were to be found the new bureaucracy of the inquisition had to create 'heretics' in order to justify its own survival. Perhaps, too, to preserve the discipline of the faithful it was deemed necessary, from time to time, that they should witness a thought-provoking execution. Characteristic victim of this policy was 'the order of the Apostles', founded by Gerardo Segarelli. Segarelli, having given all his goods to the poor, had begun his mission in Emilia in 1260. Reputed to possess miraculous powers, patronised for some time by the bishop of Parma, he preached repentance and the pursuit of 'an apostolic life' of complete poverty. But this creed attracted the hatred of two enemies. First were the Franciscans, whose own assumption of poverty was by now less than absolute and whose claims to be of the poor were consequently undercut by Segarelli's followers. Second were the secular clergy, indignant that a lay 'illiterate' (i.e. without Latin) should compete with them – and, it is clear, often with great success – in offering spiritual ministration. For these reasons, rather than for any doctrinal eccentricity, Segarelli was burnt alive in July 1300. Such persecution, however, inevitably drove the Apostles into genuine 'heresy'. Their new leader, Dolcino da Novara, preached thenceforth the future destruction of the Roman Church and its higher clergy. Fleeing to Piedmont and the protection of the counts of Biandrate, he and his followers held out in the practice of their beliefs until destroyed by a local 'crusade' in 1306–7.

'Heresy' was now nakedly equated with 'insubordination'. In the main, it had never been thought of as anything else. It is noticeable how from the earliest days of the Inquisition, its officers had pursued and punished those who, some twenty years before, as children, 'not knowing what they were doing', had fallen into 'heresy' and those who 'with their lips and not their heart' had given a purely formal assent to it. What was at issue was not doctrine or inner adherence to doctrine, but formal obedience to formal authority. It was logical, then, that the popes should, in the fourteenth century, condemn their political enemies as 'heretics'. Boniface VIII levelled the accusation against the Colonna; and John XXII (who taught what, if preached by anyone else, would have been condemned as an 'heretical' doctrine on salvation) urged his inquisitors to condemn the orthodoxy of his Ghibelline enemies in Lombardy. At this level, however, the power of the Roman *curia* faltered and declined. For the accusation of heresy was essentially a means by which the rich and powerful imposed their view of life upon the poor and impotent. Employed against the powerful themselves, it was everywhere acknowledged at once to be a mistaken and meaningless device.

II

The triumph of the Roman Church over its doctrinal opponents in Italy was not owed simply to violence. Violence, indeed, had not been a necessary part of its victory, it had been merely a demonstration of one aspect of its triumphal power. In much larger measure its authority survived external competition through its capacity to incorporate within its existing structure new movements which were potentially hostile to it. One example of this is afforded by the Umiliati, groups of townsmen, living together in religious communities, though still married and seeking normal employment in society. Despite their condemnation in 1184 (on the grounds that in preaching they usurped the office of the priest), Innocent III had been able to reconcile the movement to the Papacy and to ensure its survival as an 'order'. So too, now, not without heartsearching, nor without a radical boldness, the Church was able to bring to itself, organise, and dominate the new movements of friars: the Dominicans, Franciscans, the Augustinians (found in a united order *c*. 1265), the Carmelites (approved 1226), and the Servites (end of thirteenth century).

Among these the Dominicans presented fewest problems. St. Dominic of Osuna (d. 1221), from the minor landowning nobility of Old Castille, had founded his order specifically as a buttress to the *status quo*. In adopting a life of apostolic poverty, his followers offered no challenge to the Papacy, but sought rather to validate its claims by taking over for it the widely-admired abnegation of the 'heretics'. As one who stressed the need for obedience, Dominic proved a welcome ally to Innocent III who had the vision to see what could be made of him. In particular the Dominicans were to excel in the fields of learning and they enjoyed their greatest popularity in university towns. That learning they employed notably in preaching, in the confessional, and in theological study.

The inheritance of St. Francis of Assisi (d. 1226) was rather more difficult to deal with. Francis had adopted poverty, not like Dominic as a means but as a supreme good, and he had no interest in organisation. His extraordinary character, combined with his attempt to live according to the literal words of Christ, had won him an immense following. For the Papacy these things were dangerous in combination. If Francis, the merchant's son, identified wealth as the source of all evil, how could that insight be received by a Church which seemed to be inordinately rich? If Francis asserted the possibility of living according to the gospel in post-apostolic times, what did that imply for all those who doubted whether such a programme was, in their own day, feasible?

It was that man of remarkable talents, Ugolino Conti, later Pope Gregory IX, who neutralised the danger presented by Franciscanism to the Papacy. Inevitably, he did so by blurring and denying much of Francis's original vision, by assimilating Franciscanism in some way to both monasticism and the Dominican order. He found, for this task, many allies in the order itself. Its organisation-men wanted a constitution, government, and privileges. To attract and hold large congregations they wanted large churches and the building of convents within the main centres of population. To preach they required learning, access to books and to the universities. All this was inimical to the original Franciscan ideal; yet all this came about. A year's novitiate was established for entry to the order; an administrative structure, ruled over by provincial ministers, was established; 'friends' were allowed to hold money for the friars; and they were permitted the 'use' of property, which, by a legal technicality, was supposed to be the property of the Papacy. As a result the order itself split. The majority of its members, the 'Conventuals', accepted the new dispensation, drifted further from their roots. The 'Spirituals', by contrast, seeking to hold to their first inspiration, resisted change by appealing to the original message of their founder.

In addition the dissidents sought inspiration in the writings of the Calabrian monk, mystic, and biblical scholar, Joachim da Fiore (d. 1202). The influence of this man's teachings is to be found in many fields of religion in our period, among heretic and orthodox alike. They took firmest root among the Spirituals. Joachim had envisaged history as the unfolding of three successive 'states': that of the Father (the era of the Old Testament); that of the Son (from the events of the New Testament); and (after the tribulations of Antichrist who was to manifest himself in the near future) that of the Holy Ghost. With the coming of the third age, amidst other signs and wonders, two new orders, he taught, would appear and give to the Church a higher quality of spiritual life. By the 1240s the Spirituals were coming to apply this prophecy to the Franciscan and Dominican friars and in the next decade Fra Gerardo da Borgo San Donnino, in his *Eternal Gospel*, expanded and developed Joachite teachings on that premise. St. Francis was the Angel of the Sixth Seal, heralding the movement from the second to the third age; the turbulence of Antichrist would break forth in the year 1260. Such views were condemned as heretical; 1260 came and went without apparent changes in the world or the Church; none the less faiths in the imminence of a third age persisted. At Santa Croce in Florence, the learned Pietro di Giovanni Olvi (d. 1298, preached at one and the same time the infallibility of the popes, the coming appearance of a false pope as Antichrist, the character of the Rule of St. Francis as 'one and the same with the gospel of Christ', and the rejection of 'the carnal church' as prelude to a world renewed. His disciple, Ubertino da Casale, echoed similar beliefs in his *Arbor Vitae Crucifixae* (1305), though here were incorporated more aggressive polemics against both the papal court (identified with the Harlot of Babylon) and the Conventual Franciscans (whose imposing new convents were castigated as a robbery of the poor). Many of the beliefs of these two men, in particular their attack upon 'the carnal church', were to gain new resonance in the *Divine Comedy*.

Their leading follower, Angelo Chiareno (d. 1337), still professed obedience to Rome. But it became impossible for his disciples to do so. In the years 1322–3, John XXII formally condemned belief in the absolute poverty of Christ and of his apostles as heretical. The Spirituals who resisted the papal sentence – the Fraticelli, as they were now called – thenceforward seized upon that pope himself as their favoured candidate for the rôle of the mysterious Antichrist. Meanwhile Joachite mysticism, linked to the expectation of a 'last Emperor' and an 'angelic pope', remained a powerful influence. Followers of Chiareno were received at the courts of both Robert the Wise and his enemy, Frederick III of Sicily. Some forty years later, Cola di Rienzo was to think of Clement VI as 'the angelic pope', and when that dream failed, was, no less improbably, to hail Charles IV as the mystic emperor who would restore the Age of the Spirit. Other millenarian hopes focused on the return of the Avignon Papacy to Rome. Again, in Florence the propaganda of the Fraticelli seems to have enjoyed some official patronage during 'the War of the Eight Saints', and to have had some influence too in the revolt of the Ciompi.

In their pursuit of an esoteric, albeit mystical, learning, as in their final repudiation of obedience to the Roman Church, the Spirituals had, every whit as much as the Observants, though in different ways, wandered far from the original vision of St. Francis. The passionate unworldliness of their lives, had, it must be granted, its own beauty, a beauty best discovered in the poetry of Jacopone da Todi :

> Senno me pare e cortesia
> empazzir per lo bel Messia
>
> Elio me sa sì gran sapere
> a cchi per Deo vòle empazzire
>
> 'Courtesy, it seems, good sense's fire,
> To go stark mad for the fair Messiah.
> Great wisdom does it seem he's had
> Who seeks for God to go stark mad.'

The criticism that they had wandered too far from the claims of reason and everyday life would have been one that they themselves would have welcomed. The Conventuals, by contrast, had accepted and accommodated to the necessities of the world. Their finest spokesman was St. Bonaventura (d. 1274). Just as, he argued, Christ was no longer in the world and so, necessarily, the Church had been forced to change its course in changed circumstances, so St. Francis was no longer living and his order could no longer survive in its original form. That order, though unable to preserve the totality of his ideal, could yet hold to something of his inheritance which in itself was of infinite value. And so, if its members were to preach 'and not just preach chit-chat', they needed learning and hence books. They needed the great church of Assisi to proclaim the greatness of their saint. They needed to become an establishment, if they were not to fall into the errors of the Spirituals.

The majority of Franciscans attended to his words of, if not holy rapture, at least good sense, with enthusiasm. The characteristic Franciscan of the new age was to be Salimbene de Adam rather than Jacopone da Todi. It is something which has often been held out as a reproach to the order, though, in so far as the absolute triumph of the true Franciscan ideal would have led to the breakdown of society into bands of holy vagrants, it is difficult to see why. Reading Salimbene's chronicle it is possible, certainly, to see the wordly satisfactions open to the friar, the freedom of a formal but not over-burdensome or dangerous poverty, the licensed wandering which gratified an adventurous desire to see the world, the meeting with life at all extremes, and the adherence to a much more classless and democratically constituted society than was to be found within the monasteries, the secular hierarchy, or the lay world. At the same time one can appreciate the real service offered by such a life: its search for poetry and joy and *cortesia*, and its constant call for action in favour of justice and the good amidst a world desperate for both.[10] The conventional criticism of the Conventuals and of the other orders of friars is certainly true. As their numbers grew the quality of their membership declined. Their privileges led them into sharp conflict with the secular clergy whose monopoly of preaching and confession within their own parish they broke. Their loyalties to their own organisations led to bizarre rivalry between the different orders. Since their 'second orders' were from the beginning designed as enclosed convents along the lines of Benedictine nunneries they did nothing to improve the status of women within religious life. Yet this all said it can hardly be doubted that the orders of friars proved through the thirteenth and fourteenth centuries a most powerful force in the satisfaction of Italian popular religious needs.

At the same time, and in part for this very reason, they played a predominant part in the preservation of the authority of the Roman Church. They assumed an advisory rôle in the penitential and flagellant orders of laymen, which might always have proved centres for the diffusion of heresy and they served as inquisitors in the inquisitorial offices now permanently established in the major communes. Their devotion to the Papacy made them ideal bishops in towns where the office had been the spoil of faction, and before 1261, certainly nineteen, perhaps twenty-six, Franciscans held this post. Further afield, as papal emissaries or missionaries, they traversed epic distances in their struggle to bring their faith to the pagan world. The Franciscan Giovanni di Piano Carpini (1246) and Bartolomeo of Cremona (1253) are found as ambassadors to the Mongol Khans at Karakorum. Italian Dominican or Franciscan missionaries were established at Tiflis in Georgia, at Sarai, capital of the Mongol Golden Horde in southern Russia, in Mesopotamia, Armenia, Persia, and India. It was mainly Italian friars too, who from 1291, under the leadership of Giovanni da Montecorvino, settled at Peking in an attempt to convert the Chinese court. These courageous men had great, albeit illusory, hopes for the future of missionary Christianity. So, Friar Odorico of Pordenone, writing in 1330 in his native Udine told of the spread of the faith which he himself had witnessed at Canton and Hangchow and looked forward with confidence to the age in which the prophecy of the Psalms should be fulfilled: 'And all the kings of the earth shall adore Him'.[11]

Nearer home the friars also pursued their mission. Their skilful preaching which, following the example of St. Francis, avoided the rhetoric of the schools and concentrated not on dogma but on penitence, filled the gap, often left by the educational inadequacies of parish priests. At the same time they catered for the needs of a literate laity by the production in the fourteenth century of a large and brilliant literature of spirituality in the vernacular tongue. Under their supervision, large parts of the vernacular Bible, originally translated into Italian by the Waldensians, were reissued in revised versions and seem to have played some part, particularly in Tuscany, in the formation of lay piety.[12] As the years passed the humanisation of religion implicit in the thought of St. Francis, with its emphasis upon the incidents of the human life of Christ upon earth, was to prove a dominant influence in the evolution of popular spirituality.

Above all – though this is not at all a priority that they would have recognised – they ministered to the poor. It has been claimed that their efforts here were marked by a deep interior incoherence, an incoherence springing from the ultimately bogus character of their claim to be *pauperes Christi*.[13] The enthusiasm of the rich for the Franciscan order, the hunger of the merchant bankers of Florence to be buried in its churches, certainly give pause. The magnificent convent of S. Chiara in Naples, where King Robert was buried, to where Queen Sancia retired at the end of her life, where were established 100 nuns from among the greatest families of the Regno, can without difficulty suggest a mission primarily directed to the higher ranks of society, a band of well-fed, well-liked scapegoats taking on the sins of aristocrats and businessmen. To make too much of this is misleading. In freeing the Papacy from the threat posed by demands for a return to the apostolic age the friars had gained a new insight into those whose condition had produced those demands. Hence the alms-giving, the hospices and hospitals, the continued emphasis on the need for charity, which did something both to alleviate the condition of the poor and touch the consciences of the rich.

III

The structure of the Church had probably been little menaced by popular heresy. It was, however, threatened at a more sophisticated level by those translations from Arabic and Greek which between the mid-twelfth and mid-thirteenth centuries introduced the philosophic writings of the pagan Aristotle, the neo-Platonic Plotinus and Proclus, the Hebrew Maimonides, and the infidel Alkindi, Avicenna, and Averroës to the schools of Europe. These works brought a new era of confusion, ultimately of philosophic revolution, into the European intellectual world. Would this revolution serve too to undermine the intellectual foundations of Christianity? Could the wholly secular tone of Aristotle's *Ethics* exist side by side with the morality of the monastic life? Would Maimonides' denial of personal immortality, his doubts upon whether the concept of an essential unity in God allowed man even to predicate His existence, triumph over more orthodox beliefs? If Averroës taught the existence of the eternity of matter, did not this doctrine reflect upon the Christian story of creation? If he argued for the existence of 'the world soul', did not such a belief strike immediately at the Christian doctrines of the individuality of each created soul and so of free will?

The first instinct of the Papacy was simply to forbid that these writings be read, or to urge, as did Gregory IX in 1231, that they only be studied in expurgated texts. It soon became very clear, however, that it was impossible to forbid those who taught in universities the reading of what was the most stimulating material in existence which bore upon the subjects they professed. The Church was saved from this dilemma by a rather long-term version of Gregory IX's, at first sight somewhat unsophisticated, solution. Aristotle was made the object of a forcible conversion.

Though theology flourished in the schools of the friars, it was not taught in the Italian universities. Moreover the study of philosophy itself was largely confined to the faculties of Arts and Medicine (here, normally combined into one faculty). Aristotelianism, scholastic method, the procedure of the *quaestio*, came to the north-Italian universities only in the last years of the thirteenth century. Hence the 'christianisation' of Aristotle took place primarily in the *studia* of northern Europe. None the less 'the scholastics', the men – mainly friars – who brought it about, who sought to use human reason as an aid towards the understanding of the divine, were, very often, Italians. Among the Franciscans stand out St. Bonaventura (d. 1274) and Matteo da Aquasparta (d. 1302). Their interest was perhaps half-hearted; they adopted the trappings of scholasticism, but still sought faith through Augustinian illumination. The Dominicans, however, embraced much more enthusiastically the problems posed by the new philosophies. Pre-eminent here was the pupil of Albertus Magnus, St. Thomas Aquinas (d. 1274).

He was a second son of a nobleman of Roccasecca, from a minor branch of the counts of Acerra. At the age of five his father had offered him as an oblate to the monastery of Montecassino. For this rejection by his family Thomas was, later, to seek revenge. At puberty he attended the schools at Naples, and then, aged nineteen or twenty, against the violent objections of his family, joined the (by comparison with the Benedictines of Cassino) 'lower-class' Dominican order. For this act of defiance, he was, it could be, to spend his whole life in atonement. Having on this one occasion asserted himself against authority, he was, thenceforth, to seek always to persuade authority never again to send him away, to put all his capacity for unending work, his extraordinary memory, and his immense intelligence at the service of authority. Through the long years of study and teaching (1252–9, 1268–72, in Paris; 1259–68, 1272–4, in Italy) that remained his stubborn purpose. It would not be true to say that he had rejected an unprejudiced *a posteriori* search for the understanding of the truth; more correctly it could be said that the possibility of any other truth than that dictated by his spiritual superiors had never occurred to him. His was the position made clear in his well-known and curiously moving eucharistic hymn :

> Visus, gustus, tactus, in te fallitur
> Sed solus auditus tute creditur
> Credo quidquid dixit Dei Filius
> Nihil veritatis verbo verius. . .
>
> Plagas sicut Thomas non intueor
> Meum tamen Deum te confiteor
> Fac me tibi semper magis credere
> In te spem habere, te diligere.

(In the translation of Gerard Manley Hopkins:

> 'Seeing, touching, tasting are in thee deceived;
> How says trusty hearing? that shall be believed;
> What God's son has told me, take for truth I do;
> Truth himself speaks truly or there's nothing true.
>
> I am not like Thomas, wound I cannot see,
> But can plainly call thee Lord and God as he,
> This faith each day deeper be my holding of,
> Daily make me harder hope and dearer love'.)

Many, very many, have written of the greatness of his achievement. It would be impossible for anyone unmoved by philosophic speculation or unversed in the arcana of theological learning to assess what element of confessional sentiment might enter in such praise or to contest his right to be included in the ranks of the most eminent Italians of all time. Only those who hold to the doctrines he expounded can tell us whether the Thomist rejection of St. Bernard's voluntarist conception of faith, whether all those elaborate attempts to define the Trinity and explain Transubstantiation, are capable of reinforcing belief. If a Gentile, faced with Thomas's proofs for the existence of God, feels a sudden and wholly novel scepticism before what he had never previously doubted, that in itself is, perhaps, a part of religious feeling. Thomas was following the route sign-posted by Abelard. In doing so he became one of Europe's great system-builders. His work, too, has been interpreted as a 'humanising' influence. He accepted that the pagan thinkers might have useful knowledge in the natural order to bestow upon

Christians, and in using Aristotelian philosophic principles to buttress Christian beliefs, he gave a much wider sanction than ever before to men and their concerns.

Yet this very concern for men, this encapsulation of the divine in terms of human reason, makes him, at times, very much the spokesman of his own age and class. It is, after all, only in those terms that his views on women will not seem preposterous or his teaching on the necessity of persecuting 'heretics' criminal. Only in those terms can one understand his rejection of St.Bernard's denial of Jewish guilt in Christ's death, his claim that all Jews were stained with hereditary responsibility for the crucifixion, and his assertion that 'the Jews have sinned as the crucifiers both of Christ the man and, too, Christ the God'. Again, vowed formally to poverty though dining as an honoured guest at the table of princes, he had, when condemning 'usury', no occasion at all to wonder how a famished peasant was to feed his family without taking a loan, or the lightest concept that his very condemnation would raise the interest on that loan.

God himself, in Aquinas's *Summa Theologica*, appears as an all-powerful emperor of the time, one who wages vendetta against offending man, who has constituted, indeed, a virtue of 'vindictive justice', and who calls upon his subjects to rejoice with him over the sufferings in Hell of those who have gone against his commands. But it is above all in his political thought that Thomas reveals himself as a noble of the *Mezzogiorno*. One thinks of his definition of 'the just war', a definition aptly summarised by Erasmus as 'any war declared in any way against anybody by any prince' (and dismissed with the curt: 'Why should I be more impressed by the arguments of Thomas than the teachings of Christ?'). In his thoughts on civil government he condemns tyranny (he remarks that the tyrant prohibits *convivia*, i.e. *corti*), but conceives of tyranny as less terrible than the rule of the many, which, he remarks (and with much justice), generally ends in tyranny. The remedy against the tyrant, however, is not revolt, but fervent and continued prayer to almighty God.

For a moment he seems to bow to the experience of his own day in northern Italy:

From experience it may be seen that one city which is administered by rulers who are appointed annually may achieve more than some king who holds three or four cities and that small services exacted by kings weigh more heavily than great burdens when imposed by the community of the citizens.[14]

But this insight is swiftly abandoned. Aristotle's own preference for a polity is set aside in favour of that absolute monarchy upon earth, as it might be, of Charles of Anjou in Naples, which is supposed to mirror the perfection of God's absolute government of the universe.

The underlying social assumptions of Aquinas's thought appear most starkly when he writes of merchants. Obviously he follows Aristotle (and his sympathy with Aristotle over the centuries no doubt springs from a subconscious perception that they both come from a threatened class) in rejecting 'usury', by which he means 'any lending of money at interest'. The nobility of the southern kingdom, unlike those of the north, gained nothing from money-lending and had much to fear from it. More remarkable is his whole attack upon trade. A community, he argues, may live either by agriculture or by trade. Obviously the first alternative is preferable. Does not self-sufficiency lie close to perfection? For if import be prevented by war, the citizen will starve. Merchant-towns, again, require a 'continual social intercourse with foreigners'. Nothing, as Aristotle points out, is more likely to corrupt civic morale and disturb *civilis conversatio*, for in this case one is continually meeting people of other laws and customs. More than this, merchants are unpleasant people: cupidity burns in their hearts; all their zeal is given to gain; they turn everything to venality and all good faith vanishes in their presence. Beyond this (and moving to views which could only be held by a southern Italian wholly ignorant of the world of the northern communes), their trade is the enemy of military efficiency. Merchants seek the shade, rejoice in pleasure, grow soft in soul and weak in body. Yet, at the same time, the very society they create breeds war. More people come to the city, hence there is more possibility of conflict. It is not desirable to exclude merchants totally from cities, since the regrettable truth is that not all places give sufficient abundance for life simply from their fields. None the less, such people should be employed only 'in moderation'.

The needs of war, however, are seen as paramount. The ideal state is a province rather than a city because it has greater strength in war. It should have a temperate climate in that this is best suited to war, 'which' (a characteristic statement) 'assures the security of human society'. It should be encompassed by pleasant surroundings, but not to such an extent that the will may be softened and warlike ardour diminished. That the *De regimine principum*, which contains all this curious matter, should have been solemnly dispatched as a handbook for a real ruler in the real world (the king of Cyprus) may strike the modern reader as strange; and only slightly less strange perhaps is the thought of Fra Antonio, chaplain to King Robert of Naples, illuminating and binding the work for his master. When, at the beginning of the fourteenth century, Tolomeo of Lucca took up and completed the work, he did so, not without some bizarre clash of views, in an anti-monarchical and pro-republican form. What the citizens of the northern towns, for whose benefit the treatise was then translated into Italian, made of the final version, it is not easy to imagine.

The age when Aquinas was to be the dominant influence in Catholic theology, however, was still far away. Ironically enough his works were condemned at Paris in 1277 as 'heretical', and in the northern schools of the fourteenth century many of the scholastics moved to scepticism before the claims of reason in the exposition of faith. Yet in Italy both Thomism and Aristotelianism – notably through the influence of the Dominican order – were from early on to exercise a powerful influence. Within the peninsula an Italian philosopher and (from 1323) saint was perhaps naturally preferred to such feared and subtle *Britannici* as Scotus and Ockham. Certainly for many Thomas's *Summa Theologica* provided a system, complete within itself, unifying philosophy and theology, and providing a method or dialectic capable of encompassing the whole of intellectual life.

IV

The repression of 'heresy', the alliance with the new orders of friars, the 'baptism' of Aristotle, the continual exaltation of its power by the canon lawyers, all represented great triumphs for the Roman Church. Again, although its struggle with the empire may have in some measure tarnished its spiritual credibility, the outcome of that struggle had been successful. Ecclesiastical censures, interdict, and excommunication, though losing force, were still feared. Yet from the last quarter of the thirteenth century one senses a deep decline in the enthusiasm with which the Papacy was regarded. In the political world it failed to reverse the verdict of the Sicilian Vespers, underwent the humiliation of Anagni, retreated in some ignominy to Avignon. For Italian intellectuals who identified the Papacy very closely with Rome and who hated France and the Angevin royal house, 'the Babylonian Captivity' represented a profound humiliation for Italy itself. Commenting on that passage in *Inferno* xix (90–117) in which Dante identifies certain popes of his day as the great Whore committing fornication with the Kings, Benvenuto da Imola notes — quite gratuitously — that in his own day Petrarch has identified 'the great Babylon' with Avignon, and continues:

Avignon is indeed the mother of fornication and lust and drunkenness, full of abomination and of all filthiness, and seated upon the rushing waters of the Rhône, the Durance, and the Sorgue. And her prelates are indeed like the Scarlet Woman, clothed in purple and gold and silver and precious stones, and drunken with the blood of the Martyrs and of Christ.[15]

Yet such patriotic or xenophobic utterances were accompanied, too, by profound suspicion of that military activity undertaken by the popes which was designed to secure their return to Rome. Whatever it did or did not do, the Roman *curia* was the object of denunciation.

Nor did the great increase in the Roman Church's centralised authority and financial power, which is a continuing feature of its life throughout our period, seem to bring any general improvement in the lower echelons of its administrative structure. The reforming decrees of the Fourth Lateran Council, promulgated by Innocent III in 1215, were apparently largely ignored. If, at first sight, one is tempted to dismiss the amazing portrayals of corrupt prelates, canons, and secular priests in Salimbene's chronicle, as being the product of a pen dedicated to showing, above all, the superiority of the friars, the similar condemnations found in all other sources soon persuade the reader of their essential veracity. Almost all laymen in his city, remarked the jurist, Odofredo of Bologna, complain that they are paying tithes not to the poor, but to cathedral canons 'who live like laymen, have palfreys, falcons, and bravos'. Or again, Boniface VIII in 1302 complains that: 'Many ribalds and low fellow are received into orders'. Did anything change? Probably not or, if so, only for the worse. The institutions of the diocese were in decline. The development of the communes in the twelfth and thirteenth centuries had dealt a death-blow to the old powers of episcopal secular jurisdiction. Without this support the prestige of the Italian bishop, whose diocese was generally much smaller and poorer than anything known in northern Europe, suffered. The Italian chapter was almost invariably non-monastic, dominated by its local nobility, divided by that nobility's feuds, and unresponsive to reform movements. It was weakened both by increasing papal attempts to interfere in its running and, then again, by an expansion of a parochial system which detracted from the lustre of the cathedral itself. At the same time the formation of new parishes, the increasing division of parishes (*pievi*) into smaller units with their own churches (*cappelle*) brought no new strength to the institution of the parish as such. For the standing of both cathedral and parochial clergy was inevitably diminished by the rise of the friars whose popular esteem attracted almost all who were most learned or devout to their orders.

Even the friars, however, were the victims of an anti-clericalism which was strong among all classes. The circumstances of the ordinary parish priests made it perhaps inevitable. They were recruited almost at random and underwent no formal training. They were normally of a very low educational level, frequently unable even to read the sacred texts or expound satisfactorily the complex doctrines of their faith, often following a course of life at variance with the ideal which they were supposed to represent. That ideal was extraordinarily high, and frequent lapses from it were hardly surprising. Yet such considerations did not moderate the censoriousness of laymen before them, for what was universally desired was the manifestation of thaumaturgic powers in everyday life through the agency of men of celibacy and sanctity. And the very claim of the priesthood to be an élite, experts, mediators of spiritual powers wholly denied to laymen, their very insistence that they alone were preachers of a gospel which others were excluded from interpreting, ensured that any clerical inadequacy would be seized on by laymen with avidity.

Clerics, for their part, were as swift to condemn the laity. Humbert of Romans, drawing upon his experience of both France and Italy, remarked that: 'It must be noted that the poor rarely go to church and rarely to sermons, so that they know little of what pertains to their salvation'.[16] He was equally condemnatory of magnates and their servants; other preachers frequently attacked the scepticism and indifference to religion of all classes. These attacks should not be taken too seriously for they form an essential part of incitement to penitence in the sermon literature of any age. The truth is that in the peninsula of the day all the stages between the extremes of faith and scepticism are to be discerned. There are the asceticisms of the saints, the kissing of lepers and, beyond these, the fullest manifestations of religious hysteria. So, in the convent of S. Caterina at Quarto, one finds thirteenth-century 'devils of Loudon': no less than sixty nuns, said to be demoniacally-possessed. At the other end of the scale one reads the private letter of Niccolò Acciaiuoli to his brother, remarking of the monastery he has founded that it will increase his fame and that, 'if the soul is immortal', his, wherever ordained to go, will rejoice at the thought.[17]

The views of total sceptics, if they existed, are difficult to discover for they were or would have been dangerous to express. Accusations of 'Epicureanism', directed at men like Frederick II and Farinata degli Uberti, are generally found in a political context, and, even then, are infrequent. Rarely, if ever, are these charges levelled before the inquisitors. There did exist certainly some mockery of a 'modern' kind against the more extreme forms of piety, which merges into anti-clericalism. There are those who, seeing the devotion of the flagellants, declare: 'Let them flog themselves as much as they want, I won't be doing it'. There is the amiable Boncompagno da Signa, with his verses on Fra Giovanni da Vicenza's preaching of the 'Great Alleluia':

> And Giovanni giovangelised
> And leaping about he crossed his eyes;
> Now jumped this way, now jumped that,
> Till in Heaven he slumped flat.
> He jumped that way, he jumped this,
> Thousands jumped up with new pumped fizz;
> Jumped the lords without repletion,
> Jumped the doge of the Venetians. . .

Or again, the satirical comments attributed to the Florentines about the same Fra Giovanni: 'For God's sake don't let him come here. We've heard he raises people from the dead, and we're so full already, our city can't hold any more'.[18] Clearly sentiments akin to these were not uncommon, which is not to say that they could not merge quite comfortably with a conventional piety.

Of that piety it is not easy, given the variety of the evidence, to speak. For most, no doubt, religion consisted of a few simple things. These might be the sign of the Cross, a knowledge of the Our Father, Hail Mary, and, perhaps, the Creed, with certain charms and ejaculatory prayers ('Ora pro nobis', 'Miserere nobis'). Then there would be attendance at Sunday Mass (whose full meaning cannot have often been very apparent to most); normally annual participation in confession and communion; a hope for miracles; reverence offered to images of, and some knowledge of stories about, Christ, Mary, and the saints; a hatred of unbelievers; plus the sacraments of baptism, confirmation (though this hardly seems to loom large), and (perhaps seen by the Church as a second-rank sacrament) matrimony. Yet even after the suppression of 'heresy' one is struck by the wide variety of fuller spiritual satisfactions offered to those who desired them.

Certain forms of religious observance were clearly in decline. The monastic orders, with their withdrawal from the world, were yielding to the friars who engaged within it. The Cistercians still enjoyed popularity in the thirteenth century, but their influence seems to wane thenceforth. (In the twelfth century, forty of their monasteries were established in Italy: from 1200 to 1250, thirty; from 1250 to 1300, fourteen; from 1300 to 1350, four.)[19] Again, though Italians were prominent in the Fourth and Fifth Crusades, true crusading fervour died away amidst the plethora of secular and anti-heretical crusades of the later thirteenth century. None the less, the power which religious excitement could generate in the masses is illustrated by the five great movements which, in our period, caught up thousands in itinerant processions throughout Italy. There was the 'Great Alleluia' of 1233 and the Flagellant Procession of 1260 (significantly the year of Joachite expectation), which were both basically peace-movements. There was the general movement on Rome in 1299, which probably originated in millenarian expectations of the turn of the century, and was deftly transformed by Boniface VIII into the first Jubilee year of 1300. There was the flagellant peace movement of the Dominican Venturino da Bergamo in 1335, which was in its later stages to fall under ecclesiastical censure for indiscipline, and finally the Jubilee pilgrims to Rome of the year 1350.

In everyday circumstances the devout lay man or woman had many outlets. They could join an 'Order of Penitents', wear a distinctive habit, and in their own homes, sometimes in isolation, sometimes in fraternities, practise fasting and abstinence, celibacy if unmarried, continence, at least on feast days, if married, and other ascetic practices designed to achieve humility of spirit. It was from such an order, a group of *viri poenitentiales*, that Franciscanism itself had arisen. Alternatively they could join a Pious Confraternity, coming together, generally under the supervision of a cleric, to enlarge their spiritual experience by prayer and religious learning. These two forms of lay religion were of some antiquity in Italian life. But from the thirteenth century, both in towns and villages, they grew at an extraordinary rate. Often they were associated with burial societies, hospitals, refuges for the poor. From 1260 they were joined by the Confraternities of the Beaters, who combined the practice of penitential self-flagellation with, in the fourteenth century, the performance of *laude* or hymns to Christ and the Virgin.

It was amidst these circles, and, then again and above all, in the milieu of the Franciscans, that there grew up what still today might be recognised as an 'Italian religious sensibility'. There was a new emphasis on eucharistic devotion (the doctrine of transubstantiation had been officially promulgated only in the Fourth Lateran council) and on the succour of the poor. (There was, perhaps, some psychological connection between the idea of Christ giving his body as food and drink to man and the need to feed 'the poor of Christ'.) At the same time pietistic sentiment tended to move towards a more human religious experience and a new spiritual tenderness. It was not that God the Father or Christ the stern Judge in Majesty were no longer present, did not exercise as great power as ever, but that these images came to be increasingly balanced by softer thoughts. Men dwelt more now upon Christ the Child (an aspect which drew strong impetus from St. Francis, inventor of the crib) or upon Christ the Man of Sorrows, sharing with men a life of human joys and pains. With this went the exaltation of his human mother, *illuminatrix*, star of the sea, bitter sea, Lady of Heaven, bride of her son, mother of all the faithful. Against popular belief which tended to ascribe divine attributes of majesty and omnipotence to Mary, the theologians fought a difficult battle. A world of general sentiment is summed up in the fines in punishment of blasphemy prescribed by the statutes of Ivrea: against God and the saints, twenty shillings; against the Virgin, sixty.[20]

Within this general process of humanisation of religion, the saints too assumed a new and ever-increasing prominence. The most venerated were the Apostles and Martyrs of Christian antiquity. But there was deep-felt desire as well for the recognition of contemporary sanctity, and popular canonisations (normally of men and women who were never to enjoy anything more than a local cult) were frequent. One could perhaps calculate within the peninsula 137 in the thirteenth, 124 in the fourteenth century. The new importance of the saints is very clearly demonstrated by their proliferation in ecclesiastical art, by a vast extension of hagiographical literature, and then again by the 'anthroponymic revolution' in the Italy of the later Middle Ages. In the twelfth century names with a specifically Christian character were rare. By the sixteenth (when Germanic names had virtually disappeared) the majority of the population bore them. It is the fourteenth century which seems decisive in this change. So, for example, a recent investigation of the anthroponymy of Genoa shows 11.72 per cent of a representative sample of the population with saints' names from 1099 to 1199; 23.33 per cent in the years 1200–99; and 66.66 per cent in 1300–1401.[21]

The intense veneration of men and women esteemed for sanctity brought with it a hunger for miracles, an extraordinary cult of relics and images, and a vast increase in the practice of pilgrimage. Miracles were needed, for they were necessary to authenticate sanctity. Side by side accordingly one meets both frequent complaints that the age of miracles was past or almost past and, at the same time, very frequent reports of miracles (no less than sixty, for instance, associated with Fra Raniero of Borgo San Sepolcro between 2 November 1304 and 27 May 1305).[22]

Relics were sought out because they preserved the personality of the saint and so too his miraculous power. There presence was absolutely essential for a lawful consecration of a church. At the consecration of SS. Annunziata at Rome in 1220 the following relics were deposited within the altar:

Some wood of the Cross. Some wood of the table on which Christ dined with his apostles. Something from the tomb of the Blessed Mary and the Blessed John the Evangelist. Something of a stone on which Christ wept. Some relics of SS. Andrew the Apostle; Simon and Jude; Matthew and Lawrence, martyrs; Fabian and Sebastian; Nicando the Priest; Sixtus, Pope and Martyr; Felicissimus and Agapitus, martyrs; Cosmas and Damian; Libertinus, Paternus, and Honoratus, martyrs; Chrysanthus and Darias; the Holy Innocents; St. Herman the Martyr, SS. Dionysius, Rusticus and Eleutherius; Quintinus, Bishop and Martyr; SS. Nerus and Achilleus; S. Menna the Martyr; Felix and Adauctus; St. Thomas; the 11,000 Virgins; Secundina the Virgin; Domitilla the Virgin. Something of the column of Christ and his tomb. Something of the stone on which Christ was transfigured; of the stone on which St. Mary Magdalene did penance; of the arm of St. Maximinus.[23]

Such a combination was conceived of as radiating immense spiritual force, as did, too, images of the saints which were often believed to possess wonder-working powers. Such, in Florence, were the images of Mary in the Servite Church of SS. Annunziata, near the oratory of San Michele, and in S. Maria at Impruneta, six miles from the city. This last was most valued as a talisman against the plague and as a rain-goddess. Matteo Villani describes how in a year of drought:

The Florentines, fearing to lose the fruits of the land had recourse to divine aid, ordering the saying of prayers and continual processions through the city and *contado*. Yet the more processions they made the brighter the sky grew, by day and night. Seeing that this was to no avail, the citizens with great devotion and hope had recourse to the aid of Our Lady, and drew out the ancient figure, painted on wood, of Our Lady of S. Maria [Impruneta]. And on 9 May 1354 the commune prepared many large candles and called out the parish priests and all the clergy, with the arm of St. Philip the Apostle, and with the venerable head of St. Zanobius, and with many other holy reliques. And almost all the people, men and women and children, with the priors and the whole government of Florence, while the bells of the commune and the churches sounded out in praise of God, went to meet the painting outside the gate of San Piero Gattolino. And they looked on the painting. And those of the house of Buondelmonti, patrons of the parish, reverently bore the painting with the men of the parish. And the bishop joined them with his procession, with the relics and the people, and bore the holy figure with great reverence and solemnity to [the Baptistry of] Saint John; and from there it was followed to S. Miniato al Monte, and then taken back to its ancient place at S. Maria Impruneta. It came about that on the day of the procession the sky filled with clouds; the next day remained cloudy though previous days had been burnt up with heat. The third day it began to drizzle a little, and the fourth to rain in abundance, and continued so, day after day, continually for a week, gradually and evenly. . . Thus its controlled and helpful flow, was no less wonderful a gift of grace than the rain itself.[24]

The interest in relics was maintained through the indulgences assigned to them by the Papacy. A visitor to St. Peter's at Rome in 1377 learnt from a *Liber Indulgentiarum* that for every hour spent before the Veronica (the cloth with which, it was supposed, St. Veronica had wiped the face of Jesus), a Roman could gain 3,000, an Italian 9,000, and a foreigner 12,000 years of indulgences; before the altar of St. Peter's he gained a plenary indulgence.[25] Such opportunities were not to be missed and prompted a rapid growth of pilgrimage among the Italian peoples. Many went abroad: to the shrine of St. James at Compostella, or on 'package tours' (including transport, food and board, payment of tolls, guided tour of Jerusalem and other sites) organised by Venetian merchants to the Holy Land. Many more visited native shrines: Rome (whose importance was increased by the institution of the Jubilee); Assisi; and, enriched with the reliquary treasures taken from Constantinople, Venice.

Faced with these developments, official circles, it is clear, came often to develop a certain wary scepticism. This arose partly through the development of more elaborate canonisation procedures, and partly through the criticisms of religious orders, seeking to depreciate the miracles of their rivals. (The Franciscan Salimbene, for example, tells of how some Dominican friars set about manufacturing them.) Hence the sanctity of specific individuals and the truth of the marvels they were supposed to perform were often rejected. Again, the notorious duplication of identical relics in different places provoked thought, as did the suspicion that pilgrimages might be primarily undertaken by those seeking a holiday from local and domestic duties. Yet one cannot make a distinction between 'popular' and 'official' religion in the growth and development of these practices, for the Church never denied, but rather strongly affirmed, the reality of sanctity, the virtue of relics, the ideal of pilgrimage, and a world shot through with the constant possibility of the miraculous. And having no adequate criteria to distinguish the fraudulently miraculous, it was often forced to take it under its wing.

V

In the piety of the thirteenth and fourteenth centuries there is much of beauty and much to be admired. The administrators of the Roman Church, who channelled and directed it, could have seen in that the justification for the torture and killings for which they were also responsible. More than this the organisation of the Church provided that sense of participation in a community, of belonging to a world linked and united by the bells of Christendom. It was easy enough in these circumstances to portray the 'heretic' as an enemy of human sociability. Nor did the claims of the community inhibit the individual mystical spirituality of men like Giovanni Colombini (1304–67) and women like Catherine of Siena (1347–80).

Once the Inquisitors had done their work there were three groups of people alone in Italy who might have been tempted to stand out against the general religious consensus. First were the merchants. Yet, despite ecclesiastical condemnation of 'usury' and the Christian exaltation of poverty, the Church was itself so closely bound up with the existing economic order that accommodation between the two was easily made. It was in fact businessmen and artisans who featured most prominently in the confraternities and daily religious life of parish and diocese.

Second were men of government. For these the Roman Church had always to be treated as, in some sense, exterior to their interests. In the first place the Papal State was always a potential rival in the world of inter-communal diplomacy. Then again, as both secular governments grew in power and as papal administrative pretensions expanded, in Italy, as in the rest of Europe, politicians came to object to papal provision, taxation of 'their' clergy, and rights of appeal to Rome against judgments given in their own courts. Yet in Italy the attacks launched by Dante in the name of the empire, by Marsiglio of Padua on behalf of the commune, against all forms of temporal jurisdiction claimed by the Roman Church never came to provide the basis for a programme of political action. Marsiglio's *Defensor Pacis* (probably written shortly after 1326), with its call for the abolition of the administrative structure of the Papacy and the transfer of all its power in the world to secular rulers, was translated into Italian but found a response only in lands beyond the Alps. Influencing Wycliffe and the Hussites, and rendered into English at the command of Thomas Cromwell at a critical moment in the Henrician Reformation, Marsiglio's principal desideratum, the abolition, for good or ill, of all check and counterbalance by ecclesiastics upon the power of the secular state, was to be achieved in northern climes while rejected in his homeland.

The reasons for the comparative spirit of harmony between the two powers within the peninsula are to be explained, above all, by the fact that, normally, the secular rulers had their own way. Since bishops and canons had belonged to the same families which dominated town-governments the communes' assumption of episcopal secular rights had largely passed without severe conflict. With the rise of the *popolo* and, concomitantly, with the occasional appearance of 'foreign', particularly mendicant bishops who had been collated to their posts by the

Papacy, tensions between the lay and ecclesiastical powers had grown. But by the fourteenth century communes and *signorie* had generally a dominant influence in appointment to benefices; they laid taxes upon the Church in their domains; regulated disputes over tithes; and, occasionally, appropriated ecclesiastical property to themselves. Then again, the commune itself increasingly came, within the diocese with which it was generally coterminous, to provide for its citizens a form of, as it were, state religion. It was assisted in this by the strongly local character of a religious life in which each bishop formed his own diocesan calendar. Hence those saints whose feast-days fell on days of military victory or political triumph – as St. Anne at Florence – were by decree of government raised to a new prominence within the local pantheon, and the rhythms of the liturgical year itself came to be imbued with a markedly civic flavour. This tendency was reinforced by the commune's increasing insistence upon taking over the building of 'their' Duomo and other churches. The great cathedrals of Siena, Arezzo, and Florence were constructed, and each part of their construction supervised, under the auspices of not clerics but secular governments. And the spirit in which they were put up was summarised by the rulers of Pistoia in their decrees for the church of San Jacopo: 'neither the work nor the workers on that work shall be controlled or supervised by any ecclesiastical person'.[26]

The communal statutes, again, were drawn up in the names of the saints considered to be the defenders of the city. They prescribe those days in the liturgical year when the councils and guilds should make oblations of wax, flags, and money to the cathedral and other designated churches. (Book vi of the Statutes of Ivrea of 1324, for example, is wholly concerned with 'the festivities to be celebrated, the wax to be offered to Holy Mary and the other churches, and the alms and other solemnities to be offered'.) They lay down those feast-days on which work is to be prohibited both in the city as a whole, and in individual parishes of the city. They claim a right to supervision over the hospitals run by the confraternities, and enforce payment towards the running of hospitals which had been promised, but not made, by members of confraternities. They lay down penalties for blasphemy, for disturbance of services, and provide in all for the decorum of religious life within their territories.

The communes, that is to say, had, in a strong sense, 'their' churches, and the Catholic Church in Italy in the fourteenth century could almost be thought of as a federation of local patriotic churches, where civic feeling and religious emotion blended without conflict. In these circumstances secular rulers, like merchants, maintained harmony with the ecclesiastical order.

The third class which one would expect to have stood outside the normal religious currents of the age was composed of those men whose education was the equal of, or superior to, that of most clerics, and whose writings went to make up the distinctly lay culture or cultures of the day. One thinks here, above all, of Dante again, and (though technically both took minor orders) Boccaccio and Petrarch. Though none of these men challenged or wished to challenge the doctrines of the Church, there was none the less a real sense in which the writings of each, in their different ways, emphasised thoughts and feelings which were not easily assimilable to the current ecclesiastical ethos.

Of Dante's repeated attacks on the canon lawyers and their claims, on 'the carnal Church', on its corruption by wealth, power, and simony, it is unnecessary to speak for they are so well known. What has been less emphasised is the deep secular strain which coexisted in his thought together with his other-worldly hopes. It is half-revealed in his preoccupation with the question of the salvation of unbaptised but virtuous pagans; it shows itself most starkly in his belief in the *duplex finis* of man, his contention that happiness was not purely eternal but might be created in the social world of men. This profoundly optimistic, even doubtfully orthodox, contention was cogently underlined in the attack made upon the *De Monarchia* by the Dominican friar, Guido Vernani, in 1327:

This man did not need to discern a twofold beatitude resulting from a twofold nature, corruptible and incorruptible, for in corruptible nature there can, strictly speaking, be neither virtue nor beatitude. He says, moreover, that man is predestined to these two goals by God. Whereupon I say that man is not predestined by God to temporal beatitude as to a final goal, because such beatitude has never been capable of ending and satisfying man's hunger. Even philosophically speaking, the action of such virtues [the moral virtues] is designed with a view to a contemplative life, in order that through these virtues man, all his passions having been quelled, may more calmly and freely contemplate eternal things. . . Man is therefore predestined to eternal felicity as to his final goal, and should organise and employ all his assets – natural, moral, and supernatural – with a view to securing it.[27]

What this passage brings out with particular force is that laymen, in possession of a learning which had once been the monopoly of the clerical world, were now able to formulate aspirations which were ultimately at variance with those offered by the ecclesiastical order. Two years before Vernani wrote, Cardinal Bertrand du Poujet had in fact had the *De Monarchia* burnt at Bologna. But it was less easy to burn out the ideal contained within it, for it was bound up with a situation where the highest learning was no longer the monopoly of ecclesiastics.

Boccaccio, with all his reverence for Dante – a reverence resting not simply on an admiration for literary mastery, nor on a mutual anti-clericalism, but precisely upon the appeal of his secularity – was, clearly, totally different in character. It is not always easy to perceive the register in which his works were written, yet obviously, even at the time of his spiritual crisis of the early 1360s, they were light-years away from the religious and philosophic preoccupations of the Divine Comedy. What emerges from them is a very different strand of lay thought. In his 'human comedy', the *Decameron* (*c.* 1350), the note of secularity is accompanied by a universal mockery of clerics: monks, nuns, friars, secular clergy, and members of lay-orders, invariably portrayed as greedy, lustful, cunning or stupid, mean or contemptible. Attacks on clerics were a hallowed medieval genre and, outside their sustained vigour and artistry, there is nothing new here. What is remarkable, however, is that all popular religious practices, miracles, invocation of saints, pilgrimages, are seen as laughable, and that in this there is no indignation, no moralising. Religion, like love, we seem to be told, is just another field where people make fools of themselves.

Once again an important section of the lay world, hitherto expressing themselves only inarticulately, has found a voice. What is being prepared is the spiritual world of Machiavelli and Guicciardini. With Boccaccio's friend, Petrarch, yet another note is struck. Among his writings there is a pronounced distaste for Thomist method in theology and, notably in the unbridled attacks on the Avignon curia in the *Liber sine nomine*, a marked anti-clericalism. But there is no eager embracing of the secular, rather an unresolved tension between the demands made by the ecclesiastical order and the author's desire for glory and his admiration for the pagan *virtus* of the Roman world. Though he himself had sought the indulgences to be gathered from visits to the churches of Rome, there is too a superior and somewhat distasteful contempt for the religious practices of the uneducated lower orders. With this went suggestions of a search for inner spirituality largely divorced from the popular religious externalised practice of the day. To his brother, a Carthusian monk, he writes of how he carries out his spiritual obligations: 'solitary confessions', 'prayers to Christ' by day and night. He reiterates the theme of looking into oneself in order to seek the Divine for, 'nothing is more wonderful than the soul, than which nothing is greater'. Faced with the ills of the world, it is this path of contemplation that he recommends to Canon Stefano Colonna:

Finding in the whole world no place of quiet and solace, return to your own room and to yourself; keep vigil with yourself; speak with yourself; hold silence with yourself; walk with yourself; stand still with yourself. . . . Make for yourself at the centre of your soul a place where you may hide, where you may rejoice, where you may rest undisturbed, where Christ may dwell with you, who in your youth made you his familiar and companion in his holy priesthood.[28]

Petrarch has turned aside from the active involvement in the world, the pursuit of scholastic learning, and the externalised religious practice advocated by the friars, and has returned to the contemplative ideal of the monastic orders. It was not an ideal which was to achieve any prominence in popular spirituality in Italy. But it influenced later humanists and through them it was to play some part in the formation of that 'philosophy of Christ' preached by Erasmus and his followers in the sixteenth century.

NOTES

The most recent **general discussions** of religious life in this period are those of G. Miccoli, 'La storia religiosa' in the Einaudi *Storia d'Italia, cit.*, II', 1974 and of S. Spariò, M. Fois, and G. Cracco, in their article, 'Italie. Moyen Age et Humanisme' in the *Dictionnaire de Spiritualité* fondé par M. Villier, vol. vii, Paris, 1971. D. Hay, 'The Problems of Italian Church History' (ch. i of his *The Church in Italy in the Fifteenth Century*, Cambridge, 1977), though primarily concerned with the fifteenth century, has much to say which is also relevant to our period. An important periodical is the *Rivista di Storia della Chiesa in Italia*, 1946 ff. The Edizioni di storia e letteratura of Rome have made plans for the publication of a large collection of source material in their *Thesaurus Ecclesiarum Italiae*. Important works have already been issued by the Centro di studii sulla spiritualità medievale, established at Todi in 1957.

Much has been written on the Papacy; see particularly A. Fliche, *La Chrétienté romaine (1198—1274)*, Paris, 1950; G. Mollat, *Les Papes d'Avignon (1305—1378)*, ninth edn, Paris, 1949 (English translation by J. Lowe, 1963); and Y. Renouard, *La papauté à Avignon*, Paris, 1962 (English translation by D. Bethell, 1970).

An abundant literature on 'heresy' includes H. Grundmannn, *Bibliographie zur Ketzergeschichte des Mittelalters (1900—1966)*, Rome, 1967; *Heresies of the High Middle Ages*, ed. and trans. W. L. Wakefield and A. P. Evans, London, 1969 (with valuable bibliography and translations into English of the main sources); J. Guiraud, *Histoire de l'Inquisition au Moyen Age*, vol. ii, Paris, 1938; L. Paolini, *L'eresia a Bologna fra xiii e xiv secolo*, Rome, 1975 (an important work); *Eretici e ribelli del xiii e xiv sec.*, ed. D. Maselli, Pistoia, 1974; M. Lambert, *Medieval Heresy*, London, 1977; M. d'Alatri, ' "Eresie" perseguitate dall' inquisizione in Italia nel corso del duecento' in *The Concept of Heresy in the Middle Ages*, ed. W. Lourdaux and D. Verhelst, The Hague, 1976. The sections of *Hérésies et sociétés dans l'Europe préindustrielle: 11-18. siècles*, ed. J. Le Goff, Paris, 1968, which are relevant to Italy in this period, have now appeared in Italian translation as *L'eresia medievale*, ed. O. Capitani, Bologna, 1971. Still of great value is G. Volpe, *Movimenti religiosi e sette ereticali nella società medievale italiana: secoli xi-xiv*, 2nd edn, Florence, 1961.

On the friars see R. F. Bennet, *The Early Dominicans*, Cambridge, 1937; W. A. Hinnebusch, *The History of the Dominican Order*, New York, vol. i, 1965; Rosalind R. Brooke, *Early Franciscan Government*, Cambridge, 1959; idem, *The Coming of the Friars*, London, 1975; J. Moorman, *A History of the Franciscan Order*, Oxford, 1968; *S. Bonaventura*, ed. J. .G. Bongerol, Grottaferrata, 1974. Important periodicals are the *Archivium Fratrum Praedicatorum*, 1931 ff. and the *Archivium Franciscanum Historicum*, 1907 ff. On the issue of poverty, there is M. D. Lambert, *Franciscan Poverty*, London, 1961, and Decima L. Douie, *The Nature and the Effect of the Heresy of the Fraticelli*, Manchester, 1932. For Italian friars as missionaries there are G. Golubovich, *Biblioteca Bio-Bibliografia della Terra Santa e dell' Oriente francescano*, vols. i–v, Quaracchi, 1906–1927; *Sinica Franciscana: Itinera et Relationes Fratrum Minorum saec. xiii et xiv*, ed. P. A. van den Wyngaert, i, 1929; G. Soranzo, *Il papato, l'Europa cristiana e i Tartari*, Milan, 1930. For translations of works by or about Oderico da Pordenone, Giovanni da Montecorvino, etc. into English, H. Yule, *Cathay and the Way Thither*, 2nd edn by H. Cordier, London 1913–15 and A. C. Moule, *Christians in China before the year 1550*, London, 1930. For Giovanni Carpini's 'History of the Mongols' in English see *The Mongol Mission*, trans. by a nun of Stanbrook Abbey, ed. C. Dawson, London, 1955.

For the preaching of the friars there is C. Delcorno, *Giordano da Pisa e l'antica predicazione volgare*, Florence, 1975; for their literature of spirituality, *Prosatori minori del Trecento, Tomo I: Scrittori di Religione*, ed. G. de Luca, Milan–Naples, 1954, and G. Petrocchi, *Scrittori religiosi del Trecento*, Florence, 1974; for their early bishops, W. R. Thomson, *Friars in the Cathedral: The First Franciscan Bishops*, Toronto, 1975 (ch. v for Italy). On Joachite influence, there are, most recently, the two works of Marjorie Reeves, *The Influence of Prophecy in the Later Middle Ages*, Oxford, 1969, and *Joachim da Fiore and the Prophetic Future*, London, 1976.

For the Italian dimension of scholasticism see B. Nardi, *Saggi sull' aristotelismo padovano del secolo xiv al xvi*, Florence, 1956; E. Gilson, *Dante et la Philosophie*, Paris, 1939 (cf. the review by Nardi, 'Dante e la filosofia' in his *Dante e la cultura medievale*, Bari, 1942, pp. 207–45); and P. O. Kristeller, *Le Thomisme e la pensée italienne de la Renaissance*, Montreal–Paris, 1967. Useful is K. Foster (editor and translator), *The Life of St. Thomas Aquinas: Biographical Documents*, London, 1959.

The abundance of material on the topics so far discussed falls away to a thin trickle when considering the regular and secular clergy of **monastery, diocese, and parish**. No general works encompass these themes though much of importance can be found in R. Brentano, *Two Churches; England and Italy in the Thirteenth Century*, Princeton, 1968. Otherwise one is driven to a, still sparse, selection of local studies, such works as Catherine E. Boyd, *A Cistercian Nunnery in Medieval Italy: The Story of Rifreddo in Saluzzo 1220–1300*, Cambridge, 1943; R. Caravita, *Rinaldo da Concorrezzo, Arcivescovo di Ravenna (1303–1321)*, Florence, 1964; R. C. Trexler, *Synodal Law in Florence and Fiesole 1306–1518*, Vatican, 1971; G. Briacca, *Gli statuti sinodali novaresi di Papiniano della Rovere (a. 1298)*, Milan, 1971; N. Meoni, 'Visite pastorali a Cortona nel Trecento', *ASI*, 1971; and, more general, though, on a limited theme, T. D. Kurze, *Pfarrerwahlen im Mittelalter*, Cologne, 1966, chs. v and ix.

On **spirituality** I owe, for what I write here, a principal debt to the Edinburgh Ph.D. thesis by M. G. Dickson, *Patterns of European Sanctity: The Cult of Saints in the Later Middle Ages (with special reference to Perugia)*, 1974, the first part of which is shortly to be published. The Mass Movements are covered by four articles: V. Fumagalli, 'In margine all' "alleluia" del 1233', *BISI*, 1968; A. Frugoni, 'Sui flagellanti del 1260', *BISI*, 1963; *idem*, 'Il guibileo di Bonifacio VIII', *BISI*, 1950; C. Genaro, 'Venturino da Bergamo e la peregrinatio romana del 1355' in *Studi sul medioevo cristiano offerti a R. Morghen*, 1, Rome, 1974. G. G. Meersseman, *Ordo fraternitatis: Confraternità e pietà dei laici nel medioevo*, Rome, 1977, supersedes all written previously on the confraternities. Other interesting works are E. Delaruelle, *La piété populaire au Moyen Age*, Turin, 1975; R. Manselli, *La religion populaire au Moyen Age*, Montreal–Paris, 1975; J. Sumption, *Pilgrimage: An Image of Medieval Religion*, London 1975; R. C. Trexler, 'Sacred Images in Florentine Religion', *Studies in the Renaissance*, 1972.

On **new lay attitudes** see R. C. Trexler, *The Spiritual Power: Republican Florence under Interdict*, Leiden, 1974; J. Gilchrist, *The Church and Economic Activity in the Middle Ages*, London, 1969, and amidst a vast literature, M. J. Wilks, *The Problem of Sovereignty in the Later Middle Ages*, Cambridge, 1963, ch. iii; K. Foster, 'Religion and Philosophy in Dante' in *The Mind of Dante*, ed. U. Limentani, Cambridge, 1965; J. W. Allen, 'Marsilius of Padua and Medieval Secularism' in *The Social and Political Ideals of Some Great Medieval Thinkers*, London, 1923; P. P. Gerosa, *Umanesimo cristiano del Petrarca*, Turin, 1966; and C. Trinkaus, 'Petrarch: Man between Despair and Grace', ch. i of his *In Our Image and Likeness*, London, 1970.

1. Salimbene de Adam, *Cronica*, ed. G. Scalia, Bari, 1966, pp. 484, 925.
2. *Statuta civitatis Faventiae*, ed. G. Rossini, *RIS*, xxviii, pt. v, I, p. 341.
3. Galvano Fiamma, *Opusculum de rebus gestis ab Azone, Luchino et Iohanne Vicecomitibus (1328–1342)*, *RIS*, xii, 4, ed. C. Castiglioni, p. 16.
4. Gullielmus Durandus, *Rationale Divinorum Officiorum*, Rome, 1473, in the translation of the first book by J. M. Neale and B. Webb, *The Symbolism of Churches and Church Ornament*, Leeds, 1843, pp. 17ff.
5. *Defensor Pacis*, ed. R. Scholz, *MGH*, Hanover, 1932, II, 2, in translation by A. Gewirth, *The Defender of Peace*, New York, 1951–6, ii, p. 103.
6. *Chronicon Parmense (1038–1338)*, ed. G. Bonazzi, *RIS*, ix, 9, p. 36; G. Brucker, 'The Florentine Popolo Minuto' in *Violence and Civil Disorder in Italian Cities, 1200–1500*, ed. L. Martines, London, 1972, p. 175.
7. A. Dondaine, 'Le Manuel de l'inquisiteur (1230–1330)', *Archivium Fratrum Praedicatorum*, 17, 1947, p. 93.
8. Raynerius Sacconi O.P., 'Summa de Catharis', ed. F. Sanjek, *Archivium Fratrum Praedicatorum*, xliv, 1974, in translation in *Heresies of the High Middle Ages, cit.*, pp. 329–30.

9. Paolini, *L'eresia a Bologna*, *cit.*, ii, pp. 160–1.
10. For the best account of Salimbene see C. Violante, 'Motivi e caratteri della Cronica di Salimbene', *Annali della Scuola Normale Superiore di Pisa*, S.2, xxii, 1953.
11. H. Yule, *Cathay and the Way Thither*, *cit.*, ii, 97 ff.
12. K. Foster, 'Vernacular Scriptures in Italy', in *The Cambridge History of the Bible*, vol. 2., ed. G. W. H. Lampe, Cambridge, 1969, pp. 452 ff.
13. C.M. de la Roncière, 'L'influence des franciscains dans la campagne de Florence au XIVe siècle (1280–1360)', *Mélanges de l'école français de Rome*, 87, 1975.
14. In T. Aquinas, *Politica opuscula duo*, ed. J. Mathis, 2nd edn, Turin–Rome, 1948, I,4. (Tolomeo of Lucca's contribution starts from Bk.ii, ch. v.)
15. P. Toynbee, 'Benvenuto da Imola and his Commentary on the *Divina Commedia*' in *An English Miscellany presented to Dr. Furnivall*, Oxford, 1901, 440.
16. A. Murray, 'Piety and Impiety in Thirteenth-Century Italy', in *Studies in Church History*, ed. G. J. Cuming and D. Baker, vol. viii, Cambridge, 1972, p. 93.
17. In G. Gaye, *Carteggio inedito d'artisti dei secoli xiv-xv*, Florence, 1839-40, i, pp. 61–2.
18. Salimbene de Adam, *Cronica*, *cit.*, pp. 109, 117.
19. B. G. Bedini, *Breve prospetto delle Abazie Cistercensi d'Italia*, n.p., 1964.
20. *Statuti del Comune di Ivrea*, ed. G. S. Pene-Vidari, Turin, 1968–9, i, pp. 165–6.
21. B. Z. Kedar, 'Noms de saints et mentalité populaire à Gênes au XIVe siècle', *Le Moyen Age*, 1967.
22. See L. Kern, 'Le Bienheureux Ranier de Borgo San Sepolcro', *Revue d'Histoire Franciscaine*, vii, 1930.
23. F. Savio, *Gli antichi vescovi d'Italia: Il Piemonte*, Turin, 1899, pp. 209–10.
24. Matteo Villani, *Cronica*, Florence, 1846, iv, 7 [i, pp. 308–9].
25. Sumption, *Pilgrimage*, *cit.*, p. 242.
26. S. Ciampi, *Notizie inedite della Sagrestia pistoiese*, Florence, 1810, p. 111.
27. Quoted in E. Gilson, *Dante the Philosopher*, translated D. Moore, London, 1948, pp. 200–1.
28. Quotations from F. Petrarca, *Le familiari*, ed. V. Rossi, Florence, 1933–42, x, 5 [ii, p. 317], iv, i [i, p. 159], xv, 7 [iii, p. 153].

CHAPTER TWELVE

The difficult years, 1340–80

I

Although the thirteenth and early fourteenth centuries had been a period of great external violence and internal anarchy within the city communes, they had also been times of agricultural and commercial expansion. From the 1320s, perhaps even earlier, there is some evidence for the appearance of checks and difficulties in the Italian regional economies which some historians have interpreted as indicating a general movement downwards. Bankruptcies seem to be more frequent (though, perhaps, they are simply better-documented), and what demographic witness there is, though very fragile, might suggest a population decline in certain areas. On the whole, however, without in any way seeking to magnify the in many ways inadequate achievements of the economic revolution, the development of Italy between 1200 and 1340 could be considered only in terms of general growth and success.

The last forty years of our period, by contrast, see a series of disasters fall upon the peoples of the peninsula, which in many regions depressed the tenor of economic life, had deep effects upon society, and brought personal tragedy to vast numbers.

Though bitter enough for those who endured them, the famines which struck most of Italy in the years 1339–40, 1346–7, 1352–3, 1374–5, were not, perhaps, more severe or more frequent than those of the previous century. These famines, however, were accompanied by a large number of general wars which were to make the peninsula a byword in the northern world. (In his *Livre de Chevalerie*[1] Geoffrey de Charny, writing in the 1360s, urged those who wished to become knights to gain experience in such distant lands as 'Lombardy, Tuscany, and Apulia, and other places where men-at-arms may find wages of war'.) The development of the *condottiere* system and the new powers of taxation attained by communes and *signorie* ensured that these conflicts would be much more devastating and prolonged and would engulf much more productive wealth than those previously fought.

The military companies which were now hired grew to an impressive size. 'The Great Company', for instance, originally founded in 1342 by Werner of

Urslingen, 'Enemy', as he boasted, 'of God, Pity and Mercy', was, within ten years, a virtual mobile state. Its *signore,* the renegade Hospitaller, Fra Moriale d'Albano, dispensed justice to the 10,000 fighting men and 20,000 camp-followers who constituted his subjects. A bureaucracy, consisting of Chamberlain, Councillors, and the ever-necessary notaries, watched over the Company's interests, prudently invested with Venetian merchants the booty that it had gained, and conducted its own diplomacy with other, more static powers. Throughout the 1360s and 1370s, with occasional schisms, destructions, and re-formations, the bands of Hawkwood, Albrecht Sterz, Hannekin Baumgarten and Ambrogio Visconti dominated the military life of the peninsula. They were expensive to hire in war. In peace, when they turned on their former employers with a variety of blackmailing threats, they were likely to prove equally costly.

II

War was not the worst that Italy had to face in these years. At sowing time, October and November 1345, rain fell constantly throughout the peninsula and the Po, Taro, Parma, Enza, and Serchio all flooded. During April, May, and June in the next year there were continual rains and the harvest was considered the worst for a hundred years. Famine struck everywhere. Villani guessed ('judging in the round, for in so great a city as is Florence one can't otherwise calculate') that in Florence 4,000 died of starvation. The harvest of 1347 was better, though in some areas still poor. Famine diseases everywhere lingered on until November. It was thus an already weakened population that was to be exposed to the next disaster, the arrival from the East of that 'new and unheard-of pestilence' which later generations were to call the Black Death.

This plague, which had been extinct in Europe from the eighth century, was brought to Italy by galleys trading with Byzantium and the Crimea. It first struck in the port of Messina in early October 1347 from where it spread to Catania and throughout Sicily. By January 1348 it was at Genoa and Pisa. At Venice it began in February, reached its peak between April and July, and began to abate at the end of August. From the principal ports it spread inland. By February it was at Lucca, by March at Florence and its *contado*, by April at Piombino, by May at Pistoia and Prato. In Siena it is recorded between the end of April and September.

In Emilia it raged at Modena, Bologna (May to September), Piacenza, and Rimini (15 May to 1 December). It was present at Padua in April and in Ancona and Naples by the first week in May. In Umbria it was at Perugia by April, at Orvieto between May and September. Although described by many chroniclers as 'universal' it did not strike everywhere with uniform force. In Lombardy, particularly, and remarkably at Milan and Parma, it had on this occasion little effect. By the end of the year it had, for the moment, finished its work in Italy and was being borne along the trade routes to the rest of Europe.

Two Italian doctors who lived through the plague of 1348, and one (Gentile da

Foligno) who died within it, together with at least another twenty-six who witnessed its resurgence before 1400, have left behind tractates upon its pathology which still survive. They give a sombre testimony to the worthlessness of the medical science of the age. Remarkably uniform in character, indeed sometimes indistinguishable in substance from tracts written with reference to earlier famine diseases,[2] they normally begin by referring to God as the primal cause of all things and His known tendency to punish abominable wickedness through spectacular scourges. They continue with a discussion of the astrological conjunctions which might, as a secondary cause, be supposed to have given birth to the disease. Attention here normally centred on the meeting of Saturn, Jupiter, and Mars in the sign of Aquarius on the 14th or, as others had it, the 20th March 1345. These astral influences had led to putrefaction of air, food, and water in the sub-lunary world and from this to secondary contagion between man and man.

Given the mysterious movement of the disease, the conclusion that plague was a miasmatic infection (a conclusion first suggested by Hippocrates and accepted by the English historian, Coulton, as late as 1929), must seem, in terms of the knowledge of the age, reasonable. Until the theory of germ-borne disease had been generally accepted – and such a theory was being ridiculed in learned circles less than a century ago – nothing written was likely to approach nearer to the truth. What will strike the modern reader of these tractates as strange is not so much their conclusions as their method. The frequent failure to suggest any differences between the customary famine-plagues and this new infection is here almost invariably paralleled (and explained) by a striking failure to describe the most basic symptoms which the various forms of the illness assume in the body. In the whole of Europe only Gui de Chauliac, papal physician at Avignon, distinguished what we now recognise to be the characteristic bubonic and pneumonic forms of the disease.

With the terror that the disease provoked, the frequent refusal of doctors to visit patients, this is not perhaps remarkable. But the preference for *a priori* speculation to empirical investigation was characteristic, not of medicine alone but of most learning in the age. Not surprisingly in the circumstances no cures were suggested. As prophylactics the treatises advised the cultivation of a simple temperate life in order to ensure high bodily resistance, abstention from hot baths (against the possibility of opening up the pores to the poisonous miasma), the avoidance of corrupt air, particularly from windows facing south, and domestic fumigation through, for example, the burning of juniper branches. As best defence all advised flight from the area contaminated by the miasma and avoidance of contagion through the shunning of the sick.

In our own day epidemiologists speak with no unanimous voice on the pathology of plague, on the behaviour of those fleas and rodents which are its vectors, or indeed even on the name which should be assigned to its bacillus. These differences of opinion sometimes pose certain problems to the historian, notably when attempting to calculate the number of deaths that the disease is likely to have caused. Recently, for instance, the learned bacteriologist, Professor J. F. D. Shrewsbury,[3] has strongly stressed the primarily urban character of bubonic plague and has urged that the large number of deaths recorded in the predominantly rural Britain of 1349 must have been brought about not by that disease, as has always hitherto been believed, but by classical epidemic typhus. These conclusions have not gone uncontested. In so far as there is a consensus, however, it might be summarised as follows. *Yersinia pestis* takes three main forms. The first and most common is bubonic plague. In this the rat-flea (*Xenopsylla cheopis*), which makes its home in the black rat (*Rattus rattus*, the ship or house-rat), transmits the plague bacillus from rat to rat and from man to man. The bite of the diseased flea produces swellings of the lymphatic glands in the groin or under the armpits which develop into buboes or carbuncles. The patient suffers agonising pain. Recovery is possible (survival-rates of between 10 and 40 per cent of diseased groups were recorded at various outbreaks in the nineteenth century), though death within five days is more probable.

The black rat, whose presence is an indispensable prerequisite for the diffusion of the bubonic form of the plague, is an extremely sedentary animal. It depends upon human constructions – houses, granaries, or ships – for its food and shelter and has never been found at more than 200 metres from a building. The flea too can fly only the smallest distance from its rat. Hence bubonic plague can be spread in only two ways. The first is by human transportation of the rats in ships or carts. The second is by fleas which have separated from their rats (from whom, as most have it, they can live apart for up to six weeks) in bales of wool or cloth. In the septicaemic form of plague, however, the bacillus is transmitted directly into the bloodstream. The buboes have no time to form before the onset of death, which may occur within a few hours of the first symptoms. Here it may be that the human flea, *Pulex irritans*, is able to transmit the bacillus from a sick to a healthy human being. If that be so, the spread of the disease would be independent of rat colonisation and movement, and could take place without any prior epizootic among rats (a phenomenon to which no European chronicler refers).

If the bubonic plague alone had been present in Italy in 1348, and if, as some maintain, the human flea is in fact incapable of transmitting the bacillus, it would follow that, even taking into account the close links between city and *contado*, its most severe effects would have been limited to cities, above all ports and trading centres. The countryside would have been severely struck only had the plague assumed its primary pneumonic form. In pneumonic plague the disease is localised in the lungs, the patient coughs blood, and shows the symptoms of pneumonia. In these circumstances the plague becomes infectious, the most infectious disease known to man. The bacillus is transmitted by droplet infection which in normal speech reaches 2 metres, in sneezing or coughing 4 metres. For the patient the prognosis is invariably fatal; death comes within four days or less. Whereas bubonic plague, transmitted by a rat-flea which hibernates in cold weather, is a summer disease, pneumonic plague particularly flourishes in winter, when indeed, as some claim, the diseased saliva may remain in suspension and be inhaled over a long period of time.

Whatever might have been the character of subsequent plagues (an important question for the demographic historian), it seems, both from the severe effects which were felt in the countryside and from the observations (though never very precisely given) of Italian contemporaries, that in 1348 plague was present in the peninsula in all its three forms. How many died within it cannot be known; but the extent of the catastrophe as it appeared to men at the time can be gauged from their own, undoubtedly wildly exaggerated, estimates. Chroniclers describe the deaths of 70 per cent of the population of Venice, 68 per cent of Genoa, two-thirds of all Italy, and so on. Boccaccio's introduction to the *Decameron* (though based in part upon Paul the Deacon's account of plague in seventh-century Rome) sets the scene of fear and tragedy. On the other hand there is evidence too of great resilience. Governments nowhere collapsed under the pressure, but struggled strongly to maintain the fabric of social life. Studies of Orvieto and Siena where in 1348, it may be, half the population died, show temporary dislocation but no breakdown in administrative continuity. In each town, before the plague had fully run its course, decrees were issued to face the effects of the crisis: the doubling of penalties for crime, wage-freezes, measures to encourage emigration, special arrangements for orphans, doubling of salaries for doctors, and establishment of special courts to deal with cases of disputed legacies.

The effects of the plague of 1348, however, were not confined to that year. As a consequence of its coming then, bubonic disease was firmly rooted in Europe until the eighteenth century. Within our period contemporaries often wrote of three other plagues. In a European context the papal physician, Chalin de Vinario, writing at Avignon in 1382, recorded that the first plague of 1348 had struck at, so he believed, two-thirds of the population of which none had escaped death. The second of 1363 had struck at only one half, from which some few had recovered. In the plague of 1373, he continued, one-tenth were attacked and many of these were cured, while in 1382, out of the one-twentieth who were seized by the disease, very many recovered in health. These calculations are of course wholly arbitrary but they find a general echo in a chronicle of Orvieto which distinguishes a first plague of 1348 'which was the greatest', and, treated much more laconically, a second of 1363, a third of 1374 and a fourth of 1383.[4]

These testimonies may express some symbolic truth, but the reality behind them was more complex. For our period we may provide a check-list, which, however inadequate and requiring greater elaboration, gives something of a truer picture. It is possible that in some of those towns recorded below the *pestis* recorded by contemporaries was (as perhaps at Pisa and Lucca in 1357 and Orvieto in May 1358) smallpox or (as, possibly at Florence in 1374) one or more of the famine diseases. But it seems likely that in each of these years bubonic plague, sometimes distinguished as the *pestilenza dell'anguinaia* ('the pestilence of the loins'), had some effect. Whether septicaemic and pneumonic plague were also present is not clear.

Pestis in
1361 at Piedmont, Como, Pavia, Milan and its *contado* (spring and summer), Novara, Piacenza, the Romagnol towns (beginning lightly in January, mounting in May, ending October), the Tusco-Romagnol Apennines, Gubbio and the

Marche (winter). [Only slight effects this year in Modena, Bologna, and Tuscany]

1362   at Bologna and its *contado* (May to October), Ferrara, Forlí, Padua (summer), Mantua.

1363   at Orvieto (May), Florence, Siena, Venice (late December).

1371   at Venice (severely April to August), Padua and Treviso (less severe), Lucca.

1373   at Milan.

1374   at Bologna (January, particularly strong June to October), Florence (March to October), Romagna, Marche.

1382   at Venice (May to November), Padua, Milan, Ferrara, Bologna, Romagna.

1383   at Bologna, Lucca, Florence, Prato, Vicenza, Apulia.

From this data one gains the impression of a disease which though slackening in its power and tending to move more slowly, in more sporadic and less generalised outbreaks, still presents a constant threat – though now perhaps more in the towns than the countryside – to the peoples of Italy.

III

The conjunction of war, famine, and plague in the forty years before 1380 clearly had profound effects upon population. Firm figures are not to be looked for here. None the less it is apparent that in many rural areas the process of *Wüstungen* (the abandonment of villages and cultivated lands) was proceeding apace. In Lucania the number of villages taxed in 1277 was 148, in 1329 140, in the early fifteenth century, 96. (There is evidence here of decline before the 1340s.) In Sardinia between 1320 and 1358, 300 centres were abandoned. In 1370 the Council of Siena declared that the population of Grosseto had diminished from 1,200 to 100 *homines*, that of Magliano from 400 to 40, that of Talamone from 50 to 8. In 1373 it claimed that the population of the district of Marittima had fallen from 10,000 to 2,000 inhabitants.[5] In the countryside of Pistoia one estimate calculates 37,598 souls in 1244, 23,964 in 1344, and 14,178 in 1383.

Everywhere the same story is repeated. At San Gimignano (town and country) there were 2,539 'hearths' in 1332, 1,163 in 1350, and 564 in 1428. At Volterra (town and country) there were 3,142 'hearths' in 1326, 1,359 in 1380. At Florence, it may be that in 1348 a population of about 80,000 fell to 30,000 and by 1427 had recovered to only 37,000. Pisa, which had, perhaps, 50,000 inhabitants in 1315, had less than 10,000 in 1428–9.

Despite all the difficulties of interpretation which such isolated figures present it seems difficult to doubt that between 1348 and 1380 the population of the peninsula must have been reduced by between a third and a half. The economic consequences of such a decline are still largely uncharted and an object of controversy, nor would it be possible within the chronological limits of this present work to consider the wide-ranging debate among historians on the long-term effects of this crisis upon Italy in the fifteenth century. How far the great demographic disaster of these years constituted merely an incident, a temporary set-back in the Italian economies, how far it dealt a permanent wound, how far it served in Italy to stifle or release new creative forces, are matters which could be considered only from a later standpoint.

Confining ourselves to the period in question, the problems are difficult enough. For many commentators a point of general economic crisis had been reached in the 1340s, before the coming of the Black Death, and would have existed independently of it. Following their thesis Italy was already faced by the problem of a general decline in European production and demand. To the north the Hundred Years War disrupted trade routes, reduced wealth, accentuated xenophobia against aliens. In the east the expansion of the Ottomans in Asia Minor and the Balkans under Sultans Orkhan (1326–62) and Murad I (1362–89) brought new problems to the merchant. It might even be that the break-up of the *pax mongolica* in Persia and along the Silk Road which ended trading opportunities in Asia was of some significance. Within Italy itself large-scale general war was diverting wealth to non-productive ends. At the same time new competitors were coming to the fore: the merchants of Catalonia and clothiers of England.

By the 1340s already, the proponents of this view would continue, Florence was faced by a widespread recession. Its banking system was over-extended, its production of wool cloth was declining, unemployment and under-employment were growing. It was in the shadow of this decline that in September 1342 the patriciate had appointed Walter of Brienne, titular duke of Athens, as life *signore* of the commune. Within eleven months their hopes that the economic problem could be solved politically collapsed. At Walter's expulsion the 'pillars of Christendom', as Villani called the great banks, tumbled to disaster, dragging with them large numbers of the city's lesser investors: in 1343 the Peruzzi, in 1345 the Acciaiuoli, in 1346 the Bardi. These blows, it is concluded, at 'the most sensitive point of the [Italian] economy' introduced not merely for Florence but for Italy as a whole a long period of recession which the coming of the Black Death accentuated sharply.

Such views are, however, by no means unanimously accepted. It is obviously difficult to generalise from the economy of Florence to that of Venice or Milan. It is probably true that the 1340s were a difficult time for most cities; it is much more doubtful that they were succeeded by uniform development or contraction. At first sight it might seem that a vast fall in population – among both producers and native and foreign customers – as the result of plague must have brought with it a corresponding fall in aggregate production. If, in the manufacturing sector, on the other hand, there had existed, as seems likely, a large number of unemployed who could now both obtain work and consume, the effects would be muted. Again, there would have been a decline in *per capita* wealth only if production were to have fallen in greater measure than population.

In seeking to resolve these difficulties, one is faced by the fact that even in one city the specialists have reached different conclusions. Against, for instance, the claim of one authority that the 'pieces' of Florentine cloth produced fell precipitately throughout the fourteenth century (1309–10, 100,000 pieces a year; 1339, 70,000; 1373, 30,000; 1382, 19,000), another asserts that the value of such production (through, for instance, the use of finer English wool) was rising and goes on to hail the period 1360–1400 as 'the golden age of Florentine cloth production'. Yet another sees a surprising initial recovery in the business of the city from 1349 to 1357, recession from 1357 to 1361, followed again by depression to at least 1378.[6]

This last more-nuanced picture of alternating rise and fall has the merit of avoiding blanket judgment. But it cannot be used, of course, as a pointer to the general state of production in Italy as a whole. For even if it were assumed that the production of cloth declined in Florence, it cannot be known how far this should be balanced by the rise of new local cloth industries which took place in this period in Padua or Lombardy and the development in several cities of new textiles such as silk. Similar doubts must attend attempts to draw up an overall balance on commerce. Genoa has been portrayed as in sharp decline to the 1370s. In that decade there was a recovery in trade though its volume was still less than half that of 1284. This in turn was followed by another 'catastrophic decline' to 1400. But the evidence that Venice – victor over Genoa, it should be remarked, in the war of Chioggia (1378–81) – underwent any decline is extremely thin, while the second half of the fourteenth century seems to show a new prosperity for Milanesi merchants at the fairs of Geneva, the Low Countries, Paris, Chalons, and Dijon.

It has been urged that from the 1340s many old families abandoned trade, acquired fiefs and castles, and settled for the life of country gentlemen. In the second half of the fourteenth century, it has been calculated, only fifteen out of some fifty-one ancient Florentine families still participated directly in business. At Genoa in the same period the Fieschi, Fregosi, and Adorno abandoned commerce and became essentially a landed class. Among two of the most powerful banking families of Asti, the Scarampi of Camino and the Scarampi of Cairo, a similar process has been discerned: investments in money-lending gave way to massive purchases of land.[7] Such withdrawals have been taken to suggest a general discouragement before the prevailing economic climate. Yet these views ignore how far similar movements had always occurred and how far too other families – for instance, the Malabaya of Asti and the Alberti antichi of Florence – came forward to economic prominence. As the story of Francesco Datini of Prato shows, it was still possible to make very large fortunes by trade in the second half of the fourteenth century.

In agriculture, again, no uniform picture emerges. If, before the plague, there had been large-scale rural unemployment, it might be that workers could still be found to till most of the land which had been worked before the plague. Any land abandoned would be that which was marginal and less fertile. In these circumstances one has on the one hand clear evidence for abandonment of villages and fields in Sardinia, Latium, and Southern Tuscany, and the suggestion that in the island of Sicily the growing of grain gave way to pasturage. On the other, the Lombard plains, where rice-cultivation was introduced in these years, have been seen as entering, in the second half of the century, upon an agricultural revolution, a vast extension of agricultural profitability.

Despite the absence of statistics, the discontinuity and frequent doubtfulness of the statistics we possess, one might, if forced to a judgment on the overall problem, guess that in the thirty years after the 1340s there was economic contraction in the *Mezzogiorno*, at Florence, and at Genoa, and that, at least by 1380, losses were hardly balanced by more fortunate circumstances elsewhere. One senses a certain general economic malaise. Yet it is still not easy to calculate from this the social effects of the changes. The huge mortality must have allowed in some areas a withdrawal from marginal to more cultivable land, and have turned competition for land into competition for tenants. Against that a rise in pasturage would have worked against peasant prosperity. In towns, again, shortage of labour might be expected to have produced – and did indeed temporarily produce – a rise in wages and working conditions.

It was a situation which brought impassioned complaints from Matteo Villani:

The *popolo minuto* were fattened and became lazy after the mortality and did not want to serve at their usual trades and wished for their life the dearest and most delicate things of the real citizens, and through this they brought discord to the city. Serving girls, unskilled and without experience of service, and stable boys wanted a salary of at least 12 florins a year, and the more experienced 18 and 24 florins, and so did wet-nurses. Petty manual workers wanted three times as much or thereabouts, as they were used to, and the workers of the fields wanted all the cattle and all the seed and to work the best lands and leave the others.[8]

Any permanent advantages which might have accrued to the lower classes from the situation, however, were, it seems probable, wiped out by government and guild action, price controls, inflation, increased taxation, and, in those regions where it occurred, lower demand over the whole economy.

In the political field too the demographic fall brought disturbance but no ultimate structural change. As old fortunes collapsed new men, the hated *gente nuova*, often enriched by inheritance from those who had died in the plague, came forward to seek their share in the control of commerce and, with all the social tensions that the challenge was likely to provoke, in politics. In republics the struggle between this class and existing oligarchies heightened the climate of uncertainty, brought instability to established political élites, threw up temporary regimes of a less-oligarchical character (the *Dodicini*, 1355–68 and the *Riformatori*, 1368–85, at Siena; the guild-regime at Florence, 1378–82) and numerous working-class disturbances against authority.

The final result of these conflicts (though this is to carry us beyond the confines of our period) seems everywhere to be the same, namely the restoration of oligarchical rule and the freezing of élites into quasi-castes. Symbolic of the process is the final 'closing' of the oligarchy of Venice in 1381. The Italy of the following seventy years – it is perhaps an argument in favour of the view that the economic revolution had spent its force – sees, certainly, powerful organised violence between governments, but seems to be the scene of much greater order, stability, and internal peace within the towns than in the previous two centuries. The élites have triumphed, and with them has triumphed the new élite culture of Humanism.

It should be remarked, finally, that the coming of the Black Death in 1348 and subsequent years was not simply a factor in economic and social change. It was, for those who endured it, a profound human tragedy in which each individual from year to year was called upon to exercise his or her own courage and endurance. It is worth citing, once again, the oft-quoted words of Agnolo di Tura, recorded in a Sienese chronicle :

The mortality began in Siena in May. It was horrible and cruel, and I know not how in its frightfulness this cruelty began, for it seemed that those witnessing it were stupefied with sorrow. And it is not possible for human tongue to tell of the horror, and one can well call that man happy who has not seen it. Father abandoned child; wife, husband; one brother, another; for the illness struck both through breath and sight. And so they died. None there were who for money or friendship would bury the dead. Members of a family brought their dead to the ditch as best they would without priest or divine office, and the bell did not sound for them. And in many places in Siena huge pits were dug and the multitude of the dead were piled within them. . . And I, Agnolo di Tura, called 'the Fat', buried my five children with my own hands. And there were those so poorly covered with earth that the dogs dug them up and gnawed their bodies throughout the city. And there were none who wept for any death, for everyone expected to die. And so many died that everyone thought it to be the end of the world . . . and there was so much horror, that I, the writer, cannot think of it, and therefore will tell no more.

'Is it possible', wrote Petrarch of the mortality, 'that posterity will believe these things ? For we who have seen them can hardly do so.'[9]

IV

Towards the end of the twenty-second canto of the *Paradiso*, Dante from the sign of Gemini, looks down through the seven spheres to see below the far-distant outlines of the world :

> *l'aiuola che ci fa tanto feroci*
> 'the little threshing floor that makes us so fierce'.

From so exalted a standpoint it would be easy enough to sum-up the experience of Italy over almost two centuries. Six generations of men had been tested in this life and had attained to either salvation or damnation in the next. The empire which should have ruled the temporal conditions of their brief span was no more, and the Church, still turned from the true path, was tormented by Schism. Florence still played the harlot. A great prophetic poem had been written whose prophecies were unfulfilled : the 'Greyhound' or 'Dux' or Scipio-figure who might redeem the ill-fortunes of the world was as far-off as ever.

For those standing on the threshing floor any generalisation must be more difficult. Yet one attempt at synthesis might be this: that the leading theme of the age was the centralisation and concentration of power. The working out of the economic revolution and the rise of much more effective governments in the peninsula had ensured that life was now much more ordered and controlled. At the level of the family the slow reorganisation of domestic life on patrilineal lines had reinforced the authority of the household head. Changes in the countryside – the coming of *mezzadria* and *appoderamento* – had given new potentialities to landowners. The wealthy grew wealthier. Their introduction of such commercial techniques as double-entry book-keeping and marine insurance had gone hand-in-hand with the building of ships which were bigger and, through the compass and portolan, more mobile.

The weapons that the strong controlled – the crossbow, even sometimes the bombard – were more expensive and more destructive. The forces they raised were larger, the armour they wore thicker. Governments, though still far from having anything like the character of modern states, exercised a stronger supervision over the individual and taxed more oppressively. Within governments either one man had come to claim sole rule or oligarchies were narrowing their boundaries. Despite its decline in moral authority, the strength of the Roman *curia* had been increased by the suppression of heresy, the rise of a subservient scholasticism, and the expansion of canon law. Immense new potentialities for the ordering of life and thought had been developed: Roman law, the notariate, institutionalised education. The very diffusion of literacy had widened the gap between the literate and illiterate, and yet the development of Humanism was ensuring that only an élite among the literate should be thought of as truly educated.

Most men were now less free. The invention which could be taken as symbolising the age is the mechanical clock, the first example of a machine built to control the daily life of human beings. Clocks, of course, have their uses, as have most of the other innovations of the period. (One thinks of paper, eye-glasses, the upright loom.) It would obviously be anachronistic to read back into the Middle Ages the modern despair at each report of some new technological development or means of social engineering. So too the extension of the coercive power of governments had positive as well as negative aspects. The Campo of Siena and its Palazzo Comunale, the notarial protocol, the codifications of law, were all attempts to establish form and order. In the thirteenth and fourteenth centuries that order was being sought within an extremely violent world. In face of the violence Italians had displayed extraordinary resilience. Against the apparent mockery of plagues and famines at human impotence, peasants, poor, artisans, merchants, perhaps rulers too, had in the end achieved some form of triumph.

NOTES

On the **Black Death** as a European phenomenon see E. Carpentier, 'La Peste noire: Famines et épédemies dans l'histoire du XIVᵉ siècle', *Annales: ESC*, 1962; P. Ziegler, *The Black Death*, London, 1969; and J-N. Biraben, *Les hommes et la peste en France et dans les pays méditerranéans*, Paris–The Hague, 1975–6. In an Italian context it has been discussed by E. Carpentier, *Une ville devant la Peste: Orvieto et la peste noire de 1348*, Paris, 1962; W. M. Bowsky, 'The Impact of the Black Death upon Sienese government and society', *Speculum*,

1964 ; M. Brunetti, 'Venezia durante la peste del 1348', *Ateneo veneto*, 1909; A. Chiapelli, 'Gli ordinamenti sanitari del comune di Pistoia contra la pestilenza del 1348', *ASI*, 4s, xx, 1887 ; D. Herlihy, 'Population, Plague and Social Change in rural Pistoia, 1207–1430', *Economic History Review*, 1965; E. Carabellese, *La peste del 1348 e le condizioni della sanità pubblica in Toscana*, Rocca San Casciano, 1897. See too the works on Population referred to in the bibliography to chapter IX, *supra*, pp. 208–9.

Most of the Italian plague tractates from the period have been printed in volumes v (1912), vi (1913), and xvi (1923) of the *Archiv für Geschichte der Medizin* edited by Karl Sudhoff.

On famine, in addition to the bibliography on food policies in Chapter X, *supra*, p. 226, see G. Cherubini, 'La carestia del 1346–7 nell' inventario dei beni di un monastero del contado aretino' in his *Signori, Contadini, Borghesi*, Florence, 1974. G. Corradi, *Annali delle epidemie occorse in Italia*, vol. i, Bologna, 1863, lists some famines and plagues, but is in need of revision.

For an introduction to the debate on economic change see R. Romano, 'L'Italia nella crisi del secolo XIV', *Nuova rivista storica*, 1966 (now in his *Tra due crisi: L'Italia del Rinascimento*, Turin, 1971). For pessimistic portrayals of developments in the period see A. Sapori, *La crisi delle compagnie mercantili dei Bardi e dei Peruzzi*, Florence, 1926 ; E. Fiumi, 'Fioritura e decadenza dell' economia fiorentina', *ASI*, 1957, 1958, 1959; C. Klapisch-Zuber and J. Day, 'Villages désertés en Italie' in *Villages désertés et histoire économique: XI–XVIIIᵉ siècle*, Paris, 1965; J. Day, *Les douanes de Gênes 1376–7*, Paris, 1963; D. J. Osheim, 'Rural population and the Tuscan Economy', *Viator*, 1976; B. Z. Kedar, *Merchants in Crisis: Genoese and Venetian Men of Affairs and the Fourteenth-Century Depression*, New Haven, 1976. There are more optimistic approaches in C. M. Cipolla, 'The trends in Italian economic history in the later middle ages', *Economic History Review*, 1949; *idem*, 'I precedenti economici' in *Storia di Milano*, viii, pt. 3, Milan, 1957; D. F. Dowd, 'The economic expansion of Lombardy', *The Journal of Economic History*, xxi, 1961; G. Miani, 'L'économie lombarde aux XIVᵉ et XVᵉ siècles: une exception à la règle?', *Annales: ESC*, 19, 1964; and F. Melis, 'Firenze' in *Città, mercanti, dottrine nell' economia europea dal iv al xviii secolo: Saggi in memoria di G. Luzzatto*, Milan, 1964.

Two valuable works on the political and social changes of the period are G. A. Brucker, *Florentine Politics and Society, 1343–1378*, Princeton, 1962; and Christine Meek, *Lucca, 1369–1400*, Oxford, 1978.

1. In Froissart, *Oeuvres, Chroniques*, ed. K. de Lettenhove, Brussels, 1870–7, i, pt. 2, p.468.
2. See, e.g., the treatise of Augustine of Trent, written in July 1340 in L. Thorndike, 'A pest tractate before the Black Death', *Archiv für Geschichte der Medizin*, xxiii, 1930.
3. *The History of Bubonic Plague in England*, Cambridge, 1970; against which, C. Morris, 'The Plague in Britain', *Historical Journal*, 1971.
4. Chalin's *Tractatum* in R. Hoeniger, *Der Schwarze Tod in Deutschland*, Berlin, 1882, p. 177; *Ephemerides Urbevetanae*, ed. L. Fumi, *RIS*, xv, pt. v., p.208.
5. G. Ciacchi, *Gli Aldobrandineschi nella storia e nella Divina Comedia*, Rome, 1935, ii, pp. 316–7.
6. R. Davidsohn, 'Blüte und Niedergang der Florentiner Tuchindustrie', *Zeitschrift für die gesamte Staatswissenschaft*, 1928 ; Melis, 'Firenze', *cit.*, p. 133; Brucker, *Florentine Politics and Society, cit.* p. 15.
7. P. J. Jones, 'Florentine families and Florentine diaries of the fourteenth century',

Papers of the British School at Rome, 1956, pp. 203–4; A. Sisto, *Banchieri-feudatari subalpini nei secoli XII–XIV*, Turin, 1963, *passim*.

8. *Cronica*, 1, 57.
9. *Cronica senese*, ed. A. Lisini and F. Iacometti, *RIS*, xv, pt. vi, p. 555; F. Petrarca, *Le familiari*, ed. V. Rossi, Florence, 1923–1942, viii, 7 (vol. ii, pp. 174–9).

Index

269

Lewis, king of Hungary, 48
Liguria, 25, 122, 148
Lionardo Fibonacci of Pisa, 23
Lionel, duke of Clarence, 55, 211
Lippo di Fede di Sega, 193–4
Lodi, 134, 138
Lombard League, First, 2, 20, 30, 136
Lombard League, Second, 20, 30, 31, 39, 130
Lombardy, 25, 44, 53, 63, 97, 122, 131, 135, 137, 138, 148, 155, 163, 234, 256, 257
  economy of, 263–4
Louis IX, king of France, 41, 43
Lucania, 261
Lucca
  city of, 62, 86, 89, 154, 183
  commune of, 3, 42, 43, 66, 108, 122, 128, 148
  economy of, 53, 183, 187, 189
  plague in, 260, 261
Lucera, 19, 31
Ludovico I, king of Trinacria, 49
Lupi family, 61

Machiavelli, Niccolò, 11
magi, 16–17, 74
magnates, 118, 121–2, 123, 124, 147
Maria I, queen of Trinacria, 49
Maimonides, 23
malaspina family, 96, 217
Malatesti family, 54, 139, 149, 217
Manfred, king of Sicily, 2, 17, 39, 40–3, 45, 164, 217
Manfredi family, 102, 139, 140
Manfredo II Lancia, 128
Manfredonia, 41
Mantua, 9, 31, 83, 88–9, 106, 128–9, 183, 208, 215, 230
  Bonacolsi in, 140–5
  see also Gonzaga
manufacture, 188–9, 194–5, 263
March of Ancona, see Marche
Marche [March of Ancona], 9, 20, 33, 34, 41, 137, 139, 148, 174, 214, 261
Marchionne Stefani, 11, 107
Marco Polo, 101, 186
Maremma, 91
marriage, 65, 71, 78, 179, 245
  see also: antifactum; dowry; women

Marritima, 261
Marsilio of Padua, 229, 249
Martin da Canale, 10
Martin IV, pope, 45, 50, 94
Martino da Fano, 66
masnade, see fideles
Matteo da Aquasparta, 50–1, 239
Matteo Villani, 247, 264
Matthew Paris, 10, 22, 23, 33
medical science, 258
Medici family, 121, 201
Meloria, battle of, 4, 184
merchants, 193–4, 241–2
  see also: banking; trade
Messina, 26, 45, 183, 257
mezzadria, 160–3, 167, 169, 177, 266
Mezzogiorno, see Southern Italy
Michael Paleologus, 43, 45
Michael the Scot, 16–17, 23, 198
Michele di Lando, 11, 201–2
Michele da Piazza, 49
Milan, 9, 31, 66, 69, 90, 113–14, 128, 135, 136, 149, 150, 183, 186, 188, 211, 225
  heresy in, 232, 233
  plague in, 257, 260, 261
  see also: Torre family; Visconti family
milites, see knights
minstrels, 203–4, 213
  see also troubadours
Modena, 20, 31, 35, 68, 100, 103, 108, 118, 124, 133, 139, 140, 146, 164, 257
Monferrato family, 42, 137, 139, 170
Montaperti, battle of, 42, 120, 215
Montecchi family, 130
Montefeltro family, 54, 139, 148, 160
Moses ben Solomon, 23
Muratori, Ludovico Antonio, 4–5, 7, 8, 11–12

Naples, city of, 3, 46–7, 125, 183
  university of, 19, 223, 239
Naples, kingdom of, 9, 164
  Angevin rule of, 46–8
  popolo in, 125

national consciousness, 1–3, 38
Niccolò of Bari, 24
Nicholas III, pope, 138, 207